JOSEPH A.HORAK

JUSTICE DENIED

A Detective's Dilemma

Lt.

Thank you for your help

Joseph A Horak

July 30, 2004

Martinsville, Indiana
www.BookmanMarketing.com

JOSEPH A. HORAK

In the interest of protecting the innocent and
the privacy of individuals contained in this true story,
certain names and other descriptive details have been altered.

DEDICATED TO

Diane Compagna, Anne Psaradelis, and the innocent victims of society's crimes and to those who spend their lives in the fight for justice

JOSEPH A. HORAK

AUTHOR'S NOTE

Lives are too precious to be wrongfully stamped out and forgotten. Equally wrong is never bringing the murderer or murderers to justice to allow them to run free. This is a true story of rape and murder. The killers are still free, free because those who have vital information which would aid in bringing them to justice are afraid to come forward, free because law enforcement agencies over the years were too busy to solve this case. This story is actually a plea from two retired law enforcement officers who have dedicated over twenty years of their lives searching for clues and searching for individuals who have this vital information. Perhaps this story will touch their hearts. Let's not forget the victims. We will find the guilty and help bring justice to the innocent victims. Please come forward.

In the interest of protecting the innocent and the privacy of individuals contained in this true story, certain names and other descriptive details have been altered.

The author's career in law enforcement is quite extensive and broad in accomplishment. His career includes serving as Patrolman, Inspector, Supervisor-Investigator, Detective Sergeant, Detective Lieutenant, Captain, Chief of Police and Deputy U.S. Marshal. Most of his career has been spent in the State of New Hampshire.

JOSEPH A. HORAK

Preface

In a small town in New Hampshire, on July 12, 1973, a worried father reported his fifteen year old daughter and her girlfriend missing. Two and a half months later a hunter found two badly decomposed bodies in the woods twenty miles away - one fully dressed, the other completely unclothed. How did these girls get from Hampton Beach, where they were last seen to this deserted area forty miles from the beach? Why was only one girl unclothed? These questions have remained unanswered for twenty-eight years.

The New Hampshire State Police took the investigation out of the hands of local authorities within hours of the discovery of the bodies. Did the State Police botch the investigation and interrogation of the primary suspect? Why have they refused to press forward in the investigation all these years? Is corruption involved? Reading the text of this case history will allow armchair detectives to decide for themselves.

I was the Detective-Sergeant who took the initial report of the missing girls and conducted the fruitless investigation into their disappearance. I was also an active participant in the multi-jurisdictional task force put together by the State Police and the Attorney General's Office to investigate this crime until my forced retirement in 1976 due to injuries received in the line of duty.

Since my retirement, I've kept in touch with friends in law enforcement and with the help of Chief Robert Baker from the Candia Police Department, we have prodded authorities to keep the case active and to bring it to a conclusion by placing or eliminating the two prime suspects or any other suspects.

JUSTICE DENIED

Life is precious and it was taken away from Diane Compagna and Anne Psaradelis. Oh, we know that there are friends, relatives and others out there that know who the killers are that took the lives of these two 15 year old girls. You know who you are, just as we do. The investigation has been hampered by people who do not want to get involved or are afraid to come forward fearing the same thing will happen to them. After nearly 30 years, "Please come forward with the information you have held all these years and help to bring justice for the two young girls."

JOSEPH A. HORAK

MURDER IN CANDIA
1973

September 29, 1973

Candia, New Hampshire is a small town that consists of about 3,400 people. There really isn't what you would consider a center to the town. The small towns around us are Auburn, Chester and Deerfield. We have always tried to help each other when any kind of an emergency or disaster comes up. The Candia Police Department is run out of two rooms that are located on the second floor of Pa Pa's Country Store on Deerfield Road, which belongs to Chief Robert Baker.

Counting the Chief, the department has two female officers and eleven male officers who work only part time however, they are all certified and have been given the very best of training. The police budget for the year is $13,000; and everyone is dedicated to doing the very best job possible. Over the years the various officers have investigated just about every type of complaint or crime and have had good results.

The last week of September of every year is usually taken up with traffic control in regards to the Deerfield Fair. It's the biggest Agricultural Fair in the State. On the 29th and 30th, we have 100,000 or more people pass through our town on their way to and from the event. These people converge on Routes 43, 101B and 107A, and thus the requirement of a large contingent of officers to handle this task is needed; they come from the local police, sheriff departments, state police and other sources. There really isn't any manpower left to take care of other complaints. If something should happen, we would have to pull officers from some of the various traffic assignments.

Saturday, September 29, 1973

By 8:00 A.M., Chief Baker had just finished dropping the last officer off at his traffic assignment. It was already hot and humid and it promised to be a long busy day. You never knew if you would have a chance to eat, take a break or be pulled off your assignment for some kind of an emergency.

JUSTICE DENIED

Things went quite well all morning. The traffic flowed right along with no apparent problems, but then, it was still early and anything could happen.

"Sergeant Morse, you'll have to take over this traffic assignment while I check with the various officers to make sure they've had something to eat and allowed to take a short break."

"That'll be fine with me, Chief."

It was about 2:15 P.M., it was still extremely hot and humid and the traffic was very heavy at this intersection of 107A and 101B. A man driving a 1971 Volkswagen pulled up beside me and stopped then rolled down his window.

"Sergeant, I'd like to talk with you, it's kind of urgent."

"Sir, would you pull your vehicle over in front of the IOOF hall so you won't block the flow of traffic. I'll be right over."

"What can I do for you sir? You seem a little nervous, are you all right?"

"Sergeant, my name is Robert Lupien, I'm from Manchester. I've been scouting the woods off the New Boston Road here in Candia and not too far from the town dump. I've been looking for some good places to hunt birds. After all, the hunting season will be open soon. My attention was drawn to an area in a pine grove by some bright clothing that was lying on the ground."

"I walked over towards it and looked down towards the ground. I was shocked and couldn't believe what I was looking at."

"Are you all right Mr. Lupien?"

"Yes, Sergeant, I'm all right. To get on with my story, I was looking at a partially decomposed body of a young girl. I didn't touch anything. It was pretty spooky and the smell of death was every where. I had a feeling someone or something was watching me, so I just got out of there and started looking for a police officer when I came upon you."

While I was listening to Mr. Lupien, Chief Emerson Heald, of the Auburn Police Department, happened along in his patrol car, headed to check out the crowds at the fair. I flagged him down and reported the situation.

"Chief Heald, I have a major problem here. This is Robert Lupien from Manchester, he was scouting a wooded area for birds near the town dump when he came upon what he believes is the body of a young girl. I would appreciate it if you would contact Chief Baker on your two-way radio, since this is in the Candia jurisdiction, and advise him of the situation. Could you have him respond to New Boston Road and we'll meet him on the side of the road across from the Bell residence?"

"Will do, Sergeant Morse, and I'll take over your traffic assignment until I can get relieved by one of my officers."

"Mr. Lupien, if you don't mind, I'll ride with you and we can proceed to New Boston Road and check this out."

Mr. Lupien and I arrived back on New Boston Road. This is more or less an isolated area, and we parked on the shoulder of the road across from the Bell residence.

Once out of the car, Mr. Lupien pointed to a small opening in the stone wall that was filled with brush and saplings, and stated that he had entered into the woods from this area. We went through the opening and came upon an old logging road full of ruts and brush. We walked north for a distance and then took a turn to our right and headed toward the east. After a short period of time, we crossed over a stone wall and entered a wooded area filled with pines.

"Sergeant Morse, look over to your right, can you see the bright cloth lying on the ground?"

JUSTICE DENIED

"Yes Mr. Lupien, I can see something there, and more, I can smell that awful odor of something lying dead in there."

As we approached the spot of color, there was evidence of a shallow depression in the ground and what appeared to be a partially decomposed human, appearing to be a young female, lying naked in the dark.

It was a horrible sight, nothing left of the body but some skin stretched over emasculated muscle and bone. It was hot and muggy and the stench of death was every where. Looking down at what was left of this poor young girl didn't help.

"Mr. Lupien, you look a little on the pale side, maybe we should walk back out to the road and wait for Chief Baker."

"Good idea, Sergeant," replied Lupien. "That stench of decay is really overpowering."

Just as we were coming out of the woods and back onto New Boston Road, we could see a police cruiser approaching, Chief Baker at the wheel with Officer Mac Donald.

"What kind of a situation do we have here, Sergeant?"

"Well Chief, I went with Mr. Lupien back into the woods and there's this pine grove over behind an old stone wall. It seems Mr. Lupien is right. There's a partially decomposed body of a young female. She isn't wearing any clothing, but does have a pair of jeans she is laying on, with the remainder of her clothing folded and placed in a pile about ten inches from her right hand."

"Sergeant, I want you and Mr. Lupien to take Officer Mac Donald and myself back into the area where the body was found so that I can look at the scene myself."

After checking the remains, Chief Baker confirmed that the remains were that of a young female between the ages of 13 & 16 years old.

"Sergeant Morse, I want you to take a statement from Mr. Lupien and have Officer Mac Donald stay with the body and protect the scene. Once you finish up with Mr. Lupien, call for the crime van and then scout around the area and look for any evidence that might tie in with the crime. Don't touch or remove anything you might find or observe and above all, don't let anyone enter into the crime scene area unless you get an OK from me, is that understood? Once our crime van arrives, we will rope off the area, take photographs, measurements and conduct a proper crime scene search."

"I'm going to have to leave here now and make contact with Attorney General Warren Rudman, the County Medical Referee Dr. Hart, Roger Beaudoin from the State Police Crime Lab and others. I'll dispatch Officers Ken Howell and Walter Perkins to the scene and you can utilize them in regards to making sure the crime scene has tight security. Again, no one is to enter the crime scene unless you clear it with me."

"Understood, Chief. I'll advise you of any new developments that come up while you're out of the area."

Chief Baker left the area and I obtained a statement from Mr. Lupien. He was told that he was free to leave and I thanked him for all the assistance that he had given in regards to this matter.

"Sergeant Morse, if you need me for anything, please call. I'm willing to help in anyway I can. I sure hope you catch the person responsible for killing the girl."

Officer Mac Donald stayed with the body while I started looking around the area for any additional evidence that might tie in with the crime. I began by circling the body and expanded my search in all directions looking for anything that could be connected with the victim or the person responsible.

I was about a couple of hundred feet southeast of the body that had been found by Mr. Lupien, when my attention was drawn to an area about three feet away from a large stone wall, it was high and wide. I walked over towards whatever it was that had caught my eye. There were lots of pine trees, hard wood saplings, as well as lots of pine needles and leaves on the ground. You could really smell death every where, I got closer to the wall and observed another partially decomposed body, this also appeared to be a young girl, but this body had all her clothes on.

There was nothing but a little skin and bone, you could see her right eye still in its socket, dry and desiccated, and it appeared like she was looking right at me. It was more than a little spooky and it made quite nervous. All kinds of thoughts went through my mind and how I wished I could catch the person responsible for the murders of these two girls. I made my way back to where Officer Mac Donald and the first girl's body was found.

I informed him of my finding a second decomposed human body. Also a young girl.

"Sergeant Morse, your kidding aren't you? This is nothing to kid about."

"No Officer Mac Donald, I'm sorry to say there is another body of a young girl. At least this one has all of her clothing on. We better alert Chief Baker."

"I'll use the walkie-talkie to contact him."

"Sergeant Morse to Chief Baker."

"Come in Sergeant. What's going on?"

"Chief, be advised that we have two crime scenes now."

"Sergeant, secure the entire area, do not let anyone into it. I have Chief Heald and Officers Howell and Perkins with me, we should be at your location within four or five minutes."

It wasn't long before Chief Baker and the others walked into the area where the first body had been discovered. The Chief instructed Officers Howell and Perkins to rope off the entire area and to protect the crime scene at all costs.

"Sergeant Morse, I want you to take me to the area where you found the second body and we will secure that area as well"

"Over here Chief, the body is about three feet from that big stone wall. By the position of the body, it appears that the girl was running for her life."

"That's a horrible sight, Sergeant. The two girls must have been together; it's strange that one is nude and the other with her clothes on. We better take photographs of the two victims, take measurements of the scene while we wait for Roger Beaudoin and Warren Edmunds from the State Police Crime Lab."

Doctor Hart, the County Medical Referee was taken to the two crime scenes, he examined both bodies without disturbing either of them.

Governor Melvin Thompson, having been notified of the situation, arrived at the location and spoke with Chief Baker. He wanted information regarding the situation; he wanted a full report and was advised that Roger Beaudoin would see that he received a full report of the investigation once he had checked out both crime scenes.

Night fall was fast approaching and Roger Beaudoin and Edmunds had just arrived at the Maiden Funeral Home and requested that Chief Baker meet them there.

Chief Baker responded to the Maiden Funeral Home and met with Beaudoin and Edmunds along with several Rockingham County Deputy Sheriff's. They all drove down to New Boston Road and the crime scenes.

JUSTICE DENIED

<u>Saturday September 29th</u>
6:15 P.M.:
Chief Baker, Roger Beaudoin and Warren Edmunds had viewed the two crime scenes. Darkness had already set in and it would be difficult to do a complete crime scene investigation. There could be a chance of spoiling any evidence that might be obtained and once you move the bodies, the true crime scene is lost forever. The same thing goes for ANY evidence; once lost, it is gone forever.

"Chief Baker, I think we would be wise if we were to post a guard here, seal off the entire area until we have better light and manpower."

"I agree with you Lieutenant Beaudoin, I'll have Sergeant Morse make arrangements to have proper security and we will have the area under guard until the day light hours tomorrow, Sunday morning.

"Chief Baker, I have already set up a guard schedule for the night. Officers Gilbert, Mac Donald, Howell and I will provide coverage from 6:30 p.m. until 12:30 A.M.; relief will be provided by Officers Lovering and Perkins from our department and two officers from the Auburn Police Department."

It had been a long night for the officers assigned to make sure the crime scene and surrounding area were secure; the only good thing that happened was that Chief Baker came back during the night bringing food and coffee for everyone, donated by the Lions Club of Candia. The smell of death was everywhere. The woods were dark and spooky and every once in a while you would hear an animal moving around in the pine needles, leaves and under brush. I am sure that various thoughts were in the minds of each officer there. This was truly a dark, isolated area to be in.

<u>Sunday September 30th</u>
7:15 A.M.:
Officers Gilbert, Mac Donald, Howell and Sergeant Morse relieved the night guards and would maintain security until relieved by Chief Baker.

8:05 A.M.:
"Sergeant Morse, we'd like to go into the crime scene."

"Deputy Pickowitz, I cannot allow you and County Attorney Eldridge into the crime scene area until I receive an OK from Chief Baker."

8:30 A.M.:
All responsible enforcement agencies met Chief Baker at the Maiden Funeral Home. Medical Referee Doctor Hart had responded to the scene on Saturday and left the responsibility to Doctor Katsas for removal and autopsy of the two bodies.

Dr. Hart's representative at the scene was Deputy Medical Referee Leland Davis and Dr. Katsas. Also present to the officers were County Attorney Carleton Eldridge and Assistant Attorney General Robert Johnson III. After a discussion of the plan to be followed, Detective/Lieutenant Ralph Wilson from the State Police assumed responsibility of investigation and assigned the following teams:

SP Det/Cpl Lamy and Candia, Chief Baker - Diagram and Measurements.

Lab Sup Beaudoin and Tech/Lab Edmunds - Collection and Preservation of evidence.

SP Det/Cpl Heon and Dep/Sheriff Stony - Photographs and Video tape.

All other personnel were kept on stand-by for an eventual crime scene search.

By 10:00 a.m. the photographs and diagrams were completed on body #1 and it was time to remove it.

"Chief Baker, do you have a large piece of board that we could use in the removal of the body?"

"No, I don't, but I can go down to the lumber company and buy a couple of pieces of plywood, I am sure the selectmen won't pay for it, but I'll buy it anyway."

Body #1 was badly decomposed, almost a complete skeleton, and was completely naked, no signs of being shot, stabbed, hit over the head, tied up or any signs of a struggle. Found near the right hand were a blue and red bathing suit top, a pair of pink underpants with white lace design and they were folded and placed in a pile. A pair of blue jeans, brand name "Time & Place" was found lying partly under the left shoulder. One round silver earring was taken off the skin of the left ear and the matching earring was found lying underneath the skull and appeared to have been in proper position to have been on the right ear and fell off because of advanced decomposition of the body. The remains were placed in a plastic burial bag, then placed on the piece of plywood for removal from the scene.

By 10:45 a.m. the photographs and diagrams were completed on body #2.and it was time to remove it.

"Chief Baker, could you have that other sheet of plywood brought over here near the stone wall."

The Chief and Officer Howell carried the sheet of plywood over to where Beaudoin and Edmunds were and placed it on the ground near the body.

This body was also badly decomposed, almost a complete skeleton, but with clothing on the body. The body is clad in what appears to be a white blouse with buttons down the front, short sleeve, a multicolored halter top or bathing suit top still over the upper part of the body, but not in the regular position. Blue jeans with a leather belt and large buckle, the buckle is undone but the buttons on the jeans are not. In black print on the left front of the pant leg are the words, "Love is Beautiful".

We made an attempt to remove the body intact and upon lifting the hands away from the ground, a small chain is observed around the neck. The type a pendant might hang from; there is a ring on the left ring finger, a ring on the right ring finger and a ring on the little finger. We placed the body into a plastic burial bag and placed it on the piece of plywood for removal from the scene. We had to be careful, very careful, because the body or bodies hold the facts that will lead to the killer. Once the body or bodies are removed, the best piece of evidence is gone forever.

Both bodies were removed and taken to the Maiden Funeral Home in Candia. Doctor Katsas was called and he advised us to have the two bodies x-rayed at the hospital and then returned to the funeral home for autopsy.

11:45 A.M.:
Lieutenant Wilson, Chief Baker, Beaudoin, Edmunds, Heon and the funeral parlor help take the two bodies to the Elliott Hospital in Manchester where complete x-rays would be taken of the whole bodies. Nothing unusual was observed and the bodies were returned to the Maiden Funeral Home where Dr. Katsas was waiting.

11:50 A.M.:
State Police Troopers Lamy, Waterhouse, Caron, and other troopers along with Sergeant Morse, Officers Gilbert, Mac Donald, Howell and Perkins conducted a search of the roadsides from the Maiden Funeral Home to the crime scene and back. The search proved fruitless.

The New Hampshire Fish and Game Department brought in scuba divers and conducted a search of the waterway across the road from the town dump. A couple of old tires were found along with an old rusted rifle, bottles and other junk, nothing that would tie in with the murders of the two young girls.

2:00 P.M.:
Dr. Katsas began the autopsy on body #1 and then continued on with body #2. Lieutenant Wilson was advised that the Nashua Police Department had contacted the Merrimack Police Department and alerted them to

the fact that these two bodies could possibly be the two young 15 year old girls that were reported as missing on July 11, 1973. Lieutenant Oscar Gerlach notified Lieutenant Wilson that he had located the two dentists who had done dental work on both girls in the past and he would bring them to the Maiden Funeral home in Candia. Lieutenant Gerlach picked up Dr. Ronald Royer, DDS along with Dr. Joseph Patryn, DDS, and they both brought dental records from both victims.

They arrived at the funeral home at about 5:30 P.M.

5:35 P.M.:
"I am Lieutenant Oscar Gerlach from the Merrimack Police Department. Would Dr. Katsas be here?"

"Yes, Lieutenant. I'll get him for you."

"Dr. Katsas, this is Dr. Royer and Dr. Patryn. At one time or another, they did dental work on the two missing girls from Merrimack. We were told that we might be able to identify the bodies that have been found murdered here in Candia."

"Come in gentlemen. I'll brief you on what we have at this point."

Doctors Patryn and Royer examined the skull x-rays of the bodies and compared them with their Dental x-rays. They were then taken to the bodies and they compared their Dental Charts minutely with the teeth of the two bodies, they were identified as:

Body #1   Diane Compagna   DOB 3/26/58
Walden Drive
Merrimack, NH
Body #2   Anne R. Psaradelis   DOB 9/19/58
Harris Avenue
Merrimack, NH

Doctor Katsas had not given a real cause of death, but did indicate the possibility of strangulation. The bodies were secured at the Maiden Funeral Home and all available personnel were utilized to conduct another roadside search from 101B to the crime scene itself and back. The two crime scenes themselves had been searched several times; certain areas had various sections where the soil, pine needles, and leaves were sifted in an attempt to obtain any evidence that might have been dropped or used in connection with the two murders.

Chief Baker took several officers from his department and conducted a search of the town dump for well over three hours but the search proved fruitless.

During the entire crime scene investigation, the Lions Club members from Candia furnished every man involved with food, coffee and sandwiches; greatly appreciated by the tired, upset workers.

The investigation into the murders of these two young girls starts on October 2nd and the base of operations is at the Merrimack Police Department, Merrimack, New Hampshire. It promises to be a difficult case to investigate.

1

It's now July 2001; to tell this story we are going back in time twenty-eight years to July 1973.

We are in Merrimack a small town nestled on the banks of the Merrimack River in New Hampshire, population around ten thousand. Most people know each other and the pace of life is much slower than in a big city. The town is quiet, you can even hear the sound of cows mooing in the background.

This is a nice town with plenty of green grass and tall trees. Stoic old buildings and white steeples tower in the skyline. There are schools, stores, churches, a fire station and a police department - that's where I work.

I am a Detective Sergeant Joseph Horak. I investigate crimes of every description from start to finish. I usually work the night shift. I don't give up on a case until it is solved.

July 1, 1973

It was hot and muggy. We were preparing for the Fourth of July. The people in town get together every year and put on a celebration. The day would be filled with a parade, food, fun and games, which would culminate with a spectacular fireworks display. We had to make plans to handle thousands of people from surrounding cities and towns who would join the festivities. That meant all the full and part - time officers had to work.

JOSEPH A. HORAK

July 3, 1973

Chief Pelletier held a meeting with all the officers. Each of us was assigned a specific detail and given instructions. By the sound of it, part of my day would be spent working with the chief. I hoped he would drive the new cruiser, the old one was in pretty rough shape.

July 4, 1973

When I awoke, it was cloudy and there was some light rain. I hoped it wouldn't spoil the day for everyone. The bad weather could postpone the fireworks display and a lot of people would be upset.

9:30 a.m.

Some people were already lining the sidewalks, even though the rain had continued. Some spectators were sitting on benches, others on the rooftops of cars. I wouldn't let anyone sit on the roof of my car. I guessed they wanted to be able to see what was going on. They would have a long wait; the parade wouldn't start for another hour. We still had a lot to do.

I saw some of the officers already at their assigned posts and traffic locations. I liked directing traffic, but knowing my luck, I would catch that assignment later when the crowd started to leave after the fireworks. That would be a rough time. People would be tired and wanting to get home. They would get frustrated waiting in lines of traffic and a lot of them would get impatient. They would honk their horns or make remarks like, "Why don't you get out of the street and let the traffic take care of itself?"

I remember last year when an old man wanted to cross the street. No one in the traffic line would stop and let him cross. He went into his house, came back out, then tried to cross again. Still, no one would stop. So, he pulled a gun from underneath his shirt and pointed it at the next driver who came along. The traffic stopped and the man crossed the street, but he got himself arrested. That was a heck of a way to finish up the Fourth of July.

People just don't understand why the police have to stand in the middle of the street and take care of traffic. When they yell and complain, it's best to do your job and let it go at that.

JUSTICE DENIED

After the parade, most of the events would take place in the parking lots next to the high school. I headed over there to see how they were coming along. I thought most of the booths and rides should be set up. It would be great to know just what kinds of food they were going to sell. I hoped they would have some fried bread dough. I sure could go for a slice or two of that.

The chief was heading my way. I guessed he wanted to check things out, since they should be about ready to open the booths and rides.

"Come on, Sergeant, let's head over to the high school."

"Look at that, Chief, they have quite a few booths already up. Look at those four guys putting up the Ferris wheel. Boy, that one guy is sure heavy, but he looks strong. That food looks and smells great. Do you want a cup of coffee or something?"

"No, thanks."

There was music in the air. People were laughing and everyone was working hard to make it a joyous day. I was sure they wanted to make a little money also.

"OK, Chief, I guess I better get back to my post. It's time for the parade to start."

"Take my car, I want us to lead the parade."

A crowd had gathered and the streets were lined with people of all ages and descriptions. The rain had nearly stopped.

It would be a good parade, there were ten or so marching bands, floats of various kinds, fire engines, military units, tanks, trucks, horses, antique cars and a host of other things. They were even selling popcorn, balloons and ice cream. Everyone had a great time. The people seemed to enjoy the bands and military units best of all, they were great!

After the parade was over, I headed to the high school to see how things were going. I checked with Ted Trask, the officer on duty.

"Looks like things are going OK, Ted."

The rides were in full swing and loaded with people. They were laughing and screaming on the Ferris wheel and some of the other rides.

"I think there is going to be light rain off and on all day."

"I heard that it was supposed to clear up by mid-afternoon. They seem to be enjoying that good food, Ted. How about you and me getting a piece of that fried dough?"

"That sounds like a good deal."

"Here comes the chief and lieutenant. I wonder what they want now?"

"Hey, Sergeant, come with us, we're going out and check the back road areas to see what's going on."

"Things seem to be quiet. We haven't even run into an illegally parked car."

"Chief, let's check out the swimming hole off Bedford Road, that's usually a hangout for the kids."

1:40 p.m.

We entered the area off Bedford Road, there were fields, woods and a swimming hole. We tried to watch this area because of drinking and drug use. As we pulled in, we observed a 1963 sun-bleached beige station wagon with several people in it. Most of them were known to us. Apparently they saw our cruiser; the operator started the engine and backed into the woods. A couple of the passengers threw bottles and things out the windows into the woods. One man bolted out the back door and ran into the woods.

I jumped out of the cruiser and ran through the brush and trees in the direction of the fleeing man. After running through raspberry bushes and a host of other things, I saw the man just ahead of me. I hollered for him to stop, but he continued to run deeper into the woods. After a short distance, I caught up with him. It was Jake Johnson. I had dealt with him in the past. I placed him under arrest and advised him of his rights. Then I searched and cuffed him, and took him back to where the chief and others were waiting.

As I approached, the chief looked up and said, "Good job. We're going to take them into headquarters, but first I want you to check the area where we observed the occupants of the vehicle throwing things out the windows into the woods."

The chief and lieutenant took care of the seven boys and girls we detained. I checked the area in question and found several full containers of beer and a dozen or so half-full and empty containers. I also found two brown paper bags containing smaller plastic bags with a vegetative substance in them. I believed it to be marijuana. I marked and tagged the evidence.

Seven people were taken to headquarters. The adults were charged with contributing to the delinquency of minors and possession of a controlled drug. The juveniles were taken home and turned over to their parents, pending further investigation.

I took Jake Johnson into my office. Again, I advised him of his rights. I asked him why he bolted from the vehicle and refused to stop for me. He said he was scared. He stated the vehicle was his father's and that he didn't want to get into trouble.

I asked if he had the registration to the station wagon. He said it was in the glove compartment. I didn't have a chance to check the inside of the station wagon while we were in the wooded area. I told Johnson that I would go with him to get the registration.

I asked him for his consent to search the vehicle in his presence. I told him that he didn't have to give his consent. Johnson said, "I don't have anything to hide," and read and signed a consent-to-search card.

We walked out of the station to the rear parking lot where the vehicle had been stored. I unlocked the passenger-side door. Johnson said he would get the registration out of the glove compartment. As he opened it, a plastic bag with a vegetative substance fell onto the floor. I picked it up; it was a bag of marijuana. I then advised Johnson that I would search the rest of the vehicle myself.

At this time, I motioned for Lieutenant Gerlach to come out of the station to assist me. As the lieutenant approached, I advised him that I had just found marijuana in the vehicle and wanted him to watch Johnson while I searched the entire vehicle. Upon searching the station wagon, I found roaches in the ashtrays, a plastic bag with a vegetative substance under the front seat and two more in the cushions of the back seat. These were all marked and tagged for evidence.

Johnson was taken back into the station. He stated he wanted to give a statement admitting that most of the drugs were his. Johnson was charged with failing to stop for a police officer, possession of a controlled drug, and contributing to the delinquency of minors. He made bail and was released.

The chief and lieutenant interviewed the other adults. They were charged and bailed out.

3:30 p.m.

I was back in the parking lot next to the high school. A large crowd had gathered and everyone was having a good time. I decided to check with some of the officers on duty and give them a break.

"Hey, Ted, how about you and George Rousseau taking a break and getting something to eat? After you come back, Tom and Frank can go."

"That's OK with me, Sergeant."

Most of the people at the carnival appeared to be school aged. Some were talking and eating, others were trying out the Ferris wheel and some of the other rides. They must have been having fun because they were laughing, screaming and just plain having a good time.

I spotted Officer April across the parking lot. He seemed to be having some kind of problem with two men. I went over to see if I could help.

"What's the problem?"

"Sergeant, these two men have either been selling or giving beer to juveniles. I'm placing them under arrest for contributing to the delinquency of minors. Could you give us a lift to the station?"

"Sure, let's go."

On the way to the station, I spoke to the two men.

"I don't know when you guys are going to learn to use your heads. Look at the problems you've caused for yourselves and others."

6:30 p.m.

By the time Officer April and I returned to the carnival, all the officers had had a break. I checked some of the other areas to make sure things were going all right.

The crowd seemed larger than before. I guessed a lot of them had rested up and were ready for an evening of enjoyment. There was still a lot of food, fun and games to be had. The rain seemed to be over, so that was a big help.

We had officers all over the place, assisting with parking and the general welfare of the public. Cars, trucks and buses were starting to pile in. I was surprised that they were coming so early. I guessed a lot of them wanted to go on the rides. Some people had picnic baskets and blankets.

It sure looked like we were going to have a huge crowd. The parking lots were already overflowing. If all the officers followed through with their assignments, things should go well. There were a couple of kids drinking beer over near a red truck.

"They don't learn. Come on, Ted, let's take care of it before we have bigger problems."

9:15 p.m.

We were so busy parking cars and helping people, time sped by. The parking lots were full and we were sending late arrivals down to the fire station and shopping center to park. People were all over the place - on the rooftops of cars, in the back of pickup trucks, on benches, in chairs on lawns - any place they could find. A lot of families brought baskets of food, chairs and even radios.

A helium balloon went up in the air. That will make some little boy or girl unhappy. I heard someone shooting off fireworks in back of the school and in the parking areas. Some people were running around trying to find a better place to sit, others were looking for friends or a place to go to the bathroom. I hoped they would settle down soon, the fireworks were about to start.

The chief came around again. It seemed that every time I turned around he was there to give me something else to do.

"Sergeant, how are things going here?"

"The parking areas are filled to the brim. We sure do have a crowd. It's much larger than last year and they're still pouring in. Look at all the cars, trucks and buses. They're tucked away into every parking space, lawn and sidewalk they could find. It's going to take some time to get them out of here once the fireworks are over."

7

"By the way, Sergeant, I want you to do the traffic control down at the main intersection. Make sure you get down there ten minutes before the fireworks end."

"OK, Chief, I'll do my best to keep things from jamming up."

9:30 p.m.

The fireworks display was underway. The first rocket went up with a big bang. I would have liked to have stood around and enjoyed the fireworks like everyone else, and I was sure some of the other officers felt the same way, but we had our assignments and plenty of other things to look out for. Our main concern was to make sure everyone had a good time and to keep them safe. We would take care of any problems that arose.

As the second round of fireworks shot up into the sky, the eyes of young children were as big as golf balls. You could hear, "Oh-h-h!" "Wow!" "Really nice!" "Did you see that?" "Look at that one!" Every once in a while you could hear a little boy or girl say, "Mommy, I'm scared."

People were enjoying themselves - talking, laughing, eating food, enjoying the fireworks - just having a good time. I have often thought that when most people have off for a holiday and enjoy themselves, we police officers always seem to be working.

The fireworks had been going off for about an hour and a half. I decided it was time to get to my traffic detail.

"Hey, Ted, will you keep an eye on my area as well as your own? I'm heading down to the main intersection to do traffic."

"You got it, Sergeant. I'll take care of things here."

As I said before, I have always enjoyed doing traffic duty. It's a lot of work and a pain in the neck, but it can also be a lot of fun if you let it be that way.

The cars were starting to come out. The show was nearly over and a lot of people were walking. That meant watching out for them. Sometimes children just ran out into the streets. We didn't want anyone hurt. We just wanted to get the cars and everyone else out of there safe and sound.

The traffic seemed to be moving right along. That meant all the officers were doing their jobs, that sure helped. There were a lot of horns honking and people laughing. One little girl said, "I'm tired, Mom," as they crossed the street in front of me. I smiled at the lady and she waved good night.

After forty-five minutes of steady traffic pouring out of every possible parking area, the last few cars appeared, heading in my direction. As they went by, a couple of them honked their horns, waved and yelled, "We'll see you next year. We had a great time!"

It was time to roll up the Fourth of July for another year. The best thing of all was that no one was injured and there were no major problems. It was time to head back to the station and see if I was needed for anything else.

2

July 12, 1973

The workdays came and went. There was always something differ-ent. That's what made the job interesting. Each day brought with it something new; no two days were alike. I was busy investigating a couple of house burglaries, a stolen car, and a host of other complaints. My day should have been over when the dispatcher's voice came over my radio.

"Headquarters to unit one."

"This is unit one, go ahead."

"Sergeant, will you come into the station and take a report of a missing person?"

"Be right in."

As I pulled into the driveway, I observed a blue pickup truck parked next to the front steps. It didn't belong to anyone I knew. As I entered the station and stepped into the waiting room, I observed a man standing near the counter. He seemed nervous and concerned. He looked up and said, "Guess you're the officer I'm waiting for. My name is Marcel Compagna. I want to report my daughter as missing. Her name is Diane. She left home on July 11 with her girlfriend, Anne Psaradelis, to go swimming at the lake here in town."

He continued by stating that the Psaradelises lived on Harris Ave-nue. Mr. Compagna advised that his daughter had called home last night, July 11, to ask permission to stay overnight at Anne's house. When asked what she would do for a nightie, Diane said she would borrow one from Anne. She planned to be home by noon the next day.

JUSTICE DENIED

The next morning Mary Psaradelis, Anne's sister, called the Compagna home and asked for Anne. She spoke with Mike Compagna, Diane's brother. He told Mary that Anne wasn't there. Mike thought that Anne and Diane were supposed to have stayed at the Psaradelis house. It appeared that both girls had gotten permission to stay at the other's house. Now, no one knew where they were.

Marcel Compagna reiterated that he wanted to report Diane as missing and said he might as well report Anne Psaradelis as missing also since they were together. Mr. Compagna was advised that a missing person's bulletin could not be put out for twenty-four hours because a lot of people who are reported missing aren't really missing. They take off for a day or two and then return home.

Mr. Compagna pleaded, "Can't you at least put out a bulletin in our area?"

"All right, Mr. Compagna, I will put a missing person's bulletin out to the local areas."

"That will be great, I really appreciate it."

Mr. Compagna gave me a description of the two girls. Diane Compagna was fifteen years old. She was a white female, five-feet-five-inches tall, and weighed one hundred five pounds. She had long black hair and was wearing blue jeans, a blue-and-white peasant-type midi blouse, and brown leather sandals. She was carrying a red beach bag, a towel and a two-piece bathing suit. The suit was pink and purple.

Anne Psaradelis was also fifteen years old. She was a white female, five-feet-four-inches tall, and weighed one hundred twenty-five pounds. She had long dark brown hair. She was wearing blue jeans, a red blouse, and brown leather sandals. She was carrying a multicolored beach bag, a towel and a multi-colored, two-piece bathing suit.

"Mr. Compagna, if you'll wait a minute, I'll let you listen to the dispatcher putting out the missing person's bulletin regarding Diane and Anne."

"I really appreciate your help. I'm sure my wife does also."

"Mr. Compagna, if you should hear from either of the girls, please let me know."

11

JOSEPH A. HORAK

The investigation of the two missing girls, Diane Compagna and Anne Psaradelis, started on July 12, 1973. All the local police departments were notified to be on the alert for the girls and asked to check any areas where they might be found.

I started checking the back-road areas myself. Although I was sure the other units had already started checking, I asked them to give special attention to the ponds and lakes in their areas.

July 13, 1973

So far, we had no luck in finding the two girls. I spent all day with other officers looking around and asking people if they had seen the girls or knew where they might be. No luck. There was no sign of them anywhere.

It was time for me to go home, so I checked with the dispatcher to see if there were any messages for me.

"Hi, Richard, how are you doing tonight? I thought I'd check and see if you need me for anything."

"Hello, Sergeant, you're just the one I've been looking for. Mr. Compagna is here and would like to talk with you. He's waiting for you in the hall."

"Thanks, Richard. I'll go right out and talk with him."

I hung up the phone and walked out into the hall.

"Hello again, Mr. Compagna, sorry to keep you waiting. Is there any news on the girls?"

"No, Sergeant, I came over here to see if you found them. My wife and I are worried sick. This sure isn't like Diane. We've even checked with Jim and Ann Psaradelis and they haven't heard a thing either."

"Mr. Compagna, we've checked all over town all day and officers are still looking for them. I know it's a rough time for you and the Psaradelises, but try to keep up your courage. I'm sure they're all right and we'll find them. As you know, a missing person's bulletin has been put out and I'm sure all the police departments are on the lookout for them."

"Sergeant, would you go out with me for a few hours? I'd like to check around some of the other cities and towns. Some of the areas are pretty rough. Your being there would sure make me feel better."

"Come on, Mr. Compagna, let's see what we can do. I'll let the dispatcher know where we're going in case something turns up."

Mr. Compagna and I headed for Manchester. For four hours we drove through shopping centers, bowling alleys and every other place we could think of. We stopped and talked with several groups of kids, showed pictures of the girls, and still didn't have any luck.

"I really think we should call it a day. You have to go to work in the morning and so do I."

"You're right, Sergeant, let's head back. I really do appreciate all you've done for me."

"Mr. Compagna, just try to keep your courage up and tell your wife I'll drop by to talk with her tomorrow. I need to get a list of Diane's friends. It could help. I need to get a list from the Psaradelis family also."

When we arrived at the station, I said good night to Mr. Compagna. Then I put some gas in the cruiser and checked the oil.

"Unit one to headquarters."

"Go ahead, unit one."

"Richard, could you mark down twelve gallons of gas and one quart of oil on the slip for me?"

"Consider it done. Sergeant, by the way, Mr. Psaradelis is here in the station. He's been waiting for over an hour. Could you come in and see him?"

"Sure, I'll be right there."

Mr. Psaradelis was waiting in the hall when I walked into the station.

"Hello, Mr. Psaradelis, what can I do for you?"

"Sergeant, have you found the girls yet?"

"No. In fact, Mr. Compagna and I have just been out looking for the girls for the past four hours. We checked shopping centers and a lot of the places kids hang around. We even showed pictures of the girls. We didn't get even a hint about where the girls might be."

"Sergeant, I know it's late and you've been working all day, but do you suppose you could go out with me for a couple of hours? You know the area better than I do and I don't want to go prowling around in back alleys and get picked up by the police."

"I guess I could go out for a couple of hours."

"Sergeant, I have a feeling that Anne and Diane are here in town. Could we check around the lake and the swimming holes?"

"We've checked out these areas several times, but if it will make you feel better, let's check them again. I'll tell the dispatcher that we will be out in unit one for a few hours."

Even before I settled behind the wheel, Mr. Psaradelis started talking.

"Sergeant, I have a feeling that the girls are down near the lake. I know Anne knows people down there and some of them have camps."

"OK, Mr. Psaradelis, let's head down there."

We drove toward the lake, watching the roadway for anything suspicious as we went.

"Sergeant, see that green cottage over there? I know that Anne has been in there. That's where a boy from school by the name of Ricky Jones lives. Do you suppose we could check to see if the girls are there?"

"It's late to be knocking on doors, but I can understand how you feel, so let's go up and see if we can find the girls or anyone who knows where they are. Let me do the talking and don't argue with anyone."

"That's fine with me, Sergeant. I just want to find my daughter."

Our car doors slamming awakened someone in the cottage. A light went on and someone was at the door. As we approached, a young man began to speak.

"Yes, sir, can I help you?"

"Is Ricky Jones here?"

"I'm Ricky Jones. What do you want?"

"This is Mr. Psaradelis. His daughter, Anne, and her girlfriend, Diane Compagna, are missing. We would like to know if the girls are here or if you know where they are."

"Sergeant, I know both of the girls, but I haven't seen them since the Fourth of July. I saw them over near the high school just before the fireworks started. I didn't know they were missing. I don't have any idea where they've gone. If I find out anything, I'll let you know."

"Mr. Psaradelis and I both thank you and appreciate any help you can give us in finding the two girls."

As Jones closed the door, Mr. Psaradelis and I headed back to the car.

"Sergeant, would you mind checking one more place? Anne has been to some parties in one of the other cabins not too far from here."

"It's kind of late to be waking people up, Mr. Psaradelis, but I guess since we're right here, we might as well try."

"Thanks, Sergeant."

We had driven only a short distance when Mr. Psaradelis identified the cabin.

"That's the house over there. All the lights in the house are on. Look at the cars, there must be a house full of people."

While walking up to the front door, I heard someone holler, "It's the police." Someone else said, "You answer the door."

I knocked on the door. It was opened by a girl I knew to be Faith Buck.

"Are we making too much noise?"

"No, we're looking for two missing girls by the names of Anne Psaradelis and Diane Compagna."

Faith said, "I know them, but they aren't here. I didn't know they were missing."

"Faith, I'm Anne's father. Do you think that I could come in the house and look around? You seem to have an awful lot of kids in the house by the sound of it."

"Mr. Psaradelis, the girls aren't here, but if you want to come in and look through the house, you can."

"OK, as long as you don't mind."

Mr. Psaradelis' inspection of the house brought no new evidence. When we were back in the cruiser, I talked with Mr. Psaradelis.

"Well, Mr. Psaradelis, we checked out the house and spoke with twenty or so of the kids. Not one person knows where the girls are or why they left. That's all we can do right now. Maybe one of the kids will come forward in a day or two and tell us something."

"It's hard for me to believe that someone doesn't know something about where the girls are or why they took off."

"We've been out nearly three hours, Mr. Psaradelis. I don't know about you, but I think we better call it a night. If any of the other officers locate them, you will be notified. I'll take you back to the station and you can pick up your car."

"That will be fine, Sergeant. I really do appreciate all you've done. By the way, Mr. Compagna and I are going out looking for the girls tomorrow night after he gets off work."

As I parked the cruiser at the station, I put in one last call to the dispatcher.

"Unit one to headquarters."

"Go ahead, unit one."

"Richard, are there any messages for me or any news about the girls?"

"No messages and nothing on the girls, Sergeant."

"Thanks, I'm going home and get a few hours sleep."

3

July 14, 1973

I had a lot to do, including a couple of cases in court, so I looked over the paperwork related to the trials, then went to talk to the lieutenant.

"Good morning, Lieutenant, how long do you think we'll be in court today? I sure have a lot to do once I get out of here."

"Sergeant, we should be finished by mid-morning. By the way, have you turned up any leads about where the girls might be? Have you put out that all-points bulletin on the girls yet?"

"I'm planning to do that as soon as I get out of court. I've already cleared it with the chief. The chief told me to make sure the alert goes over the entire country. You know, sometimes we can put an alert out and it doesn't help at all. There are so many missing, lost or wanted people out there that the officers can't keep up with all the alerts with all the other things they have to do, but all it takes is one officer to remember and he could locate the girls or a wanted person.

"You know, Lieutenant, I've been spending a lot of time with Mr. Compagna and Mr. Psaradelis, attempting to locate the girls. So far, it has been pretty discouraging. We've talked with all kinds of people, as well as friends of Anne and Diane. It just seems strange to me that someone doesn't know something."

"All we can do is keep looking, Sergeant, they're bound to turn up. We better go into court, it's about to start."

When court was dismissed, I called the dispatcher.

"Unit one to headquarters."

"Come in, unit one."

"I'm clear from court. Are there any messages for me?"

"Sergeant, no messages, but Mr. Compagna and Mr. Psaradelis are here and would like to talk with you."

"Please tell them I'll be right in."

It was a short trip to the station. I found the two fathers waiting for me in the hall.

"Good morning, Mr. Compagna and Mr. Psaradelis. Sorry to keep you waiting, but I had a couple of cases over at court."

"Sergeant, we want to know if there is any news about Anne and Diane."

"I'm sorry to say no, but as soon as I finish talking with you, I'm going to have a bulletin put out on the girls that will cover the entire country. I still think they're around here, probably in the house of someone they know. I'm sure by now they know you're angry with them for not coming home. The longer they stay away, the harder it will be for them to face you."

"Sergeant, we're not mad, we just want the girls to come home wherever they are."

"I know that, but the girls need to know that too. Please try and keep your courage up. They're going to show up. It's just a matter of time."

Mr. Compagna and Mr. Psaradelis wanted me to go out with them and check around the shopping malls and other places the girls might hang out. They wanted to talk with people and show the girls' pictures. I checked with the chief and he agreed that I should accompany the two fathers. I put some gas and oil in the cruiser and we were on our way.

We headed north of town, toward the beach. We looked around every house and yard. Each of us expected one of the others to say, "There they are," but that didn't happen.

Mr. Psaradelis suggested we check out the large shopping mall. We spent nearly two hours making our way through the crowd of shoppers, talking with all kinds of people, both young and old, and showing the girls' pictures. Not one person had seen the girls.

We left the mall and headed toward the big park at Mr. Psaradelis' suggestion. It was only a couple of miles from the mall.

The mild weather had brought many people to the park. They were running around, some were in the pool, others were eating. I pulled the cruiser over to the side of the road and we all got out. We started walking around and talking with various people. Mr. Compagna and Mr. Psaradelis showed pictures of the girls to each person we met. As we walked deeper into the park, we could see a camping area. We separated and covered the area thoroughly, checking the rest rooms and around the hot dog stand. The girls were nowhere to be found

Heading back toward the cruiser, Mr. Compagna and Mr. Psaradelis discussed further search plans.

"We might as well start checking restaurants and gas stations."

"We can stop by and check the bus terminal and taxi cab companies."

Our search was turning up no clues. I tried my best to comfort the two men.

"We've been out here for seven hours now. We really need to start heading back to town. I know that it's pretty discouraging, but the girls will turn up."

I contacted the dispatcher at headquarters to report that we were back in town and asked if there were any messages. I was advised that the missing person's alert had been put out and should cover the entire country.

Weeks started to slip by and we had talked with hundreds of people. There was nothing to go on. We heard people say, "I saw them down at the mall," or "I saw the girls go into a four-story building up in Manchester," or "I've seen them. They jumped into a red car with two men." There were all kinds of stories, but not one ever proved to be true. I don't know why people say they see or do something that really isn't true. I think they just want to feel important or want to have us chase around for nothing. But we had to check out every lead, whether it sounded good or not.

I was really surprised that we hadn't found the girls yet. I tried to encourage the parents, but I didn't have a good feeling about their being gone all this time. I was concerned and really worried. Why hadn't we turned up a lead? We had done everything possible to locate Anne and Diane. Why were so many people sending us in the wrong direction?

I decided to talk with the parents of both girls again, as well as some of their classmates and friends. I really needed to know if anyone knew where the girls might have gone or why they left. Were there family problems? Did they drink or use drugs? Did they know anyone who might want to harm the girls? I had a host of questions. My thoughts were interrupted by the dispatcher's voice coming over my radio.

"Headquarters to unit one."

"Unit one, go ahead."

"Please come into the station. There's someone here to see you."

"Be right in."

I parked the cruiser in front of the station and went in to speak with the dispatcher.

"Evelyn, why did you want me?"

"Sergeant, Dorothy and Marcel Compagna are in the waiting room and would like to talk with you."

"Thanks, I'll take care of them. We'll be down in my office."

I walked into the waiting room and greeted Diane's parents.

"Hello, Mr. and Mrs. Compagna, hope you weren't waiting long. What can I do for you?"

"Sergeant, we want to know if you have any leads about our daughter and Anne Psaradelis. You know, they've been gone for quite a while. We just want to know that they're all right."

"First of all, Mr. and Mrs. Compagna, I'll try to answer your first question. No, we haven't received any leads. Oh, we've had calls from people who say they've seen the girls over at the beach, others say they've seen them hitchhiking down toward Boston. We've tried to check these stories out as best we could, but haven't found any of the reports to be reliable.

"Since you're here, you've saved me a trip to your house. I wanted to talk with you both and ask you some questions."

"What do you want to know, Sergeant? We'll help you in anyway we can. We just want our daughter back."

"I need to know how Diane got along with you and the rest of the family. Was she afraid of anyone?"

"First of all, Sergeant, we love Diane. We got along great and always did things together. Her father would take her anywhere she wanted to go. We all have a great relationship. Diane was not afraid of anyone that we know of."

"Did she smoke, drink or use drugs?"

"Diane did smoke, but not in the house. She didn't swear. Maybe she would use the word 'damn' once in a while, but she sure wasn't a bad girl. Diane didn't use drugs or drink."

"Did Diane go out with Anne very often? One of the big questions is, do you have any idea where the girls went or who they might be with?"

"We did hear that she hitchhiked once in a while. No, we don't know where the girls went or who they might be with. We would have told you if we knew."

"Mr. and Mrs. Compagna, I know you would have told us. I don't mean to offend you with some of the questions I might ask, I'm just trying to find something or someone who caused the girls to leave home. I want you to keep your courage up. We'll find the girls. They have to be staying with someone since neither girl has any money, a car or anything else. It could be as simple as the girls staying away one night, and knowing that they would be in trouble with you, they stayed away another night. Now that they've been gone weeks and weeks, it's much harder for them to face you. It's going to take someone they're with to convince them that the best thing is to come home and face up to what they have done."

"Well, Sergeant, we've taken up enough of your time. We know you and the rest of the officers are doing everything possible to find the girls. We really appreciate it. Will you keep in touch with us if anything turns up? Day or night, please let us know."

"Mr. and Mrs. Compagna, as soon as I hear something, I'll contact you. That's a promise."

After talking with the Compagnas, I headed over to meet with Mr. and Mrs. Psaradelis.

"Hello, Mrs. Psaradelis, hope you don't mind my coming by so early in the morning."

"Of course not, Sergeant, come in. Have you any good news for us?"

"I wish I could say yes, but there isn't a sign or a clue about where the girls are, but we'll find them."

"Jim, come out here, the Sergeant is here and wants to talk with us."

"I'll be right out. Give him a cup of coffee."

"Hello, Sergeant, any word on the girls?"

"No. The way things are going, it makes me think they're staying with someone. The question is, who? I'm here because I'd like to ask you a few questions."

"Go ahead, Sergeant, ask them."

"I'd like to know if Anne had any family problems?"

"No problems that we can think of. She gets along with everyone and is especially close to her father."

"Do either of you know if she was afraid of anyone?"

"No, Sergeant, not that we know of."

"Did Anne use drugs, drink or smoke?"

"All we can say, Sergeant, is that Anne is a good girl, that she likes boys, that she does smoke, but not in the house. We really don't know if she drank or used drugs."

"My husband and I really don't think that anyone would want to hurt her. We can't understand why the girls took off and don't know where they would go. As you know, Sergeant, my husband has been going out day and night looking for the girls. He's even seen them on a third-floor porch at a large apartment house down in Nashua. By the time he contacted the police so they could go to the apartment with him, the girls were gone."

"I know what you're talking about, Mrs. Psaradelis. I was one of the officers who checked out that third-floor apartment several times. We didn't find anything to indicate that the girls were there at any time. I don't know if the lieutenant told you or not, but I, as well as other law enforcement officers, have received twenty or so telephone calls from various unknown people saying they saw or heard the girls were in Nashua, Lowell, Boston, Salisbury Beach, and even down in Florida. These so-called leads had to be checked out the best way we could. We haven't found even one of them to be true. It really doesn't sound like anyone wants us to find the two girls. So far, this has been a very tough missing person's investigation. Usually we have some kind of lead revealing why the person or persons took off. So far, we have nothing. Well, Mr. and Mrs. Psaradelis, I want to thank you for taking the time to talk with me. Just know that we're doing everything possible to locate the girls. If you need me for anything, please feel free to call day or night."

When I returned to the station, I decided to speak with the chief. It was Sunday and I was glad to see that he was in his office.

"Chief, I've just come back from talking with the parents of Anne Psaradelis and Diane Compagna. I really feel sorry for both families. I'm sure they are more than upset, wondering where their daughters are and if they're safe. I'd like permission to spend the rest of the day out of town. It's a nice warm day and I'd like to check as many camping areas, lakes and ponds as I can. Our girls might be at one of them."

"Yes, Sergeant, of course you can go. It's the lieutenant's day off, why don't you see if he wants to go with you?"

"I will. Thanks, Chief."

I called the lieutenant and he agreed to join me in searching for the two girls. During our phone conversation we made plans for the day.

"Why don't you drive for the first couple of hours, Lieutenant, then we can switch off. I think we should head north and start checking everything, then we can head over to the coast. We have a full day ahead of us, but if we find the girls, it will be worth the effort."

We approached one of the nearby campgrounds and noticed that it was packed with people.

"Boy, Lieutenant, this looks like the kind of place we might find the girls. Drive slowly as we work our way through the park. You pay attention to everything on your side of the car and I'll take this side. Look at the people. It makes you wonder if anyone works. It looks like they have a couple of swimming pools over there. How about checking them out?"

"OK, let's check everything that looks good, Sergeant. That's why we're out here."

Unfortunately, there was no sign of the girls in the campground and we decided to move on to the next place on our list.

"You must be tired of driving, Lieutenant. How about me driving for a few hours? We've checked a dozen places so far and haven't seen one person we know. That shows me that it's going to be tough to find the girls. If we realize that, then the girls also realize it. That would make them feel they could go to a pond or lake and not be seen."

"OK, Sergeant, you drive for a while. Why don't I pull into the next gas station and we'll change over. We can also get a cold drink, I'm a little thirsty, how about you?"

"I could go for that. Let me pay for your drink since you're out here on your own time. Lieutenant, would you mind showing the pictures of the girls to the clerk in case he's seen them?"

"I was planning to do that, Sergeant."

"I know you were. You're usually way ahead of me."

We didn't realize there were so many campgrounds, ponds and lakes in the area. It was getting late and we weren't far from the coast, so we decided to head over to the beach. If we didn't find the girls there, we planned to head home. We wanted to get back before midnight.

The people on the beach were packed in like sardines. They were all over the place sitting on the hoods of cars, on the grass areas, on benches, just about anywhere they could find. We parked the cruiser and decided to check this one out on foot. We walked through the crowd for nearly three hours and found no sign of the girls. Then suddenly, we spotted a couple of kids from town and stopped to talk with them.

"Hi, Tom, who is that with you? Mike?"

"Yeah, you know who he is. What are the police from our town doing over here?"

"We're looking for two girls who are missing. Do you know Anne Psaradelis and Diane Compagna?"

"I know both of the girls, Sergeant. Are they the ones who are missing?"

"Yes, they are, Tom. Have you seen them here today or do you know where they might be?"

"To be honest with you, no, I didn't even know they were missing. Mike and I have been here since early this morning. If they had been here, we would have seen them."

"Well, thanks anyway. If you do happen to see them, would you give me a call?"

"You got it, Sergeant."

The Lieutenant and I looked another twenty minutes, then headed back to town. It was just about midnight when we arrived at the station. We had put a lot of mileage on the cruiser. I shared my frustration with the lieutenant as I filled the car with gasoline.

"I can't understand why someone doesn't come forward with a lead. Everything we've received so far takes us in every direction but the right one. It's almost like someone doesn't want us to find the girls."

The lieutenant agreed. I placed one last call to the dispatcher before calling it a night.

"Unit one to headquarters."

"Go ahead, unit one."

"Richard, would you mark down twenty gallons on the gas sheet for me?"

"Consider it done, Sergeant."

"Any calls for either the lieutenant or myself?"

"No sir, nothing."

"We're going home. See you in the morning."

4

July 30, 1973

Almost a month had passed since the girls were reported missing. I didn't have a very good feeling about how this was going to end. I prayed we would find the girls safe and sound. I knew everyone was doing everything they could to solve this case.

While sitting at my desk in the station, I was notified that there was a call for me on line two.

"Hello, who am I speaking with?"

"I would rather not say at this time."

"Why?"

"I have information about the two missing girls."

"Who are you talking about?"

"Diane Compagna and Anne Psaradelis."

"What do you know that you think would help us find the girls?"

"Well, I don't want to get involved. I just want to pass on some information I thought might help you."

"All right, let me have the information, please."

The unknown male told me that Tom Jefferson had been with Diane Compagna on the night of July 4 and that he was supposed to have raped Diane. The caller also stated that another person was with Anne Psaradelis and the same thing was supposed to have taken place. This man told me that the girls were supposed to be some place in Massachusetts.

"Sir, can you tell me in what city or town they are supposed to be?"

"No, Sergeant, I can't. This is just hearsay. All I know is some-place in Massachusetts. If I hear anything else, I'll call you back. I want to help find the girls."

"Thanks a lot. I hope you will call back."

I immediately went to the chief's office and told him what the caller had told me.

"Chief, that was quite a telephone call. The man on the phone didn't want to identify himself, but he gave me some good informa-tion. It could be a lead. He stated that he heard that Diane Compagna could have been raped during the evening of July 4 by a person named Tom Jefferson. I'm pretty sure that Jefferson lives off Amherst Road. The caller also said that he heard the girls were some place in Massa-chusetts. If this is true, it could explain a lot of things. I'll have to do some research into the possible rape. Would it be OK to pull Detective Tom McQuarrie off the case he's working on now to help me?"

"Go ahead, Sergeant. If you need him, pull him off that other case."

I contacted Detective McQuarrie and asked him to come into my office

"There you are, Detective McQuarrie, come on in. I really need your help with this one. I'm sorry I had to pull you off the case you were working on, but we might have a good lead about why Diane Compagna and Anne Psaradelis are missing. We really need to get right after this one. It sounds like the first good lead we've had."

"What do you want me to do, Sergeant?"

" Tom, I'd like you to check all the files and find out all you can about a Tom or Thomas Jefferson, who is believed to be living in our town. There's a Jefferson family living on Amherst Road. He could be their son. Please give me everything you can find out about him - friends, vehicle, record check, everything. I need this like yesterday, so do the best you can."

"I'll get right on it, Sergeant."

I passed the lieutenant's office on my way down the hall and no-ticed that he was at his desk.

"What are you doing here, Lieutenant? I thought this was your night off and you were having a cookout at your house."

"We are, but the chief told me that you might have a good lead about why the girls took off. I wanted to come in and help. I want to find the girls just as much as you do. You know, Sergeant, I have three daughters and they could be the ones who are missing. I think about that often. Where do we start?"

I told the lieutenant about the phone call I had received around six o'clock that evening.

"This man wouldn't identify himself and stated that his information was just hearsay. If he hears anything, Lieutenant, he said he would call us back. All he wants to do is help us find the girls. It sure sounds good to me. I have Detective McQuarrie running a background check on this Tom Jefferson. I think the next step is to call the Compagna home to see if they know or have heard of this Tom Jefferson. In fact, I'm going to call them right now."

"That's a good idea, Sergeant. Let me know if there's anything I can do to help."

I returned to my office and placed the call to the Compagna house.

"Hello, is that you, Mrs. Compagna?"

"Yes, it is."

"Well, this is Sergeant Horak."

"Don't tell me you've found the girls."

"No, I'm sorry, we haven't, but I need to ask you a question. Does Diane, you, or anyone in the family know someone by the name of Tom Jefferson?"

"Why, yes, Sergeant. Diane was with Tom Jefferson for a short time on the Fourth of July. What is this all about?"

"Nothing really, Mrs. Compagna, we're just trying to check out some information. If anything turns up, I'll contact you. I'm sorry to bother you so late."

"Don't worry about it, Sergeant. We really appreciate everything that the police department is doing to help us out."

After I hung up the phone, the lieutenant stepped into my office.

"Well, Sergeant, how did you make out with that phone call?"

"Lieutenant, Mrs. Compagna stated that Diane had, in fact, been with Tom Jefferson for a short time on the Fourth of July. I think we should go to the home of Linda Caron. She's a close friend of Diane's and might be able to help us. She lives over on Valley Street."

"Sounds like a good idea."

"It's getting late, Lieutenant, but I think we should go over and interview her now. The sooner we do this, the sooner we'll find the girls."

"You're right, Sergeant. Let's go."

The lieutenant wanted to accompany me on the interview and offered to drive his car. As we approached 20 Valley Street, we noticed that the lights were on in the house. Our knock on the door was answered quickly.

"Can I help you?"

"Yes. This is Lieutenant Gerlach and I'm Sergeant Horak. Is this the Caron residence?"

"Yes, it is. Can I help you?"

"Is your daughter, Linda, at home?"

"Why yes, in fact, she's sick in bed. Why do you need her?"

"Mrs. Caron, we're working on a missing person's case and we think Linda can help us. We won't take much of Linda's time, we just need to ask her a few questions."

"Who's missing?"

"Diane Compagna and Anne Psaradelis."

"Gosh, I know them both. Come on in, I'll get you a cup of coffee and then I'll get Linda. I'm sure she will help in any way she can."

When Linda entered the room, the lieutenant and I introduced ourselves. I reminded Linda that we had met at the Compagnas' house a couple of weeks ago.

"I don't know what I can do to help, Sergeant."

"Well, Linda, you know that Diane and Anne are missing. We're trying to find them. We'd like to know why they left and where they are."

"Sergeant, all I know is that they're missing. I don't have any idea where they are or why they took off."

"Linda, do you know anything about the possibility of Diane having been raped or having had relations with a male subject?"

"Well, Sergeant, I was with Diane during the evening of July 4 and I know what took place between her and Tom Jefferson. I really don't want to say anything more about it. I don't want to get involved. I will say that I don't know where the girls are or why they took off."

"Thank you for letting us impose on you this late at night. If you think of anything you haven't told us or come across anything that might help us find the girls, please call us, day or night."

The lieutenant and I returned to the station to find out how Detective McQuarrie was making out with Tom Jefferson's record. McQuarrie was in his office.

"Well, Tom, how are you coming along with that record check on Jefferson?"

"Sergeant, I checked all of our files and also ran a records and motor vehicle check with the state police. He has three vehicles registered in his name. Not much of anything else turned up, only a few speeding tickets. I also made a few phone calls. Jefferson drinks a lot. He has a bad temper and thinks he's a lady's man. I'll do some more searching and see what I can come up with."

"Thanks, Tom. Be sure to give me a copy of your report listing all the vehicles and anything else you turn up. Use the case number we have on the missing person's report."

"You'll have the report in the morning, Sergeant."

I asked the lieutenant to join me in Detective McQuarrie's office. I wanted to talk to both of them at the same time.

"I really think we need to move on with this investigation tonight. I know it's late, but I'm thinking about the girls. If we put things off, it could cause the girls to be hurt or worse. We have our first real lead and I say, let's go forward. If you agree, I'm going to give Jefferson a call and see if he'll come in and talk with us. We really can't take the chance of something happening to the girls because we didn't act on a lead."

McQuarrie and the lieutenant agreed and I placed the call.

"Hello, is this the Jefferson residence?"

"Yes, it is."

"May I speak with Tom if he's there?"

"Just a minute, I'll get him."

In only a few seconds, I heard a male voice answer the phone.

"Hello, is this Tom Jefferson?"

"Yes, it is."

"Well, this is Sergeant Horak. I know it's late, but could you come down to the station? I really need to talk with you."

"What's it about?"

"Tom, I would rather talk with you in person if you don't mind."

"No, I don't mind. I'll be there in about ten minutes."

Jefferson arrived at the station only minutes later. I asked the lieutenant to be present while I interviewed him. When Tom Jefferson was shown to my office, I introduced the lieutenant and myself, then began questioning him.

"Tom, we want to thank you for coming down here. I'm going to advise you of your rights. I always do this before an interview, whether they're a victim, a witness or a suspect. It protects the person I'm talking with, as well as myself.

"Tom, you have the right to remain silent. You have the right to have legal counsel before you do or say anything. If you don't have the proper funds to hire an attorney, one will be appointed for you. Any statement that you make can be used for or against you. You have the right to stop talking with me any time during the investigation. Do you understand your rights, Tom?"

"Yes, I do."

"Are you willing to talk with me?"

"Yes, I am, Sergeant."

Tom Jefferson signed a rights card and the lieutenant acted as witness.

"Sergeant, what do you want to talk to me about?"

"I want to talk to you about Diane Compagna."

"Is this about a rape?"

"Yes, it is, Tom. That's the problem at hand. Do you want to tell me about it?"

"On July 4, 1973, at approximately 9:00 p.m., I met Diane Compagna for the first time. I was walking around the celebration with Jimmy Smith, but spent a lot of time by myself talking to different people I knew. I met Diane through Linda Caron, who I've known for some time. I saw Linda off and on all day. So, when the dance started that evening, I met Diane and Linda. I asked Diane if she wanted to go for a walk. She said, not right away, because Linda would get mad with her. So, I went off and danced a couple of dances, then went back over to where the two girls were standing. I stood there for a while, then Linda went off to talk to someone. That's when I asked Diane if she wanted to dance. She refused and suggested we go for a walk instead. We went out behind the school and watched the fireworks for a couple of minutes, then we headed back to the dance. We stopped halfway and started kissing. I started feeling her, then went lower. There was no response on her part, so I started undoing her pants. Then she said no. I asked her why. She said that someone might see us. So I suggested we go down to the edge of the woods and she agreed. We lay down in the tall grass and I proceeded feeling and kissing her. I undid her pants and took them down, then I undid my pants. I put her hand on my penis and she played with me. Then I lay on top of her and was ready to enter when she said no again. I asked her why and she said, 'Cause.' So I made my entry with no physical struggle or molesting involved. I started laying her. When it came time for me to shoot my load, I pulled out. When I was finished, she said, 'OK, let's go,' and got up and dressed herself. We walked back to the dance and went our separate ways. The next thing I knew, Linda came up to me and said that Diane was telling everyone that I raped her. That's the first and last time I saw Diane."

"Tom, do you want to write out a statement in your own handwriting about what you just told us?"

"Yes, Sergeant, I would like to do that."

I gave Tom the appropriate form. He wrote his statement and the lieutenant and I witnessed it.

"Tom, since the incident on July 4, have you seen Diane Compagna?"

"No, but I've been looking for her. She's been going around telling everyone that I raped her. I want to find her so I can get things squared away."

"Tom, you're not under arrest at this time. Once we locate the girls, I'll get Diane's side of the story. If she says you had intercourse with her, with or without consent, you'll probably be charged with statutory rape. I'll contact you if we need you. If you see either of the girls or hear anything about where they might be, contact me or someone from the department."

"Sergeant, I'm not under arrest, right?"

"No, Tom, you're free to go."

"Sergeant, if I hear anything, I'll let you know."

The lieutenant and I went upstairs to talk with Detective McQuarrie. I gave him Tom Jefferson's statement and asked him to read it.

"Well, Tom, what do you think?"

"Well, Sergeant, I would say that Tom Jefferson could be the reason Diane and Anne took off."

"That's the same conclusion the lieutenant and I came to. It really makes sense when you think about it. If, according to Jefferson, Diane was going around on the night of July 4 telling everyone that Jefferson raped her, I'm sure he was more than upset.

"I'm sure the Compagnas must be wondering why I called earlier tonight regarding Tom Jefferson. Lieutenant, even though it's late, I think we better go over and talk with them. I'm sure Tom Jefferson is already calling his friends about coming into the station. I would bet that one of them will call the Compagnas to find out what's going on. It's really better that we talk to them tonight and let them know what the story is."

"You're right, Sergeant."

"You've put in a full day, Lieutenant, and it's supposed to be your day off. Why don't you go home? Tom and I can go over to the Compagnas'."

"Yes, I am a little tired, so I'll take you up on your offer."

When Tom and I approached the Compagna house, we noticed how nicely they kept their home. It was painted white. We were sure it looked even better in the daylight. Mrs. Compagna must have seen our headlights. She opened the door even before we knocked.

"Come on in, Sergeant. I just called the station and the dispatcher told me you were on the way over. Is everything all right? Have you found the girls?"

Mr. Compagna quickly interrupted his wife.

"Dorothy, let them get into the house before you start asking a lot of questions."

"I'm sorry, won't you come in? We were just going to have a piece of apple pie and coffee, would you like some?"

"That would be great."

I introduced Detective McQuarrie and we all sat down at the table. As we ate pie and drank coffee, we discussed the case.

"What's going on with your investigation of the girls? Why did you want to know if we knew Tom Jefferson?"

"First of all, there really isn't anything new on the girls. However, this thing with Tom Jefferson could shed some light on why the girls took off. I still have a feeling that the girls are somewhere close by, probably in someone's apartment or house. They aren't just wandering around the streets, someone would have found them by now."

I told them about the anonymous phone call I received that lead to our interview with Jefferson. They were surprised by what Tom Jefferson told us about the evening of July 4.

"'She didn't mention anything about a rape to me. Marcel, did Diane say anything about that to you?"

"No, Dorothy, she didn't say a thing."

"You know, folks, we didn't come over here to upset you. We promised to keep you informed about what was going on as much as we could."

"We know, Sergeant. What's going to happen to Tom Jefferson if he did rape our daughter?"

"Our prime concern now is to locate the girls. That has to come first. I'm thankful that we have a possible reason for the girls taking off. I don't like the reason any better than you do, but at least now we have a clue. I'd appreciate your not telling anyone about Tom Jefferson and the things we discussed tonight. We're going to talk with a lot of people. Maybe one of them will give us some information that will help bring the girls home.

"I've told you and the Psaradelises many times to keep your courage up. I know that's easier said than done, but please do your best to do just that. We'll be in touch as soon as we know something."

"By the way, Sergeant, I'm off work for the next five days. I'd appreciate it if I could ride in the cruiser with you while you're checking out various areas in town."

"I'll clear it with the chief, Mr. Compagna. I'll call you by noon tomorrow."

I checked with the dispatcher during the drive back to the station. There were no messages. Detective McQuarrie and I headed home to get some sleep.

5

<u>August 1973</u>

I was becoming more concerned with each passing day about the length of time the girls had been missing, but I couldn't let the Psaradelises or Compagnas know that. I had to try to give them encouragement and support. The only real clue we had was the Fourth of July incident and we really couldn't do much with that until we located Diane and Anne.

I went to the chief's office to talk with him about my concern.

"Good morning, Chief, can I come in and talk with you about our missing girls?"

"Come on in and pull up a chair."

"You know, Chief, it's been a month since the girls were reported missing and we don't have any kind of clue, except the one involving Tom Jefferson. In our interview with Linda Caron, she stated that she knew what happened on July 4 between Tom Jefferson and Diane Compagna. We have the information from the man who refused to identify himself, telling us that Tom Jefferson is supposed to have raped Diane Compagna. And, we have tom Jefferson himself who stated he had sex with Diane, but that he did not force her in anyway. I really thought someone would come forward with more information that would lead us to the girls, but that hasn't happened. It seems that no one wants to get involved. Maybe there're afraid to come forward and tell us what they know." "I know, Sergeant, it's frustrating."

"Chief, beyond this Tom Jefferson thing, we've received telephone calls from men, women and children reporting that they've spotted the girls in places like Nashua, Salisbury, Lowell, Boston, Hampton Beach, Florida, and even New York. We've received other reports, placing the girls in an apartment house on Main Street in Nashua, a cottage on Elm Street in Lowell, a camp, and many other places. We've had calls saying the girls have been seen hitchhiking toward Boston and other places, others saying the girls got into a car - a red one and a black one. Mr. Psaradelis himself has called and come into the station at all hours of the day and night saying he saw them go into a building or run up an alley. He even says he's chased them over rooftops. Our department, as well as other police departments in the area, has checked all these reports and never found even one of them to be true. I know Mr. Psaradelis is worried about his daughter, but it doesn't help things if he thinks he sees them and has us chasing all over the place. For all the so-called leads that he and others have given us, it almost seems like no one wants us to find Diane and Anne. It sure is a strange case, Chief. It makes me think there's more than meets the eye.

"I really feel bad for both families. I know a lot of the officers feel the same way. We all try to encourage them as much as possible, but all we can do is keep looking.

"Chief, I've spent so much time with the two families that they asked if they could call me by my first name. I said, 'Why not. We're all in this together, so call me Joe if you want to.'

"Chief, I have a feeling that something is wrong, more than just missing girls.

"By the way, Mr. Compagna is taking some time off work so that he can look for his daughter. He wants to know if he can go out in the cruiser with me for the next five nights."

"Go ahead, let him go out with you."

The dispatcher interrupted my conversation with the chief. There was a woman calling on line two. I answered the call in the chief's office to save time.

"Hello."

"Is this Sergeant Horak?"

"Yes, it is. What can I do for you?"

"I'm not going to give you my name. I just want to tell you that I saw those two missing girls. Ten minutes ago they went into an apartment at 20 Granite Street in Nashua."

"Are you sure it's them?"

"Yes."

"All right, we'll check it right out. Thank you for calling."

I got the dispatcher back on the line and asked her to contact the Nashua PD and have them meet me at 20 Granite Street.

"Chief, do you want to go with me to Nashua?"

"Yes, Sergeant. Let's use my car."

The apartment building in Nashua was surrounded by the local police when the chief and I arrived. We knew that if the girls were there, we would find them.

I introduced Sergeant Fred Powers of the Nashua PD to the chief.

"How are you, Chief? We just arrived. I put officers around the building just in case the girls try to run away. We wanted to wait for you because we don't know which apartment the girls are supposed to be in."

"Sergeant Powers, we don't know which apartment the girls went into either. All we can tell you is that a woman called a short time ago and said she saw the two girls run into the apartment house."

"Chief Pelletier, this apartment house has ten or more apartments in it. We'll check them all out.

"Sergeant, why don't you and the chief check out the apartments on the second and third floors with some of my officers? I'll leave a couple of officers outside to watch the building."

We agreed and went into the apartment building. Although it took very little time, our investigation of the first floor was thorough.

"We checked all four apartments, Chief. Not a sign of them. I'm surprised people let us come in and look around, but I suppose they wanted to help find the girls."

"I wonder how the other officers are doing. Let's go up to the second floor and see if we can help."

We met Sergeant Powers and the other officers as we were ascending the stairs.

"How did you make out, Chief?"

"No luck, Sergeant."

"We didn't have any luck either. We even checked out the attic and roof area."

"I wonder about these people who call in tips, but we have to check out any possible lead. We really appreciate your help, Sergeant Powers. Please thank the other officers for us."

"I will. Good luck."

During our drive back to the station, the chief and I talked about the investigation.

"You know, Chief, this is the same problem we've been having throughout this entire missing person's investigation. Some unknown person calls and gives us information. It never turns out to be true. I know that I've said it before, but it's almost like someone is trying to throw us off track. These people are taking us in every direction but the right one. I wonder how they would feel if they were missing, or if it was their brother or sister. I bet they'd want help from everyone."

"All we can do, Sergeant, is keep looking and keep checking out any leads that might come in."

Mr. Compagna and I went out every night and day, searching for Diane. We checked hotels, motels, barrooms, shopping centers, bowling alleys, back-road areas, ponds, lakes, just about anywhere that kids might hang out. We talked to all kinds of people, put up posters, and showed the girls' photographs. There wasn't a sign of them anywhere.

"Someone has to be hiding them, Mr. Compagna. I can't understand why the girls would want to hide from all the people who love them. I do suppose there's a chance that the girls might think that since they've been away from home all this time, they might get into trouble for being away and are afraid to come home."

"No, Sergeant. Diane would know better than that. She knows that we love her and would stand by her no matter what."

"All we can do is keep looking and praying to God that they return safe and well."

The days and weeks slipped by. I wondered if we would find the girls alive. I prayed to God we would.

I checked with the parents every day to find out if they had received a post card, a letter, a telephone call, or even a message from a friend. Nothing.

Both the Psaradelises and the Compagnas were receiving prank phone calls, some even came during the night. The phone would ring, but there would be no one on the other end of the line. Even worse, sometimes the person calling would say, "This is Anne. Help me." I wondered what kind of sick person could do that kind of thing. I also wondered if someone was trying to cause the investigation to go in another direction.

Tomorrow will be the last day of August. The girls have been missing for nearly two months. It was really hard for me to understand why we haven't been able to locate them.

I wanted to bring Tom Jefferson in and have another talk with him, but I decided to wait until we locate the girls and bring them back home.

In keeping with my daily routine, I called the Compagnas.

"Hello, is this Mrs. Compagna?"

"Yes, it is."

"This is Sergeant Horak."

"Hey, I thought we were going to call you Joe."

"Sorry about that. Well, anyway, if it's all right with you, I'd like to go over to the high school and see if someone will open up Diane and Anne's lockers. I'm going to call Mrs. Psaradelis, but I wanted to check with you first."

"It's OK with me. I'm sure it will be fine with the Psaradelises. We'll do whatever it takes to get our girls back."

When I arrived at school, Mrs. Compagna had already called the office to give me permission to check the girls' lockers. Mr. Stone, the janitor, took me downstairs to the locker area.

"Locker number forty-eight belongs to Diane Compagna and number sixty-four belongs to Anne Psaradelis. Here are the keys to both lockers. If you need me for anything else, I'll be in my office."

"Thanks, Mr. Stone, I'll return the keys when I'm finished."

JUSTICE DENIED

I checked the lockers of both girls and found only schoolbooks, papers, a couple of candy bars, and some cookies. There was not one thing that would help us.

I returned to the station and reported my findings, or lack of findings, to the chief. As I was walking toward my office to do some paperwork, the dispatcher caught me. Mr. Psaradelis was in the station and wanted to see me. The paperwork would have to wait.

"Hello, Sergeant, you're just the man I want to see."

"What can I do for you, Mr. Psaradelis?"

"Have you located my daughter yet?"

"No, Mr. Psaradelis, we're still looking and doing everything possible to locate her."

"Well, Sergeant, I quit my job today so I can spend more time looking for Anne. Can you go out with me tonight? We can check the shopping malls again. The girls just have to be around some place."

"Yes, Mr. Psaradelis, I'll go with you. Be here at five o'clock."

"Thanks a lot, Sergeant. I'll be here."

Our night of searching brought no new clues.

The next day Detective McQuarrie and I decided to visit as many police departments in the state as we could. We needed help and wanted to talk with them about our missing girls. Issuing bulletins and making phone calls weren't the same as talking with someone in person. We wanted to put a fire under the officers so they would make a bigger effort to contact the public. We wanted them to talk to people in the streets, in shopping malls, anywhere they might pick up a clue. We wanted the officers to show photographs of the girls and plead for help.

We drove from police station to police station. We had never heard of some of the small towns before, but we were determined to do whatever we could to find the girls. After nine hours, we stopped for a hamburger and something to drink. Then, we returned to our mission and continued driving until 5:00 a.m.

We received good responses from all the officers we talked to, personal touch is the best thing every time, but we wouldn't know if we really accomplished anything for a few days. Only if we found the girls would we know that our trip was worthwhile.

6

September 1973

The weeks sped by. It was difficult to believe that the middle of September had come so quickly. Where could the girls be? We've had very little cooperation from the public. Everyone who gave us information seemed to push the investigation in another direction. Something was wrong. There must be people out there with information about why Diane and Anne took off and were still missing. Not wanting to get involved was not a good reason to withhold information that could save them from injury or even death.

Mr. Psaradelis and Mr. Compagna continued to accompany me in the evenings, searching for their daughters. I knew it would be a lot easier for the parents if they knew the girls were safe and well.

September 28, 1973

We were still looking for our girls and not having much luck. Everyone, including the parents of Diane and Anne, had done everything possible to find the girls. The investigation had become a large part of everyone's life - especially mine. It was hard to know what to do.

I felt bad for the parents. I knew they wondered if they would ever see their daughters again, because that's the way I felt. I was determined not to let them know about my fears. I tried to encourage them and be there when they needed me.

I continued to check the lake area and the swimming hole off Bedford Road. I talked to everyone I could and continued to hear rumors that the girls were in Massachusetts. The story gathered more detail as the weeks passed. It was now reported that the girls were living with two boys and that one of the girls was pregnant. It was suggested that the girls were afraid of someone, which was preventing them from returning to town.

During one of my searches, I received a call from the dispatcher. The lieutenant was with me.

"Headquarters to unit one."

"This is unit one."

"Could you check out a report of burglary in progress at John's Texaco Station?"

"Sure. We're on our way."

We approached the gas station and noticed the owner's pickup truck parked near the front door. John was inside. The lieutenant got out of the cruiser to investigate and I swung around the rear of the building. There was nothing suspicious to report. The lieutenant found out that the owner had locked his keys inside the garage and had to break the window to get in.

The lieutenant and I continued our patrol. It was unusually quiet for a Saturday night. We had a couple of hours left on duty, so we decided to go into the back-road areas and beat the brush, hoping to turn up something about the girls.

"Lieutenant, it's such a hot muggy night, maybe the kids are having a big party somewhere. I think we should try to find it. I keep thinking that our luck will change. If we talk with the kids long enough, maybe one of them will come forward with information that will help bring the girls home. Somebody has to know something. If we keep trying, maybe we'll find the right person."

"I agree with you. Let's take a swing down near the reservoir and gravel pit areas. Maybe we'll run into something."

We came upon a dirt road packed with cars. It was an area known to all of us as Mud Road. There was the glow of a fire in the distance. It was worth investigating. We knew we would never be able to drive the cruiser through the congestion of cars, so we set out on foot with our walkie-talkie.

As we neared the area in question, we spotted teenagers we knew from town - Jimmy Brown, Sam Moses, and a group of girls who looked familiar. They were leaning against a truck, talking. There were empty beer and soft drink cans thrown all over the ground.

We walked closer to the fire and observed several cases of beer and soft drinks stacked on the ground. Some of the kids were eating hot dogs and hamburgers; others were singing and laughing. It seemed like everyone was having a good time, until they spotted us.

Someone yelled, "The police! Let's get out of here!" Then, kids started running in all directions, trying to get away.

"Hold on, boys and girls, we want to talk with you."

"We didn't do anything wrong. Why are you stopping us?"

"You know, we could arrest you for a variety of charges-trespassing, burning without a permit, drinking. I'm sure you realize that or you wouldn't be trying to run away. So, just listen up.

"We're sure you all know that Anne Psaradelis and Diane Compagna are missing. They've been gone since July 12. Most of you probably know them and we need your help. Does anyone know where the girls are or why they took off?"

There was no answer.

"How would you feel if you were missing and none of your friends stepped forward and told what they knew? You wouldn't feel very good, would you? You know, true friends are there when you need them, not just during good times. They're there during bad times as well. If you're a good friend of the girls, you really need to tell us what you know. You might save the girls from serious injury or death."

Still, no one came forward.

"If you change your mind, please call the lieutenant or myself. You can come to the station day or night. Everything you say will be kept in strict confidence. I'm not going to kid you, we really need your help. Please think over what we've said and help us."

It was apparent that no one was going to talk to us in that environment, so we dropped the questioning.

"We want you to have a good time, but we're going to confiscate the beer. We'll be back a few more times tonight. If there is drinking or a problem of any kind, some arrests will be made."

I couldn't help adding one more plea for information.

"Remember, any help you can give us will be appreciated."

The lieutenant and I confiscated the beer and headed toward the station.

"Lieutenant, I think we did the right thing tonight by not arresting anyone at that so-called party. We probably wouldn't have been able to get the people who purchased the beer. "At least we confiscated the beer and we had a talk with quite a few kids. Who knows, maybe we'll benefit from it. I'll go back down there a few more times tonight. If there is beer, drugs or trouble, arrests will be made."

"OK, Sergeant, I think I'll head home. If anything turns up, call me."

After I delivered the confiscated beer to the station, I checked a few buildings and swung back down to Mud Road. The fire was out and the area was abandoned.

September 30, 1973

It was Sunday morning. Even though it was my day off, I decided to stay at the station for a couple of hours and do some paperwork. As usual, I was interrupted by a telephone call.

"Hello, is this Sergeant Horak?"

"Yes, it is."

"This is Sam Moses. Could I come into the station and talk with you?"

"Yes, of course, you can."

Sam knocked at my office door within minutes.

"Come on in, Sam. I saw you at that party last night off Mud Road."

"I know you did, Sergeant. We thought you and the lieutenant were pretty decent to us."

"What can I help you with, Sam?"

"I have something I want to tell you about Diane Compagna, but it's just hearsay, it's not something I know from my own personal knowledge."

"That's OK, just tell me about it."

"I heard that Tom Jefferson was with Diane on July 4 and that he was supposed to have raped her. I don't know any more than that, but

I'm going back to the person who told me and see if I can find out anything more. I'll try to get this person to come down and talk with you, if I can. I don't know if this information will help, but I heard what you and the lieutenant said last night. I know both girls, but, like most people, I don't really want to get involved."

"Sam, I want to thank you for coming in. If you hear anything else, please let me know."

As soon as Sam left, I called the lieutenant to let him know about our conversation.

"I know we already have this information, Lieutenant, but at least someone has come forward on their own to help. I think we should have Tom Jefferson come into the station and have another talk with him."

"You're probably right, Sergeant. Why don't we ask him to come in tonight or tomorrow?"

"OK, Lieutenant, I'll try to make contact with him. If I do, I'll notify you."

It was almost noon and I was still in the office. I wasn't able to contact Tom Jefferson. On my way out of the station, I left a message for the lieutenant that I would continue to call Tom Jefferson to arrange an interview.

7

6:15, September 30, 1973

The phone rang. I wondered who it was. I never received calls unless it was bad news or something about a case.

"Hello, Sergeant, this is Leutenant Gerlach."

"Hello. What's going on?"

"They just found our girls. Anne Psaradelis and Diane Compagna were murdered."

"Murdered! Murdered! You must be joking."

"No, Sergeant, I'm not joking. The girls have been found murdered."

"I can't believe it. I just can't believe it. When did this happen? Where were they found?"

"Hold on, Sergeant, one question at a time. They found the bodies of two girls yesterday, September 29. A positive identification was made today - they're the bodies of Diane Compagna and Anne Psaradelis."

"Where did this happen?"

"About twenty miles from here, over in Candia. I'm going back there in about ten minutes, I'll pick you up in five."

"I'll be ready, Lieutenant."

When the lieutenant picked me up, I was in a state of shock and didn't know what to say. Having received all the false leads, I knew something was wrong, but I couldn't believe the girls had been murdered. I finally gathered my thoughts enough to start asking the lieutenant some questions.

"If the bodies were discovered yesterday, why weren't we notified until today?"

"The only thing I can say for sure is that they didn't notify our department because they didn't have a positive identification of the two bodies."

"Come on, Lieutenant, I'll bet we're the only place in the state that has two girls missing together. Our bulletins on Diane Compagna and Anne Psaradelis have been out since July 12. We've contacted just about every police department in the state. Everyone knew we had two missing girls. Why didn't they contact us?"

"I don't know, Sergeant."

"When were you contacted, Lieutenant?"

"I got the call around two o'clock this afternoon."

"I'm really upset. Why didn't you call me?"

"Well, this is your day off. You haven't had a free day in quite awhile. I didn't want to bother you."

"Come on, Lieutenant, it's after six o'clock. Give me a break. You know that I've lived this investigation day and night for the past eighty-one days. How could you think I would rather have a day off than do my job? You should have let me know. I should have gone over to the crime scene with you right away. By the way, Lieutenant, who was with you when you first went to the crime scene?"

"I took the corporal so he could take photographs."

"Boy, that sure makes me feel good," I said sarcastically. "You know, Lieutenant, when an investigator can go to a crime scene before everyone moves in, it really helps. When things have been moved around and damaged, it gives a different picture of what really took place. From what you've told me, that's what happened over in Candia. It'll be interesting to see what's left to investigate. Are the bodies still there?"

"No, they've been moved to the Maiden Funeral Home."

6:30 p.m., September 30, 1973

As the lieutenant and I drove to Candia, the cruiser was deathly quiet. There was nothing left to say.

The crime scene was on New Boston Road. By the time we arrived, the road was roped off and a state trooper and two local police officers were guarding the area. One of the officers motioned for us to stop and walked up to the window.

"Lieutenant Gerlach, I thought you left here a couple of hours ago."

"I did, Officer, but there are a few things that need to be finished up here. Besides, I wanted Detective-Sergeant Joe Horak to look over the scene."

"Well, there are still quite a few police officers up there. Go ahead, you know where to go."

As we drove up the road, I kept looking from side to side. There were woods and ditches on each side of the road. We crossed a section of road that had water and wetlands on both sides. I scanned the area, not really sure what I was looking for, but trying to identify anything that might be connected to the girls and their deaths. Farther on, there was a dump off to the right side of the road. As we neared the crime scene, there were police cars of every description parked all over the place. The lieutenant pulled the cruiser in front of a state police van.

We were in a pretty isolated area. I spotted a house about eight hundred feet from a gravel pit. It was the first house we'd seen since we left the main road. The area was surrounded by a stone wall. There was an opening in the wall and we headed toward it.

"This is probably where the killer parked the car, truck, or whatever vehicle was used."

"You could be right, Sergeant."

I stopped for a moment and stood there, looking over the gravel pit. It wasn't very big and didn't appear to have been used very much. As I looked around, I kept thinking I might find something that someone else had missed.

Figure 1: New Boston Road, Candia, NH

Figure 2 abc: Composite of wetland on New Boston Road

*Figure 3: Crime Scene entrance from
New Boston Road*

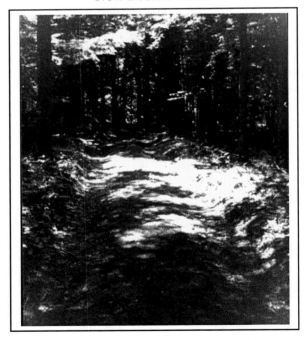

*Figure 4: Old logging road off
New Boston Road*

Figure 5: Looking from gravel pit to New Boston Road

Figure 6: Area in which the body of Anne Psaradelis was found

Figure 7: Stone wall at Crime Scene

Figure 8: Chief Baker

JUSTICE DENIED

"Come on, Sergeant. We have to go this way."

The lieutenant pointed toward a wooded area ahead.

"It's pretty warm, isn't it, Sergeant?"

"Yes, and you can feel death in the air. It's not a nice feeling. The air is stifling, there isn't even a breeze."

As we walked through the woods, my thoughts wandered to our poor girls who were murdered in this awful place. It wasn't long before we approached another opening in the stone wall. We walked through and met two officers coming out of the woods. They gave us a wave of their hand and shook their heads in disgust.

Within a few seconds we entered a grove of pines. There were three or four officers in a group talking and a couple of others walking around.

"This is part of the crime scene, Sergeant. The bodies were found over there."

The lieutenant motioned toward an area covered with pine needles. I observed the impression of a body burned into the needles and the ground beneath them. I was filled with sadness and anger. I was more determined than ever to find the person or persons who took the lives of these two young girls.

"Lieutenant, which girl was found here?"

"Diane Compagna. Anne Psaradelis was found about three feet from the stone wall."

The stone wall was about three hundred feet away. The crime scene didn't tell us very much. I was pretty discouraged and wished someone had notified me right after the bodies were discovered. I would have liked to have searched the scene for evidence before so many things had been moved around. There was no way of telling how many people, including law enforcement officers, had been in the area since the bodies were discovered.

Finally, the lieutenant described the details associated with finding the bodies.

"A man by the name of Robert Lupien approached a Candia police officer who was on traffic duty at the intersection of Routes 101A and 107. Mr. Lupien told the officer, who has been identified as John Morse, that he was bird hunting in the woods near the town dump when he came across a partially decomposed human body. Lupien's attention had been drawn to the body because of its bright clothing.

"About this time the Auburn police chief, Emerson Heald, came along. Sergeant Morse stopped him and requested that Heald contact Chief Robert Baker and ask him to respond to New Boston Road near the dump.

"Chief Heald and Sergeant Morse went to the area of New Boston Road where Robert Lupien had entered the woods. They walked in a northerly direction along an old logging road. They had traveled only a short distance when they found a shallow depression in the ground, created by what appeared to be a decomposed human body. There were no clothes on the remains.

"Heald and Morse returned to the road. Chief Baker and Officer Ed Perkins had just arrived. The entire group went back to the site and confirmed that it was indeed, a human body, very badly decomposed. The officers remained with the body, while Chief Baker left to contact the medical referee.

"Sergeant Morse scouted around and found a second body about one hundred fifty feet away. He advised Officer Perkins, then continued to search the area.

"Chief Baker was told about the new discovery when he returned. He ordered the area to be roped off. The chief took photographs of the two bodies and the locations in which they were found. He also took measurements from New Boston Road. The officers were ordered to secure the scene while Chief Baker left to meet the medical referee and to notify the attorney general and the state police.

"Word spread fast through governmental offices. Eventually there were representatives from the attorney general's office, the state police crime laboratory, the fish and game department, the sheriff's department, the state police, the Candia Police Department, and the Auburn Police Department on the scene.

"When the state police crime laboratory people arrived, Roger Beaudoin, the supervisor, recognized the complexity of the case. He recommended that the bodies not be removed until morning when better light would prevail. Chief Baker concurred and requested that Sergeant Morse set up a guard schedule to protect the scene for the night.

Officers Perkins, Gilbert and Jennings provided coverage from 6:30 p.m. until 12:30 a.m., when they were relieved by Officer Jones from the Candia Police Department and Officers Shaw and Gilbert from the Auburn Police Department.

"Chief Baker returned with support personnel at 8:45 a.m. They mapped the area completely with photos and measured the scene from permanent positions on New Boston Road to the bodies. The first body located by the hunter was labeled Body #1 and the body near the stone wall was labeled Body #2.

"Both bodies were examined by Roger Beaudoin from the crime laboratory and Carlton Eldredge the assistant county medical referee, although there was little to examine. The bodies were so badly decomposed that they were little more than skeletons. They made notations of the information gathered, then placed the bodies into plastic bags. They used plywood slabs to remove the bodies from the scene and take them to Maiden Funeral Home.

"Several officers conducted a search of New Boston Road from the scene to the intersection of Routes 101A and 107. They found nothing.

"That's all I can tell you right now, Sergeant. As for me, I was home this morning when I received the phone call from the Nashua Police Department around 9:30. Sergeant Everett Costa advised that two female bodies had been found in Candia and it was suspected that they were our missing girls.

"I called Candia, but couldn't contact Chief Baker. So, I called Chief Emerson Heald from the Auburn Police Department, since it's the next town over. I gave Chief Heald the information on Anne Psaradelis and Diane Compagna.

He told me that he would contact Chief Baker right away and relay the information to him.

"Sergeant, I guess the chief called me back around 11:10 this morning. He advised that the bodies could be the two girls missing from our town. He added that one girl had on a blue ring and the other, silver earrings.

"Chief Baker requested that someone from our department respond to the Maiden Funeral Home in Candia with whatever information we had on the girls some time after 2:00 p.m. this afternoon.

"Around the same time, I received a telephone call from Sergeant John Gates of the state police crime lab, asking if I could find out who the girls' dentists were. They needed the dental charts, x-rays and anything else the dentists might have at the funeral home.

"I went to the homes of the Compagnas and Psaradelises and obtained the information I needed. Both girls were patients of Dr. Joseph Patryn and Dr. Ronald Royer. They responded to Candia with the material, as requested. That was about two o'clock this afternoon. Corporal Hudson and I went to the funeral home ourselves, and then to the crime scene."

I had listened as long as I could without saying something.

"That really isn't fair, Lieutenant. I was doing paperwork at the station all morning. If you could call the corporal, you sure could have called me."

"Well, Sergeant, I needed him to take photographs at the scene. Besides, I don't have to explain to you."

"No, you're right, Lieutenant, you don't."

"It's getting dark out, we better head back to town. I still can't believe the girls were murdered. I guess now our investigation goes from missing girls to murder. If we thought we had our work cut out for us before, we really have it cut out for us now."

"Lieutenant, how did the parents take the news about their girls being found murdered?"

"Sergeant, I really think after all this time of looking, praying and false leads, they almost expected it to end this way."

"Lieutenant, when we get back to town, would you mind taking a few minutes to stop by the Compagna and Psaradelis homes?"

"Of course not, Sergeant."

"Thanks, I would really appreciate that. It's going to be hard to know what to say, but I'd like to say something to them."

"I know the feeling, Sergeant."

As we drove back to town, I talked with the lieutenant about what we had viewed at the crime scene.

"I doubt that the killer or killers parked their vehicle on the road. There's a home about eight hundred yards or so from the gravel pit entrance. The vehicle had to be parked for some time; the killer or killers couldn't have accomplished what they did in just a few minutes. I feel the vehicle used was parked close to the gravel pit, off the road. It would have stuck out like a sore thumb if it had been parked on the road. The people in that house would have seen it."

"Sergeant, what makes you say killer or killers?"

"Well, Lieutenant, one person wouldn't be able to control two girls, especially if they were in fear of their lives. They would either scream, run, or both. If it were just one killer, the girls would have put up a good fight. It doesn't look like that happened.

"Then, Lieutenant, we have two crime scenes. One girl was found naked in the pine grove. The second girl was clothed and found in an area of heavy brush and hardwood trees."

"So, what are you trying to say, Sergeant?"

"Of course, Lieutenant, since I didn't see the entire crime scene before everyone got into it, I don't have a clear picture of this; but from what you've told me, I would say that we're looking for someone who knew the girls."

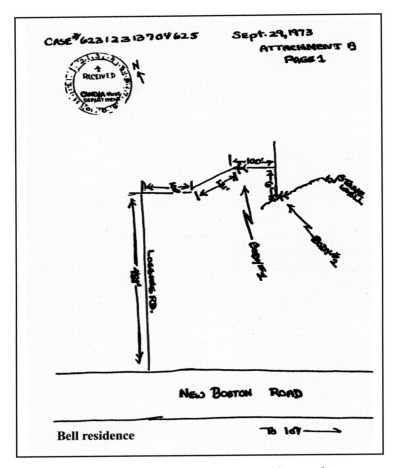

Figure 9: Plat of Crime Scene (General)

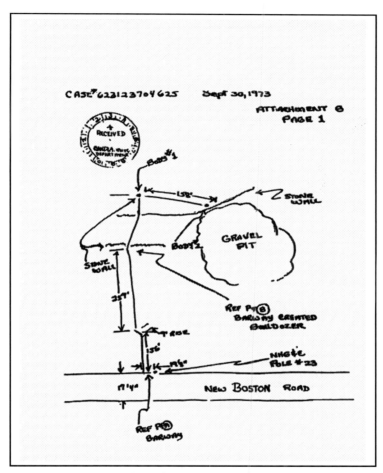

Figure 10: Plat of Crime Scene (Specific)

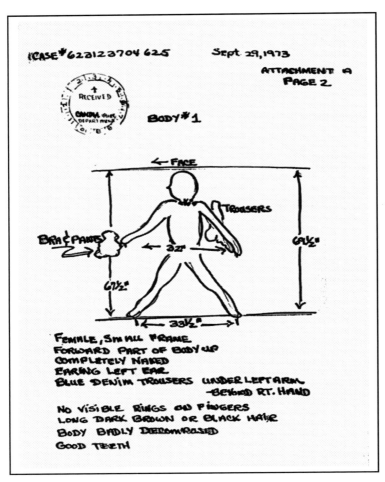

Figure 11: Body #1 (Police Description)

Figure 12: Body #1 (Artist Rendering)

Figure 13: Body #2 (Artist Rendering)

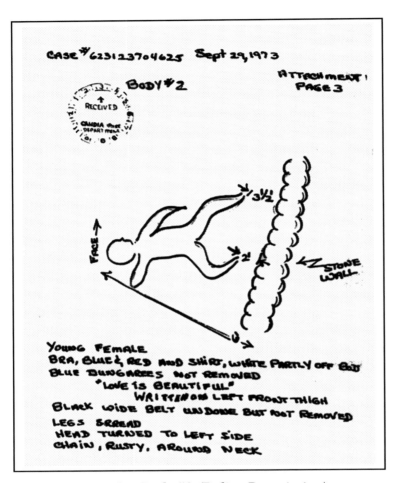

Figure 14: Body #2 (Police Description)

"Well, Sergeant, there's supposed to be a meeting in the attorney general's office in the State House. It's my understanding that they're going to formulate plans to conduct the standard homicide investigation procedure. The base of operations will be at our headquarters in Merrimack. That means the investigation should be in full operation by Tuesday."

"We're close to the Psaradelis home, Lieutenant. Maybe you should drop me off for a minute. I'll be right out."

The visit to the Psaradelis house was pretty rough. I asked the lieutenant to accompany me at the Compagna home, but it wasn't any easier. It was really hard to face the girls' parents. For eighty days we had been telling them to keep up their courage, that the girls would be found safe and sound, but it didn't work out that way.

September 30, 1973
10:00 p.m.

I placed the call when I returned to the station and arranged the interview for that evening.

"Hello, Linda, come on in. I really appreciate your coming down here so late." Although it was late, I felt it was important to re-interview Linda Caron as soon as possible.

"Sergeant, I just heard about Anne Psaradelis and Diane Compagna being murdered. I just can't believe it. I'll help you in any way I can. What do you want to talk with me about?"

"Well, Linda, you know that the lieutenant and I talked with you some time ago regarding the incident between Tom Jefferson and Diane Compagna that took place on the evening of July 4."

"Yes, Sergeant, I remember that."

"Well, Linda, at the time you really didn't want to talk about it or get involved in any way. As I told you on the phone, I really need your help and hope you'll reconsider talking with me about what happened. Will you do that for me?"

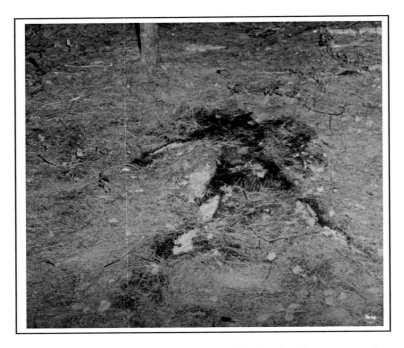

*Figure 15: The eerie shadow left by the decomposed
body of Diane Compagna*

"Yes. On July 4, Diane Compagna and I met at the Merrimack High School. We were going to the carnival in the large parking lot near the school. I don't remember what time it was, but it was a couple of hours after the parade."

"Linda, was Diane alone at that time?"

"Yes, I think she was. Diane told me she had seen Tom Jefferson and wanted to talk with him. She thought he was really cute."

"Then what happened?"

"I noticed Tom was standing in the parking lot with a beer in his hand. Diane and I walked over to him and started talking. Diane wasn't wearing a bra, just a midriff. Tom looked her over the whole time we talked with him."

"Linda, what do you mean, he looked her over?"

"He was looking at the way she was built, you know, the way some men look at women. Well, anyway, Tom acted like he had some-place to go, so we left him standing there. Diane and I walked over to the games, but we didn't play, we just walked around. Not much was happening, so we decided to go home for supper and return later on. I don't know what time it was, only that I could hear the band playing.

"When we returned, Diane spotted Tom Jefferson and Ted Smith walking toward us. I remember telling Diane that she better watch out for Tom. When he drinks, he's fresh and wants to get you in the bushes."

"What do you mean by that, Linda?"

"Well, he would try to have sex with you."

"I see. Then what happened?"

"When Tom and Ted joined us, Tom asked Diane to dance. Both boys had a bottle of beer in their hands. At that point, Ted tried to kiss me, but I pulled away. Tom and Diane were gone when I turned around."

"Linda, do you know where they went?"

"No, Sergeant. All I know is that I was scared because I knew Tom was drinking. I suspected he would take Diane to the bushes behind the school and try to have sex with her."

"Linda, did you try to find Diane?"

"Sergeant, I walked all over the place looking for her. The only place I didn't look was in back of the school. I didn't go there because I was afraid of the dark. I ran into Frank Davis and told him what had happened. He joined me in searching for Diane. We looked around the games and rides, out in the parking lots, and in the fields. We never did find her.

"Later on, Diane showed up with Frank. Diane told me she was really mad because Tom Jefferson took her over to the bushes. She said that even though she said no, he kept trying to pull down her pants."

"Linda, did Diane say anything else about what took place in the bushes?"

"Well, Sergeant, she said she sort of let him pull down her pants, but he started to hurt her, so he told her to relax. Diane told me that she thought Tom tried to rape her. She said they had relations in the woods behind the school. Diane was very upset. I told her if Tom did try to rape her, she should press charges against him. Diane didn't say anything."

"Did you and Diane go home then?"

"No, I told Diane that I was going to talk with Tom Jefferson. When I left, Diane was talking to someone else. I know she told a lot of people what happened between her and Tom Jefferson."

"Linda, did you have that talk with Tom?"

"No, I couldn't find him, so I went back to where Diane was. It had started to rain, so I didn't look for him any more. Diane and I walked back to where the band was playing in front of school and talked about Tom. She told me that she didn't mind what Tom did. She was upset because she probably wouldn't see him again. I told Diana she was right, she wouldn't see Tom again.

"Then I spotted Tom and walked over to him. I asked him if he raped Diane. He said, 'What are you talking about?' Tom told me that he took Diane into the bushes but he didn't rape her. She was with him of her own free will. He was really drunk and swearing."

"Linda, what did you say when he told you that?"

"I told Tom that I believed him. He isn't that forceful. Tom wouldn't push anyone if they didn't want to do it. I don't know if his being drunk would make a difference.

"I left Tom and went back to talk with Diane. She was standing by the band, listening to the music. I told Diane what I had said to Tom. She kept saying she wished she would be able to see him again. I told her she never would. Then we left and headed down to the gas station to use the bathroom. After that, I dropped Diane off at her house.

"Sergeant, I did see Tom Jefferson sometime after Diane disappeared. He was coming out of Pizza By Golly. I told him that Diane was missing and he said, 'Who is Diane?' I said, 'Diane Compagna.' Tom still didn't know who she was, so I described what she looked like. Then he said, 'Oh, yeah, I think I remember her.' Tom asked why she had left. I replied that I didn't know. Tom acted as if he could care less and said he had to go.

"I did hear that Tom Jefferson is going to get married because he has a ready-made family. The girl is about twenty-two. I want you to know Sergeant that's only hearsay.

"That's really all I can tell you, Sergeant. If I think of anything else, I'll come in and see you."

"Linda, I want to thank you for coming in and talking with me."

It was late and I was tired. It had been a long day. I was sure the days and weeks to come were going to be more than busy. I hoped we could catch whoever murdered the girls fast. If he murdered two girls, he could do it again.

Monday, October 1, 1973

I drove to the station with unanswered questions swimming through my head. Who? What? Where? When? How? Why? If we knew the answers to these questions, we could solve the case.

The meeting with the attorney general's office was scheduled for tomorrow at 10:00 a.m., officially turning the investigation over to our department.

I was eager to get started interviewing people to try and turn up some leads. I really wanted to talk to Tom Jefferson first, but knew I should probably hold off. Instead, I called Greg Moses and arranged a meeting for later that morning.

"Come on in, Greg."

"What did you want to talk with me about?"

"Well, Greg, I'd like to know if you saw Diane Compagna during the evening of July 4."

"As a matter of fact, Sergeant, I did. Do you want me to tell you about it?"

"Yes, Greg, I'd like to hear what you have to say."

"Well, Sergeant, I was walking around the grounds of the Merrimack celebration and met a friend of mine, Linda Caron. Diane Compagna was with her. While I was talking to Linda, I noticed that Diane seemed upset. I asked Linda what had happened and she told me that Diane had just had sexual activities with Tom Jefferson.

"While I was talking to Linda, Diane left to look for Tom Jefferson. She found him and they talked for a few minutes, then Diane returned to where Linda and I were. Diane seemed more upset than ever. She told me she was with Tom in the wooded section by the high school and they had sex. Diane was upset because she thought she might be pregnant. She didn't know what to do. I saw a friend of mine and left. I never saw Diane again. I don't really know anything else. If I hear something, I'll let you know."

"Thanks for coming in, Greg. I really appreciate it."

At this point in the investigation, it was like starting from scratch. I decided to review all the paperwork we had accumulated on the case to see if I could come up with anything we had overlooked. The name Anne Psaradelis hadn't meant anything to me when the missing person's report was filed, but suddenly I remembered another incident involving Anne Psaradelis. I went directly to the chief's office to tell him about it.

ua Telegraph

Weather
Fair Tonight
Cloudy Tuesday

...mpshire's Largest Evening Newspaper . . .

...ASHUA, NEW HAMPSHIRE, MONDAY, OCTOBER 1, 1973 — Second Class Postage Paid At Nashua, N. H. — Price: TEN CENTS

Bodies Of Merrimack Girls Found In Candia

CANDIA, N.H. (AP) — The decomposed bodies of two teen-age girls discovered in woods here this weekend have been identified as those of Diane Compagna and Anne Psaradelis, both 15 years old from Merrimack.

"The probability is almost complete that this is a double homicide," said Atty. Gen. Warren Rudman, whose office is coordinating the investigation.

Missing Since July 11

The girls reportedly were last seen July 11, when they left their homes to go swimming at Baboosic Lake.

Dr George Katsas, a forensic pathologist from Boston, was unable immediately to establish the exact cause of death, Rudman said.

The bodies were discovered about 300 feet apart Saturday afternoon, officials said.

A hunter discovered the first corpse about 2:30 p.m. near the intersection of New Hampshire 107A and New Boston Road.

Police found the second body a short time later.

Officials said the first body appeared to be unclad. A halter top and a pair of underpants reportedly were found a few feet away.

The second body appeared to be clad in dungarees and a halter top.

No weapon was found at the scene, officials said.

The bodies were left at the scene until a complete evaluation of the crime scene was made Sunday, then they were taken to a hospital in nearby Manchester for tests.

The Compagna girl, daughter of Mr and Mrs Marcel Compagna of Walden Road, and the Psaradelis girl, daughter of Mr and Mrs James Psaradelis of Harris Avenue, Merrimack, had been reported missing by their parents since July 11, when they failed to return home from Baboosic Lake where they had reportedly gone swimming.

In a report published in the Telegraph July 28, the two girls were reportedly seen at Hampton Beach and were also reportedly to have been seen later in Nashua on several occasions.

Merrimack police had been checking out numerous reports of the girls' whereabouts, including the reports in Hampton Beach and Nashua, but were unable to locate them.

With the discovery of the bodies here, authorities are going on the theory that the girls were taken from Baboosic Lake to Hampton Beach. This led Atty. Gen. Rudman to again issue a strong warning about the high risk run by both young girls and boys who hitchhike.

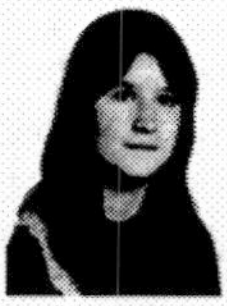

Diane Compagna

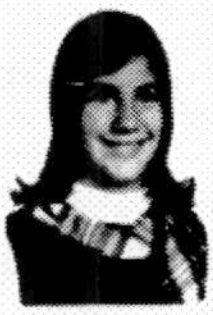

Anne Psaradelis

"I know that many parents do warn their children," Rudman said, "but to no avail. I am so concerned about the number of cases I have seen in the past three-and-a-half years, that I am considering some sort of educational program in the schools about this because homicides involving hitchhiking can be avoided."

Figure 16: Nashua Telegraph article on murders

"Chief, do you remember that incident on July 4 at the swimming hole off Bedford Road - the one involving the 1963 Chevy station wagon?"

"Yes, Sergeant, I do."

"Well, one of the people involved was Anne Psaradelis. I think we should interview everyone who had anything to do with it. Maybe one of them can help."

"Good work, Sergeant. Get right on it."

The first person I contacted was Lynn Tamworth. She was caring for her brother and sister and couldn't come down to the station, so I made arrangements to meet with Lynn at her home. I knocked on the door at 5 Railroad Street about twenty minutes later.

"Sergeant Horak?"

"Yes, it is."

"I'm Lynn Tamworth, won't you come in? Would you like a cup of coffee or something?"

"No, thank you."

"Can you tell me what this is all about, Sergeant?"

"Lynn, I'd like to talk with you about Anne Psaradelis and Diane Compagna."

"Oh, those are the two girls they just found murdered. Everyone is upset. I don't know why anyone would do a thing like that. How can I help?"

"Well, first of all, Lynn, did you know the girls?"

"I knew Diane Compagna, but I didn't know Anne Psaradelis. Diane and I were friends since last year. I saw her mostly during school hours and once in a while outside of school."

"Lynn, when was the last time you saw or spoke with Diane?"

"It was sometime after July 4 at the coliseum in Manchester. Diane was with another girl from Merrimack, but I don't remember her name."

"Did Diane give you the impression she was worried or afraid?"

"No, Sergeant, but while I was talking with her, Diane told me she might be pregnant. She also told me the name of the boy, but I really don't remember it. She said he was about twenty years old and wasn't from Manchester or Nashua. I think Nancy Johnson might be able to tell you more about that."

"Lynn, did Diane say anything else?"

"Well, Sergeant, she gave me the impression that it just happened, like about five days ago. She seemed kind of worried, but not upset. I got the impression she liked this boy, but he wasn't interested.

"Sergeant, I've heard all kinds of rumors, just like a lot of people have. I heard that two girls are supposed to know where Diane and Anne went, but I can't remember their names. I know that Donna Green knows the names of the two girls, but I really don't believe Donna will tell you. She doesn't want to get involved and have the police start a big mess."

"You know, Lynn, I wonder how Donna would feel if one of her family members was missing or murdered?"

"Sergeant, I really don't know anything else. I'll call you if I hear anything that might help catch the person who killed the girls."

"Lynn, I really appreciate your help. Thanks for taking the time to talk to me."

I contacted the dispatcher from my cruiser to report that I was leaving the Tamworth resident and was en route to the station. I wanted to talk with the lieutenant.

"Have you got a few minutes, Lieutenant?"

"Sure, Sergeant, what's on your mind?"

"Well, I want to have another talk with Tom Jefferson. He could be a prime suspect in this case. When you think about it, Lieutenant, he really does have a motive."

"Why do you say that, Sergeant?"

"Well, look at what was supposed to have taken place between Diane Compagna and Tom Jefferson at the Fourth of July celebration. If it's true and he is charged with rape, he could be convicted and end up in prison. There's also a rumor that he intends to marry in the very near future. Getting arrested could spoil things for him. I think we should have another talk with him."

"Sergeant, you better hold off until we meet with the attorney general's office tomorrow."

"OK, Lieutenant, if that's what you want."

"Sergeant, I think you and I should stop by the Psaradelis and Compagna homes to see if there's anything we can do. I know they were pestered by reporters. We should ask them to keep a record of people who call them for the next couple of weeks. Strange things have been happening in this case. Someone may try to get information from them regarding suspects or how the investigation is going."

It was hard talking to the parents about their daughters. I knew they appreciated everything we had been doing, but it didn't change the fact that the girls were found murdered. They were holding up better than I thought they would. They're really special people. I hoped we could wrap up this case soon.

Diane Compagna

Anne Psaradelis

*Figure 17: Photographs of Diane Compagna and
Anne Psaradelis*

8

Tuesday, October 2, 1973

A line of police cars rolled up to the State House for the meeting with the attorney general. Some were from the state police; others were from the sheriff's department and Candia Police Department.

Assistant Attorney General Robert Johnson III was assigned as overall coordinator for the homicide investigation. When we were all settled around the table, he explained how the investigation would be conducted.

"The base of operations will be at the Merrimack Police Department. The investigation will be conducted by teams of investigators consisting of two investigators per team. At the close of each day, we'll all sit down and compare notes and see what progress we've made.

"I'm sure you all know the two victims are Diane Compagna and Anne Psaradelis. They've been missing from their homes since July 11. Their bodies were recovered in a wooded area in the Town of Candia on September 29.

"A complete crime scene search was conducted by twenty assigned personnel and nothing was found. The search included sifting the area where the bodies were found. The cause of death indicates the possibility of strangulation.

"Lieutenant Wilson will be in charge of all the material brought in by the investigation. If you have any questions, contact Lieutenant Wilson or myself."

JUSTICE DENIED

I was assigned to work with Chief Robert Baker. After the meeting, we sat down and talked about the case. I told Chief Baker that I had already identified a possible suspect and detailed the incident between Tom Jefferson and Diane Compagna on July 4. I told him there was a possibility of Jefferson being charged with statutory rape since Diane was under age. I also repeated the rumor about Jefferson planning to get married and that if Jefferson had to go to jail, he would lose everything. Chief Baker suggested I report this information to Lieutenant Wilson, which I did.

"Lieutenant, Tom Jefferson had motive enough to do something like this. I'd like to interview him right away."

"No, Sergeant, we won't interview him now. We can do that later on."

Needless to say, I was frustrated with Lieutenant Wilson's reaction and shared my feelings with Chief Baker.

"You know, Chief, I really can't understand Lieutenant Wilson. I thought he would want to check out Tom Jefferson, but I guess he wants it to be his idea."

Chief Baker made no comment about my remarks. Instead, he suggested we start interviewing the people on our list who might have information about the case.

The first person we contacted was Carol Burke. The Chief and I conducted the interview at her home located at 23 Pine Street.

"Carol, this is Chief Baker and I'm Sergeant Horak. We'd like to talk with you about Diane Compagna and Anne Psaradelis."

"Oh, I heard on the radio that they were murdered. Isn't that terrible? Who would want to do anything like that?"

"Carol, did you know the girls?"

"Well, I really just knew them by name and face. I never hung around with them."

"Did you happen to see or know where the two girls were after July 11?"

"Well, sometime around the middle of July I went to Hampton Beach with some of my friends. We left Merrimack about 8:00 a.m. and got home some time after 5:00 p.m. Susan Beach told me she saw the girls at the beach when we were there. I don't remember when it was, but sometime later the girls were reported missing.

"Officers, I really don't know of anyone who would want to hurt Diane Compagna or Anne Psaradelis. I think any of the kids from school would help you because everyone liked the girls."

"Carol, do you know Tom Jefferson?"

"Why, yes, I do. He's liberal, carefree and wants to do what he wants, when he wants to do it."

"Carol, when did you last see the girls?"

"Sergeant, I saw the girls at the end of school in June. You know, I really think that it was a stranger who killed the two girls. I've heard rumors like everyone else. I think the girls were hitchhiking and were picked up by a single person. I heard that one of the girls was raped and shot. When the second girl got scared, the guy went after her and shot her too. I've heard all kinds of rumors. I don't know anything else I can tell you. If I hear of anything I'll contact you."

"Carol, here's a card with our names and phone numbers. Please feel free to call us day or night if you hear anything."

We didn't learn much from Carol Burke.

I knew the next person on our list. It was Ruth Donovan who lived on Tyler Street. As we approached the Donovan residence, a lady on the curb was waving her hands, telling us to stop.

"Sergeant Horak, I thought that was you."

The woman was an acquaintance of mine, Mrs. Nelson.

"Wasn't that a terrible thing that happened to the two girls? I want you to know that I've picked up bits and pieces of information about Diane Compagna and Anne Psaradelis."

"Mrs. Nelson, would you like to tell us what you know?"

Figure 18: Hampton Beach, Hampton, NH

"Well, once the kids found out about the two girls being murdered, they started talking. My daughter told me she knows who drove the girls to the beach. She's afraid to tell. She thinks whoever murdered the girls might hurt her.

"I also heard that Diane and Anne got into a little red car over in Hampton Beach. Some of their friends saw them at the beach on July 12.

"Sergeant, I don't know why two girls would go that far into the woods unless they knew who was with them. Of course, they could have had a gun. I really think the girls knew the person who murdered them.

"That's all I can tell you right now, Sergeant. As soon as I find out anything else from the kids, I'll let you know."

"Thanks a lot, Mrs. Nelson."

After talking with Mrs. Nelson, the chief and I proceeded to 39 Tyler Street to talk with Ruth Donovan.

"Ruth, Chief Baker and I would like to talk with you. May we come in?"

"Of course you can, come on in. What's this all about? I haven't done anything wrong, have I?"

"No, Ruth, we'd like to talk with you about Diane Compagna and Anne Psaradelis."

"Isn't that terrible. I just can't believe they were found murdered."

"Ruth, did you know either of the girls?"

"Sergeant, I didn't know Anne Psaradelis at all, but I've been friends with Diane Compagna for many, many years."

"Ruth, can you tell us anything that might help with our investigation of their murders?"

"Diane was bored in Merrimack and wanted to go to the beach. She wanted to do something different. I don't think Diane really knew Anne very well. I was under the impression that she had only gone out with Anne a few times.

"Sergeant, I know that I last saw Diane in June. It was in downtown Manchester. She was fine and didn't seem to have any problems. She liked her family and never complained. She was just bored in Merrimack.

"I was over in Seabrook when I heard that Diane was missing. I went to the beach every day to look for her, but I never found Diane."

"Ruth, do you know anyone in the beach area who has a cottage, a camp, or even an apartment where Diane and Anne might have gone?"

"No, Sergeant, I don't know of any place they could have gone over there. As I told you, I checked the beach every day and there wasn't a sign of her.

"Sergeant, I would like to say that Diane was a normal, everyday, fifteen-year-old girl. She was good looking and had lots of friends. There really isn't anything else I can tell you. If I hear anything, I'll call you."

The chief and I stopped for a cup of coffee before our next interview. We decided to speak with the girl Carol Burke had talked about, Susan Beach. We wanted to find out if Susan really had seen the girls at Hampton beach.

Susan's mother answered the door. It took only a minute for Susan to join us. The chief and I introduced ourselves, then proceeded with the interview.

"Did you know Diane Compagna or Anne Psaradelis?"

"I knew of them."

"Susan, where did you last see them?"

"At Hampton Beach. As I said, I knew both girls, but I really just knew Anne by name and sight. I said hello to her once in a while. Now, Diane Compagna, I knew quite well. She and I were on the same softball team. Diane was very quiet and modest. I don't know if she ever drank or used drugs. I don't think she had a boyfriend."

"Susan, when was the last time you saw Diane?"

"It was at Hampton Beach and Anne Psaradelis was with her. It was in July. I'm sure it was around the middle of the week, either a Wednesday or a Thursday. Both Jean Littlefield and I saw them. I walked up to Diane and Anne, and said, 'Hi, having a good summer?' or something like that. They both seemed normal, nothing seemed to be bothering them."

"Susan, what were the girls wearing?"

"Diane had on a bathing suit and some kind of white top. As for Anne, she had on a lightweight T-shirt with some kind of design on the front. Anne might have been wearing blue jeans. Neither of the girls had shoes on. I don't think they were carrying anything."

"Susan, were there many people at the beach that day?"

"It was cool that morning and there weren't a lot of people around, but it warmed up in the afternoon and there was a bigger crowd. I guess I saw the girls between one and two o'clock. I didn't see anyone with them. Diane and Anne didn't say how long they'd been there and I really didn't ask. I don't know how they got to the beach, I thought they were with one of their mothers. If they hitchhiked home, they could have been picked up by one guy, or a group of guys, gotten raped and dumped in the woods. It really scares me just thinking about it."

"Susan, did you see Diane or Anne again that day or anytime after you came back to Merrimack?"

"No, Sergeant, I never saw the girls again. I sure hope you get the bastard who murdered them. If someone kills once, they could do it again. That sure scares me. If I hear anything at all, I'll contact you right away, Sergeant."

The Beach house was in close proximity to the station, so Chief Baker and I decided to stop by and see how things were going. As we approached, we noticed that the parking lot was filled with cruisers of every description. I couldn't believe that many officers were already finished for the day.

I checked with the dispatcher when we arrived and found out there were no messages for me, but there was a message for the chief to call his office. While Chief Baker used my office to make his phone call, I talked with Chief Pelletier and Lieutenant Wilson.

"Sergeant, what's on your mind?"

"Chief Baker and I interviewed several people today. It seems strange that both girls had some kind of problem on Fourth of July and now they're both dead. I really think this whole thing began on July 4, not July 12 when the girls were reported missing.

"Chief Baker and I would like to interview Tom Jefferson again, he's someone who has a motive, but Lieutenant Wilson wants us to hold off for now."

"Well, Sergeant, the lieutenant is in charge. He's calling the shots."

"I understand, Chief, but I feel like we all have to realize that this problem could have very well started on July 4. If all the investigators know that, it might aid them in the questions they ask when they're interviewing people."

"Sergeant, I appreciate your concern and I'll advise all the investigators to keep this in mind during their investigations and interviews."

"Thanks, Lieutenant."

Chief Baker had just completed the call to his department when I entered my office. He had arranged an interview with a woman from his town who thought she might have seen Diane Compagna and Anne Psaradelis in the area of New Boston Road sometime during July. The chief was going to check it out on his way home.

The rest of the group called it quits for the day, but Chief Baker and I decided to interview as many people as possible before it got too late. We knew there was time for at least one interview, maybe more. The next person on our list was Susan Bell. Chief Baker and I went to the cruiser and headed for 43 Kelly Street.

"Hello, we're looking for Susan Bell."

"I'm Susan Bell. What can I do for you?"

"Well, Susan, this is Chief Baker and I'm Sergeant Horak. We'd like to talk with you about Diane Compagna and Anne Psaradelis."

"I kind of expected you, Sergeant. Susan Beach is a friend of mine and she told me you talked with her. She thought you'd also want to talk with me. It's terrible, Sergeant. Who would have done such a horrible thing? I don't know anyone that disliked either of them."

"Susan, did you know both Diane Compagna and Anne Psaradelis?"

"Yes, but I knew Anne better."

"When was the last time you saw them?"

"Well, I had an appointment at Rainbow Alley in Hampton Beach on July 15 to have my portrait made. I wasn't going to be able to keep the appointment, so I decided to cancel it."

"Susan, did you call Rainbow Alley to cancel the appointment?"

"No. Some of the girls invited me to go to the beach with them and I thought I could cancel the appointment then."

"When did you go to the beach?"

"Well, I went with Carol Burke, Susan Beach, Doris Morse and Janice Garnett. It was either on Wednesday, July 11, or Thursday, July 12."

"Did you or any of the other girls see or talk with Diane or Anne?"

"We talked with both of them. We saw the girls between two and three o'clock. I asked Anne Psaradelis if she and Diane wanted a ride home. She said they had just hitchhiked to the beach and were going to stay there for a while. I asked them a second time if they wanted a ride home, and they said no."

"Susan, do you remember what the girls were wearing?"

"Yes, I do. Both Diane and Anne were wearing halter tops and bathing suits. They weren't wearing anything on their feet, but I'm pretty sure they were both carrying sandals."

"Did they have a beach bag or anything like that?"

"No, the only thing they were carrying were sandals. After we talked with Diane and Anne, we took off and did the things we wanted to do. I went over and took care of changing the date to have my portrait done."

"Susan, did you ever see Diane or Anne again?"

"Yes, I did. There weren't very many people on the beach that day because the weather was cloudy and cool. I ran into the girls again while they were walking along the beach. We stopped and said hello again. They seemed just like I would see them in school. They didn't appear upset. Anne was a nice girl and had an outgoing personality. She was someone like I would have known for thirty years. I'm sure you've met those kinds of people in your lifetime."

"I guess we all have, Susan."

*Figure 19: Board walk, Hampton Beach (site where
Diane Compagna and Anne Psaradelis were last seen
alive on July 12, 1973 at about 4:30 p.m.)*

"Diane was a quiet girl. She was very pretty and everyone liked her. We asked the girls again if they wanted a ride home and they refused. I would say it was about 4:30 p.m. when we headed back to Merrimack.

"Sergeant, I've heard all kinds of rumors about Diane and Anne and I don't believe in gossip. I just hope you catch the creep that murdered them. He deserves to be hung."

By the time we finished the interview with Susan, it was pretty late. Chief Baker still had to interview the woman back in Candia, so he headed home. We made plans to meet early tomorrow morning at the crime scene.

I planned to visit with the Compagnas and Psaradelises later that evening to give them the latest information on our investigation, so I stopped by Lieutenant Gerlach's office to find out when the girls' bodies would be released to their parents. The lieutenant thought it would be within the next day or two. He told me that he had arranged for the parents to come into the station tomorrow to identify some clothing and jewelry that the girls were wearing.

While I was there, I talked to the lieutenant about the personnel assignments.

"Lieutenant Gerlach, can you arrange it so I can work mainly with Chief Baker as my partner during this investigation?"

"Why do you want to do that, Sergeant?"

"Well, I know it's good to work with other investigators, but I feel that if this case isn't solved right away, most of the investigators will have to go back to their own departments. Since Diane Compagna and Anne Psaradelis came from Merrimack and they were murdered in Candia, we need to do the bulk of the investigating. If you have a good team, you can do anything."

"I see what you mean, Sergeant. I think I can work that out for you."

"Thanks a lot."

I stopped by the Psaradelis house on my way home and let them know that the attorney general's office, state police, sheriff's department, and the Candia and Nashua police departments were joining us in the investigation. I assured the Psaradelises that we would find the person responsible for their daughter's murder and asked them to contact me if they discovered any new information.

A visit to the Compagna home was next on my agenda.

"Hello, Mr. and Mrs. Compagna. I thought I'd drop by and see if there is anything I can do for you."

"Well, Sergeant, first of all, you need to stop calling us Mr. and Mrs. Compagna. You've been over here so often, you're like part of the family, so please call us Marcel and Dorothy."

"All right, if that makes you feel better."

"Sergeant, we're going to call you Joe since that's your first name."

"That's OK. Just don't do it in front of the chief. He might not understand."

"Well, anyway, Joe, is there any kind of news about who took the lives of our girls?"

"There really isn't, Dorothy, but we have a good team of investigators and they're all working very hard to come up with the person responsible. You know, I still can't believe this happened. I know you must be devastated. I think we all are. Please know that I'll never let go of this case until it's solved. We owe that to you and to the girls.

"It's late, folks. I should get going. If it's all right with you, I'd like to come back in a day or two and interview you. That is, if you feel up to it."

"Sure, Joe, that would be fine."

After leaving the Compagna home, I contacted the dispatcher. There were no messages. Tomorrow was going to be an early day, so I headed home to get some rest.

9

5:45 a.m.

I left word with the dispatcher that I was en route to the crime scene in Candia and would be back at the station around 10:00 a.m. for the lieutenant's meeting. I was surprised that Chief Baker was at the scene when I arrived.

"I can't believe it, Chief, you're already up and ready to go."

"It was easy to get here early. I only live a stone's throw away from New Boston Road."

"Has this whole section of road been searched?"

"Yes, it's been searched by over twenty law enforcement people and they haven't come up with a thing."

"How about the dump, has anyone checked in there?"

"Yes, Sergeant, it's all been checked out."

I parked just inside the stone wall, facing the gravel pit, and joined the chief on the road. As we looked up and down New Boston Road, we noticed there wasn't any place to pull all the way off the road.

"Sergeant, someone would have noticed a car parked along the side of the road."

"You're right, Chief. But if they parked close to the gravel pit, like I did, they probably wouldn't have been seen."

"I tend to agree, Sergeant. I can't see your cruiser from here."

The chief led the way to the crime scene. As we walked, I could feel death in the air and it made me angry.

"You know, Chief, if you come in this way instead of from the old logging road, it's quite a distance to travel. Do you know if the logging road was checked to see if a vehicle had been parked there?"

"Yes, it was checked. The entrance was overgrown with brush and young trees. They found no sign of a vehicle having been there for a couple of years. They also checked the roadway and didn't turn up a thing."

We walked a bit farther without saying a word. Then, the chief broke the silence.

"Sergeant, this is where the first girl was found."

The area looked like a pine grove. The ground was covered with pine needles.

"Sergeant, we've checked this area thoroughly, we even sifted the soil, but let's look around to see if we can find anything that's been missed."

We found nothing but a feeling of death lingering in the air.

The chief and I walked to the site where the second body was found. This area was full of brush and a lot of young hardwood trees mixed in with pines.

"It appears that this girl was running for her life. I would say she was about to go over that stone wall when she was grabbed from behind and brought down to the ground. It doesn't appear that either girl put up a struggle."

"Chief Baker, let's give this area another going over in case someone missed something. It would be pretty easy to do with all this underbrush, leaves and pine needles covering the ground."

The chief and I inspected the area thoroughly but found nothing.

"You know, Chief Baker, the first body was found naked with blue denim trousers under the left arm, and a bra and panties only one foot beyond the right hand. The dungarees and bra had not been removed from the second body, but the white shirt was partly off. The more I look at the crime scene and the location of the bodies, it makes me think that the girls knew the killer."

"I have to agree with you, Sergeant."

We decided to go back to New Boston Road and search for clues. The girls' beach bags and sandals hadn't been found and we thought locating them would be important to the investigation.

The chief took one side of the road, and I took the other, paying special attention to the dump area. After searching for two hours, we had found nothing.

"Chief, even though we didn't find anything, I feel better knowing we checked it. The girls' beach bags and sandals have to be someplace. I think we need to come back another day and check farther back from the roadway."

The chief agreed.

My shoes and feet were soaking wet. I vowed to wear boots and old clothing the next time we searched out here.

We spent more time at the crime site than we intended and were concerned about missing Lieutenant Wilson's briefing. We were an hour late when we arrived at the station.

"Sorry we're late, Lieutenant Wilson."

"From now on, you two better be on time like everyone else."

"Yes, sir."

"All right, men, today we're going to change assignments. Each man will have a different partner. Remember to gather as much information as you can about Diane Compagna and Anne Psaradelis. Someone out there must know something. It's up to us to find out what that is. So, let's get out there and find something that's going to help us solve these murders."

I was assigned duty with Detective-Sergeant Donald Bazin. The first person on our list of people to interview was Frank Gorman from Nashua. I knew Frank's father, Bob Gorman, and was able to drive directly to their home.

"Hi, Bob, is your son, Frank home?"

"Yes, he is."

"Could we talk with him, please?"

"Has Frank done anything wrong, Sergeant?"

"No, Bob, we just want to talk with him about the two girls from Merrimack who were murdered. We hope he might be able to help us in some way."

Bob called Frank to join us. He introduced us to his son and added his support.

"Frank, help them out if you can."

We appreciated the father's comment and proceeded with the interview.

"Did you know Diane Compagna or Anne Psaradelis?"

"I didn't know Anne Psaradelis at all, but I knew Diane."

"Frank, how long did you know her?"

"I used to go with a friend of Diane's. Her name was Barbara Casey. Diane used to come down to Nashua once in a while, when Barbara came to see me. I guess I saw Diane about six or seven times, usually at the bowling alley."

"What did you think of Diane?"

"I thought she was a real nice girl. She was friendly and well dressed. You know, Sergeant, Diane really was very, very nice. I hope you guys catch the murderers."

"Frank, when was the last time you saw Diane Compagna?"

"Well, it was a couple of weeks before the Fourth of July. I never saw her again."

"Frank, do you know anyone who wanted to harm either of the girls or anyone they were afraid of?"

"No, I can't think of anyone who wanted to harm them. I did hear lots of rumors, like everyone else. I've heard lots of talk, such as, the girls were drowned and their throats were cut. I think they could have been murdered by someone they knew, or I suppose it could have been a stranger."

"Frank, what else can you tell us about Diane?"

"Well, Diane was a neat person. She took care of her clothing and cared about the way she looked. I noticed that she always carried money in her pocket, not in a wallet.

"I don't know why anyone would want to murder her. She was liked by everyone, as far as I know. There really isn't anything else I can tell you, but if I hear anything, I'll let you know.

"Oh, before I forget, can you tell me when the funeral will be? I'd like to pay my respects."

JOSEPH A. HORAK

"Frank, I believe it's going to be the first of the week. We want to thank you for taking time to talk with us."

When Detective Bazin and I returned to the cruiser, the dispatcher was calling on the radio. We were asked to interview Shirley Armstrong at 26 Ridge Road. We had planned to get a cup of coffee, but decided the interview was more important.

When we arrived at the Ridge Road address, a woman answered the door. She identified herself as Shirley Armstrong. Bazin and I introduced ourselves and proceeded with the interview.

"What can we do for you, Mrs. Armstrong?"

"I received a suspicious phone call about 8:15 last night regarding my daughter and Diane Compagna. My daughter Phyllis is fifteen years old. I don't want anything like what happened to those poor girls to happen to my daughter. You know, Officers, Phyllis used to hang around with Diane last year at school. I think she may have seen her this summer.

"Anyway, the man who called sounded like he was middle aged, I'd say around forty. He identified himself as Everett Gray, the coach of the girl's softball team at the high school. He asked for Phyllis. I told him she wasn't home. Gray said he checked the telephone book for Phyllis's name, but it wasn't listed. I told him the number was listed under her stepfather's name.

"Gray said Diane Compagna was one of the girls on his team. He said he knew that one of the girls on the team hung around with Diane, but he wasn't sure which one it was. This Mr. Gray said he asked some of the girls on his list if they hung around with Diane and Phyllis's name stuck in his head. I asked Mr. Gray where he got this so-called list, but he made me so nervous, I don't remember what he said. He did say something about his own daughter, but never mentioned her name. Anyway, this man said the police investigators were going to school tomorrow to talk with the girls. He said, 'Tell Phyllis to tell them what they want to know.' This man really made me nervous, so I called you."

"You did the right thing, Mrs. Armstrong. We'll locate this Mr. Gray and see what this is all about. Please call the station if you need anything else or if you hear anything that will help us catch the people responsible for the murders."

"I will."

Detective Bazin and I decided to stop by the high school to investigate Mr. Gray. We talked with Mr. Johnson, the principal. He identified the softball coach as Everett Gray.

"He's a nice guy. He lives on Grant Street. If you'll wait a minute, I'll get him on the phone for you."

Mr. Johnson placed the call and handed the phone to me.

"Mr. Gray, this is Sergeant Horak from the police department. I'd like to ask you a question or two, if that's OK with you."

"What do you want to know, Sergeant?"

"Mr. Gray, did you call Mrs. Armstrong in the past day or two?"

"Why, yes, I did, Sergeant. I've been checking with various girls who played on the softball team with Diane Compagna last year. I wanted them to cooperate with the police and tell them anything that might help catch the people responsible for murdering Diane Compagna and Anne Psaradelis. I hope I haven't caused any problems. I just wanted to help in any way I could. My daughter was friends with Diane. I keep thinking, what happened to her could have happened to my daughter. I didn't mean to upset anyone. Should I call Mrs. Armstrong and apologize?"

"No, Mr. Gray, you better let me square that away."

The detective and I stopped by the Armstrong home and explained Mr. Gray's intentions. Mrs. Armstrong was relieved and offered us a cup of coffee. We gratefully accepted.

Our next interview was with Michelle Brown at 22 James Street. Michelle's mother answered the door and invited us into her home.

"Michelle, when was the last time you saw either Diane Compagna or Anne Psaradelis?"

"Sergeant, I guess the last time I saw both girls was around July 10. They were at the sub shop on Main Street. It was in the afternoon. We talked for a while, but they never mentioned anything about going to the beach or any other place. I never saw the girls again, but Linda Caron told me the girls were living in Nashua with some guy. Linda didn't know his name.

"Diane wasn't the type of girl who went out on dates, she just hung around cars and talked with the boys. Anne's brother, Jimmy, had a nice car and took the girls everywhere. He's a great guy."

"Michelle, do you know anything about either of the girls' home life?"

"Diane and Anne very seldom got grounded for anything they did at home. I never heard either of them say they wanted to run away. I don't know anyone who would want to murder them. Both girls were liked by all their friends. I'll do anything I can to help catch the people who did this."

Detective Bazin and I headed back to the station for a briefing with Lieutenant Wilson. We were surprised there weren't more cars in the parking lot when we arrived. We found out that Chiefs Baker and Heald were interviewing people in Candia, Lieutenant Gerlach and Detective Gates had gone to the coast area, and a couple of others were down in Massachusetts. They all arrived a short time later and the briefing got underway.

"Lieutenant Wilson, have any decent clues been turned up by the interviews that have been conducted so far?"

"No, we really haven't turned up much of anything. It seems like people don't want to get involved. The only thing we know for sure is that Diane Compagna and Anne Psaradelis made it to Hampton Beach and were alive on July 12 at 5:00 p.m."

"Lieutenant, have the bodies of the girls been turned over to their parents yet?"

"No, Sergeant, that should take place tomorrow. The parents are supposed to be here at the station in about twenty minutes to identify some clothing and jewelry found at the scene. I'd like you to join Chief Pelletier when that takes place."

"Sure, Lieutenant."

I thought this was as good a time as any to bring up the Jefferson interview again.

"Lieutenant, I'd like to talk with Tom Jefferson again. If we don't interview him now, we can't charge him with statutory rape for the incident that occurred on July 4."

JUSTICE DENIED

"No, Sergeant, you don't have a victim to testify about what took place. We're not going to interview Tom Jefferson at this time. Are there any more questions? If not, continue with your interviews."

As the meeting was breaking up, we were advised that the Compagnas and Psaradelises had arrived. Chief Pelletier requested that they be shown to his office for the identification hearing. Also present were Detective-Sergeant Bazin, Assistant Attorney General Robert Johnson III, and myself.

"Folks, we're going to show you some clothing and jewelry found at the crime scene. It's in plastic bags and marked for evidence. Please inspect the articles carefully to see if any of it belongs to your girls."

The articles in evidence were described in detail.

1. Pair of silver earrings, pierce type
2. Silver bracelet
3. Ring, green in the center, surrounded with a gold band
4. Wedding-type gold ring
5. Gold ring, large oval gold piece on top of the ring with initial "A" in center of the ring
6. Bathing suit, two-tone purple in color
7. Bathing suit, two-piece, yellow print
8. Cut-off blue jeans with the words "Love is Beautiful" printed in black ink
9. Belt, large brown, found around cut-off blue jeans

Mr. and Mrs. Marcel Compagna identified the silver pierced earrings as possibly belonging to their daughter. They also identified the two-toned purple bathing suit found next to the body of their daughter.

Mr. and Mrs. Jim Psaradelis were also shown the items in the same rotation. They identified the silver bracelet, the gold ring with the green center, the gold-type wedding ring and the gold ring with the initial "A" in the center as belonging to their daughter. The Psaradelises also identified the yellow print bathing suit, the cut-off blue jeans and brown belt as being their daughter's.

All the items found at the crime scene were identified.

Lieutenant Wilson advised the parents that their daughters' bodies would be released tomorrow. I asked if I could stop by the victims' homes after funeral arrangements were complete.

"I'd like to be in a position to see who stops by your homes and comes to the funerals in case the people who did this have enough nerve to show up. Sometimes it does happen."

"That will be fine, Sergeant. Thank you."

Figure 20: Red Cross Station at Hampton Beach

10

<u>October 6, 1973</u>

It was hard to believe that a week had gone by since the girls were found and we didn't know anything more than we did before.

While I was tied up with the chief and lieutenant, Detective Bazin conducted an interview, but learned nothing new. I joined Bazin in the cruiser around mid-morning. We proceeded to 89 Elm Avenue to interview Cynthia Powers.

"Ms. Powers, we'd like to talk with you about Diane Compagna and Anne Psaradelis. When was the last time you saw them?"

"Well, I went to Hampton Beach with my sister, Jean Litchfield, sometime in July. I know it was after July 4, because Diane was still here in Merrimack then. I think we went to the beach during the middle of the week, I believe it was a Tuesday or a Wednesday."

"Cynthia, did you or your sister see either of the girls at Hampton Beach?"

"Yes, we saw both of them. It was around 1:00 p.m. Diane and Anne were on the beach near the Red Cross Center, near the casino."

"Do you remember what they were wearing, Cynthia?"

"Yes. Diane had on a two-piece bathing suit, it was purple and pink."

"Did you talk with the girls?"

"Yes, Jean, Debra Ross and I talked with both Diane and Anne for a few minutes. We said 'hello, how are you?' Just general conversation. I'd say Diane did most of the talking, Anne more or less looked on. Diane said they'd been at the beach overnight and had told each other's mother a different story. Diane told her mother she was staying at Anne's house, and Anne said she was staying at Diane's."

"Cynthia, did either of the girls have anything else to say?"

"Yes, Diane said they met a guy at the beach. He had a sister with a young baby and all of them stayed at her place overnight. We told them they should call home and tell their parents where they were. The girls said they would call."

"Cynthia, did you see them again while you were at the beach or anytime after that?"

"We saw them about five minutes later. They told us they had called home. As I remember, one of the girls was carrying a beach bag, but neither of them had shoes on. They both looked hungry. Diane was working at a restaurant in Merrimack and they were trying to make it home in time for her to get to work. I think she was supposed to be there at 5:00 p.m. that day. The girls said they were going to hitchhike back to Merrimack. That's the last time I saw either of them. A couple of days later I heard that the girls never came home. I was shocked to hear that Diane and Anne were found murdered. What an awful thing to happen. If I can help in any way, please call me."

"Thanks for taking the time to talk with us, Cynthia."

As Detective Bazin and I walked out to the cruiser, I couldn't help remarking, "If Diane and Anne had taken a ride home with Cynthia and her sister, they would be alive today." It was a sad situation.

Debra Ross was the next person on our list. She lived at 43 Windy Hollow Road. A young woman answered the door.

"Hello, are you Debra Ross?"

"No, I'm not. Debra's down in the cellar doing the laundry. I'll get her. Why don't you come in and wait in the living room?" "Thank you, we will."

Within a few moments, Debra entered the room.

"You wanted to see me? Did I do something wrong?"

Figure 21: Casino at Hampton Beach

"No, you didn't do anything wrong. I'm Sergeant Horak and this is Detective Bazin. We'd like to talk with you about Diane Compagna and Anne Psaradelis."

"Gosh, I knew both of them. I still can't believe they were murdered. Who could do a thing like that? He must be a terrible person. I don't know how someone could live with themselves after taking the lives of two young girls. How can I help you?"

"Well, Debra, we'd like you to tell us about the last time you saw either of the girls. Do you know anyone who wanted to harm them? Anything you can tell us might help."

"Well, I did see Diane and Anne at the lake in Hollis, but it was quite a while before the girls were missing. I'd gone to the lake with Phyllis Henry, Nancy Johnson and a couple of other girls. We got there around noon, Diane and Anne were already there. We walked over and talked with them. They said they had hitchhiked to the lake. While we were talking, Diane told us about a man at the lake who was following them around. They didn't want anything to do with him. Diane said the man was fat and had a blond ponytail and beard. They thought he was between twenty and twenty-two years old. They said the man appeared to be alone. I left the lake before Diane and Anne, my mother came to pick me up for work."

"Debra, did you ever see the girls again?"

"Yes, I went to Hampton Beach with Phyllis Henry sometime between the ninth and seventeenth of July. I think Phyllis could give you the exact date we were there. Anyway, we arrived at the beach around 10:00 a.m. and saw Diane and Anne. We yelled to them and they walked over to us. While we were talking Diane and Anne said they had called each other's mother and told them they were staying overnight at each other's house, but they really didn't. The girls said they had spent the night at Hampton Beach. I thought they must have been there at least a day or two before."

"Debra, did the girls say anything else? Did they appear to be afraid of anyone? Were they with anyone while you were talking with them?"

"No, they were alone, as far as I could tell. They didn't appear to be nervous or afraid of anyone. In fact, the girls laughed and joked

about having fooled their mothers again. I felt as though they were going to stay at the beach even longer, especially after making phone
calls to their mothers."

"Debra, do you remember what the girls had on?"

"Yes, Diane had on a two-piece bathing suit and nothing else. It
was purple and pink. Anne had on a bra or bathing suit top with some
type of T-shirt over it. The shirt had some sort of print or picture on
the front of it, nothing on the back. Each of the girls had a towel and
beach bag with them.

"You know, Officers, I don't understand why the girls called our
attention to them if they were running away from home. It would have
made more sense if they had tried to hide from us. I really don't know
what to make of it all."

"Debra, did you go to the July 4 celebration in Merrimack?"

"No, I didn't, but I did hear a lot of rumors about Diane being
pregnant because she had been with some guy on the Fourth of July.
Apparently, she was pretty scared.

"You know, when we said good bye to the girls at the beach, none
of us ever thought that it would be true. It doesn't seem possible that
they were murdered and we'll never see them again.

"There really isn't anything more I can tell you. I don't have any
idea who would have wanted to harm either girl. If I can help in any
way, please let me know."

Detective Bazin had to appear in court that afternoon or his case
would be dropped. So, I took him back to the station and wished him
good luck with his case. While I was there I stopped in to talk with
Chief Pelletier.

"Could you spare me a little of your time, Chief?"

"Come on in, Sergeant, what can I help you with?"

"Well, Chief, I'd like to talk with you about the Compagna-
Psaradelis murders. As far as I can tell at this point in time the officers
conducting interviews have contacted approximately sixty people. To
be honest, Chief, we aren't really receiving any more information on
the murder investigation than we did on the missing person's case.
Most of what we've gotten is rumor. No one really wants to get involved. Maybe they're afraid. It's as though everyone wants to throw

us in a different direction. Some of the same people we interviewed before are telling us now that they knew the girls hitchhiked to the beach, some even saw them there. Why didn't someone tell us sooner? It might have saved their lives. It's pretty sad when you think about it.

"Chief, I still think that whoever murdered Diane and Anne is from our town. I don't want to sound like someone who harps and complains all the time, but I still think we should interview Tom Jefferson again. Ever since the end of July when we found out he had intercourse with Diane, I've wanted to charge him with statutory rape. Everyone from our court to the county attorney's office says we can't do it because we don't have a victim. I don't understand that. Diane told lots of people about what happened. Why can't we use that as evidence?"

"I understand what you're saying, Sergeant, but that's the county attorney's decision and I have to abide by it."

"I'd still like to re-interview Jefferson. I can't think of any better way to move this investigation along, but all I hear is, 'not right now.'"

"Sergeant, Lieutenant Wilson is running the investigation, so you'll have to comply with whatever he tells you to do, or not to do."

I knew this issue was a dead end, so I changed the topic of the conversation.

"Chief, I'd like to position myself at the funeral so I can monitor everyone who comes to pay their respects. You never know, the killer might show up there. Things like that do happen. I'll have to keep out of sight since most people know me."

"I think that's a good idea, Sergeant. Go ahead and cover that."

"Thanks, Chief."

I hated sitting around until the end of my shift, so I decided to interview the next person on our list while Detective Bazin was in court. Richard Greentree's home was on Marina Drive. His father answered the door and called Richard from upstairs.

"Hi, Richard, do you remember me?"

"Yes."

"Can I come in and talk with you?"

"I didn't do anything wrong, did I, Sergeant?"

"No, Richard, I just need your help and thought you might be able to tell me something about Diane Compagna and Anne Psaradelis."

"Finding them murdered is really something. I knew both girls, but I knew Anne better. I hang around with her brother, Jimmy."

"Richard, can you tell me the last time you saw them?"

"I last saw Diane and Anne on July 11, sometime between 11:00 and 11:30 a.m."

"How do you remember that?"

"Well, I was riding around with Jimmy Psaradelis, we were heading toward his house on Harris Avenue. As we drove near the swimming hole on Bedford Road, we saw Diane and Anne. We stopped the car and talked with them for a while. They were both laughing. Anne said they were supposed to be at the lake, but they were going to Hampton Beach instead. Anne told Jimmy, 'Don't tell Ma.' The girls wanted us to take them to the beach, but Jimmy said he was heading home and didn't want to go over there. We picked the girls up near the swimming hole and took them to Main Street. We let them out near the store so they could get some cigarettes. They told us they planned to hitchhike to Hampton Beach. Diane added that they'd be back by 5:00 p.m. so she wouldn't be late for work at the restaurant. That's the last time I ever saw the girls."

"Richard, were the girls going to meet someone at the beach?"

"They didn't say anything about meeting anyone. They just wanted to go to the beach and have a good time. I don't think Jimmy told his parents about it. He wanted to protect Anne."

"Richard, do you remember what they were wearing the last time you saw them?"

"Well, Anne was wearing dungarees and a light shirt, sort of a summer type. I'm not sure if she had on shoes, but she was carrying a beach bag. I'm not sure what Diane was wearing, but she was carrying a beach bag too. That's all I know, Sergeant. Oh, I've heard rumors that they were in Nashua, Lowell, and Boston, but nothing really good. If I find out anything, Sergeant, I'll call you."

"Thanks for your help, Richard."

11

October 12, 1973

I placed a call to the Compagna home as soon as I arrived at the station.

"Hello, Mrs. Compagna?"

"Yes, it is. Who is this?"

"Dorothy, after all this time you still don't recognize my voice?"

"Oh, it's Joe. You'll have to excuse me. I have so many things on my mind."

"I know you do. Don't worry about it. I thought that you and the Psaradelis might be making funeral arrangements today and I'd like to drop by and talk with you about monitoring people who will be stopping in to pay their respects."

"That will be fine, Joe. I'll see you later."

Lieutenant Gerlach joined me on my visit to the Compagna home. We were relieved to see the Psaradelis' car parked in the driveway. We wanted to talk with both families at the same time. We hated walking into the families' unhappiness, but realized it was our unhappiness too. Mr. Compagna met us at the door.

"Come on in, don't stand out there. Is there anything new regarding the investigation? We hope you'll keep us abreast of what's going on."

"There really isn't much to tell you at this time. The investigators are working hard trying to come up with the answers. Folks, we're doing everything possible to bring this case to a conclusion. How are the funeral arrangements coming along?"

"We're going to the funeral home as soon as we finish talking with you. Both Diane and Anne are going to be at George Rivet Funeral Home. We're planning visiting hours tonight and tomorrow afternoon and evening."

"We want you to know that there will be security there. We'll monitor everyone coming and going. Don't let us hold you up. We'll check in with you later in the day."

The lieutenant and I headed back to the station. I was assigned to work on the investigation with Deputy Sheriff Carl Leavitt during the morning. He had a court appearance scheduled in the afternoon, which freed me up to visit the Compagnas later in the day.

After talking with Mrs. Nelson the other day, I scheduled an interview with her daughter Betty for first thing this morning. Mrs. Nelson sat in on the interview because Betty was a little nervous about talking with us.

"Betty, did you know both Diane Compagna and Anne Psaradelis?"

"Yes, I knew both girls. It's really horrible to think they were murdered. I knew Anne very well because we used to live near her, I only knew Diane by sight. The last time I remember seeing Diane was on a Monday during the last part of June. She was walking south on Main Street.

"You know, Sergeant, a lot of the kids are hesitant to say anything because they're afraid something will happen to them."

"Do you feel that way, Betty?"

"Yes, I do."

"Betty, what else can you tell us about the girls?"

"For one thing, Sergeant, I don't know if Diane or Anne drank or used drugs, but they both liked boys. Diane was very quiet in school, but when she got outside, she was just like everyone else."

"Betty, do you have any idea what happened to the girls?"

"Well, Deputy, I think the girls got a ride to the beach with someone they knew. I think they probably hitchhiked home since they'd been seen at the beach.

"I don't know how Diane and Anne were killed, but I think one of them was raped because when the bodies were found, one was naked and the other was fully clothed. I don't think one person could handle both girls. I don't know what happened, maybe they raped one of the girls, then got scared. I've heard all sorts of rumors like everyone else. I do know that I'm scared and don't want that happening to me. I really don't know anything else. If I hear anything, I'll let you know."

"Betty, I'd like you to do one thing for me. When you talk with your friends, let them know we need their help. If they have any knowledge or suspect anyone of killing the girls, ask them to come forward and let us know. We'll protect them from harm."

Back in the cruiser, the deputy and I talked about our interview with Betty Nelson.

"Sergeant, I think Betty's scared. She probably knows a lot more than she told us."

"The thing that bothers me, Deputy Leavitt, is that during the eighty-one days we were looking for Diane and Anne, we didn't receive any help from their friends. All we got was information that sent us in another direction. The kids were scared then, and now that it's turned into a murder investigation, I think they're even more afraid. I think they're afraid of someone here in town."

The deputy and I had time for one more interview before going our separate ways. John Brothers lived close by, so we drove to his house. He was entering the side door when we arrived.

"Hi, John. May Deputy Sheriff Leavitt and I come in and talk with you?"

"I didn't do anything wrong, did I, Sergeant?"

"No, John, we want to talk with you about Diane Compagna and Anne Psaradelis. Did you know the girls?"

"Yes, Sergeant, I did. Come on in."

John showed us into his home and we continued our conversation.

"John, you said you knew Diane and Anne. Tell us about them."

"I knew Diane better than Anne. I guess I've known Diane for at least three years. She had nice parents and they took her anywhere she wanted to go."

"John, do you remember the last time you saw either of the girls?"

"I saw Diane during the afternoon of July 4. I never saw her again.

"Sergeant, I've heard rumors like everyone else, like they were in Nashua, Boston - all over the place. Ever since they were reported missing, I felt that Diane and Anne would be found dead. Diane wasn't the type of girl to run away, she had too much going for her."

"There's nothing I can tell you. If I hear anything I'll come in and see you."

"Thanks, John, we appreciate your taking the time to talk with us."

I dropped the deputy off at the station so he could make his court appearance, then I went by the Compagnas' house to talk with them about the funeral arrangements.

"Visiting hours will start at 6:00 p.m. tonight. We've set aside to-morrow afternoon for students to pay their respects. Then we'll have regular hours again tomorrow night. The burials will take place on Fri-day morning. Diane will be laid to rest in Manchester and Anne, here in Merrimack."

"Mr. and Mrs. Compagna, I want you to know that Chief Pelletier has instructed me to help in every way possible. We'll take care of se-curity and traffic control, and tomorrow we'll have officers near the funeral home to handle all the students, teachers and friends who might show up. If you need anything else, please let us know."

"Sergeant, we want to thank you and all the other officers who have helped us through this ordeal. It's been rough on all of us."

I checked in with the chief to let him know about the funeral ar-rangements, then went home to get something to eat.

After a late lunch, I went to the funeral home. I wanted to look over the rooms where the girls were before people started to arrive. I also wanted to say a little prayer for both of them. While paying my respects, I promised both girls that I would get the people who took their lives, no matter how long it took.

It wasn't long before family members started to arrive. Officers Stavenger and Rousseau weren't far behind. They had donated their free time to handle traffic, parking, and security so the families could mourn their loss in peace.

A lot of people came to the George Rivet Funeral Home. Most ap-peared to be family and close friends. It was a sad night, but the offi-cers did a good job of keeping everything under control. When the last car left the parking lot, my day was finally over. I headed home to prepare for tomorrow.

October 13, 1973

At this point in the murder investigation we had interviewed approximately one hundred people and didn't have much more information than when we were investigating the missing person's report. People seemed afraid to come forward with information, or they didn't want to get involved, although rumors about the July 4 incident involving Tom Jefferson continued. The people we interviewed didn't think much of Jefferson, they used words like bully, rough person, and bum to describe him. A lot of people repeated the story that Diane Compagna told them she was raped by Tom Jefferson and thought she was pregnant.

Providing security and directing traffic for the afternoon visiting hours at George Rivet Funeral Home took three officers - Officers Rousseau and Stavenger and myself. The school kids created so much traffic we closed down one lane of the road so no one would get run over. A lot of the kids were crying.

When the lines from the afternoon visitation started to shrink, I went home to change clothes. I thought wearing civilian clothes to the evening viewing would help me blend into the crowd so that I could monitor people coming and going without being noticed.

A lot of people attended both viewings, but I didn't notice anything out of the ordinary or anyone who looked suspicious. All the officers involved did a great job handling the people who came to pay their respects.

October 14, 1973

We expected a large procession for the girls' funeral and planned to block off the south-bound lane of Main Street to allow it to pass. Several officers were assigned traffic control, others were assigned to lead the procession in cruisers.

Before I headed to the funeral, I stopped in to talk with the chief.

"Good morning, Chief."

"Come on in, Sergeant, and have a seat. How's the investigation going? Are you people making any headway?"

"Everyone is working hard, Chief. We've interviewed about one hundred people so far, but I'm sure there are hundreds more to be interviewed. Every time we interview someone, they talk about other people and that means we have to interview them. The list seems to grow and grow. I wish all the investigators could know more about what's going on."

"What do you mean by that, Sergeant?"

"Well, Chief, the whole group never gets together to discuss how their interviews are going or to talk about their thoughts. Some teams have been assigned to investigate the coast area, some head down to Massachusetts, and others are scattered around the state. I think we need to work closer together."

"Sergeant, I'll talk with Lieutenant Wilson and see if we can take care of that problem."

The crowd gathering for the funeral was enormous, many were standing in lines, waiting to get into the funeral home. I was sure the services would be delayed to accommodate so many people. When the Psaradelises and Compagnas arrived, they entered through the side entrance.

Forty minutes behind schedule, the lieutenant moved his car to the head of the procession to lead the line of cars to the church where the service would take place. I followed at the end of the line. The entire funeral was uneventful. I felt bad for both families and hoped it wouldn't be long before we found the people responsible for the murder of their daughters. The cemetery where Anne Psaradelis was to be laid to rest was across the street from the church. After the service, the procession went to this cemetery first and then to the cemetery in Manchester where Diane Compagna was to be interred.

After the funeral I relayed a request from the Compagnas and Psaradelises to Chief Pelletier. The parents wanted to visit the crime scene in the next day or two. The chief checked with Lieutenant Wilson and gave his approval.

I was assigned to work with Deputy Sheriff Leavitt for the remainder of the day. Our first interview was with Suzette Brown. She was a close friend of Anne Psaradelises. The interview took place in Suzette's home on Ballerina Drive.

"Suzette, can you tell us anything about either Diane Compagna or Anne Psaradelis?"

"First of all, Sergeant, I didn't know Diane Compagna at all, but I knew Anne very well. We talked about anything and everything."

"Suzette, how long did you know Anne?"

"I knew Anne at least two years. She didn't seem to have any problems, but she was sort of boy crazy, like the average fifteen-year-old girl."

"Suzette, when was the last time you saw or talked with Anne?"

"I last saw Anne on July 11, but when I talked with her on July 10, she told me she was going to Hampton Beach with Diane the next morning. I told Anne it was supposed to rain and it wouldn't be a very good day to be at the beach. Anne said she didn't care, they were going to the beach anyway. Then, I saw her the next morning, July 11, between 10:30 and 11:00 a.m. Anne was in her yard and said she was going to Hampton Beach with Diane. Mrs. Compagna was going to give them a ride."

"Suzette, do you remember what Anne was wearing the last time you saw her?"

"She was wearing dungarees with a couple of patches on them. As I recall one of them said 'Love is beautiful.' She also had on a midriff top, I think it was blue and white. Anne wasn't wearing glasses, but she did have on some rings. She was barefoot, but was carrying the brown sandals she used to wear all the time and a red-white-and-blue beach bag."

"Suzette, did Anne say anything else to you?"

"Yes, she told me that she had told her mother that Mrs. Compagna was taking them to the beach. I was at the Psaradelis home on July 11 when Mrs. Psaradelis received a phone call from Anne. She asked permission to spend the night at Diane's house. Anne said she would be home by 10:00 a.m. the next morning."

"Suzette, do you know if the girls were planning to meet anyone at the beach?"

"I don't really know, Sergeant, Anne didn't say. I liked Anne and trusted her enough to have her baby-sit for my kids. I don't know of anybody who wanted to murder the girls, but if I hear anything, I'll call you."

"Thanks for your time. We'll be in touch."

Deputy Leavitt had to appear in court, so Detective Bill Dodge from the state police was assigned to spend the remainder of the day with me. Our first assignment was to re-interview Greg Moses. Mr. Moses answered the door and called his son to talk with us.

"You know, Sergeant, you already interviewed me."

"I know, Greg. This type of thing happens quite often in a homicide investigation. Sometimes we need to clarify facts or statements. It helps us put the puzzle together or eliminate pieces that don't belong."

"I understand, Sergeant. I'll do my best to help."

"Greg, why don't you start with the Fourth of July celebration and tell us what you know about Diane Compagna and Anne Psaradelis?"

"Well, I was at the celebration with Bill Corbitt. We were in the high school parking lot where all of the events were taking place. Bill and I ran into Linda Caron and talked with her for a while. We noticed Diane walking around. She seemed upset, so Linda went over to Diane and talked with her for a few minutes."

"Greg, did Linda tell you why Diane was upset?"

"Well, Sergeant, when Linda returned, she didn't say anything, but later she told us that Diane had gone for a walk in the rear of the high school with Tom Jefferson. Apparently, they went into the woods and something happened. Later, Diane came over and started talking with us. She seemed worried and upset. Diane repeated the story Linda had told us and said she hadn't planned on Tom doing that to her. After a while Diane left us so she could search for Tom Jefferson. A bit later Diane returned and said she had found Tom. I think Diane said she thought she was pregnant, she really didn't know what to expect. Diane knew she could have been pregnant from what happened with Tom Jefferson. She was really worried about that."

"Greg, did you see Diane Compagna or Anne Psaradelis after July 4?"

"No, I never saw Diane again. I didn't know Anne Psaradelis until I saw her picture in the papers."

"Greg, do you know anyone who wanted to hurt either of the girls?"

"No. That's all I can tell you. If I hear of anything, I'll call you."

"Greg, thanks for taking the time to see us again."

Detective Dodge and I had one more interview scheduled. It was with Edward Bask. We stopped for a cup of coffee on our way to the Depot Street address. Edward immediately invited us into his home. He didn't want the neighbors to talk about our being there.

"Ed, when was the last time you saw Diane and Anne?"

"Well, Officers, I knew both girls for about two or three years. The last time I saw Anne Psaradelis was in school during the last week of June. I never saw her again after that. Now, as for Diane Compagna, the last time I saw her was on July 10. She was watching a baseball game at the high school and I said hello to her. I never saw her again. I don't know why anyone would want to hurt either of the girls. Everyone liked both of them. I've heard a lot of rumors, like everyone else, that they were in Boston and Hampton Beach, even New York. There really isn't anything else I can tell you. I just hope you get the people who murdered them."

"Thanks for taking the time to talk with us. If you hear of anything that might help us, call day or night."

On our way back to the station, the dispatcher advised that Lieutenant Gerlach wanted to speak with me in his office. I replied that I would be there as soon as possible.

"Lieutenant Gerlach, you wanted to see me?"

"Yes. We just received a telephone call from Linda Caron. She wants us to meet her at the entrance to the drive-in theater right away."

When we arrived at the drive-in, Linda was with a group of people near a red truck. We parked the cruiser and Linda came over to talk with us. She had been crying, so I offered her my handkerchief.

"Linda, what's the problem? Things can't be that bad."

"Well, I came early so I could watch the movie. I saw David walking by and said hello to him, then he came over and we started to talk."

"Linda, who is David?"

"David Collins."

"What happened that's upset you so?"

"Well, while David and I were talking, Diane and Anne's names came up. I told David that they were friends of mine and David said, 'I know who did it.' I tried to find out more, but David left and went back to his car. I was upset and started crying. A few minutes later David returned and talked with me again. This time David said that it was two guys and he knew their names. He also said the whole thing started on July 4th."

"Linda, did David tell you who these two guys were or anything else that might help us?"

"No, Sergeant, he wouldn't tell me anything else, he just went back to his car. I thought I should tell you about what he said."

"That was the right thing to do, Linda. Don't talk about this with anyone right now. We'll check it out. If you hear anything else, please call us, day or night."

"All right, Sergeant. Thanks for coming down, I feel a lot better now."

When we returned to the station, I made arrangements with the lieutenant to have one of the other investigators check the David Collins story, since I planned to spend most of the next day with the girls' parents at the crime scene. I couldn't help mentioning Tom Jefferson one more time while I was there.

"Lieutenant, I still think we need to talk with Tom Jefferson again about the July 4 incident and a few other things. I've already asked several times and the only answer I get is, 'not now' or 'later on.' I don't understand what we're waiting for.

"I know I shouldn't cry over spilled milk, Lieutenant, but I wish I'd been able to view the crime scene before everyone else got there, moving things around and walking all over everything. I haven't even seen a good photograph or video.

"From what I have seen, I think the people who murdered the girls are local, not strangers. The girls weren't running away from home. If they were, they would have gone someplace where no one knew them, not a place where they could bump into friends.

"Even the crime scene indicates they knew the people who murdered them. There's no sign of a struggle, especially from the victim who was found naked. I've never heard of a rapist letting a victim take her clothes off and put them in a pile, then letting the victim put her jeans on the ground so she could lay on them.

"Then there's the second victim. There was no sign of a struggle there either. It looks like she just tried to outrun the killer.

"I could be wrong, Lieutenant, but I think the girls knew their killer or killers."

"Sergeant, I tend to agree with you. All we can do is keep investigating and hope we come up with a lead or some kind of evidence."

When I finished talking with the lieutenant, it was too late for any more interviews, so I went to my office to catch up on paperwork.

12

October 16, 1973

I stopped by Lieutenant Wilson's office first thing in the morning to make sure Lieutenant Gerlach had cleared our taking the Compagnas and Psaradelises to the crime scene. He assured me the visit had been approved by the attorney general's office.

I ran into Lieutenant Gerlach a short time later.

"Hi, Lieutenant, have you been waiting for me?"

"No, Sergeant, I've been talking with the chief about the Compagna-Psaradelis investigation. The chief and I are both surprised that not one person has come forward with any type of lead. I guess none of us can understand."

"I know, Lieutenant, the only thing we do know is that they were alive on July 12 at 4:30 p.m. It appears they were murdered that night."

"Sergeant, if the case isn't solved in a couple more weeks, the state police and sheriff's office will pull their people out, leaving the bulk of the investigation with our department and Candia's. I spoke with the chief about you and Chief Baker working as partners."

I was pleased that someone was finally taking my advice.

Lieutenant Gerlach and I picked up the Compagnas and Psaradelises and drove them to the crime scene. Chief Baker met us at the intersection of Route 107 and New Boston Road and led the way from there.

As we passed the dump and wetlands Mrs. Psaradelis asked if we had checked the areas for the girls' beach bags and sandals. I told her that in addition to twenty police officers checking the area, Chief Baker and I checked the area four times ourselves. I told her we even put on hip boots and went into the water, but found nothing but old bottles and a couple of tires. I assured Mrs. Psaradelis that we checked the gravel pit as well.

I explained that although you could get to the crime scene from the logging road, through the wetlands, or by walking a couple of miles through the back woods, we felt the killers brought the girls into the woods through the gravel pit. After looking over the area, the parents agreed with us.

When we arrived at the pine grove where the girls' bodies were found, we left the parents to roam through the area alone. I knew it was a difficult time for the Compagnas and Psaradelises. The smell of death still remained in the area. It made us all angry.

This visit to the crime scene was one of the hardest things any of us had done. When we dropped the parents off at their homes, they thanked us for our time. Mrs. Psaradelis added, "I felt kind of sick when you showed us where the girls were found, but we just wanted to see the place for ourselves."

"You don't have to explain, Mrs. Psaradelis. I understand."

Deputy Sheriff Leavitt was waiting for me when I returned to the station. He wanted me to accompany him on an interview with Lilley Preston. She lived at 98 County Road.

"Lilley, when was the last time you saw Diane Compagna?"

"It was in June when we got out of school. Diane, Linda Caron and I were riding around. We went to Manchester and rode around some, then we looked in some of the store windows.

"Come to think about it, Sergeant, I did see Diane on July 4, in the afternoon. She was with Linda Caron. I didn't talk with them, but they seemed to be having a good time."

"Lilley, do you know Tom Jefferson?"

"Yes, Sergeant, I know Tom. I went out with him for eight or nine months. I was supposed to go out with Tom on the Fourth of July. I saw him for a little while in the afternoon, but I had to go to Nashua for lunch. When I came back to Merrimack, I saw Tom again. He was drinking with Ted Smith. They're close friends and live near each other. Tom was going to take me home around 7:00 p.m., then Ted spoke up and said he had to go to Nashua to get some speed. Tom told me he was going to take me home first because he didn't want me to be arrested if they got caught by the police. I didn't see either of them again that night.

"Tom Jefferson got married sometime after that. I think he married a girl who lived next door to him. I think she was Ted's sister."

"Lilley, did Tom Jefferson drink a lot?"

"Yes, in fact, he was a heavy drinker."

"How did he act when he was drinking?"

"He was a loving-type person to me, but he would pick fights with other people. Oh, he'd try to get fresh with me. He said things like, 'Come on, you can trust me,' and things like that.

"Can I ask you a question, Sergeant?"

"Of course, you can."

"Was Tom Jefferson involved with the two girls who were murdered?"

"Lilley, let's just leave it this way, he knew the girls just like a lot of other people did."

"If I hear anything, Sergeant, I'll call you. I hope you catch the person who killed the girls. I can't understand why anyone would want to hurt them."

"Thanks for taking the time to talk with us, Lilley."

Time passed quickly. October turned into November and we didn't know much more than we did a month ago. Tom Jefferson was our only suspect and we hadn't re-interviewed him. I talked with the Lieutenant Wilson about my frustrations.

"I've wanted to charge Jefferson with the rape that was alleged to have taken place on July 4. At least ten people have stated that Diane Compagna told them that Tom Jefferson raped her, but the answer I get from everyone, right up through the attorney general's office, is, 'You can't charge him because you don't have a victim.' How can I come up with a victim when she's been murdered? If we had some answers from Jefferson, it might help our investigation."

"Well, Sergeant, we've heard so many stories and rumors, we're going to start running people on the polygraph to try to eliminate some of them. We'll bring Tom Jefferson in and interview him. Just be patient. It will all work out."

Officer Rousseau caught me on my way out of the lieutenant's office.

"Hey, Sergeant Horak, have you heard about the suicide?"

"No."

"Well, it took place on Friday, November 9."

"Who was it?"

"A twenty-year-old boy by the name of Wayne Powers. I thought it might be of interest to you."

"Thanks, Officer Rousseau, I'll track down the paperwork and find out what it's all about."

I got the report from Chief Pelletier and went to my office to familiarize myself with the case. No sooner had I finished reading the report than Lieutenant Gerlach asked me to join him in the chief's office to discuss the case.

"Chief, I was shocked by the way the case was handled."

What do you mean, Sergeant?"

"Well, Chief, statements weren't taken from people who were in the house and out in the yard at the time of the incident, they were just part of the officer's report, not real interviews. There was no mention of looking for a suicide note or asking the victim why he shot himself, if in fact he did shoot himself. When Officer Hudson arrived, he didn't protect the scene well. Don't get me wrong, Officer Hudson did the best he could, but evidence from the scene was destroyed.

"Chief, the biggest thing that bothers me is that Wayne Powers was conscious for quite a few hours before he died. Why wasn't our department notified? One of our investigators could have talked with Powers and found out a lot of answers. I think we need to investigate this further. There has to be a good reason why Powers shot himself. I have a feeling it's tied in with the Compagna-Psaradelis murders."

The chief took my suggestion seriously and assigned Detective Dodge and me to the investigation. I filled Dodge in on the details.

JOSEPH A. HORAK

"At 9:08 a.m., November 9, Officer Hudson received a message from our dispatcher to respond to the Powers home on Gate Way Lane to assist an ambulance. When he arrived at 9:10 a.m., he was met at the back door by a woman who said, 'He's upstairs.' Officer Hudson ran upstairs to one of the bedrooms and found Mrs. Powers wiping blood from the eyes and nose of a boy lying in bed. There were blankets and a sleeping bag on top of him. Although there was blood all over his face and head, the boy was still breathing. While attempting to stop the bleeding, Officer Hudson observed a small hole in the left side of the boy's head. He also observed a rifle and some shells on the floor.

"Chief Pelletier and the ambulance arrived at the Powers home a few minutes later. The boy was taken to Memorial Hospital. When they arrived at 9:34 a.m., the boy was still conscious. The doctors determined he had a gunshot wound on the left side of his head. At 11:35 a.m. Officer Johnson called headquarters and advised that the boy was holding his own. At 7:17 p.m. Dr. Valley advised the Merrimack Police Department that Wayne Powers had expired a few minutes earlier.

"During the investigation it was discovered that Wayne Powers was twenty years old. His mother advised that her son had been treated for a nervous breakdown at the Memorial Hospital from October 2 through 26.

"Detective Dodge, I think we need to find out why this happened. Since the scene was corrupted by the family, ambulance people and others, we'll have to go back to October 2 and find out what contributed to Powers's nervous breakdown.

"You know, Detective, I'm sure some of the investigators will think we're wasting our time, but I have a feeling that there's a link between the Compagna-Psaradelis homicides and the suicide. Once we do our investigation, we'll know one way or the other."

I found out that Wayne Powers went to the Vo-Tech school in Nashua. Detective Dodge and I started the investigation by talking with the school's director, Professor Hildebrand.

"Professor, we'd like to talk with you about Wayne Powers, one of your students."

"We're all shocked about his death. How can I help?"

"Professor, we'd like to know anything you can tell us about Wayne Powers."

"Wayne was a good student. Everyone considered him to be a good kid. One peculiar thing did happen during the week of September 3. He was quite upset and walked out of class and went to his car to cry. From that time on Wayne changed.

"On October 2, Wayne came into my office."

"Professor, did you call him into your office?"

"No, Sergeant, Wayne came in on his own. I had a large picture of my Marine Corps class hanging on the wall. When Wayne saw it, he started talking irrationally about the Corps. He wanted to know about DI's. He told me he was at Parris Island all summer when, in fact, he wasn't.

"I talked with Debra Wilders, Wayne's girlfriend, about the situation. The two of us finally convinced Wayne that he should go for some help. He agreed. Professor Currier, Debra Wilders, and I took Wayne to Memorial Hospital in Nashua. On the way, Wayne told us he thought he was going crazy. When we arrived at the hospital, Wayne started doing pushups. Wayne was examined by a couple of doctors and, at one point, ran out of one of their offices."

Professor Currier learned that we were asking questions about Wayne Powers and joined the interview.

"I visited Wayne in the hospital nearly every day. I was pretty upset when I found out they were going to discharge him on October 26. I didn't feel Wayne had made sufficient progress to be released. Professor Hildebrand and I have talked about this and we can't understand why Wayne took his own life. It just doesn't make sense."

After interviewing Wayne's professors, Detective Dodge and I felt we were onto something. Our next stop was the Bise's IGA where Wayne used to work. We talked with Ron Boyer.

"We all thought a lot of Wayne."

"Ron, tell us about Wayne. Did you notice a change in him before the incident?"

"Wayne Powers was an especially good worker and an excellent employee until the beginning of July. Then he appeared somewhat flaky. He was moody and his directions to fellow employees were inconsistent. It was obvious that Wayne was having some kind of mental problem, so I called Professor Currier, the guidance counselor at Nashua Vo-Tech. I thought Wayne might be taking drugs, but Currier said no. He thought Wayne was under some type of mental strain.

"I asked Wayne if anything was wrong, if there was anything I could do to help. He replied that he was there to help me.

"Wayne had some type of construction job for a while and asked if I could adjust his hours so he could work both jobs.

"Something strange happened on September 30. Wayne had been at work about a half hour when he received a phone call and got really upset. Joe Kachoki, one of the other employees, called me at home. He said there was trouble and asked me to come to the store. I arrived about ten minutes later. It was obvious that Wayne was having serious mental problems, so I sent him home."

"Ron, can you check your records and tell us if Wayne worked July 12?"

"Sure, Sergeant, I have his card right here. Wayne was off on July 12."

I asked for a copy of Wayne's time card for the days surrounding July 12. Ron's secretary, Gloria, obliged by giving us Wayne's time card for the week before July 12 and the week following.

We interviewed Debra Wilders, Wayne's girlfriend, next. I had known Debra since she was a little girl and hoped that would make the interview easier for her.

"Debra, we'd like to talk with you about Wayne Powers. We know it must be difficult for you to talk about him right now, but if you could help us, we'd appreciate it."

"It's all right, Sergeant. I'll talk with you and Detective Dodge."

"Thanks, Debra. Please start by telling us about your relationship with Wayne Powers."

"Well, I've been going with Wayne for a couple of years. Last March I broke up with him, but we went back together in June. We went to the same school. Wayne wanted to manage a store sometime in the future."

"Debra, did you notice a change in Wayne?"

"I didn't notice anything strange until September."

"What happened in September?"

"Wayne started yelling a lot and was always starting fights with people. It really scared me. He was sick and needed help. It peaked around October 2 when he flipped out at school and had to be taken to the Memorial Hospital.

"Wayne stayed in the hospital quite a while. When he came home at the end of October, I went to his house every day. He seemed to be doing pretty well, until one day he couldn't walk or shave or do anything. I really don't know what happened. It was apparent something was bothering him, but he didn't tell me what it was."

"Debra, do you know if Wayne worked on July 12?"

"Not that I know of, Sergeant, but I can't tell you where he was or what he was doing.

"You know, Sergeant, I can't think of any reason why Wayne wanted to kill himself. He had everything going for him."

After the interview, I took Detective Dodge back to the station so he could appear in court. Something suspicious had happened to Wayne Powers around July 12 and we both thought his suicide had something to do with the Compagna-Psaradelis homicide investigation.

13

November 15, 1973

Detective Dodge and I decided we needed information about Wayne Powers's mental situation, so we decided to interview Dr. Dennis Hughes, who had treated him.

"Dr. Hughes, we understand you treated Wayne Powers around September 30."

"Yes, I did see Wayne Powers. I diagnosed his problem as acute castoria schizophrenia and prescribed a couple of things for him to take."

"Doctor, what might have led to this kind of problem?"

"It could happen to anyone, at anytime. I would say that no amount of counseling or oral discussion could help a problem like his."

"Dr. Hughes, I'd like you to answer a question for me, but I really don't know how to word it. Say that you and I are together and we've been friends for a long time, yet I'm a little afraid of you. Then one day you ask me to go for a ride with you and I agree. I jump in your car and we take off. Who knows where we're going, maybe you do, but I don't. For all I know we're going to the country, over to the coast, or just about anywhere. Dr. Hughes, say that we see two girls hitchhiking and you either know them or you don't, but you stop and pick them up. At some point we stop in a lonely and very dark area. Then we pull off the road into the woods, much like the Compagna-Psaradelis crime scene. You persuade one of the girls into going for a walk, leaving the other girl in the car with me. Some time later you come back to the car and tell us the girl fell and you need our help. We go into the woods and see that the girl is dead. The other girl runs. You go after her and kill the other girl too.

"My question, Dr. Hughes, is, if this took place between you and me and I was already afraid of you, would this put me in a position where I couldn't handle the guilt and fear? After all, now I'm a part of the crime."

"No, Sergeant, that wouldn't cause you to take your life. That's all I can tell you."

On the way back to the cruiser, Detective Dodge and I discussed the interview with Dr. Hughes.

"Detective, do you believe what we just heard?"

"I sure don't."

"I'm not a doctor, but I know that if I was somehow involved in one murder, never mind two, I wouldn't know how to cope with it. I can see how it would cause a person to commit suicide. So much for that interview. Let's get on to the next one."

Lyn Jacoby, a nurse at Memorial Hospital, was on duty in the emergency room when Wayne Powers arrived on November 9. Our interview with Ms. Jacoby took place in her home.

"There really isn't a lot I can tell you, Sergeant. I was working in the emergency room when the ambulance came in with a boy who had a gunshot wound to the head. It was around 9:40 a.m."

"Nurse Jacoby, do you remember the boy's name?"

"Yes, I do, Sergeant. His name was Wayne Powers. I stayed with him for about an hour before they transferred him to the intensive care unit."

"Did Powers say anything to you during the time you were with him?"

"Sergeant, Wayne was conscious right up to the time they transferred him to intensive care, then he went into a coma. Wayne did talk with me, but he didn't make any comments about shooting himself or about any personal problems he had."

It frustrated both Detective Dodge and me that Wayne Powers was conscious from the time he was found in bed, around 9:08 a.m., until around 11:00 a.m. and no one from law enforcement attempted to question him. If they had, we might have some answers that would help.

Our next interview was with Charles Allen, a close friend of Wayne Powers. He lived at 32 Temple Street in Litchfield.

"Charles, we'd like to talk with you about Wayne Powers. We've been told you were good friends."

"Wayne and I were friends for a long time, but I haven't seen him lately. I'm in the Marine Corps. I was at Parris Island for three months, followed by three months at Camp Lejeune. It was pretty rough. I got back home sometime between July 8 and 14, but I didn't see Wayne much then. When I did see him, I thought Wayne had changed. It seemed like something was bothering him, but he wouldn't talk to me about it.

"When he was at my house one time, he spotted my Bible and asked if he could borrow it. Wayne kept it about a month. He told me he read it and even wrote down things from it. I never did find out what he wrote, but I'll check my Bible and let you know if I find anything."

"Charles, when did you see Wayne Powers again?"

"Well, Sergeant, I guess the last time I saw him was in late July. Wayne and I went to Montreal for a few days vacation."

"Charles, is there anything else you can tell us about Wayne Powers?"

"I think Wayne might have been into drugs a few years ago, but I really don't know for sure. I do know he smoked grass once in a while. Wayne liked to go to the mountains and Hampton Beach a lot, but I can't think of anything else I can tell you. I can't understand why he took his own life. It's really too bad."

Detective Dodge and I interviewed half a dozen people and we were convinced that Wayne Powers's suicide was connected to the Compagna-Psaradelis murders. We felt so strongly about it, we decided to report our findings to Lieutenant Wilson.

"The individual pieces of information we have don't tell us a heck of a lot. We know that Diane Compagna and Anne Psaradelis were both alive and well on July 12, they were seen at Hampton Beach between 4:00 and 5:00 p.m. We know that a hunter found one of the bodies in Candia on September 29 and the second body was found in the same vicinity later that day."

"Yes, Sergeant, I'm aware of those facts. What makes you think Wayne Powers's suicide had anything to do with the murders?"

"The first thing is that Wayne Powers's time card, supplied by his boss Ron Boyer, indicates that Wayne did not work on July 12.

"During our interviews we found out that something happened in early July that changed Wayne's life. Whatever it was caused his life to fall apart. By late July Wayne was having problems at school and on the job. His attitude and outlook on life changed.

"Throughout August and into September things got worse for Wayne Powers. He cried a lot and was reported to have started fights with several people. Everything was going down hill. He even began to read the Bible.

"On September 30 Wayne received a phone call at work. It upset him so much that he was sent home and later visited a doctor. Interestingly, it was on September 30 that the identities of the two bodies were released and the news media reported it to the public.

"Powers was hospitalized on October 2 for emotional problems. He was released on October 26 and took his life on November 9."

"You know, gentlemen, when you look at the whole picture, I understand why you think there's a connection between the suicide and the homicides. I'll have someone look into this theory of yours and see if they can tie the two together."

"Thanks, Lieutenant. By the way, have they started to run the polygraph on any of the people we've interviewed?"

"Yes, we've started the polygraph stage of the investigation."

"Lieutenant, are you going to interview Tom Jefferson and run him on the polygraph?"

"Yes, Sergeant, we'll be talking to Jefferson within the next few days."

I was relieved that the lieutenant was finally taking me seriously.

I wanted to go over the crime scene again to see if anyone had been around there. I also wanted to check the roadway and wetland areas again before winter set in and covered everything with snow. I called Chief Baker to see if he wanted to accompany me. He did. We made arrangements to meet the next day.

November 22, 1973

Chief Baker was waiting in his car when I arrived. I told him about Wayne Powers's suicide and my theory that it was connected to the murders.

"Chief, have you turned up any new leads?"

"No, Sergeant, we've interviewed all kinds of people but haven't learned anything new. The people in Candia are quite nervous about two young girls being murdered so close to home. I've received several phone calls from mothers asking if it's safe for their children to play outdoors. I tell them it's OK, but they're still nervous. Some of them have said they're keeping their children in the house until we catch the killers."

As we moved into the crime scene, I could still smell death in the air. I could almost feel the presence of Diane and Anne telling us not to give up and to find the people who murdered them.

Chief Baker brought a metal detector with him, hoping it would help with our search. He also brought a camera. If we found anything, he could take a picture of it before we marked it for evidence and removed it from the scene. His efforts were in vain. We searched every inch of the crime scene and surrounding areas and found nothing.

We still hadn't found the beach bags and sandals the girls were carrying. In an attempt to reenact the actions at the crime scene, I brought along two beach bags and placed a towel and pair of sandals in each of them. We stood on New Boston Road and threw both bags as far as we could into woods. Then we searched the area where they landed, but found nothing.

It was a frustrating day. We'd spent eight hours turning over every leaf and rock we could find. I even wore hip boots so that I could inspect the water thoroughly. Still we found nothing new. As the chief and I walked back to our cars, we couldn't help venting one more frustration.

"Chief, I noticed we don't have as many investigators working on the case as before."

JUSTICE DENIED

"I suppose they have other investigations to work on. You know how it is sometimes, Sergeant, when a case is fresh, everyone wants to work on it. When the case gets cold, everyone walks away from it."

14

The day I had waited for finally arrived. We were going to interview Tom Jefferson. Sergeant Floyd Potter, a polygraph technician with the state police, was scheduled to administer the polygraph test. I spoke with Lieutenant Wilson before the interview.

"Lieutenant, I think Sergeant Potter should come right out and ask Jefferson, did you have anything to do with the deaths of Diane Compagna and Anne Psaradelis?"

"Sergeant, Potter is the polygraph operator. I'm sure he knows his job without your telling him what to do."

"Lieutenant, I'm not trying to tell anyone what to do. I just think we need to identify Tom Jefferson as a suspect or eliminate him."

The lieutenant didn't seem interested in my advice, so I took it upon myself to speak with Sergeant Potter personally.

"Sergeant Potter, can we sit down and talk before Tom Jefferson arrives?"

"Sure we can. What's on your mind, Sergeant?"

"Well, Sergeant Potter, we hope you're going to be able to either identify or eliminate Tom Jefferson as a suspect in the Compagna-Psaradelis murders. I, for one, believe he had motive as well as opportunity to commit the crime."

"I'll keep that in mind during the interview. Although you and Detective Dodge will be able to see and hear everything that happens, neither of you will be in the room."

"That's all right with me, Sergeant Potter."

The interview with Tom Jefferson got underway at 10:30 a.m. Sergeant Potter conducted the questioning.

"Just relax, Tom. I'm going to advise you of your rights. I do this with everyone I interview. It protects everyone involved, including me. Tom Jefferson these are your rights under the Miranda Warning. I am a state police officer for the State of New Hampshire and I want to advise you of your rights.

"1. You have the right to remain silent and not make any statements at all.

"2. Anything you say can and will be used in a court of law.

"3. You have the right to talk to a lawyer for advice before we ask you any questions and to have him present at all times during questioning.

"4. If you cannot afford a lawyer, one will be provided for you before any questioning, if you wish.

"5. If you decide to answer questions now, without a lawyer present, you will still have the right to stop answering at any time you want.

"Tom Jefferson, do you understand your rights as I have explained them?"

"Yes, I do, Sergeant Potter, and I'm willing to talk with you."

Tom Jefferson read and signed a waiver card, then the interview continued.

"Tom, why don't you tell me what's been going on in your life since June?"

"Well, Sergeant Potter, since the beginning of June I've seen my present wife Gloria on a daily basis, the only exceptions were around September 17 or 18. We got married on September 21 and moved to 150 Grant Street in Manchester."

"Tom, what kind of work have you been doing this past year?"

"I've been cutting wood with my father all summer, until two weeks ago when I started to work at John's Better-Built Homes in Nashua. My father always paid me in cash, so there's no record of when or where I worked."

"Tom, do you go to church or anything like that?"

"Well, Sergeant, I've been studying to be a Jehovah's Witness. We have study time at my house on Mondays, around 7:00 p.m., and I go to Kingdom Hall on Sundays."

"Well, Tom, it sounds like you have your life pretty much in order. That's more than I can say for a lot of people.

"Tom, I've heard a lot about an incident that occurred on July 4. You don't have to tell me about it if you don't want to, but I'd be interested in hearing about it."

"I don't mind telling you want happened, Sergeant. Diane went willingly. She jerked me off by hand first, then she helped me slide her jeans down around her legs, but she didn't take them off. I felt she had done it before. When I was interviewed before, I told Sergeant Horak that I didn't use any force at all, but I did use a little force.

"Later that night I heard that Diane was making comments to people about my raping her. I looked around for her girlfriend, Linda Caron, and told her to tell Diane that she better shut her mouth.

"Some time after July 4 some of my friends stated that they heard I had raped Diane Compagna."

"OK, Tom. Why don't we move along and get to the polygraph test. I'm not going to ask you any questions that we haven't talked about before the test. There are no hidden questions, so don't worry about anything coming up that you aren't prepared for. Just relax and don't move around. All you need to say is yes or no."

Sergeant Potter ran two charts. It was evident that Tom Jefferson was not telling the whole truth. It appeared that he attempted deception on two questions.

"Tom, why don't you tell me what the problem is, then we can do another test."

"Well, Sergeant Potter, the first statement I gave to the police about Diane Compagna was not entirely correct. I used a different approach to get Diane to submit. She did experience some discomfort during intercourse."

"Tom, let's run another test."

"OK, Sergeant."

The third test indicated Tom Jefferson was still attempting deception on the same questions.

"Tom, do you want to talk about it?"

"Well, Sergeant, Linda Caron came to me and said that Diane Compagna was claiming rape. I told Linda to tell Diane to keep her mouth shut or I would kick her in the ass, or something to that effect."

Sergeant Potter ran another polygraph test. This time Tom Jefferson appeared to answer each question truthfully. I reported the results to Chief Pelletier.

"Sergeant Horak, are you satisfied that Tom Jefferson isn't involved in the murders of Diane Compagna and Anne Psaradelis?"

"To be honest with you, Chief, I'm pretty discouraged. I'm not happy with the questions Sergeant Potter asked."

"What do you mean, Sergeant?"

"I thought the questions were too general, but my main concern is what Jefferson said when Sergeant Potter told him the interview was complete. He said, 'Does that mean I'm no longer suspected of murder?' I doubt that we'll ever be able to talk Tom Jefferson into taking another polygraph. We sure can't eliminate him, that's for sure."

"Sergeant, have you talked with Lieutenant Wilson about this?"

"No, Chief Pelletier, I haven't. I spoke with Lieutenant Wilson prior to Jefferson's test and suggested some questions, but he more or less put me in my place. The lieutenant told me Sergeant Potter was the technician and he knew what questions to ask and didn't need me telling him how to do his job."

15

<u>January 10, 1974</u>

The new year brought with it new dedication to finding the murderers of Diane Compagna and Anne Psaradelis. We had conducted over five hundred interviews and had volumes of reports, yet the whole picture was still unclear. Chief Baker and I decided to review every interview and every piece of paper accumulated during the investigation to make sure nothing had been overlooked.

It was a typical New England winter day with snow predicted to fall all day and into the night. When Chief Baker arrived in my office, ten inches of the white stuff had already accumulated on the ground.

"Chief, I see you made it. How bad are the roads?"

"Well, Sergeant, they're passable now, but if it gets much worse, I may have to cut our meeting short and head back to Candia early."

"I understand, Chief. I guess we'd better get to work."

Each of us took a couple of the files and started reading through them. We made a list of items that needed further attention so we could look into them later. It was Chief Baker who broke the silence and brought one of the reports to my attention.

"Hey, Sergeant Horak, do you remember the attempted kidnapping you and Lieutenant Gerlach investigated on October 3?"

"Let me see the report, Chief. Yeah, I remember this one. A woman by the name of Stephanie Pigg called our dispatcher and stated that she was at the Franklin residence on Baxter Springs Road. Ms. Pigg advised that she was walking on Baxter Springs Road when a man stopped his car and asked if she wanted a ride. Before she could answer, the man tried to force her into the car. He said, 'You heard what happened to the girls from Merrimack.' Ms. Pigg asked, 'Will that happen to me?' He replied, 'You'll see.' Ms. Pigg was frightened and began to scream. At this time another car came down the road, causing the man to let her go. Ms. Pigg ran to the nearest house and called us.

"Lieutenant Gerlach and I responded to the Baxter Springs Road address. When we knocked on the door of the Franklin residence, a small white-haired man came to the door. He acted nervous and a bit surprised to see the police. We explained the incident Ms. Pigg told our dispatcher and stated that she had placed the call from his home. He replied, 'I've been home all evening and no Stephanie Pigg has been in this house.' He didn't recognize the name at all. The lieutenant and I checked the entire area and found nothing out of the ordinary.

"About thirty minutes later our dispatcher advised us that he had received a second call from Ms. Pigg. She stated, 'I'm at the last house on Baxter Springs Road, is anyone coming?' Lieutenant Gerlach and I were still in the area and arrived at the house Ms. Pigg described, the home of Robert Elwood, within a minute or two. There were no cars parked in the area and no one walking on the road. The Elwoods stated that they knew nothing about the incident Ms. Pigg described. They had been home all evening and no one had come to their door.

"After we left the Elwood home, Lieutenant Gerlach and I checked the entire area again, even the gravel pits at the end of the road. We found no sign of Stephanie Pigg.

"Chief Baker, you're going to find several phone calls like this one throughout the case. It's similar to reports we received during the missing person's investigation. It seems like someone wanted to throw us off track. That's what makes me think the murderer was not a stranger to the girls. If he was, we would have received more help from their friends and people the girls went to school with."

The storm intensified with each passing hour. The nor'easter brought with it gale winds and much heavier snow than had been ex-pected. Chief Baker left early so that he could make his way home safely, leaving me to review the remaining stack of reports by myself.

The next morning I stopped by to talk with both the Compagnas and the Psaradelises on my way to the station. I wanted to stay in touch with them and let them know what was going on. Above all, I wanted to make sure they knew we weren't putting the murders of their daughters on the back shelf.

When I arrived at the station, I checked with Chief Pelletier about interviewing Tom Jefferson's father, Frank. The chief's response was, "Do whatever you think should be done. That's what you get paid for." I called Frank Jefferson and arranged the interview. He arrived at the station about an hour later.

"Thanks for coming to the station, Mr. Jefferson. I'm Sergeant Joe Horak."

"Oh, you're the one who's been picking on my son Tom."

"Mr. Jefferson, I want you to know that no one has been picking on Tom, but I do want to talk with you about him. I'm going to do something that I very seldom do, I'm going to tell you a little bit about the case I'm investigating, because I need your help. I'm working on the murders of Diane Compagna and Anne Psaradelis."

"Sergeant, what has that got to do with Tom? He's already been interviewed by the police a few times, apparently for nothing. I call that picking on him, don't you?"

"Mr. Jefferson, why don't you listen to what I have to say, then you can decide if we're picking on Tom or not."

"I guess that would be fair, Sergeant. Tell me what you have to say."

"I'm going to be honest with you, Mr. Jefferson. I can't tell you everything we know, but I'll tell you enough so you'll understand. Tom is alleged to have raped the Compagna girl on the evening of July 4, 1973. He's given a written statement admitting to having intercourse with her. With or without the girl's consent, that's statutory rape because of the girl's age."

"Tom never said anything about that."

"As I told you Mr. Jefferson, I can't tell you everything, but I want you to understand what's going on so that you can help us resolve the case."

"Sergeant, are you saying Tom is a suspect in this case?"

"Mr. Jefferson, I'm saying that at this point in the investigation we need to either place or eliminate Tom as having involvement in the case."

"Sergeant, didn't Tom take a polygraph test?"

"Yes, Mr. Jefferson, he did. He admitted to using force to have intercourse with Diane Compagna, but I'm not satisfied that Tom was asked the proper questions about the murders of Diane Compagna and Anne Psaradelis."

"What do you want from me, Sergeant?"

"Well, Mr. Jefferson, our investigation is at a standstill. We can't place or eliminate Tom's involvement. Tom had a motive."

"What motive, Sergeant?"

"I'll try to explain. If Tom was charged with statutory rape and convicted, he could go to prison. It would spoil his reputation and it might have affected his plans to marry the girl he was going with."

"Mr. Jefferson, I'm not saying Tom was involved, I'm just asking for your help in trying to resolve some of the questions. I'm hoping you can talk Tom into submitting to another polygraph test with a different operator. Then we could get this squared away so we can move on with the investigation."

"I understand, Sergeant. I'll talk with Tom and get back to you. It would be good to resolve this situation."

After my interview with Mr. Jefferson, I stopped by Chief Pelletier's office to tell him about my hopes of retesting Tom on the polygraph.

"That's great. Keep up the good work, Detective-Lieutenant Horak."

"Chief, what do you mean 'lieutenant'? I'm a sergeant."

"Not any more. You've just been promoted to detective lieutenant. Congratulations! You more than deserve it. I wish I had ten more just like you."

"Thanks, Chief."

"By the way, Detective-Lieutenant Horak, there's more news. Lieutenant Gerlach has been promoted to become our first deputy chief and we've hired a new detective sergeant by the name of John Bennett. He'll start work tomorrow."

JOSEPH A. HORAK

Some of the officers in our department were familiar with Bennett's work in Massachusetts. He was known to be pretty sharp. It would be good to have a fresh eye look at the case. I was hopeful that Bennett might be able to pick up something from the files that we'd overlooked.

16

<u>June 28, 1974</u>

Deputy Chief Gerlach and I were congratulating each other on our promotions when I received an unexpected phone call.

"Hello. Who am I talking with?"

"This is Chief Stone of the Boscawen Police Department. I think I may be able to help you. I understand two fifteen-year-old girls from your town were found murdered in Candia in September 1973, is that correct?"

"Yes, Chief Stone, the case is known as the Compagna-Psaradelis homicides."

"Well, Lieutenant Horak, we're working on a rape and assault case. We have a possible suspect by the name of William Johnson. During our investigation we found a scrapbook among his possessions that contained clippings about the two girls from Merrimack. I thought you might be interested."

"Indeed I am, Chief Stone. Can you give me more details?"

"William Johnson was born June 24, 1946, and has an extensive criminal record. He was released from the New Hampshire State Prison in July 1973.

"Recently, Johnson picked up a female hitchhiker and attempted to rape her at knife point. The girl was able to break free and left the scene.

"We arrested Johnson soon afterward and obtained a search warrant for his vehicle, a 1966 Buick Skylark, blue in color. The warrant listed a knife, glasses, and a cap as items we were searching for. We found the knife and glasses, but not the cap.

"We also found other questionable items in the vehicle - horror books, masking tape, binoculars, nylon rope with tape on each end, and two chests filled with magazines and additional magazines stacked next to them. The magazines bordered on being pornographic. It wasn't the nature of the magazines that was suspicious, the investigators felt the magazines could have been purchased at any newsstand, it was the newspaper clippings that were inserted between the pages that caught our attention. The clippings were from daily and weekly newspapers from around the state. The articles were about girls in their preteen and early teen years. Johnson's collection covered spelling bees, 4-H, Girl Scouts-anything having to do with young girls.

"Apparently, Johnson had a special interest in homicide and placed clippings in this regard in a scrapbook. That's where we found the articles about the murder of the two Merrimack girls. I thought you might want to know."

"You were right, Chief Stone, I'm glad you called. I'd really like to take a look at what you have."

"We thought Johnson may have a connection with other sex crimes around the state, so we've set up an area here in the Boscawen Police Station where all the articles can be viewed by any law enforcement agency. Feel free to stop by any time."

"Thanks, Chief Stone. I'll get in touch with Chief Baker from Candia and we'll be right over."

I called Chief Baker to tell him about the discovery the Boscawen Police Department had made, but he too had received a call from Chief Stone and knew all about William Johnson. I offered to pick up Chief Baker on my way to Boscawen. He accepted my offer. When we arrived, Chief Stone showed us to the room where the confiscated articles were on display.

"Look at all this stuff, Chief Baker, this guy must be weird. It looks as if he liked young girls with long dark hair. Why would anyone want to cut out clippings of young girls?"

The articles concerning Diane and Anne were among hundreds of other clippings about young girls. These particular clippings may not be connected to our investigation at all, but it made us wonder about this guy. He's not someone anyone would want living in their neighborhood.

I requested permission from Chief Stone to take a roll of the masking tape found in Johnson's vehicle. I wanted to send it to the state police laboratory as a possible match to the piece of masking tape found at the crime scene in Candia. Chief Stone gave his approval and asked me to complete the appropriate forms so that a chain of evidence could be maintained. Of course, I did as he asked.

"Chief Stone, do you know anything more about William Johnson?"

"Well, Lieutenant, I know the story one girl reported to us. She was hitchhiking and Johnson stopped to pick her up. When she got into the car, the girl noticed Johnson had on white socks and black shoes. Music was playing on the radio, but he didn't say a word. She felt uncomfortable about his not talking.

"They rode on and passed another girl hitchhiking, but Johnson didn't stop to pick her up. He just kept driving, not saying a word.

"Later, they came to a road and Johnson told her he had to drop some pants off at his mother's house. He promised to drop the girl off in town after stopping at his mother's. She didn't like the idea, but she agreed. She told herself that she should have said, 'let me out,' but she didn't.

"They passed a shoe factory, but there weren't many houses on the road. Johnson slowed down the car and pulled to the side of the road. The girl told me that she knew her time had come. She had heard about this happening to other girls and now it was happening to her.

"As soon as the car came to a stop, the girl opened the door and tried to get out of the car, but Johnson grabbed her and told her not to be foolish. When she started to struggle, he pulled a sharp wooden pencil from the pocket of his shirt. She stopped struggling and a great calm descended upon her. She thought, I guess it doesn't matter now, I'm going to die.

"Johnson said, 'That's better,' and reached into his pocket and took out a metal pencil.

"She asked, 'What are you going to do now?'

"Johnson said, 'Take off your pants, but not your undies, leave them on.'

"She unbuttoned and unzipped her pants. Johnson seemed mad, so she hurried and pulled them down around her knees. Then, he started to kiss her. She thought she was going to die, so she responded, hoping it might calm him down.

"Then, Johnson told her to take off her coat and shirt, but to leave her bra on. She didn't want to make him mad, so she acquiesced. She wasn't wearing a bra, so Johnson started touching her breasts and unzipped his pants.

"The girl was really scared. She thought it might calm him down if she was nice to him, so she stroked his hair. She told me he had dandruff and his hair was dirty and greasy.

"Then, Johnson told the girl to kiss his penis, so she did. When she stopped, he got agitated and insisted she put it in her mouth. The girl was so afraid, she did as he instructed.

"Johnson told her to pull her underpants down and he touched her pubic area with his hands. Her jeans were hanging around her knees, so she decided to remove them in case she got a chance to run. Johnson opened the door and pulled her legs across the seat. He laid on top of her and started kissing her again. She was trapped under his body. He started rubbing his penis over her genitals and told her to make him hard, so she touched his penis with her hand.

"Johnson was about to enter her when he was startled by a car coming down the road. She took advantage of the situation and pushed him away from her. She ran toward the car, screaming for help. The car stopped and she jumped in. The people in the car drove her to a friend's house and gave her some clothes, then they called the police.

"Lieutenant, this guy is capable of anything."

"Chief Stone, can you give us a copy of your investigative reports on William Johnson? It sure would help us a lot."

"Sure. It'll just take a few minutes to copy the paperwork for you."

Chief Baker and I spent the next few days studying Johnson's files and interviewing people who knew him. He had no car or driver's license and very little money. He put in a full day's work on July 12, the date we suspected the girls were killed. It seemed improbable that

JUSTICE DENIED

Johnson was connected with the Compagna-Psaradelis homicides. We concluded that Johnson had the newspaper clippings about Diane and Anne because he liked young girls, especially girls with long dark hair.

Attention Hampton Beach Visitors

July 5, 1974

HAMPTON — Police in the following towns, Diane and Ann were picked up by some unknown person or persons investigators from the towns of Candia and Merrimack, New Hampshire, are interested in talking with any person or persons that spent their vacation at Hampton Beach last year between July 11 to 13 and might have seen the two girls pictured.

The two were last seen on July 12 and were found murdered in Candia in September 1973.

Diane Compagna, 15, Waldon Brive, Merrimack. White female, five foot-five inches, pounds, long jet black hair; wearing blue jeans, peasant-type midi-blouse, colored blue and white; brown leather sandals; and carrying a red beach bag with a large beads loved and a two piece bathing suit purple and pink in color.

Anne Psaradelis, 15, Harris Avenue, Merrimack. White female, five foot-four inches, 115 pounds; long dark brown hair; wearing blue jeans, red blouse; brown leather sandals; carrying a large beach towel, multi-colored beach bag, and a two piece, multi-colored bathing suit.

The investigators have found

and were picked up by some unknown person or persons known person or persons.

Then on September 28th, 1973 a man was out hunting near an abandoned road just off Route 101 in Candia. He decided to take a woods and met came upon a body lying through some small hard-decomposed body. The hunter immediately called the Candia police. Officers soon found a second body not far from the first and they were identified as those of Diane and Anne.

The investigators would be in-

terested in talking with anyone that might have seen the girls at the beach or anyone that gave them a ride or might have seen them being picked up. They would also like to talk with the people that the girls are supposed to have spent the night with on July 11, 1973.

The investigators would be interested in anyone that might have observed the girls, a suspicious person (or persons) or vehicle in the New Boston Road area of Candia between July 11th

and September 26th, 1973.

The investigation has been hampered by people who do not want to get involved in a case involving two murdered girls. You could help so please come forward with any information you might have.

If you have any information please call Chief Robert Baker of the Candia Police Department at 483-2555 or Detective Sergeant Joseph Horak at the Merrimack Police Department at 424-2278.

Diane Compagna   Anne Psaradelis

Figure 22: July 1974 – Attention Hampton Beach Visitors

JUSTICE DENIED

17

July 5, 1974
One year after Diane Compagna and Anne Psaradelis were reported missing, we placed this article in *Foster's Daily Democrat.*

ATTENTION HAMPTON BEACH VISITORS

Police investigators from the towns of Candia and Merrimack, New Hampshire, are interested in talking with any person or persons who spent their vacation at Hampton Beach last year between July 11 to 13 (1973) and might have seen or been with Diane Compagna and Anne Psaradelis.

Diane Compagna, fifteen, from Merrimack. White female, five-feet-five-inches tall, one hundred five pounds, long jet black hair; wearing blue jeans, peasant-type midi-blouse, blue and white in color, brown leather sandals; and carrying a red beach bag, red towel, and a two-piece bathing suit, purple and pink in color.

Anne Psaradelis, fifteen, Merrimack. White female, five-feet-four-inches tall, one hundred twenty-five pounds, long dark brown hair; wearing blue jeans, red blouse, brown leather sandals; carrying a large beach towel, multi-colored beach bag, and a two-piece multi-colored bathing suit.

The investigators have found the following facts: Diane and Anne were last seen in the area of the casino and the Red Cross Station at about 4:30 p.m. on July 12, 1973. The two girls are supposed to have spent the night of July 11, 1973, at a camp or cottage with a male per-

son, his sister and a small child. Apparently they slept on the floor. The two girls were waiting for some person or persons they knew in the Hampton Beach area when they were picked up by some unknown person or persons.

The two were last seen on July 12 and were found murdered in Candia in September 1973.

On September 29, 1973, a man was hunting near an abandoned road off New Boston Road in Candia. He found a badly decomposed body among some small hardwoods. The hunter immediately called the Candia police. Officers soon found a second body not far from the first. The bodies were identified as Diane Compagna and Anne Psaradelis.

The investigators are interested in talking with anyone who might have seen the girls at the beach or anyone who gave them a ride or might have seen them being picked up. They would also like to talk with the people the girls are supposed to have spent the night with on July 11, 1973.

The investigators are interested in talking with anyone who might have observed the girls, a suspicious person or persons, or a vehicle in the New Boston Road area of Candia between July 11 and September 29, 1973.

The investigation has been hampered by people who do not want to get involved in a case involving two murdered girls or who are afraid to come forward, fearing the same thing will happen to them.

You could help, so please come forward with any information you might have.

If you have any information, please call Chief Robert Baker of the Candia Police Department at 555-2255 or Detective Lieutenant Joe Horak of the Merrimack Police Department at 555-3366.

In addition to the *Foster's Daily Democrat*, the *Manchester Union Leader* also ran articles encouraging the public to come forward with information concerning the case, however, this coverage was sporadic. We were disappointed that the press and radio and television stations weren't more aggressive in reporting the on-going findings of our investigation.

It seemed as though even those charged with overseeing the investigation lost interest. As months passed, the weekly meetings originally planned to discuss information and leads gained through interviews became nonexistent. There was no forum for investigators to share their experiences or organize information related to the case.

I was still frustrated that Tom Jefferson wasn't charged with statutory rape. Diane Compagna told at least ten people about the incident of July 4, yet everyone from the district court right up to the attorney general's office contended that we couldn't charge Jefferson without a victim.

It became more and more evident that if the murders were going to be solved, Chief Baker and I were going to have to do it ourselves. Although our days were filled with investigating breaking-and-entering cases, domestic complaints, drug investigations and the paperwork that accompanied them, the chief and I made time to include the Compagna-Psaradelis homicides in our daily routine. We continued to visit the crime scene, hoping the murderers might return and give us a lead. We also stayed in contact with both girls' parents to keep them abreast of the investigation.

18

September 12, 1974

I received an alarming phone call from Officer Robert Brooks with the Nashua Police Department.

The officer told me that he was on patrol at 8:45 a.m. near the river and observed a man sitting in his car, reading. He was so engrossed in what he was doing, the man didn't even look up as the cruiser drove by. Officer Brooks thought the man was waiting for someone, so he resumed his patrol.

At 10:50 a.m. the officer checked the river area again and noticed that the car was still parked in the same place, but the driver was not present. Upon closer inspection of the area, Officer Brooks saw a man emerging from the woods and recognized him as the man he had seen behind the wheel earlier. The officer approached the man and asked for identification. The man identified himself as Jim Psaradelis of Merrimack, New Hampshire, and stated that his daughter had been raped and murdered in Candia in 1973.

When asked what he was doing in the river area, Mr. Psaradelis stated that he was merely sitting in his car waiting for time to pass. Officer Brooks reported that Mr. Psaradelis seemed very nervous. The officer approached Psaradelis' 1969 Chevrolet and observed a brown paper bag containing several paperback books on the front seat. He received permission from Mr. Psaradelis to inspect the books and found the titles to be pornographic in nature.

At this time Mr. Psaradelis voluntarily revealed that he had a firearm in his possession and produced a permit for the officer's inspection. Mr. Psaradelis also stated that he knew Detective LeBlanc from the Nashua Police Department.

Officer Brooks decided the situation needed further investigation and requested that a detective be sent to his location. Detective LeBlanc, Lieutenant Brown and several other officers arrived on the scene a short time later.

Lieutenant Brown received permission from Mr. Psaradelis to inspect his car. The inspection revealed a pair of handcuffs in the glove compartment, a ten-inch rubber hose and hunting knife under the front seat, and a bag of pornographic pictures on the front floorboard.

Detective LeBlanc assisted Brown in his inspection of Psaradelis' trunk. When itemized in their report, the articles found in the trunk filled ten pages. The most suspicious items were a large cardboard box filled with pornographic material, a pair of glasses, and fake eyebrows, mustache and beard.

Lieutenant Wilson and Detective Dodge were notified and requested to respond to the Nashua Police Department, where Mr. Psaradelis was taken. Upon arrival, Psaradelis was advised of his rights. He signified that he understood them and signed a rights waiver.

Mr. Psaradelis was interrogated in depth about the homicide of his daughter Anne. He denied any involvement in the murder and agreed to take a polygraph test. Jim Psaradelis was released and went voluntarily to state police headquarters to be tested on the polygraph, which he passed.

I was pleased that Officer Brooks had informed me of the situation with Mr. Psaradelis, but troubled about the continuous lack of coordination in the case. I spoke with Chief Pelletier about my frustration.

"You know, Chief, I don't understand the way Lieutenant Wilson and some of the other detectives handle things."

"What do you mean by that, Lieutenant?"

"Well, Chief, I think we should all work together to solve these murders. That means letting each other know what's going on in the investigation. The situation with Malcolm Gilbert is a good example. Lieutenant Wilson interviewed Gilbert about the Compagna-Psaradelis murders and didn't say a word to me about it. Now, there's the situation with Jim Psaradelis. Officer Brooks of the Nashua Police Department took the time to keep me informed, but not Lieutenant Wilson or Detective Dodge. It's almost like they want to solve the case and make the arrest themselves. It doesn't matter who makes the arrest, only that an arrest is made. The murders will never be solved if we don't work together on this investigation."

Since I had the chief's attention, I thought this was as good a time as any to air another concern I had about the investigation.

"You know, Chief Pelletier, I don't mean to complain, but I'd like to talk about Tom Jefferson for a minute. As you know, I've wanted to charge Jefferson with statutory rape ever since we first found out about the Fourth of July incident in 1973. Everyone has said, 'No, it can't be done because we don't have a victim.' I still don't understand that. Diane Compagna told at least ten people that Tom Jefferson raped her.

"I've also wanted Tom Jefferson to take another polygraph test with another operator so that we can ask him about the murders, but no one wants to get involved.

"Two years ago I talked with Tom's father, Frank Jefferson. He seemed interested in getting things cleared up and said he would talk to Tom about taking another polygraph test, but I haven't heard another thing from either of them. I'm going to write a letter to Mr. Jefferson today and find out why he hasn't called me back."

"Lieutenant Horak, why don't you call Jefferson instead of writing?"

"I can't, Chief. Frank Jefferson has moved to California."

This is what I said in the letter to Frank Jefferson.

Dear Mr. Jefferson:

I am writing to you regarding the Compagna-Psaradelis homicides. I have spoken with you in the past about this investigation and would like you to know that the case remains unsolved.

When we last talked, you advised that you would speak with Tom about taking another polygraph test. I have not heard from either you or Tom in this regard. I do not want to cause

Tom problems, but the investigation is at a standstill until we can eliminate him one way or the other.

I would appreciate any cooperation you can give me in this matter. I know how you feel about Tom, after all, he is your son. I also know that you are interested in clarifying whether Tom is involved in this case or not.

If I receive any information regarding this problem, I will inform you right away.

Before I mailed the letter, I showed it to Chief Pelletier.

"This is a good letter, Lieutenant."

"I wonder if Mr. Jefferson will reply."

"All you can do is try, Lieutenant. Just stick with the case. I know you can solve it sooner or later."

"Thanks, Chief. I appreciate your confidence in me."

March 6, 1975

I received a phone call from Chief Baker. He was excited because he thought there might be a break in the case.

The chief had received a phone call from Janice Lumber in Auburn, New Hampshire. She wanted to talk with us about the Compagna-Psaradelis murders, but didn't want to come into the station. She requested we conduct the interview at her home. Since Chief Baker was familiar with the Rattlesnake Road address Ms. Lumber gave, he offered to drive us to her home. I met the chief in his office and we started our journey to Rattlesnake Road.

Ms. Lumber's home was in the backwoods of Auburn. We turned off the main highway onto an old logging road that was so bumpy, I thought the car's springs would give way. The farther into the woods we traveled, the narrower the logging road got. After fifteen minutes of inching our way along, we came upon a sign that was nailed to a post. It read, "Lumber's Inn." A short distance away, was a shack with a heavy-set woman and huge dog standing in the doorway.

"Who's there?"

"Mrs. Lumber, it's Chief Robert Baker and Lieutenant Joe Horak."

"Wait a minute, I'll have to tie up the dog. He doesn't like strangers."

While Mrs. Lumber secured the dog, the chief and I slowly and cautiously approached the house.

"The dog's OK now, come on in. I appreciate your coming all the way out here because I want to talk with you about my husband. I don't know for sure, but I have this feeling he might have something to do with the deaths of those two girls they found murdered in Candia."

"What's your husband's name?"

"James Lumber."

"Where is your husband now?"

"James is in a mental clinic for treatment, but he's going to be released in a few days."

"Mrs. Lumber, why don't you start by telling us about your husband."

"OK. James has been arrested in several towns here in New Hampshire and even served time in prison over in Vermont."

"What were the crimes your husband was charged with?"

"He was charged with being drunk and disorderly, and assault. Then, there were some sex charges - some of those even involved his own children!"

"Mrs. Lumber, what makes you think your husband had anything to do with the Compagna-Psaradelis murders?"

"Well, I'll start at the beginning. James and I were married in 1972. In April 1973 I had to take him up north to the hospital. While we were there, I had to go into the trunk of the car for something and I noticed blood all over the place. I asked James about this and he told me he had killed a deer out of season. Between you and me, if James had killed a deer, he would have kept it."

"Mrs. Lumber, can you describe the car in which you found the blood?"

"Sure. It was a light blue, 1969 Ford LTD. It was registered in both our names. We sold it in 1973 to some auto body shop in Manchester."

"Mrs. Lumber, is there anything else that makes you suspect your husband was involved in the girls' murders?"

"Yes, there is. My husband and I have separated several times since we've been married. Every time this happened, he went to Hampton Beach. I don't know how long he stayed or what he did there, but he went to Hampton Beach, I'm sure of that.

"I'm also sure my husband is dangerous. I fear for my life. He's already tried to kill me over this. He had a knife and made me promise not to tell anyone. I just think you should check my husband out. That's all I can tell you right now."

The first thing Chief Baker and I did was contact Chief Emerson Heald at the Auburn Police Department. Although he probably already knew about James Lumber, he needed to be aware of how frightened Mrs. Lumber was.

We tried to arrange an interview with James Lumber while he was still in the clinic, but he refused to talk with us. Lumber said he hadn't done anything wrong and was tired of the police picking on him.

We ran a check on James Lumber and his record went all the way back to 1939. In addition to escaping from jail two times, his record included lewd and lascivious behavior, motor vehicle violations, fugitive from justice, grand larceny, desertion, nonsupport, and carrying a loaded gun.

We ran a check on the car the Lumbers sold in 1973, but were unable to locate it. We concluded that the car ended up in a junk yard and was sold for parts.

At this point, our hands were tied. Both Chief Baker and I hoped we would hear from Janice Lumber again.

19

March 20, 1975

I heard that Tom Jefferson and his wife Marie had been divorced. I thought talking with his ex-wife might help us gather more information about Jefferson's involvement in the case, so I contacted Marie. I found out she was using her maiden name, Major, rather than Jefferson. She consented to an interview. I asked Officer Litchfield, a policewoman, to accompany me to Marie Major's apartment in Nashua - no sense in getting into trouble during the interview.

When we arrived, Marie was cleaning and asked us to excuse the smell of bleach. She was extremely nervous and offered us a cup of coffee. Officer Litchfield and I told her not to go to any trouble, but Marie insisted, stating she needed a cup herself to calm down.

I showed Marie newspaper clippings about the Compagna-Psaradelis homicides and some photographs of the girls. She stated that she remembered reading about the murders, but that she knew nothing more about it.

"The murders took place back in 1973. Why did you wait so long to talk with me?"

"Marie, we interviewed Tom right after the bodies were found, but he didn't want you to know anything about it because the two of you were about to be married. After you were married, I thought you might not want to talk with the police, so I didn't bother you. Now that you're alone, I thought you might be able to give us some information. Please know that anything you tell us will be held in strictest confidence."

"Is Tom a suspect in the case?"

"No, Marie, we just need to clear up a few things and eliminate all possibilities."

Much of the interview continued with Marie asking me as many questions as I asked her. Although I tried to be truthful in giving her answers, she was not as candid. Most of her answers were "I don't know" or "I don't remember." She was extremely evasive, she answered as though she was pleading the Fifth Amendment.

I felt certain that Marie knew more than she told me. One of the questions I asked was, "Did Tom ever beat you up?" Marie hesitated before answering and said, "No." She reconsidered her answer, then said, "Well, he gave me a couple of bruises on my arms now and then."

I left the apartment with the impression that Marie was afraid of Tom Jefferson.

May 15, 1975

Chief Pelletier stuck his head in my office and said, "Sergeant Bennett just took a missing person's report. You'll never guess who it was - Jim Psaradelis!"

According to Sergeant Bennett, Jim Psaradelis came home from work one day last month and parked his car in the driveway. As he walked into the house, his wife Ann asked for his help in taking care of one of their children. Apparently, Psaradelis just looked at his wife and said, "I have things I have to do."

Ann Psaradelis watched her husband load some plastic bags into their blue and white, 1969 Chevrolet Impala. She had no idea what was in the bags. After Jim finished putting things in his car, he walked over to Ann and said, "I forgot to make the night deposit for work, so I have to go back to Manchester." That was the last time Ann Psaradelis saw her husband. Psaradelis left wearing a soiled white shirt, green trousers with grease on them, and a blue waist-length jacket.

When asked about her husband's state of mind, Ann Psaradelis stated, "Jim was despondent." She added, "He had a .38 caliber hand gun in his possession."

Later in the day, the dispatcher advised that there was a call for me on line three. When I picked up the phone, a woman said, "Hello, Lieutenant Horak," and hung up. I didn't recognize her voice. The phone call seemed suspicious.

It had been another long day, so I headed home with the idea of getting a good night's sleep. I had been in bed only a short time when the phone rang. I looked at the clock, it was 10:00 p.m.

"Lieutenant Horak, I can't give you my name, but I have information about the Compagna-Psaradelis homicides."

"Please, go ahead."

"I was talking with a man around May 7. He told me that the person who picked up Diane Compagna and Anne Psaradelis at Hampton Beach came from Merrimack and that he had something to do with the deaths of the two girls. This man further stated that the person planned to kill one of the girls, because she had something on him. This person hadn't planned to kill both girls, but since they were together, the second murder was unavoidable."

"Miss, would you give me your name, please?"

"No, Lieutenant, I'm afraid this man or some of his friends will harm me if they find out I've talked with you."

"Miss, would you give me the name of the man who gave you this information?"

"No, Lieutenant Horak, I can't give you his name. If I find out anything more, I'll contact you by telephone."

"Miss, I'd really like to talk with you in person. It could help with the investigation. No one has to know."

"I'm afraid these people will harm me, but I'll think about it, Lieutenant."

Another lead to nowhere. We continued to get bits and pieces of information about the murders, but no one was willing to talk with us and fill in the details.

Months passed and still no one was willing to come forward with specific information about the Compagna-Psaradelis homicides. I continued to stay in touch with Mr. and Mrs. Compagna and Mrs. Psaradelis to assure them we hadn't forgotten their daughters. As far as we knew, no one had seen or heard from Jim Psaradelis since he disappeared in April.

June 5, 1975

Nearly two years had passed since Diane and Anne were reported missing. It had been over a year since we received any information on the case. Then, out of the blue I received a phone call from Diane's mother.

"Lieutenant, this is Dorothy Compagna. Something strange has happened and I thought I should tell you about it."

"What happened, Dorothy?"

"Well, Lieutenant, a friend of mine placed a bouquet of carnations on Diane's grave yesterday. When my husband and I visited the cemetery today, we noticed that someone had tampered with the flowers."

"Please give me specific details, Dorothy, so that I can investigate the situation."

"OK, Lieutenant. One pink carnation was removed from the bouquet, along with a pink ribbon that had the name Diane inscribed in gold lettering. They couldn't have fallen off, the entire bouquet is wired together. I think someone took them."

Sergeant Bennett and I visited the Manchester cemetery that afternoon to investigate Dorothy Compagna's report. We talked with Harvey Dickerson, the caretaker. During questioning Dickerson stated that he had not seen anyone suspicious in the vicinity of Diane's grave, but he assured us he would keep a sharp lookout in the future. The sergeant and I investigated the grave site ourselves and found the situation to be exactly as Mrs. Compagna had reported it.

Since this peculiar occurrence happened at Diane's grave, Sergeant Bennett and I decided to check Anne Psaradelis' grave to see if anything similar had happened there. Our inspection found nothing out of the ordinary.

July 3, 1975

Detective Charles Henry from the Salem Police Department informed me that they were working on a case involving kidnap and rape that might tie in with the Compagna-Psaradelis homicides. Chief

Baker, Sergeant Bennett and I drove to Salem to investigate the possible link ourselves.

"Detective Henry, we appreciate your calling us. We've been working on the Compagna-Psaradelis homicides for two years and still haven't had a break in the case."

"Well, Lieutenant, we aren't sure the two cases will tie in with each other, but this guy kidnapped two young girls and raped them. One of our officers remembered your case and suggested I contact you. We thought you might like to interview the man we have in custody."

"What's the name of the person you have under arrest?"

"Malcolm E. Gilbert, Jr. We've transferred him to the Brentwood County Jail."

Detective Henry contacted the Brentwood sheriff and arranged an interview with Gilbert. We took a copy of Detective Henry's file on Gilbert with us.

Upon arrival at the Brentwood County Jail, we learned that Gilbert wouldn't be available until 6:30 p.m., after the evening meal. Since it was quite a wait, Chief Baker, Sergeant Bennett, and I decided to have dinner ourselves at a local Italian restaurant. While we waited for our spaghetti, we talked about the case.

"Chief Baker, are people in your area still talking about the murders of Diane and Anne?"

"Not really, Lieutenant. What I do hear some people saying is that they can't understand why the case hasn't been solved yet. They don't think we put enough time into the investigation."

"If they knew how much time we've spent on the case, they wouldn't believe it. People tend to think whatever they want. I guess that's the way life is."

After dinner we returned to the county jail. We interviewed Malcolm Gilbert in a conference room.

"Malcolm, before we talk with you, I'm going to advise you of your rights. I do that with everyone I interview, whether they're a witness, a suspect, or a person charged with a crime. It protects everyone involved, including me."

I read Gilbert his rights. He agreed to talk with us and signed a waiver and Miranda warning card.

"Malcolm, we'd like to talk with you about two girls from Merrimack who were found murdered in Candia, New Hampshire, in July 1973. The victims were Diane Compagna and Anne Psaradelis."

"Lieutenant Horak, I'm going to tell you the same thing I told Lieutenant Wilson. I didn't have anything to do with the murder of those two girls."

"Malcolm, do you ever pick up hitchhikers?"

"I pick up a lot of hitchhikers, some of them are girls. I've never been in Candia as far as I know, but I've been in Auburn, New Hampshire, a few times. I've picked up girls and taken them to Auburn, done what I wanted to them, then dropped them off in Massachusetts."

"Malcolm, did you know that Auburn is pretty close to Candia?"

"Lieutenant, I don't remember going to Candia."

I showed Gilbert photographs of Diane Compagna and Anne Psaradelis.

"Malcolm, have you ever seen these two girls or picked them up?"

"I have a very good memory and I know that I didn't have anything to do with these two girls. I already told you that I pick up a lot of girls from all over the area, but I didn't pick up the Compagna and Psaradelis girls. I did hear something about them, but I don't remember where I heard it."

"Malcolm, will you take a polygraph test to demonstrate that you weren't involved with Diane Compagna and Anne Psaradelis?"

"I'd like to consult my attorney before agreeing to a polygraph test. His name is John Ford."

When we consulted Gilbert's attorney, he said, "No way. I won't let Malcolm Gilbert take any test or let him admit to taking the lives of two girls." Ford added, "Mr. Gilbert may be involved in other cases since the one he's charged with went off so easily, but I feel there's something wrong with him. I'm going to have Malcolm examined by someone from the state hospital. If I'm not satisfied with the results, I'll have someone else examine him."

Needless to say, we were disappointed with the attorney's attitude. When lawyers need help from the police, they not only ask for it, they expect it, but they offer no assistance in return. There's something wrong with the system.

20

September 29, 1975

Sergeant Bennett and I were assigned as a team to investigate the homicide of John Dufrane. Unlike the Compagna-Psaradelis homicides, we were called to the crime scene as soon as the body was discovered, giving us the advantage of gathering evidence in the case before anyone tampered with the scene. The investigation went smoothly. We had the murder weapon in our possession and a possible suspect.

The Dufrane homicide was the first occasion I had to meet with the new attorney general, David H. Souter. Souter had the reputation of being a pretty square shooter. After a meeting to discuss the Dufrane homicide, I decided to talk with Souter about charging Tom Jefferson with the statutory rape of Diane Compagna. I explained the situation in detail, including my frustration with not having charged Jefferson, although we had at least ten people who would testify that Diane had told them Tom Jefferson had raped her.

"Lieutenant Horak, not only could you have charged this man when the incident occurred, but you still can. Once you finish the Dufrane homicide investigation, contact County Attorney Cloutier at the superior court and ask him to take you before the grand jury to get an indictment against Tom Jefferson for statutory rape. Tell Cloutier that I'm familiar with the case and recommended that you talk with him."

Finally, I felt as if we were moving ahead with the Compagna-Psaradelis investigation. Once we got him back here, hopefully he could be persuaded to take another polygraph exam, one with questions asked that would finally either eliminate or place him as a suspect, but all too soon we experienced another delay that was beyond our control.

We were about to conclude the Dufrane homicide investigation and Assistant Attorney General Tom Wingate called the investigators into his office to discuss the case. During that meeting it was decided that we would reenact the Dufrane homicide to make sure we had all the details straight. Sergeant Bennett was late and didn't arrive at the meeting until 6:00 p.m. He had missed most of our conversation, so I tried to fill in the details for him.

"Sergeant, we're talking about reenacting the homicide at 1:00 a.m. because that's when various people have stated they heard gun shots. We're going to need your help."

"You jerks don't know what you're doing. I'm going home with Gloria."

I couldn't believe Sergeant Bennett's attitude or that he was dating the chief's secretary. If I were chief, I would have fired him right on the spot. Attorney Wingate could see my frustration and said, "Forget it, Lieutenant. Maybe we should think about doing things earlier."

"I suppose you're right, Attorney Wingate. Let's get things ready and do it right now."

Taking two cars, the investigators and Attorney Wingate proceeded to the crime scene. Detective Buxton and Attorney Wingate rode with me. As we drove down Naticooke Road, we were involved in a head-on collision. I sustained a head injury and didn't remember anything about the accident, but Detective Buxton described what happened this way.

"Lieutenant Horak was driving and Attorney Wingate and I were passengers in the car. All of a sudden Lieutenant Horak said, 'Look at those headlights coming at us.' Then he pulled the cruiser to the side of the road and stopped. The car that was approaching us came off the pavement over the crest of a hill and landed on the front end of the cruiser.

"Attorney Wingate was thrown out of the passenger's door with such force that he ripped the radio equipment out of the vehicle. I was thrown over the front seat, onto Lieutenant Horak.

"I don't know how he did it, but Lieutenant Horak pulled a portable radio from under the front seat and called in the accident.

"The two guys in the other vehicle were drunk and walked away from the accident without a scratch."

I was unconscious when the ambulance arrived at the accident scene and I remember nothing of our trip to the hospital. I awakened briefly when we arrived in the emergency room.

"Where am I? What am I doing here?"

"Take it easy, Lieutenant. You were in an accident and you're in the emergency room. The doctor will be right in."

I was surprised the next morning when I woke up in a hospital room with Detective Buxton and Attorney Wingate in beds next to me. I was still groggy and still couldn't remember the accident.

"All I remember is leaving the meeting and heading out to the crime scene. I remember some bright headlights and pulling over to the side of the road. I don't remember being in any kind of accident. Maybe it's just as well that I don't remember."

"I understand that all three of us are being released in a few hours, Lieutenant. How do you feel?"

"I don't really feel too great, Detective Buxton, but I guess I look even worse. I'm just thankful that we're all going to be OK."

One of the nurses stuck her head in the room and announced that I had visitors. It was Mr. and Mrs. Compagna.

"Lieutenant, as soon as we heard you were injured in an accident, we rushed right over. The doctor told us that you're being released from the hospital this morning. We've talked it over and want you to come to our house so we can take care of you during your recovery. We won't take no for an answer, in fact, we're here to take you home with us."

"Mr. and Mrs. Compagna, what can I say but thank you."

The first few weeks that I was out of the hospital were spent trying to regain my strength, although I tried to stay in touch with progress on the Dufrane homicide investigation by phone. When I started feeling better, Mr. and Mrs. Compagna drove me everywhere I needed to go - to the doctor's to have my stitches removed and twice, to Chief Pelletier's house to visit him after his bypass surgery. During my visits with the chief, I updated him on what I knew about the Dufrane homicide investigation. I also told him about the circumstances of my accident.

"You know, Chief, I often think that if Sergeant Bennett had done his job the way he should have and we had reenacted the crime scene at 1:00 a.m. as we planned, I never would have been involved in that accident. I guess there's no sense in crying over spilled milk."

I spent four weeks with Mr. and Mrs. Compagna and I'll always remember how well they treated me. The gash I received on my head healed quickly, but I still had bad headaches and trouble with the vision in my right eye. The doctor released me to return to work for only four hours a day until such time as I was completely finished recuperating.

I immediately returned to my investigation of the Dufrane homicide and followed up the idea of talking to the grand jury about charging Tom Jefferson with statutory rape.

As Attorney General Souter recommended, I contacted County Attorney Cloutier. I explained the incident of July 4, 1973, thoroughly. I told Mr. Cloutier that we had ten people who would testify that Diane Compagna told them Tom Jefferson had raped her. I added that Tom Jefferson had given us a written statement saying that he had intercourse with Diane Compagna.

"Attorney Cloutier, this is not hearsay evidence."

"What do you want from me, Lieutenant?"

"Well, Mr. Cloutier, when I spoke with Attorney General Souter, he told me that Tom Jefferson could have and still can be prosecuted for the crime of statutory rape. He told me to come to you and request that you allow me to go before the grand jury to seek an indictment against Jefferson."

"Listen here, Lieutenant Horak, there's no way I'm going to let you go before the grand jury. I don't care who sent you here."

Needless to say, I was shocked by the county attorney's attitude. I decided that I needed to pressure him a bit more.

"All right, Attorney Cloutier, if that's the way you feel, I'd like a letter from you stating that you refuse to let me go before the grand jury, thus, preventing the Compagna-Psaradelis investigation from going forward."

Attorney Cloutier suddenly changed his mind.

"All right, Lieutenant Horak, I'll set things up and advise you of the date and time that you're to appear before the grand jury."

I felt like we were finally moving forward with the investigation. I wanted to make sure everyone involved with the Compagna-Psaradelis homicides was informed, so I called Chief Baker and told him the good news. Chief Pelletier was still at home recuperating from his surgery, so I stopped by his house to let him know what was going on. I tried to visit Chief Pelletier as often as I could because I knew how lonely it could be while you're recuperating.

My recuperation was coming along pretty well and I was feeling much stronger - much stronger than Sergeant Bennett seemed to think. I was surprised when Deputy Chief Gerlach told me what Sergeant Bennett had said about me.

"He told me you're still having bad headaches and your vision isn't too good. He also said that you forget things and tire out easily."

"Deputy, I don't know about Sergeant Bennett. What kind of trouble is he trying to start? I'm OK. It just takes time to recover from injuries. I think I'm more than doing my job. Sergeant Bennett is supposed to be my partner. I don't appreciate his talking about me behind my back. You tell Sergeant Bennett to talk to me if he has problems with my work."

"Lieutenant, I don't think Sergeant Bennett is trying to start trouble. I think he's just concerned about you."

"Well, whatever it is, Deputy, you'd better talk with Sergeant Bennett or I will."

A few days later I stopped by Chief Pelletier's house to see how he was feeling and to tell him about my grand jury appearance. It was a friendly conversation, we ate apple pie and drank milk as we talked. That's why I was surprised by the questions Chief Pelletier finally asked me.

"How have you been feeling, Lieutenant?"

"Why do you ask, Chief?"

"Well, Sergeant Bennett has been telling me that you're having severe headaches, your vision isn't too good, your right eyelid droops, your memory isn't too good, and you get tired easily."

"Chief Pelletier, does Sergeant Bennett tell you how many times I go to the bathroom, too?"

"What are you mad about, Lieutenant?"

"Well, Chief, I just heard the same thing from the deputy a few days ago. What is Bennett trying to pull? I'd appreciate your telling Bennett to get off my back. If he's afraid to work with me, please reassign him."

March 22, 1976

Our suspect in the Dufrane homicide investigation was tried and convicted of murder. Everything seemed to be returning to normal, until one day a commotion at the dispatcher's desk disturbed the entire station.

"That Deputy Gerlach and Lieutenant Horak are a couple of sons of bitches! They're a bunch of bastards!"

The person shouting sounded like Chief Pelletier's wife. I went out to the dispatcher's desk to find out what was going on. As I rounded the corner, I saw that it was Mrs. Pelletier. When she saw me, she shouted even louder.

"There's the bastard!"

The dispatcher was unsuccessful in trying to calm Mrs. Pelletier, so I stepped in.

"Calm down, Mrs. Pelletier. Let's go into my office so you can tell me what's wrong."

Mrs. Pelletier agreed to talk and followed me into my office.

"Mrs. Pelletier, please sit down and tell me what the problem is."

"Lieutenant, you and Gerlach are a couple of sons of bitches."

"Use your head, Mrs. Pelletier, and calm down. Tell me what's wrong."

"Sergeant Bennett told my husband that you and Gerlach are after my husband's job. I can't believe that you've picked a time like this when he's sick!"

"Wait a minute, Mrs. Pelletier, I've been chief of police, a captain, and a lieutenant. I like being a detective. I don't want your husband's job and I'm sure Deputy Gerlach doesn't want it either."

"Well, I'll tell you, my husband will get you for this."

"Mrs. Pelletier, if I wanted your husband's job, why would I visit and try to give him the moral support and encouragement he needs to get better? If you'll think about it, it really doesn't make sense. Put your mind at ease and don't listen to Sergeant Bennett. The deputy and I don't want your husband's job. Why don't you let me drive you home?"

"No, Lieutenant, I'll drive myself home."

<u>April 8, 1976</u>

My appearance before the grand jury went smoothly. I presented all the information I had about the incident on July 4, 1973, between Diane Compagna and Tom Jefferson. They listened attentively to everything I had to say and brought an indictment against Tom Jefferson for statutory rape. Tom Jefferson had moved to California, so I prepared the necessary paperwork to have him brought back to stand trial in Merrimack.

I stopped by Chief Pelletier's house and told him the good news about the grand jury indicting Tom Jefferson. While I was there, I tried to straighten out the misunderstanding Sergeant Bennett had created.

"I really came over to see how you're doing, but I think you and I need to square away the problem our famous Detective Sergeant John Bennett has created. Chief Pelletier, I'm not trying to take your job away from you and I'm sure Deputy Gerlach isn't either. If I was trying to take your job, do you think that I'd come over here nearly every day to see you? No, I wouldn't. I'd stay as far away from you as possible. You might not know it, Chief, but I'm pretty loyal to you. I try to do the very best job I can for you. If you don't realize that, then something is wrong. I think you need to take another look at Sergeant Bennett."

"Why do you say that, Lieutenant?"

"Think about it, Chief. Sergeant Bennett is still telling you and everyone else that I'm unfit for my job because I'm not well, that I get tired easily, have severe headaches, can't remember things, and so on. Why is he doing that? Why has he told you that the deputy and I are after your job? Sergeant Bennett is up to something. It isn't me you have to be afraid of, it's him."

"Lieutenant, I'm not mad at you or the deputy. Why don't you sit down and visit with me for a little while. I'll even give you a piece of homemade apple pie."

"That sounds good to me, Chief. I hope we have this job thing all squared away and that there are no ill feelings."

"Everything is fine, Lieutenant. I'm coming back to work on Monday, so I'll see you then if not sooner."

The chief told me everything was OK, but when I looked into his eyes and face, they told me something different. I hoped I was wrong.

April 28, 1976

Several weeks passed and I hadn't heard anything about the progress being made to extradite Tom Jefferson, so I made an appointment to talk with the county attorney. My partner, Sergeant Bennett, accompanied me to the meeting.

"Attorney Cloutier, I wonder what progress is being made to bring Tom Jefferson back from California?"

"Lieutenant, you have to be kidding. I'm not going to spend one cent to send you or anyone else out to California to pick up Tom Jefferson. I'm surprised that you thought we would ever bring this case to trial."

"Sir, I don't mean to be fresh or wise, but I not only expected Tom Jefferson to be brought back to stand trial, but I expected that he would be found guilty of statutory rape and sent to prison."

"Lieutenant, why don't you just forget it?"

"I can't forget it, Mr. Cloutier. If you don't want to help me, then please give me a letter stating that you refuse to bring Jefferson back to face the charges against him."

"Lieutenant, I don't like your attitude."

Attorney Cloutier paused for a moment as if contemplating what I had said and then continued.

"I'll tell you what, Lieutenant, I'll send two deputies out to California to pick up Jefferson, but you're not going to be one of them."

"Sir, I really don't care who goes to California to get him, I just want Tom Jefferson brought back here to stand trial. I don't mean to cause problems, but I've been trying to resolve this case for the past three years and no one seems interested enough to help. If your daughter was raped, wouldn't you want the man responsible brought to justice?"

Attorney Cloutier did not answer.

When we left Attorney Cloutier's office, Sergeant Bennett asked, "Why don't you let me drive home, Lieutenant?"

"Why, Sergeant? Don't you like my driving?"

"Lieutenant, you look tired and your speech is slurred. Do you have a headache?"

"Get off it, Sergeant, I don't know what you're trying to prove. I'm getting fed up with your telling everyone that I'm sick, that I can't think straight, that I have severe headaches, and that I'm tired all the time. Why weren't you concerned about my welfare the night we were going to reenact the Dufrane homicide? You walked off like some kind of jerk. You'd probably be better off asking the chief or deputy to change your work hours."

21

June 13, 1976

Several months had passed since the grand jury handed down the indictment for statutory rape and still Tom Jefferson had not been extradited from California. I knew the county attorney was not happy about bringing the case to trial and it seemed as though he was stalling.

Though it had been three years since Diane and Anne were murdered, we continued to receive sporadic phone calls about the case. The most recent call was from Janice Collins who lived in the New Boston Road area. She contacted Chief Baker, claiming to have seen something suspicious near the gravel pit and town dump. The chief and I arranged to interview Ms. Collins in her home.

"Ms. Collins, please tell us what you saw near the gravel pit and town dump."

"Well, my friend Dorothy and I went to the dump to get rid of some rubbish. As we were leaving, we noticed two men dressed in brown and gray clothing. They looked around, then walked rapidly into the gravel pit area. Since that's where those two girls were murdered, I thought they might have something to do with it. Dorothy and I wrote down the license plate number and got out of there."

Janice Collins's story wasn't much to go on, but we checked out every detail just in case it might be a lead.

The first thing we did was inspect the crime scene. Nothing had changed, even the feeling of death still remained.

We ran the license plate number through records and found out the vehicle belonged to Frank Parker. He lived at 38 South Street in Auburn. Chief Baker and I stopped by the Parker home unannounced.

"Are you Frank Parker?"

"Yes, I am. What can I do for you?"

"Mr. Parker, were you in Candia at any time during the last couple of days?"

"Yes, I was. Just the other day a friend and I were looking for birds near New Boston Road. It's almost hunting season and we wanted to get a jump on the things by locating good spots to hunt."

"Mr. Parker, would you describe the clothing you and your friend were wearing?"

"Why, yes. We both had on gray and brown camouflage clothing."

"I guess that's all we need, Mr. Parker. Thanks for your help."

The call turned out to be another dead end. Janice Collins had seemed upset during our conversation and we wanted to put her concerns to rest, so Chief Baker and I returned to the Collins home and told her why Frank Parker and his friend were in the vicinity of the gravel pit.

On my way back to the station I received a call from the dispatcher.

"Lieutenant, please respond to Wire Road. We've received three burglary reports this morning in the same neighborhood. The reports were filed by Philip Onsruth, Jean Smith, and John Dwyers."

"I'm on the way."

Before I reached Wire Road, I received another call from the dispatcher.

"Lieutenant, Chief Pelletier wants you to respond to the station right away. He's assigned someone else to investigate the burglaries on Wire Road."

"OK, I'm on the way."

It was strange that the chief pulled me off an investigation and I wondered what it was all about. I must have done something wrong, but I couldn't begin to think what that could have been. When I arrived at the station, Chief Pelletier was standing on the front steps. It looked like he was waiting for me.

"You wanted me, Chief Pelletier?"

"Yes, Lieutenant. Give me the keys to your cruiser. I can't let you drive that unit anymore or go out on investigations. You might hurt yourself or someone else."

"You have to be kidding, Chief."

"I'm not kidding, Lieutenant. Give me the keys and come into the station while I make a few phone calls."

I was shocked and had no idea what was going on. I decided to talk with my secretary to see if she knew anything.

"Jackie, do you know what the heck is going on? The chief just took the cruiser keys away from me and told me that I couldn't drive it any more or go out on investigations because I might hurt myself or someone else. He has to be kidding. I've been back at work for six months or so. Why hasn't he said something long before this?"

"Lieutenant, between you and me, they've all been talking about you. Even the chief's secretary put in her two cents' worth, but Sergeant Bennett has been the most outspoken. He told the chief that you're tired all the time, that you can't think straight, and that you don't remember things. He's afraid that you might hurt yourself or someone else. I think Sergeant Bennett is after your job."

"I appreciate your talking with me, Jackie. You've always been a good and trusted secretary. I'm lucky to have you."

I waited nearly six hours for the chief to "make a few phone calls," whatever that was supposed to mean. Finally, I decided to approach the chief and find out what was going on.

"Chief, you've kept me waiting for nearly six hours, that doesn't seem fair. What's the story?"

"Well, Lieutenant, I want you to go out and write a letter requesting retirement."

"Chief, I don't want to do that."

"Well, Lieutenant, I'm ordering you to go out and write that letter."

It appeared that I had no choice. I had received an order from the chief and had to obey. I called my secretary into my office.

"Jackie, I need you to write a letter for me to the retirement board, per order of Chief Pelletier."

"What do you want me to say, Lieutenant?"

"Jackie, write whatever you think is proper, but be sure to include that I feel it's up to the retirement board whether I should retire or not. It shouldn't be up to me, or even Chief Pelletier."

Jackie wrote the letter for me. Even though it was written against my will, I felt I had to give the letter to the chief as he requested.

"Chief, here's your letter, but this isn't something I want to do."

I handed the letter to the chief and he read it.

"What the hell do you think you're doing, Lieutenant? What are you, a wise guy?"

"What do you mean by that, Chief Pelletier?"

"Take this goddamn letter out and do it over. Take out the part where you say it's up to the retirement board and retirement doctor whether you retire or not."

"Well, Chief Pelletier, it certainly isn't up to me, it's up to the retirement board. Isn't that what they're for?"

"Lieutenant, get out of my office and take this letter with you. Have it retyped as soon as possible. I'll be waiting for it."

The chief sure was mad. I thought he was going to blow the roof right off the station. It seemed as though I had little choice in the matter and had to rewrite the letter.

"Jackie, rewrite the letter, but I still think it's up to the retirement board to make the decision about whether or not I should retire. It really isn't up to me. Rephrase the part where I say that I want it to be the retirement board's decision whether or not I should retire, but somehow I want that in the letter."

The second letter sounded good to me, so I took it to the chief.

"Chief Pelletier, here's the letter you wanted."

The chief read the second letter, then blew up again.

"You son of a bitch. Lieutenant, do you think you're smart or something? Take this goddamn letter out and do it over. Take out the part about the retirement board."

I asked Jackie to redo the letter. "Work on the part about the retirement board. I know the chief won't like it, but it's very important to me." When Jackie finished, I took the third letter into the chief. It wasn't long before I was back at Jackie's desk.

"Jackie, I guess you heard everything the chief said, he won't accept the letter the way it's written. I guess we'll have to retype it."

"OK, Lieutenant, let me see what I can do."

When the chief read my fourth letter, I was sure his comments could be heard all the way over in the town hall. I worked with Jackie to compose a fifth letter, but was determined this was going to be the last one. I asked Jackie to stay, even though it was past her quitting time. The chief was a vindictive person and I thought I might need a witness.

As I headed toward the chief's office with the fifth letter, Jackie asked, "Why do you think this is happening to you, Lieutenant?"

"Well, Jackie, I think it's a combination of two things. Number one, look at how the chief has acted toward me since he's been back at work. I think Sergeant Bennett has the chief all worked up, thinking that the deputy and I want his job. I think the second thing is that Sergeant Bennett's been buttering up the chief, the selectmen and the chief's secretary. There's no question about it, Sergeant Bennett wants my job and by the looks of it, he's going to get it. That's why I want the retirement board to make that decision."

I was more forceful about my point of view when I handed the chief the fifth letter.

"Chief, here's your letter. You'll have to take it the way it is. I've written five letters and I'm not going to write another one. You can throw it away or use it, that's your decision to make.

"You know, Chief, I've been a hard worker and more than loyal to you and you're treating me badly. I wonder how would you treat your enemy? All I know is that I've lost the respect I had for you.

"I've always thought that if you were injured in the line of duty, the department would take care of you. I was wrong."

I left the chief's office and went to talk with Jackie.

"Jackie, you might as well go home. I don't know what the chief will do, but I'm not going to rewrite that letter. I know he's going to get me one way or the other."

"It's pretty sad, Lieutenant. I can't believe the chief is doing this to you. If there's anything I can do, please let me know."

"You know, Jackie, I wonder what will happen to me. The chief has taken me off investigations and won't let me drive any of the cruisers. It's pretty unfair if you ask me.

"You'd better head home, Jackie. Thank you for taking your time to help me."

22

<u>October 2, 1976</u>

Deputy Chief Gerlach stopped me in the hall and asked, "Hey, Lieutenant, what's going on with you and the chief?"

"Come on, Deputy, I'm sure you know all about it."

"Lieutenant, the only thing I know is that the chief's secretary and Sergeant Bennett have been bending the chief's ear about your being unfit to do your job around here. I heard Bennett say he's afraid that you'll get him killed or someone else hurt. Bennett told the chief that you've had such severe headaches that you can't even think straight. He said that you used to have a super - good memory and now you can't even remember what happened yesterday. Bennett also said that your vision is poor. Of course, the chief's secretary is going to back up Bennett. Sergeant Bennett and the chief's secretary have painted a pretty bleak picture of you.

"Lieutenant, I think the chief is going to have you ride around with Sergeant Bennett and have you help him with the cases you're work-ing on and instruct him about the way you do things."

"That's a good one, Deputy Gerlach. I'm not well enough to do my job, but I'm good enough to teach Sergeant Bennett the things that I know."

"Don't get me involved, Lieutenant, I have enough problems of my own."

My conversation with the deputy was interrupted by a phone call.

"Lieutenant, this is Jean from the county attorney's office. Attor-ney Cloutier asked me to advise you that Tom Jefferson has been arrested and is out on cash bail. By the time Jefferson's attorney files all his motions to do this or that, the trial probably won't come up until sometime in 1977. We'll advise you when the trial will take place."

"OK, Jean, thank you for calling."

As soon as I hung up the phone, Chief Pelletier asked me to step into his office.

"Lieutenant, you're going to be working with Sergeant Bennett until I hear from the retirement board. I want you to give the sergeant all the information you have on the cases you're working on, plus any that are coming up in court."

"Chief, I hope you realize that you're spoiling my life, but it's plain to see that you just don't care. No matter what, as long as I'm here, I'll do the very best job I can. I wouldn't begin to give you the chance to belittle me in front of anyone. I'm sure that's just what you and Bennett would like to do. I'm a better man than both of you put together."

October 21, 1976

Weeks slid by. It wasn't easy working with Sergeant Bennett. I was sure he and Chief Pelletier wanted me to quit, but I wouldn't give them that satisfaction.

Chief Pelletier called me into his office.

"Lieutenant, I was just talking with people from the retirement board. They advised me that your retirement date is November 6."

"You have to be kidding, Chief Pelletier. How can they do that when I haven't been examined by a doctor from the retirement system or interviewed by anyone from the retirement board itself? Something's wrong with the system if they can do this to me.

"What's going to happen with the Compagna-Psaradelis homicide investigation, the Tom Jefferson investigation, and all the other cases I've started?"

"Lieutenant, that won't be your worry after November 6. Sergeant Bennett will handle everything. He's told me that he'll solve the Compagna-Psaradelis investigation. He thinks it should have been solved a long time ago and that you've been dragging your feet."

"Well, good for Sergeant Bennett. To be honest with you, Chief, I don't care who solves the case, just as long as it gets solved."

"Lieutenant, you'll have to go over to town hall on Monday and sign some paperwork. You can turn in your equipment to me on Tuesday."

October 28, 1976

It was my day off and I needed to talk with someone, so I decided to visit Chief Baker.

"Chief Baker, you'll never believe what's happened. My whole life as a police officer will be destroyed on November 6. I'm really sick over the whole thing. I don't know what to do.

"To be honest with you, Chief, I wonder if there's been some kind of agreement or conspiracy among the county attorney, Chief Pelletier, and Sergeant Bennett to get me out of the Merrimack Police Department."

"Why do you say that, Lieutenant?"

"Well, Chief, each of them has something to gain by getting rid of me.

"It doesn't make sense. I've been working nearly a year, four hours a day since I was injured, and I've done a good job. Now, all of a sudden Sergeant Bennett and the chief's secretary paint a bleak picture of me to the chief, telling him that I'm unfit to be a police officer and can't do my job. Of course, Sergeant Bennett wants my job and rank. He goes with the chief's secretary, so who's in a better position to help him?

"Chief, Mrs. Pelletier said to my face that the chief would get me because Sergeant Bennett told them that the deputy and I were after his job.

"Then there's the county attorney. He's upset about my pushing the Tom Jefferson investigation. He didn't want that case to go forward and I'm sure he still doesn't.

"I'm not ready for retirement, Chief Baker. If I decided that I wanted to retire in five or six years, then I could work toward it, but now my career's been taken away overnight. I just don't know how to handle that."

"Lieutenant Horak, there isn't any better police officer than you. You give one hundred percent, plus."

"Chief Baker, I'll be done next Monday, but I already feel like a lost soul. It's like I haven't finished the job I was meant to do. Can you understand that?

"Chief, I want you to know that the Compagna-Psaradelis homicide is the only case I haven't brought to a conclusion. I'd like you to make me a promise."

"What's that, Lieutenant?"

"Well, Chief Baker, I will never feel good about myself or my job as a police officer until the Compagna-Psaradelis homicide is solved. I want you to promise me that, even though I'll be retired from police work, you'll work with me on this case until it's solved, no matter how long it takes or how much pressure there will be to back off the investigation in the future. I just have to solve this one, but then, I know you already understand that."

"OK, Lieutenant, you have my promise that even if no one else wants to work on the case, you and I will finish it, even if it takes twenty years.

"Lieutenant, what are you going to do after next Tuesday?"

"I don't know, Chief. My whole life has been law enforcement, that's what I'm good at. Right now, I'm just lost. I really felt that if you got injured in the line of duty, your department would help you instead of throwing you out on the street. It makes me wonder how many other police officers have been in the same position that I'm in now. It's pretty sad when you think about it.

"I should let you get back to work, Chief Baker. I just had to talk with you about the Compagna-Psaradelis homicide investigation. I don't think anyone else will bother with it. Just check the names on the investigation reports. That alone will tell you who has worked on the case and who is still working on it.

"Oh, Chief, I forgot to tell you that Sergeant Bennett has told Chief Pelletier that the Compagna-Psaradelis case should have been solved a long time ago. He thinks I've been dragging my feet on the case because I wanted the overtime. Bennett also said that he'd solve the case soon, that it's the kind of case he likes to work on.

"Well, I guess I'd better get out of your way, Chief. I'll be in touch with you soon. Thanks for taking the time to talk with me. Don't forget, we aren't going to give up on the case. We'll stick with it until it's solved."

After I talked with Chief Baker, I decided to stop by and talk with the Compagnas and Mrs. Psaradelis. I wanted to let them know what was going on. I didn't want them to think I had just walked away from the investigation.

November 4, 1976

Deputy Gerlach greeted me as I walked into the station.

"How are you doing, Lieutenant Horak?"

"Not very good, Deputy. How would you feel if the job you loved was coming to an end because a chief and a sergeant didn't care about anyone but themselves? I know one thing, Deputy, you'd better watch out for your job. Remember, Sergeant Bennett told Chief Pelletier that both you and I were after his job."

"Don't worry, Lieutenant, I'll handle Sergeant Bennett."

"Sure you will, Deputy."

As the chief had instructed, I went to the town hall to sign the papers necessary for my retirement.

"Hello, Mrs. Armstrong, how are you doing today?"

"Good, Lieutenant, how can I help you?"

"Well, Mrs. Armstrong, Chief Pelletier sent me over to sign some papers."

"Just a minute, Lieutenant, I'll get them. You're the first police officer to retire from the department, so we're really not sure what to do. Sign these papers and if we need anything else, we'll contact you."

When I returned to the station, Chief Pelletier called me into his office.

"Lieutenant, have you been to the town hall to sign those papers yet?"

"That's all done, Chief. I hope you're proud of yourself. You really are spoiling my life. If the truth were known, I'm in better health than you are."

180

"Lieutenant, you better go out and finish up the day with Sergeant Bennett. He has to check out a burglary at Merrimack Metals."

Sergeant Bennett was out in the cruiser, so I had to wait until he returned to the station. We drove to Merrimack Metals and took a report on the burglary. When we were back in the cruiser, Sergeant Bennett asked me to fill him in on my cases.

"By the way, Lieutenant, you haven't filled me in on your active cases, don't you think you should?"

"Well, Sergeant Bennett, I'm not a vindictive-type person like you and Chief Pelletier appear to be. To show you that I'm much more of a man than either of you, I'll take the rest of the day and tomorrow morning to help you with any of the cases you still have questions about. I guess that I can't be any more fair than that. I wonder if either of you would do that for me if you were in my shoes."

November 6, 1976

When I arrived at the station, I asked Richard, the dispatcher, if Sergeant Bennett had come in yet.

"Lieutenant, I think he's down with the chief. They both left here with smiles on their faces.

"Lieutenant Horak, I'm sorry to see you leave. I know what a good police officer you are. They don't make them like you anymore. I wanted to take up a collection and get you a retirement present, but the chief and Sergeant Bennett didn't think much of the idea, so I didn't do anything. There's no sense in getting them on my back. You know how that is better than anyone else in this department."

"I appreciate that Richard. Don't worry about not getting me a retirement gift or whatever they call it. I really don't expect anything."

As Richard and I were finishing our conversation, Sergeant Bennett joined us at the dispatch desk.

"Sergeant Bennett, if you want me to help you for the next three hours, we'd better get started now."

"OK, Lieutenant, let's go to my office. There are quite a few things I need to know about some of the cases we haven't gone over."

I spent the next three hours giving Sergeant Bennett details about my open cases. Before I left his office, I couldn't help asking him to do one thing for me.

"Sergeant, there's one thing I'd like you to do - solve the murders of Diane Compagna and Anne Psaradelis. The chief told me that you believe you can solve the murders in the near future. I sure hope you're right."

"Lieutenant Horak, I'll solve the case, you can bank on that."

The dispatcher let me know that Chief Pelletier was waiting in his office to talk with me.

"Come in, Lieutenant Horak."

"This isn't a very happy day for me, Chief, so here's my badge, my gun, and other equipment. I'll leave now. I just hope you're pleased with what you've done to my life."

Before I left, I made sure to say good-bye to my secretary, Jackie, and some of the other officers.

"Jackie, I want to thank you for being such a great person and secretary. You made things easier for me. I'm going to miss you."

"Lieutenant, most of us will miss you, that's for sure. You were good with everyone."

"I guess I'd better get out of here. This is pretty hard for me to handle. Now, the question is, what do I do with my life?"

Sergeant Trask was sitting at his desk, working hard as usual.

"Sergeant Trask, don't you ever rest? It seems like all you do is work."

"Hello, Lieutenant Horak."

"You don't have to call me that any more, Sergeant Trask. You can call me Joe."

"Oh, no, you'll always be Detective Lieutenant Joe Horak to me. I really think you got a bad deal and we all know who to blame for that."

"Sergeant Trask, I just dropped by to let you know that I'll be out of town for a couple of weeks, I'm going to Canada to see some friends of mine. I need a change of pace. The trip will allow me some time to think. I have to put my life back in some kind of order."

"OK, Lieutenant, I have the telephone number from the last time you went to Canada. Will you be at the same number?"

"Yes, I will, Sergeant."

23

December 7, 1976

I spent a month in Canada visiting my friends. It was a good break from the things that were happening in New Hampshire. I had a chance to think things out and prepare myself for what lay ahead.

The status of my health insurance was the first concern that needed attention. I went to the town hall to speak with Jean. I knew she would have the answers I needed.

"Hello, Jean, it's me again."

"Gee, Lieutenant, I haven't seen you for a while. Where have you been?"

"As you know, Jean, I'm not with the police department anymore and I've just come back from spending a month in Canada. I need to find out how I stand with my health insurance."

"Just a minute, Lieutenant, I'll check."

Within a few minutes Jean returned with my file.

"Lieutenant, would you believe your insurance has run out? You could have picked up the coverage within the first thirty days of your departure, but too much time has passed and the policy has lapsed."

"Just what does that mean, Jean?"

"Lieutenant, it means you don't have health insurance."

"Jean, why wasn't that taken care of when I retired?"

"Lieutenant, you're the first person to retire and we didn't know all of the things that were supposed to be done."

"That really helps me a lot. What am I supposed to do now?"

"Lieutenant, we'll try to get you into another plan, but it will cost you more since it won't be a group plan."

"That doesn't seem fair, but I have to have health insurance. Jean, would you try to get me as good a rate as possible?"

"Of course, Lieutenant."

My next concern was employment. Law enforcement was the only thing I knew and I was good at it. It seemed the natural line to pursue. I knew that the retirement system would prohibit me from working in New Hampshire, so I decided to contact police departments in Maine and Vermont.

March 5, 1977

Months passed and still I had no job. I contacted nearly every police department in Maine and Vermont. All I heard was, "If you're on disability retirement, we can't hire you." It hardly seemed fair, because I was in good health and could do a good job for whomever hired me.

While I was at home one morning, the doorbell rang.

"Hello, are you Lieutenant Joe Horak?"

"Yes, sir, I am. How can I help you?"

"Lieutenant, I have a subpoena for you to appear in the superior court in Manchester on March 7, 1977, at 1:00 p.m. It's regarding the State vs. Thomas Jefferson."

"OK, Deputy, I'll be there."

It had taken a long time for this case to come to trial, but I was pleased that something was finally happening. I contacted Chief Baker because I thought he might be interested in sitting in on the trial. I was right, the chief wanted to attend. We arranged to meet at the courthouse at noon on March 7.

When the chief and I arrived for the trial, we were surprised to see how crowded the courtroom was. Tom Jefferson and his father were sitting together and gave us dirty looks when the chief and I entered the room. The only witness we saw was Steve Moses. At least nine other witnesses should have been there, something was wrong.

I found out that John English was the prosecuting attorney.

"Sir, are you Attorney John English?"

"Yes, I am. Want do you want?"

"Well, Attorney English, I'm here for the Thomas Jefferson rape case."

"Who are you?"

"Sir, I'm retired Detective Lieutenant Joe Horak. I'd like to know where the other nine witnesses are. The only one I see is Steve Moses."

"Lieutenant, you need to mind your own business. I'm handling this case."

"What do you mean by that, Attorney English?"

"Just what I said - I'm handling the case, so mind your own business."

"Wait a minute, Attorney English, this is my case. I want to know where all the other witnesses are. We need every one of them to show the true picture of what took place between Tom Jefferson and Diane Compagna on July 4, 1973. Having only one witness and myself to testify isn't going to do that."

"You heard me, Lieutenant, mind your own business."

After talking with Attorney English, I felt like they wanted to lose the case. Maybe they did because of all the pressure I put on the county attorney to have it brought forward. Another thing that bothered me was Tom Jefferson waiving his rights to a jury trial. It didn't make sense to me.

The trial proceeded in an orderly manner and Tom Jefferson was found guilty of raping Diane Compagna. The judge didn't give Jefferson any time in prison because it had taken so long to bring a complaint against him. It almost seemed as though the case had been decided before it went to trial.

It seemed that Chief Baker and I were the only ones still interested in the Compagna-Psaradelis homicides. Before leaving the courthouse, we renewed our promise to stick with the case until it was solved.

I dropped by the Merrimack Police Station to let everyone know how the trial went. The chief and Deputy Chief Gerlach didn't have much to say about Tom Jefferson being found guilty, they didn't even seem surprised that he wasn't given some kind of time in prison. I decided, the heck with them all, at least I know that I did my job and that's all that counts.

I wanted to make sure that the girls' parents knew about the outcome of the trial, so I stopped by the Compagna home first. Mrs. Compagna's reaction surprised me.

"Lieutenant, it really wasn't worth all your effort, was it? I guess we would have been better off just letting it go."

"No, Mrs. Compagna, we did the right thing. We can't let people get away with things like this."

Then I went to see Mrs. Psaradelis. After I told Mrs. Psaradelis about the trial, I asked her if she had heard anything from her husband. She hadn't.

I assured both the Compagnas and Mrs. Psaradelis that I was going to continue working on solving the murders of their daughters, even though I was retired. Since I was planning to be away for a couple of months looking for a job, I asked them to contact Chief Baker if they received any new information about the girls.

April 3, 1977

Since I couldn't find work in the local area, I decided to work my way out to Arizona, hoping to find a police job somewhere between here and there. I didn't care if I had to start over at the bottom of the ladder, because I knew I wouldn't stay there long. I was a good police officer and I wasn't afraid of work, I just needed someone to give me a chance to prove that I could be an asset to their department.

I checked with a couple hundred police departments in the next three months. Still, I couldn't find work. I contacted a police department outside Phoenix. They gave me an appointment for an interview.

"Mr. Horak, I'm Captain Stanley Wickey. You will be asked various questions from the other gentlemen in this room. You may also ask them any questions you may have.

"Mr. Horak, it's hard to know what to ask you since you've been and done just about everything in law enforcement."

"If that's the case, gentlemen, I'd like to ask you a question."

"Go ahead, Mr. Horak, ask us anything you want."

"Gentlemen, if I'm allowed to join your department, and I don't care if it's even as a patrolman, I would like to know if I can do police work and treat everyone the same way, and that goes for making arrests, or are you going to tell me not to touch this or that or make this or that arrest?"

"Mr. Horak, of course, you could do your job and treat everyone alike. There wouldn't be pressure or orders to do your job any other way."

"Sir, that makes me feel good. That's the way I like to do police work."

"Mr. Horak, my name is Captain Johnny Russell. I would like to ask you a question."

"Go ahead, Captain, ask anything you would like to know."

"Well, Mr. Horak, if you are allowed to join our police department, what would you like to be?"

"Captain Russell, I wouldn't mind starting off as a patrolman, but someday I'd like to be like that sergeant over there, the lieutenant sitting next to me, like you, Captain Russell, or even the chief."

There were no more questions from the panel. Captain Wickey advised me that I would be notified if I was selected for the position. I felt sure I wouldn't get the job. I saw the looks on their faces when I said I wanted to be a sergeant, lieutenant, captain, or even chief. I think they thought I wanted their jobs. But I couldn't answer any other way. I wouldn't want to hire a police officer if he wanted to be a patrolman all his life.

My trip to Arizona was disappointing. I still didn't have a job. On my trip back to New Hampshire, I took a different route and stopped at various police departments and filled out applications.

When I arrived back in Merrimack, I stopped in to see the Compagnas.

"Well, look who's here - it's Lieutenant Horak. How are you, Lieutenant? You look tired."

"I just finished driving across the country. I filled out at least fifty job applications on my way back and still don't have a job. It's been pretty discouraging. When I told them I was on disability retirement, most departments didn't want to waste their time having me fill out an application."

"I'm sorry to hear that, Lieutenant."

"Mrs. Compagna, are there any new developments about the girls? I was hoping Sergeant Bennett had solved the case by now."

"We haven't heard a single thing from Bennett, although about six weeks ago we did read in the paper that Sergeant Bennett is now Detective Lieutenant Bennett."

"Bennett must be happy and proud of that. I don't really want to see anyone from the department. It makes me feel bad that I'm still not a police officer here or any place else. You know, Mrs. Compagna, this has been the hardest time in my life. I look back at all this mess and wonder why it happened. I never even received a retirement card. I know some people really cared, but they couldn't show it because they didn't want to get into trouble with you know who."

"Lieutenant, you know you can always stay here if you need a place."

"I really appreciate that, Mrs. Compagna, but I'm all set for now."

Before my trip to Arizona, I left some paperwork at the superior court. I stopped by to see if it was still there. I was pleased to run into Fred Powers during my visit.

"Well, look who's here, Lieutenant Horak. I was sorry to hear about your retirement. They certainly didn't treat you right. Pelletier and Bennett are going to get what's coming to them someday. I haven't seen you in six or seven months, how are you doing?"

I told Fred about my trip to Arizona and my on-going search for a job. Then, I asked him a favor.

"Fred, we've done a lot of good work together over the years and I'd like to ask a favor of you."

"Sure, Lieutenant. What is it?"

"Well, Fred, you know how much it would mean to me to solve the Compagna-Psaradelis murder case. There are several detectives already helping me, but nothing is getting done. Do you have some time to devote to the case? I even have a suspect for you - someone who's been a suspect right from the start."

"Lieutenant, I have about an hour before I have to go into court. Let's go into one of these rooms and talk."

I told Fred everything I could about the Compagna-Psaradelis investigation, including my suspicions about Tom Jefferson. Fred agreed with me that the case could be solved.

"I'll tell you what, Lieutenant, I'll try to borrow the case books from either Merrimack or the state police. I'll do everything I can to help you."

"Boy, Fred, I'd appreciate that more than you realize. Thanks, Fred."

I hadn't seen Chief Baker since I returned from Arizona, so I decided to stop by for a visit.

"Hi, Chief Baker."

"Where in the world did you come from, Lieutenant? I thought you were still out in the western part of the country."

"I just got back, Chief. I've been to so many police departments looking for work that I can't even count them. It's been pretty discouraging. I'm going to start looking in another part of the county in another month unless we get some kind of break in our homicide case. With everything I was told when I left the Merrimack Police Department, I thought Bennett might have solved the case by now, but I see that he hasn't."

"No, Lieutenant, there isn't anything new to tell you. I haven't heard a single word from Bennett. I assume he hasn't solved the Compagna-Psaradelis homicide like he said he would. I was surprised to learn that he made Detective Lieutenant. I guess you were right. Bennett was after your job."

"You know, Chief, I can't believe it's 1978 and we're no closer to solving the murders than we were five years ago. I realize that when an investigation cools off, so to speak, it sometimes gets put on the back burner. I feel a double homicide that's five years old is just as important as one that's committed today. I guess I'd feel better if we could at least place or eliminate the suspects we have, but that won't happen unless you and I do it. I know we have gone over the details many times, but I would like to tell you my conclusions as to what happened the day Diane and Anne were murdered. As you know, Chief, our list isn't very long. In fact, I would have to place just three people on the list at this time - Thomas Jefferson, Wayne Powers and Jim Psaradelis. I know that we have to work just as hard to show that the suspect is innocent as to prove they're guilty. I would like to see us either place or eliminate each man as a suspect and move on with the investigation, depending on the outcome of such placing and/or elimination."

"Lieutenant Horak, come on into my office in the back of the store and we can hash over your conclusions."

We went into his office and sat down. "Well, Chief, I really feel that whoever murdered Diane Compagna and Anne Psaradelis knew both girls and came from Merrimack. There are lots of things that make me feel this way and some of my thoughts go back to the missing persons part of our investigation. At times it appeared that any information we obtained from any person or telephone call always seemed to push us in another direction and we had very little help from the general public. They just didn't want to get involved because of fear or whatever. Chief, even after all the time and effort that has been put into this investigation, people seem afraid to come forward and get involved. We even have law enforcement people that shy away from the case and refuse to help us with the investigation in any way. It sure makes me wonder why.

"And then there's the crime scene. We really have two different crime scenes. Diane Compagna is found nude, she has a pair of blue jeans partially spread out under her body and her other clothing is found folded up in a pile about a foot away from her right hand. Look at the body itself, there are no signs of a fight or a struggle. She's just lying there. This in itself tells me she knew her killer.

"Now look at the body of Anne Psaradelis and you can tell she was running for her life. The poor girl might have made it out of there if she had gotten over that stone wall. You don't see any signs of either girl fighting off her attacker(s) and you don't see any signs of either girl being tied up, hit over the head, shot, stabbed or anything else. Anne even has her clothing on. There is no sign that she was raped and none of her clothing was torn."

"You're right, Lieutenant. I agree with you. I also think the girls knew their killer(s)."

"If you don't mind listening a little longer, I would like to tell you my theory about how the murders took place. Just remember - it's only my theory. Like every other investigator, I have my own ideas about what took place. I could be wrong, but I really don't think so.

"Let's look at the facts. On July 4th, Diane Compagna was said to have been raped by Tom Jefferson. We know that at least ten people were told by Diane that Tom Jefferson had raped her and that some of these same people went to Jefferson and advised him as to what Diane was going around telling everyone. He was upset about this and re-marked that he would 'shut her mouth and give her a kick in the ass.'

"We know that during the week between July 4th and the day the girls disappeared, July 12th, Jefferson was going around the town looking for Diane. We have a written statement from Jefferson admitting that he had sex with Diane Compagna. We now know that even though Jefferson had raped Diane, she was still attracted to him, that she was afraid she might be pregnant and was worried that she might not see him again.

"We know that the girls were reported as missing on the 12th of July 1973 and that both girls were alive over at Hampton Beach at 4:30 p.m., the same day. I believe that Diane and Anne were murdered that night of July 12, 1973. We also know that both Tom Jefferson and Wayne Powers were off from work on the 12th of July.

"Now for my theory, Chief. I still believe that the girls knew their killers and that they both come from Merrimack. The reason that I keep looking in the direction of Tom Jefferson and Wayne Powers is because Tom Jefferson had both motive and opportunity, and he and Powers were friends.

"Oh, I know a lot of people look at me and ask, 'What kind of a motive could Jefferson possibly have?' Well Chief, if Jefferson had been arrested for the rape of Diane Compagna, he would have been tried, found guilty and most likely sent to prison. He would have lost his reputation and more importantly, he would have lost the woman he wanted to marry. In fact, Jefferson married that woman nine days be-fore the bodies of Diane Compagna and Anne Psaradelis were found.

"Lieutenant, how about Wayne Powers? Why do you have him as a possible suspect?"

"Well, Chief, think about it. Wayne Powers and Tom Jefferson were friends. They associated with each other and would even go over to Hampton Beach together every so often. Powers was afraid of Jefferson even though they were friends, because Jefferson is a drinker and a bully, but he hung around with him anyway. Something happened to Wayne Powers in the early part of July 1973 that changed his whole life. He was a good student, had a job, was a hard worker, had a nice girlfriend and it looked like he would have a good future.

"We know, Chief Baker, that the bodies of Diane Compagna and Anne Psaradelis were found over in your town on the 29th of September and were identified on the 30th. September 30th was also the day the news media reported the two girls had been murdered. We know that Wayne received a telephone call on the morning of the 30th while he was at work. He flipped out and had to be taken home and then to the doctor. Within a few days he was admitted into the hospital with a mental breakdown. He stayed in the hospital for 26 or 27 days, was released and sent home, about nine days later Wayne took his own life.

"Chief, I believe that the ones responsible for the murders of Diane and Anne were looking for the girls and found that they had gone over to Hampton Beach, so they left Merrimack and headed over to the beach with the expectation that they would locate the two girls. I would say that Jefferson and Powers made contact with the girls at the beach and offered them a ride home. You have to remember that even though Jefferson had raped Diane, she was still attracted to him. Diane could have been flattered and accepted the offer of a ride home. Diane probably got into the front seat with Tom Jefferson and Anne got in the back seat with Wayne Powers. It is also possible that the girls got into someone else's car that they knew but I doubt it.

"Go on with your theory, Lieutenant."

"Well, Chief, I believe the four of them headed back toward Merrimack, but while they were passing near your town Jefferson probably decided that he would stop someplace so they could talk or do whatever was on his mind.

"They pulled into the entrance to a small seldom used gravel pit off New Boston Road. They probably sat there for a few minutes and then Jefferson might have said that he and Diane were going to take a walk, that they had some things they wanted to talk about. Diane and Jefferson got out of the car and left Wayne and Anne still in the back seat. I think that Jefferson walked Diane into the woods and as they walked, he probably started saying nice things to her. They ended up in an area that reminds you of a pine grove, an area that is more open with a blanket of pine needles covering the ground. I think he probably told her that he'd been looking for her, sweet-talked her and kissed her a few times and convinced her to have sex with him. Then she took her clothes off, spread her jeans on the ground, folded up her other clothes and put them in a pile."

"Lieutenant, why would Diane fold her clothes up and put them in a pile and why would she put her jeans on the ground?"

"Well, Chief, Diane was a very neat person. Her family told me she would always fold up her clothes no matter if they were soiled or clean. It was just her way of doing things. She probably placed her jeans on the ground so she could lay on them and not have the pine needles sticking in her back, This also tells me that Diane and Anne knew who their killers were. How often do you see or hear of a rapist allowing the victim to fold their clothes up and then lay a pair of trousers on the ground so that the leaves and pine needles don't scratch the victim's back? The rapist couldn't care less about the victim. He is only interested in himself.

"I do think that once Jefferson had Diane on the ground, that they had sex. I don't think he forced her because there doesn't appear to have been any struggle. Just look at the photographs of the body and that will tell you a lot. I do think that at some point while Jefferson was on top of Diane, that maybe she asked him a question or said something to him in a reply to a question he might have asked her, such as 'You aren't going to tell the police about the 4th of July incident are you?' or Diane might have told Jefferson that she thought she was pregnant.

"At this point, I think Jefferson was still on top of Diane and had her pinned to the ground with his body, and he strangled her. I doubt he planned on doing this, but she had the rape on him and it could have spoiled everything for him.

"Jefferson must have been in a state of panic, thinking, I've killed Diane and now I have to kill Anne.

"Jefferson probably ran through the woods, back to where he had parked his car, where Wayne and Anne were still waiting for him and Diane to return. He probably said something like, 'Wayne, Anne, you need to come with me. I need your help. Diane fell down and injured herself bad. Come quick. We have to help her and bring her back to the car and we should get her to the hospital as soon as possible.'

"Wayne and Anne would have jumped out of the car and followed Jefferson into the woods. Once they were all in the woods, Jefferson might have dropped back to allow Anne and Wayne to walk in front of him. They crossed between an opening in the stone wall and worked their way through the woods to the right of the stone wall. Up ahead was the clearing.

"All of a sudden, Anne screamed, Wayne looked over towards her and they both saw Diane on the ground. She was nude and appeared to be dead. Anne turned around for a brief second and saw Jefferson starting towards her. She turned and bolted into the woods with Jefferson right behind her. Wayne followed and watched as Jefferson caught up with Anne just as she was about to go over the stone wall. He grabbed Anne from behind, brought her to the ground and strangled her.

"Jefferson then got up, leaving Anne right on the ground where he just murdered her, looked over to where Wayne was standing and said, 'You better keep your mouth shut and never say a word to anyone about this or the same thing will happen to you. Come on, let's get out of here.'"

"You know, Lieutenant, that really could have been the way the murders were done. If two strangers had picked up the girls with the intention of raping them, both girls would have been nude and besides, if that was the case, Diane wouldn't have been brought that far into the woods. The two guys would have just raped them, left them by the wayside and gotten out of there."

"Chief Baker, Tom Jefferson is the one who had motive and opportunity. I feel Wayne Powers was just in the wrong place at the wrong time with the wrong company.

"Chief, you know I have discussed my theory with many people in law enforcement and yet no one is willing to step forward and help us place or eliminate Tom Jefferson and Wayne Powers as suspects in this case.

"Chief Baker, another possible suspect, as you know, is Jim Psaradelis, and I really think we need to keep him in mind, but I think that Jefferson and Powers need to be placed or eliminated first, since they are our prime suspects.

"Jim Psaradelis acted strangely throughout the entire missing persons stage of the investigation and even into the investigation involving the murders of his daughter and Diane Compagna. Mr. Psaradelis would come to the station at all hours of the day and night, or call by telephone, advising that he had just chased the girls down an alley in Nashua, up a fire escape, over a rooftop and into various apartments. We never found any evidence to support his claims. How could they be true, when we now know the poor girls were already dead?

"At one point, Mr. Psaradelis quit his job because he said he wanted to help us find the girls. Maybe he did or maybe he just wanted to know how the investigation was going. At the time, I thought he was just looking for sympathy and attention. Even though the State Police and the Nashua police checked Mr. Psaradelis out, I think that we need to keep him as a possible suspect and either place or eliminate him. Why did Jim Psaradelis take off? There has to be a reason why he's been gone all these years. He needs to be located and questioned again.

"Chief Baker, I think that these three and any other suspects we or any law enforcement agency might have in regards to these double murders should be placed or eliminated. And how do we do that? We have been trying to accomplish this all these years and so far, no luck. We'll just have to continue the investigation on our own."

"It certainly looks that way, Lieutenant."

Although Chief Baker and I had inspected the crime scene at least fifty times, I suggested that we drive over and look at it one more time.

There was always the faint hope that the murderer would return to the scene of the crime and leave some kind of clue - that does happen every so often. Chief Baker agreed.

"This area really hasn't changed much in five years, Chief. The only difference is that the gravel pit has been expanded and someone's placed four boulders in front of the entrance so no one can drive in."

The Chief and I walked to the area where Diane Compagna was found, then over near the stone wall where Anne Psaradelis was located. We noticed that if the stone wall hadn't been there, Anne probably would have gotten away. It was sad to think about.

"It's strange, Chief, every time I come here, I can still feel the presence of death. It might sound strange, but I can almost feel the presence of the girls, telling us not to give up.

"As much time as we've spent on this investigation, I still think the girls knew the people who murdered them. If Lieutenant Bennett knows so much, why hasn't he solved the case?"

Chief Baker and I checked everything related to the crime scene while we were there. We inspected the logging road and concluded the girls weren't brought into the pine grove from that direction because they would have had to climb over the stone wall. We took another look at the entrance of the logging road on New Boston Road. There was a house right across the street. If someone had driven in that way, they would have been noticed either coming in or going out. The same thing was true of parking on New Boston Road itself. There wasn't room on the shoulder to park a car. If someone had parked there, the car would have obstructed the road and someone would have seen it. The thing that was evident was that the crime scene was much closer to the gravel pit entrance than it was to the logging road. It was probably a waste of time checking the area again, but at least it made me feel better.

After Chief Baker and I said good-bye, I headed to Manchester and then back to Merrimack. I stopped by Diane and Anne's grave sites to renew my promise that I would solve this case no matter how long it took.

JOSEPH A. HORAK

24

June 24, 1977

I was at Zyla's Auction House one morning, when I spotted Officer Stavenger heading my way. I noticed that he had been promoted to sergeant.

"What do you say, Lieutenant? I haven't seen you in a long time. How are things going?"

"Oh, they're going pretty good. Of course, I miss police work and I won't feel complete or good about myself until I finish the Compagna-Psaradelis murder case. Do you know where the investigation is now?"

"Lieutenant, that case is collecting dust in the closet. No one is going to touch that one because it means so much to you."

"That's pretty foolish. How would you like to solve it yourself, Sergeant?"

"Lieutenant, that would be nice."

"Well, come on, Sergeant, let's sit down and I'll talk with you about the case. I'll even tell you the first person you need to re-interview."

"OK, Lieutenant, I have a little time."

"All you have to do is dig those books out of the closet and read the whole case with an open mind. The first person you should interview is the woman Officer Gloria Litchfield and I interviewed. If you read through the case and really want to solve it, you'll know who this woman is."

"OK, Lieutenant."

"You know, Sergeant, if you solve the Compagna-Psaradelis murder case, it would be a feather in your cap and it would sure give me peace of mind. I hope you'll look into it."

I felt bad running into police officers I knew because I should still be one of them. I felt cheated by Chief Pelletier, Lieutenant Bennett, and the system, but that's the way life goes sometimes. If the Compagna-Psaradelis case was solved, it would mean everything to me. It would give me peace of mind to know that I completed the job.

I was still looking for a police job, but wasn't having any luck. I didn't have much money, so I picked up odd jobs now and then, cutting lawns and painting - anything to get by.

December 28, 1978

I had driven eighty thousand miles around the country looking for a police job, but still couldn't find anything. I guess the old saying, "You can be anything you want," really isn't true. All I could do was keep looking.

I was making plans to head for the Midwest in a couple of days, when I received a phone call from Chief Baker.

"Any good news for me, Chief Baker?"

"No, Lieutenant, not one thing on the case. Nothing's being done on the investigation as far as I can see. I haven't heard a single word from Lieutenant Bennett or anyone from the Merrimack Police Department, the state police, or anyone else. It's almost as though they've buried the case and aren't going to investigate it any further. I'm sure they're glad you're looking for work out of state."

"Well, Chief, we aren't going to give up. Someone out there has to be willing to help us. I appreciate your checking in with me and letting me know what's going on. I'll continue to let you know where I am and how you can reach me if something turns up. I've written letters to people I know in law enforcement to try to get them interested in helping us solve the case, but so far none of them have written back. All we can do is keep trying.

"Chief Baker, I'll be back in New Hampshire for a week in September so we can continue our tradition of going to the crime scene and cemeteries. Thanks again for calling. I'll write soon."

JUSTICE DENIED

Weeks and months sped by, but still I couldn't find a police job. I cut lawns, polished cars, and did odd painting jobs. It wasn't much, but at least I was getting by. I never realized how much the word disability could affect someone's life. I had to keep trying. Something had to turn up.

<u>December 22, 1981</u>

I received a note from Tom Hurst asking me to call him.

"Hi, Tom, this is Joe Horak. I just received your note, what's up?"

"Joe, I've got a job for you if you can get down here to Florida by January 22. This isn't a police job, Joe, but it's a good job, with good pay and benefits. A large hospital in the area needs a security supervisor-investigator. You could take it and still look around for a police job. At least you'd have something. It sure beats chasing all over the country like you've been doing for the past couple of years. My wife and I would like to see you settle down."

"Tom, I was planning to leave here in a couple of weeks to start looking someplace else. I'll be down there by January 15, if that's OK."

"That's great, Joe, we'll see you then."

The climate in Florida was just like summer, it sure beat the snow and cold I was used to. The hospital Tom had told me about was big, five stories high, and had two, four-story parking garages. When I went for the interview, I noticed they had a large security force. I seemed to be exactly what the hospital was looking for, they hired me on the spot for the three-to-eleven shift.

I liked my job at the hospital, they were good to me. I was lucky enough to have an apartment in the nurses' residence right across the street from the hospital. It was very convenient being so close to work.

Even though so many years had passed since the murders of Diane Compagna and Anne Psaradelis, I still stayed in contact with Chief Baker. We wanted to place or eliminate the suspects we had. I really couldn't understand why this case wasn't solved. All we needed was someone from law enforcement interested enough to help us.

I had been working at the hospital three years when I received a letter from the director of the New Hampshire retirement system. It was the first time I had heard from them in eight years. The director informed me that he had received information that I was working, which violated the rules regarding people on disability retirement. He stated that I had to pay back over eleven thousand dollars.

What a mess. I didn't have eleven thousand dollars. That meant I had to give up my job at the hospital, hire an attorney, and go back to New Hampshire to fight with the retirement system. It had taken me years to put my life back into some kind of order. Now, I had to start all over again.

September 19, 1984

As soon as I arrived in New Hampshire, I made an appointment with the director of the retirement system.

"Good morning, Mr. Descoteau, I'm Joe Horak."

"Mr. Horak, you owe the retirement system between eleven and thirteen thousand dollars."

"Mr. Descoteau, why do I owe the retirement system money? What has my working got to do with money you claim I owe the system?"

"Well, Mr. Horak, you've been earning more money than the retirement systems allows for extra income."

"Listen, Mr. Descoteau, when I retired I never saw anyone from the retirement board, not even a doctor. I was never told that I couldn't work. I'm pretty upset, Mr. Descoteau. I just gave up a twenty-one-thousand-dollar-a-year job that took me over two years to find."

"That's not my problem, Mr. Horak. You knew you weren't supposed to get a job that paid that much money."

"I'm going to tell you once more, Mr. Descoteau, I never saw anyone from the retirement board or a doctor connected to the retirement system. I was never told that I couldn't work or was limited to what I could earn.

"I'll tell you what, Mr. Descoteau, why don't you just give me back my job with the Merrimack Police Department. I would be more than happy with that."

"Wait a minute, Mr. Horak, I want to look through your records." Mr. Descoteau looked through my file, then continued. "Mr. Horak, who is Doctor James French?"

"That's my doctor, Mr. Descoteau."

"Who is Doctor Todd Conrad?"

"That's my doctor, Mr. Descoteau."

"Well, anyway, Mr. Horak, you knew that there was a limit to the amount you could earn."

"No, Mr. Descoteau, I didn't know. I was never told of anything like that."

"Oh, yes, you were, Mr. Horak. Every person who is on disability retirement has to fill out a form every year. You've been given these forms like everyone else."

"Mr. Descoteau, I've never received any such form, in fact, I've never heard of any such form."

"Oh, yes, you have, Mr. Horak. Let me check your file and I'll show you that you filled one out and sent it back every year that you've been retired."

"No, sir, I haven't."

Mr. Descoteau looked through my file, then said, "I guess you haven't, Mr. Horak."

"Mr. Descoteau, what do you think I've been trying to tell you? If I had known about these regulations, I wouldn't be in this position. I lost a good job because of this."

"Mr. Horak, I'll bring this matter up before the retirement board. It will probably take a couple of months. No matter what, you're going to pay that money back to the retirement system. I'll make sure of that."

"Mr. Descoteau, let me ask you one question, if I may."

"What is it, Mr. Horak?"

"Mr. Descoteau, I would like to know why a police officer who is not injured can go out and get a job that pays big money when he retires. Why is a police officer who is injured in the line of duty restricted from making a decent living the same as the officer who retires uninjured?"

"That's beside the point. You have to repay the retirement system the money you owe. You'll be hearing from me. The girl at the desk can give you some forms advising you how much money you can earn over the amount you get from the retirement system each month. You can get a job based on those income limitations. From now on you'll receive a form that requires you to advise us how much additional money you make each year."

"Mr. Descoteau, thanks to you, I'll have to look for an attorney and another job. Who told you I was working in Florida?"

"Mr. Horak, that's none of your business."

The situation was a big mess, but I didn't let it get me down. I started looking in the want ads right away and found that the U.S. Marshal's office was hiring people with a minimum of six years of law experience for the security staff at the federal court. I interviewed for the position and was offered the job. The pay wasn't great, but at least I would be able to talk with a lot of police officers and attorneys from around the state. I hoped I would be able to find a good attorney to handle my problem with the retirement system. I might even find someone who would help with the Compagna-Psaradelis homicide case.

There were probably a lot of people who thought I should forget the Compagna-Psaradelis murder case, but there hadn't been a day in the past ten years that I didn't think of the girls. I just couldn't walk away and let their killers get away scot-free. It was something I just had to finish.

I liked the position at the federal court and was determined to do the best job I could. I had been working there a month when I met an attorney I thought was right to handle my problem with the retirement system. His name was Steve Gordon. One morning I decided to talk with him.

"Good morning, Attorney Gordon. Do you have a few minutes to spare?"

"Sure, Joe, how can I help you?"

"I'm having a problem with the retirement system. They want me to pay back between eleven and thirteen thousand dollars. They even caused me to lose a good job in Florida. I really need some help because I don't have any money."

"Listen, Joe, don't give it a second thought. I'll take care of the whole thing and it won't cost you a cent."

"Attorney Gordon, I don't expect you to help me without getting paid."

"Don't worry about it, Joe, I'll take care of everything."

"You know, Attorney Gordon, this is the first time in the past ten years that I've been treated decently. I want to thank you for that."

"I'll get back to you in a couple of days, Joe."

A few days later I saw Attorney Gordon at the federal court.

"Good morning, Attorney Gordon, nice day, isn't it?"

"Yes, it is, Joe. By the way, I've taken care of that problem you had with the retirement system, so you can just forget it. Don't worry about having to pay them anything."

"Boy, that's great news. How can I ever thank you?"

"Joe, just keep doing such a great job. Everyone here likes you a lot."

25

I had been working at the federal court for four years. During that time I talked with all kinds of detectives, police officers, and attorneys about the Compagna-Psaradelis homicide case. Although many of them seemed interested in helping, none of them ever did. It was pretty discouraging at times. I often wondered why no one wanted to get involved in solving the case.

It was the fifteenth anniversary of the murders of Diane Compagna and Anne Psaradelis. As we've done each year, Chief Baker and I went to the crime scene first, and then, to the cemeteries to pay our respects.

"Chief Baker, this place hasn't changed much in the past fifteen years. I wonder if the killer or killers have ever come back here. Stranger things have happened, you know, so it is possible that they've been back. That's why I like to recheck the area. You never know if something new might turn up.

"I don't know about you, Chief, but I can still feel death and the presence of the girls here. I guess that won't change until we solve their murders."

Chief Baker and I drove from the crime scene to the cemeteries. As we passed the Merrimack Police Department, I couldn't help sharing my feelings with Chief Baker.

"You know, Chief, I really dislike going past the Merrimack Police Station. It makes me feel bad that I'm not there doing my job. I really feel cheated. Over the years I've run into various detectives and police officers from the Merrimack Police Department, including Lieutenant Bennett. I've asked them to read over the case and help solve it. They all say yes, but they never do anything. That case is still in the bottom of a closet collecting dust. That's pretty sad."

Everything looked normal at the cemeteries. There were fresh flowers on Diane's grave, but Anne's was bare, which made me glad I had brought a little something to put on it. Chief Baker and I said a prayer at each grave and vowed to keep working toward solving the murders.

<u>June 1, 1991</u>

I hadn't seen Chief Baker in a while, so I decided to drop him a note.

> *Hi, Chief Baker:*
>
> *It's just me again. I know that I must sound like a pest, but we really need to get the Compagna-Psaradelis investigation back on track. The years seem to have dragged by and we're no closer to solving it than we were in 1973.*
>
> *I really wish we could find someone in law enforcement who is interested enough to work on the case and solve it once and for all. I've asked a lot of people, but haven't had any luck finding anyone to help. All we can do is keep trying. I know I'm not going to give up on the case.*
>
> *I think we should put something in the newspapers next month. It might help. Let me know if you have any ideas. I'll drop over to see you soon.*

A lot of time had passed since the homicides and I thought I should re-interview Ann Psaradelis.

"Hello, Mrs. Psaradelis, may I come in and talk with you?"

"Why, Lieutenant Horak, come on in. It's been quite a while since I've seen you. Is there anything new on the girls?"

"No, Mrs. Psaradelis, I just thought I'd do a follow-up interview with you to see if you have any information that might help me with the investigation."

"Are you still with the police department, Lieutenant?"

"No, Mrs. Psaradelis, I retired some time ago, but Chief Baker and I are still working on the investigation. We won't stop until the case is solved."

"Of course, Lieutenant, you know that my children are grown up and married. I live here alone now. Over the years I've heard different people say things about how the girls died, but it's not anything that would help."

"Mrs. Psaradelis, have you ever heard from your husband Jim since he took off?"

"Lieutenant Horak, I haven't seen or heard from my husband since about 1974 or 1975. I can't even remember the year he left. You know, I've always felt that my husband might have had something to do with the deaths of Anne and Diane."

"Why do you say that, Mrs. Psaradelis?"

"Well, Lieutenant, my husband was never the same after Anne's death. His attitude and actions made me feel as if he had something to do with the girls' deaths."

"To be honest with you, Mrs. Psaradelis, I've given some consideration to Jim's being involved in the case. Almost right from the start things seemed strange to me. When Mr. Compagna reported Diane as missing, he said he might as well report Anne, too, since both girls were together. Then, during the missing person's part of the investigation, Jim was in the station asking questions every time we turned around.

"Mrs. Psaradelis, there was another thing that bothered me. Your husband reported that he saw the girls go into an apartment building, a house, and down an alley. Not once did the police turn up anything that proved these sightings to be true. As you know, the girls were murdered on July 12, 1973 - your husband's sightings couldn't have been true."

"You know, Lieutenant, I thought it was strange that my husband took my youngest daughter to the scene where the girls were murdered. That didn't seem right."

"Lieutenant, I've tried to locate my husband through his Social Security number. The people at Social Security told me they couldn't locate him and told me I couldn't receive benefits unless I could produce a death certificate for Jim."

"Mrs. Psaradelis, why don't you give me a photograph and full description of your husband? I'll do what I can to help locate him. I'll do some checking and get back to you."

"Thank you, Lieutenant, I'd appreciate that."

November 9, 1991

Chief Baker retired from the Candia Police Department and operated his country store.

The investigation wasn't going anywhere, so I decided to talk with the chief about moving things forward. First, I told him about my interview with Mrs. Psaradelis, then I mentioned some of my ideas.

"Chief Baker, if we don't do something soon, the possible suspects and witnesses will be dead and gone. The case will never be solved unless we move forward with it."

"Lieutenant, how do you plan on doing that? We've tried for seventeen years to get someone to help with the investigation. What makes you think we can change that now?"

"I don't know, Chief, I just know that we have to pull out all the stops and do it now or never. I think we should start by talking with Chief Pelletier's replacement at the Merrimack Police Department and ask him for his help to bring this case to a conclusion. I think Chief Devine will help since the girls came from his town. If we don't have any luck with Chief Devine, I think we should move right up the so-called ladder until we get the help we need to either place suspects into the crime or eliminate them so the investigation can move forward."

"That sounds like a good idea, Lieutenant. By the way, I almost forgot to tell you that I heard Lieutenant John Bennett isn't with the Merrimack Police Department any more. He moved on to greener pastures."

"That's really something, Chief. Bennett said he was going to solve the Compagna-Psaradelis murder case, but as far as I know, he didn't do one thing on the investigation after I left the department."

I called Chief Devine's office to make an appointment to speak with him, but found out he was on vacation for two weeks. Rather than making the appointment, I decided to write the chief a letter so it would be waiting on his desk when he returned to work. This is what I said.

November 12, 1991

Dear Chief Devine:

I am sure you must remember me. I used to work for the Merrimack Police Department.

I am writing to you regarding the Compagna-Psaradelis murders that took place in July 1973. Chief Baker, now retired, from the Candia Police Department, and I have been working on this case for the past seventeen and a half years. We have always had suspects in the case and have tried to find some law enforcement person or agency interested enough to bring this case to a conclusion.

Chief, since the two girls came from your town and since our department has been involved in the investigation right from the start, I would like you to help Chief Baker and me either place or eliminate the suspects we have in the case. We have to do it now or the case will never be solved. Won't you please help us?

Chief Baker and I would be happy to talk with you at your convenience. We hope to receive your reply in a timely fashion.

<u>February 1992</u>

Two months passed and Chief Devine hadn't replied to my letter. I was determined to talk with him, so I called the chief's office and made an appointment to see him.

"Good morning, Chief Devine. I don't know if you remember me or not, but I've talked with you a few times."

"What do you want, Lieutenant Horak?"

"Well, Chief Robert Baker and I have been working on the Compagna-Psaradelis murder case for the past eighteen years. I wrote you a letter in November, asking for your help in either placing or eliminating the suspects we have in the case. I haven't received a reply.

"I've come here today to talk with you in person and ask for your help. This case can be solved. We just need help from someone like you."

"Lieutenant Horak, I'm good friends with Mike Compagna and his father Marcel. We go out once in a while."

"Chief Devine, will you help Chief Baker and me with the investigation of the Diane Compagna and Anne Psaradelis homicides?"

"Lieutenant, that's not my problem!"

"Chief Devine, how can you say that? The girls both came from Merrimack and this department has worked on the case since day one."

"You heard me, Lieutenant, that's not my problem!"

"I don't know how you can say that, Chief Devine, but thanks for your time."

Needless to say, I was shocked by Chief Devine's attitude.

Since I was in Merrimack, I decided to stop by the Compagnas' to see how things were going.

"Good morning, Mrs. Compagna. I was in the area, so I decided to stop by and say hello."

"Where have you been, Lieutenant?"

"Oh, I just came from seeing Chief Devine."

"Mike and Marcel are friends with the chief. Mike even went on vacation with him."

"You would never know it, Mrs. Compagna. I just asked Chief Devine to help Chief Baker and me with the murders of Diane and Anne. His reply was, 'That's not my problem.' That's quite a friend they have."

"Lieutenant, I'll have to talk with Marcel about that. The chief didn't say anything to Marcel or Mike last night about your having an appointment with him today."

"Mrs. Compagna, I can't understand why Chief Devine won't help since the girls were from here and you're friends. It doesn't make sense to me.

"You know, Mrs. Compagna, this investigation is beginning its nineteenth year. I'll be honest with you, Chief Devine and the rest of the gang can say that they won't help investigate anymore, but that isn't going to stop Chief Baker and me."

"Lieutenant Horak, I want to ask you a question."

"Go ahead, Mrs. Compagna, ask it."

"Lieutenant, if you think you can solve this case, why didn't you do it nineteen years ago?"

"What a question for you to ask, Mrs. Compagna. You should know better than anyone else how much time and energy Chief Baker and I have devoted to solving the murders. Look how long and hard we've been fighting the system to get some law enforcement person or agency to help us. We haven't given up and we won't, until the case is solved.

"I feel bad that you're starting to think and feel like all the others. If it was my daughter who was murdered, I'd be thankful there were police officers out there who were still working on the case. I wouldn't want the killer to get away with taking the lives of my daughter and another girl. Maybe this person has even killed again.

"No, Mrs. Compagna, no matter how you or anyone else feels, this case has to be solved. I, for one, will never be satisfied until we can either place or eliminate the suspects we've had all these years. I don't see how you or the Psaradelises could feel any other way."

"Well, Lieutenant, I'm going to ask Marcel to talk with Chief Devine the next time he sees him. I'm not mad with you, Lieutenant. Of course, we want to see the murderer caught. Do whatever you think you should."

"OK, Mrs. Compagna, I guess I'd better get going. I'll let you know if anything develops."

I didn't know what to think. Maybe the Compagnas had talked the case over with Chief Devine. There was no other reason why Mrs. Compagna would be dissatisfied with the investigation after all these years. I always tried to keep her informed about what was going on in the case. I felt problems coming up in the future. I hoped I was wrong.

May 28, 1992

My conversations with Chief Devine and Mrs. Compagna were so distressing, I needed to talk with someone. Chief Baker was my natural choice.

"Chief Devine isn't going to cooperate with us, Chief. I think we might even have a problem with the Compagnas before long. I know you've contacted the new Candia police chief a few times, but he never came to talk with you. Do you think he'll help?"

"Lieutenant, I don't know."

"Well, Chief, if you'll give me the new chief's name, I'll approach him. We have to do something."

"Lieutenant Horak, the new chief's name is Steven Agrafiots. I don't know how much luck you'll have with him, but it's worth a try. This is a weekend and Monday is a holiday, so I don't know when you'll be able to catch up with Chief Agrafiots."

"Chief, I've already written a letter, all I have to do is fill in the chief's name. I'll stop by the Candia Police Station and try to see Chief Agrafiots. If he's not in, I'll leave the letter for him."

I left Chief Baker and drove to the Candia Police Station. The new gray and white building that the town had built was quite a change from Chief Baker working out of his home. There were police cruisers parked at the rear of the station, so I thought someone must be there. I was right. There was a woman sitting behind the front desk. I thought she was either a police dispatcher or a secretary.

"Hello, is Chief Stanley Agrafiots in the station today?"

"No, he isn't. Can I help you?"

"I'm retired Detective Lieutenant Joe Horak. I'm working on a homicide case and I'd like to talk with Chief Agrafiots."

"I already told you the chief isn't in. Can I help you?"

"No, but I'd like to leave a letter for him. When will the chief be in?"

"Lieutenant, since Monday is a holiday, he won't be back until Tuesday."

The dispatcher sure had a bad attitude. She acted as though she was the chief of police.

Tuesday was a long way off, so I thought I'd try to find the chief's home address and go over to see him. It didn't take long to find out that Chief Agrafiots lived at 96 Pearl Street in Hooksett.

When I arrived at the Pearl Street address, I knew I was at the right place, a Candia police cruiser was parked in the yard. I rang the bell and knocked on the door, but no one answered. Since I lived quite a distance from Candia, I decided to sit in my car and wait for a while. It didn't take long for one of the neighbors to stop and talk with me.

"Sir, are you looking for Chief Agrafiots?"

"Yes, I am."

"That's the chief coming out of his house now."

The neighbor pointed to the Agrafiots house and, sure enough, a man was walking out of the door.

"Sir, are you Chief Stanley Agrafiots?"

"Yes, I am. What can I do for you?"

"I'm retired Detective Lieutenant Joe Horak. I've been working with retired Chief Robert Baker on a double homicide that took place in Candia in 1973. We've been trying for years to get someone from law enforcement interested enough to help bring this case to a conclusion. So far we've had negative results. Chief Agrafiots, we'd like your help in eliminating the suspects we have regarding the murders of Diane Compagna and Anne Psaradelis.

"Chief Agrafiots, before you answer, I'd like to tell you about the case and the possible suspects."

I spent the next two hours telling the chief everything I knew about the investigation.

"Well, Lieutenant Horak, I know Captain John Barthelmes with the major crime unit of the state police. I could talk with him and see if he'll help."

"What about you, Chief Agrafiots? You're the one who could help us from this end."

"To be honest with you, Lieutenant, I cannot investigate homicides."

"You have to be kidding. Aren't you the chief of police in Candia?"

"Yes, I am."

"I can't believe a chief of police can't investigate a homicide. If that's the case, something is wrong with the system. So, what you're saying, Chief Agrafiots is that you can't help Chief Baker and me with any investigation regarding this double homicide."

"That's correct, Lieutenant. I cannot investigate homicides."

"Well, Chief Agrafiots, would you like some of the paperwork that we've done on the case? I can give it to you if you like."

"That would be great, Lieutenant Horak."

"I'll deliver the paperwork to your office. Thanks for taking the time to talk with me on your day off."

On my way home I stopped by to tell Chief Baker about my meeting with Chief Agrafiots. I told him that it didn't appear we were going to receive any more help from Agrafiots than we have from any other law enforcement agency.

Tuesday, May 31, 1992

I stopped by the Candia Police Department to drop off the paperwork on the Compagna-Psaradelis homicide case. It didn't appear that the chief was in yet, so I talked with the same dispatcher I had seen over the weekend.

"Good morning, is Chief Agrafiots in, please?"

"No, he isn't, Lieutenant. By the way, when you left the letter for him, I thought I told you the chief wouldn't be in until Tuesday. How did you find him? Why didn't you wait until today to see him?"

"Well, miss, it really isn't any of your business, but I'm an investigator and homicide investigation has to be done when you can do it. I just can't let time pass without accomplishing something. You have to do things when you can, not when it's convenient.

"Would you please see that Chief Steven Agrafiots receives these reports?"

As I was handing the paperwork to the dispatcher, Chief Agrafiots walked through the door.

"Good morning, Chief, I was just giving these investigation reports to your dispatcher. I hope they'll help in some way. If you decide that you can help Chief Baker and me with the investigation of the Compagna-Psaradelis murders, please advise us."

"I'll do what I can to help, Lieutenant Horak, and I'll speak with Captain John Barthelmes of the major crime unit. I think I can get him to help, because we get along pretty well."

While I was in Candia, I decided to drop in on Chief Baker.

"Hi, Lieutenant Horak, it seems like you're always around the area."

"Well, Chief, I just dropped off the paperwork for Chief Agrafiots as I promised. I doubt very much that he'll help us in the investigation."

"You know, Chief Baker, it's almost July again and I was wondering if we should put something in the newspapers over on the coast and in Manchester. It's the nineteenth anniversary of Diane Compagna and Anne Psaradelis being reported missing."

"We probably should give some thought to that. Do you think we should have some law enforcement agency involved in the investigation before we do that? It's really up to you, Lieutenant. If we can't do it this year, let's plan to do a big article next year for the twentieth anniversary. With a lot of hard work and cooperation, we might have the case solved by then."

"Amen to that, Chief Baker. I really don't know what we can do to bring this investigation to a conclusion. We've tried everything possible. Did you have any luck with the sheriff's department?"

"No, Lieutenant. They gave the impression they wanted to help, but that's as far as it went."

"By the way, Chief Baker, don't forget that we have a trip to the crime scene and the two cemeteries pretty soon. You know, it's our annual project."

"I won't forget, Lieutenant."

26

JUSTICE DENIED

<u>November 1992</u>

I thought it was time to speak with someone at State Police Head-quarters, either the colonel or someone from the major crime unit. There wasn't any sense in getting Chief Baker involved in this one, so I handled it myself.

"Good afternoon, ma'am. Is Colonel Presby in his office?"

"No, I'm afraid he isn't. Is there any way I can help you?"

"Well, I'm retired Detective Lieutenant Joe Horak. Retired Chief Robert Baker and I have been working on the Compagna-Psaradelis homicides that took place in 1973. This case involves two, fifteen-year-old girls from Merrimack, New Hampshire. They were found murdered in Candia, New Hampshire, on September 29, 1973.

"Chief Baker and I have been trying to find some law enforcement officer or agency that would help us bring this case to a conclusion. There are suspects in the case that haven't been placed or eliminated from the investigation. We've contacted nearly everyone we can think of to help solve this case, but not one person or agency has come forward to help us."

"Lieutenant Horak, why don't you go down the hall to the major crime unit and speak with Captain Tom Winn. He might be able to help you."

The name Tom Winn sounded familiar. It seemed to me that we had worked together on several cases. When I saw him sitting at his desk, I recognized him immediately, and he recognized me too.

"Well, hello, Lieutenant Horak, I haven't seen you in about ten years. What are you doing here?"

"Well, Captain Winn, I'm here regarding a double homicide case that Chief Baker and I have been working on for the past nineteen and a half years. We've been trying to find someone from law enforcement to help bring this case to a conclusion. We've always had suspects and still do. We just need some help and you're our last chance."

"Do you still work for the Merrimack Police Department?"

"No, Captain, I'm sorry to say that I'm retired, but even though I'm retired, I'm not giving up on this investigation."

"Lieutenant, you came at the right time. I have a man who is pulling old homicide cases and reviewing them for possible leads that might help solve the cases. Go down the hall and see Detective Sergeant Roland Lamy. He'll help you."

"Captain Winn, I know Sergeant Lamy. He's a big guy with less hair than I have, and that makes him pretty bald, but he's a good guy. I'm sure he worked on the Compagna-Psaradelis homicide case."

I walked down the hall and found Sergeant Lamy.

"Hello, Sergeant Lamy, you're just the man I'm looking for. Captain Winn just told me you're pulling old homicide cases that haven't been solved. I need some help with a double homicide case you worked on back in September 1973."

"What case is that?"

"The Compagna-Psaradelis homicide over in Candia."

"Well, you are lucky, Lieutenant Horak. I'm going to pull these old cases and review each one of them to find leads that may have been overlooked. Let's sit down and talk about your case."

I spent four hours detailing the Compagna-Psaradelis case for Sergeant Lamy. He took quite a few notes.

"Lieutenant, if I can find the case number, I'll pull the file and read it over."

"Sergeant Lamy, what do you mean, if you can find the case number? You people have the case number in your files, plus there's a copy of the entire case right here at state police headquarters."

"Lieutenant Horak, if I can find the case number, I'll pull the file, read the case, and get back to you in a week - if I can find the number."

"Sergeant Lamy, don't worry about finding the number. I'll call you with the number within the next half hour. What's today's date?"

"Lieutenant, it's November 17, 1992. Why do you need the date?"

"Well, Sergeant, you told me if you had the number of the case, you would pull the file, read it, and get back to me in a week. You'll have the number within the hour. How about getting back to me around November 30? That will give you nearly two weeks."

"That sounds all right to me, Lieutenant Horak. I'll get back to you by the end of the month."

"Thanks for taking the time to talk with me, Sergeant Lamy. I hope you'll help us solve the Compagna-Psaradelis murder case. I don't even care if you leave Chief Baker's and my name off the investigation reports, just as long as the case is solved. That's all that matters to us."

December 10, 1992

Dear Chief Baker:

It's just me checking to see if we're making any progress with Detective Sergeant Roland Lamy. We haven't heard a word from him as you know. I'm eager to know if he'll give us a copy of the complete case and allow us to help with the investigation.

Like you, I really don't care who gets credit for solving the case, I just want to see it solved once and for all. It's been going on much too long. I hope you will do whatever you can to keep us both involved in the case.

No news on this end. I really hate being a pest, but I'm sure you must feel the same way.

I'll be in touch with you soon.

January 11, 1993

I still hadn't heard anything from Sergeant Lamy. He wouldn't even return my phone calls. I wondered if the state police was going to help us. I decided to write a letter and share my concerns with Chief Baker.

Hi, Chief:

I hope this note finds you well and that 1993 will be a good year for you. I hope we'll be able to bring the Compagna-Psaradelis homicide case to a close this year.

I've been hoping to receive a note from you, updating me on progress with our investigation. Have you heard anything from Detective Sergeant Roland Lamy? It seems like we've been placed on the back burner. Maybe you could call him again. I know he has lots of cases, but ours is just as important as the others.

February 25, 1993

I received a letter from Captain Thomas Winn, commander of the investigative bureau of the state police.

Dear Joe:

I am writing in regard to your letter to Colonel Presby about the Compagna-Psaradelis homicides.

I have spoken with Sergeant Lamy and he is of the opinion that there are several areas of the previous investigation that should be scrutinized again. However, at the present time we cannot reopen this case due to the extreme demands placed on our detective personnel.

You can be assured that you and Chief Baker will be contacted when any type of activity is initiated in this matter.

I called Chief Baker right away and read Captain Winn's letter to him.

"Lieutenant Horak, it doesn't sound like we're going to receive any help from the state police."

"Well, Chief Baker, I guess we'll have to consider the next move. Let's contact the attorney general's office in Concord. I know one of the assistant attorney generals. I could write to him and ask for help. Let's think it over and then I'll write the letter."

March 3, 1993

Dear Attorney John Davis:

I hope this letter finds you well and that you are enjoying your job with the attorney general's office.

We (Chief Robert Baker, retired, and Detective Lieutenant Joseph Horak, retired) are writing to you regarding the Compagna-Psaradelis homicides that took place in Candia, New

Hampshire, in 1973. The victims were from Merrimack, New Hampshire.

The investigation of these two homicides was conducted by members of the attorney general's office, the state police, the sheriff's department, and the Candia and Merrimack Police Departments.

We have been trying to bring this case to a conclusion since 1973. Many, many attempts have been made over the past seventeen years to find someone interested enough to re-open this case and devote the time and effort required to solve it. So far, we can't seem to find anyone interested enough to reopen and investigate the case.

John, this is a solvable case. Even though Chief Baker and I are retired, we are dedicated men and hate to see this case go unsolved.

John, no one knows this case any better than Chief Baker and me. We really need to sit down with an investigator who would be interested in solving the case and come up with a plan to solve it.

John, we realize that there are many people who need to be interviewed or re-interviewed. Some polygraph work is also required. We have always had suspects in the case and still do. We have knowledge about various facts that could help in the investigation that haven't been known until now.

If there is any kind of help you could give us in solving this crime, it would be appreciated. I am sure that the state police and the Merrimack Police Department have copies of the case if you need it.

It would be a credit to any law enforcement agency that could solve a double homicide that is now twenty years old. Chief Baker and I don't care who gets the credit, we just want to see the case solved. If possible, we would like to be part of any further investigation regarding this case. We hope you will give us an early reply.

March 17, 1993

Two weeks passed and I hadn't received a reply from the attorney general's office. I wrote a note to Chief Baker to see if he had heard anything.

> *Dear Chief:*
>
> *I hope things are going OK. I wonder if you've heard any-thing from the attorney general's office regarding the letter we sent to Attorney John Davis. I know I haven't heard from him or anyone else from that office. I'm sure it takes time to look up the case and read it, but we should have received some kind of response.*
>
> *I wonder if anyone really wants to solve this case. If we don't hear something from the attorney general's office by the first of next month, we'll have to go back to the drawing board.*

April 21, 1993

Chief Baker called to tell me he wasn't having any luck with Sergeant Lamy or anyone from the state police. He suggested that we make an appointment with the attorney general. I agreed. Later in the day I followed up our phone conversation with a letter.

April 28, 1993

I watched the television program, *Unsolved Mysteries.* They featured a psychic by the name of George Anderson on the show. He was really good. I wondered if he might be able to help with the Compagna-Psaradelis homicide case. They didn't give George Anderson's address, so I wrote to *Unsolved Mysteries*, hoping the show could put me in touch with him. It was worth trying anything at this point.

May 5, 1993

I received a letter from *Unsolved Mysteries* giving me George Anderson's address. I immediately wrote Mr. Anderson a letter.

> *Dear Mr. Anderson:*

You don't know me, but I saw you on Unsolved Mysteries on April 28, 1993. I was really caught up with your psychic knowledge and powers.

Chief Robert Baker, retired, and I started working on a double homicide twenty years ago this coming July. After watching you on Unsolved Mysteries, we talked things over and decided to write to you to see if there is any way you could help us solve the murders of these two young girls.

I want you to know that we are both retired police officers, but even though we're retired, we are dedicated men. We need to have this case solved. Over the years, we have tried to obtain the aid of any law enforcement agency that would help us get the investigation started again and stick with the case until it is solved. So far, we haven't had much luck.

Mr. Anderson, we want you to know that we don't have any funds to spend on this investigation, our income is limited. However, we do know that if we were to give up on this case, it would never be solved. That would be a sad thing, not only for us, but especially for the two victims themselves, who were very young when their lives were taken away.

Mr. Anderson, if there is any way you could use your psychic powers to help us with this investigation, it sure would be appreciated. Thank you for taking the time to read this letter. Please know that we are sincere.

<u>June 4, 1993</u>

I still hadn't received a reply from Detective Roland Lamy, so I wrote a letter to Colonel Lynn Presby of the state police.

Dear Colonel Lynn Presby:

I am writing in reference to the Compagna-Psaradelis homicides of 1973 and your letter of February 25, 1993, which referred us to Captain Thomas Winn, commander of your investigative services.

Chief Robert Baker, retired, from the Candia Police Department and I have been working on this investigation for

*twenty years. Having been injured in a homicide investigation,
I have been retired since 1976. Although we are retired from
service, both Chief Baker and I are dedicated police officers.*

*In the past eighteen years we have tried to find some law
enforcement officer who would be interested enough to continue our investigation. Thus far, we have had negative results.*

*At the outset, Assistant Attorney General Robert Johnson
III was assigned to the case. Detective Lieutenant R. Wilson
was assigned as lead investigator along with officers from
various departments.*

*We realize that your office is extremely busy, however, time
is running out. Due to attrition and the age of the case, much
evidence may already be lost. Chief Baker and I feel that we
know this case better than anyone. If you are willing to assist
us, we are at your service.*

*In speaking with Sergeant Lamy in November 1992, he as-
sured us that he would look into the case and it would be
investigated. Nothing has happened.*

*Chief Baker and I are eager to solve this case and really
feel that we would be able to do so with your help. In the event
you are unable to assist us, we would appreciate your referring
us to someone other than the people we have already contacted.*

Since I was writing letters, I decided to write to Attorney General
Jeffery Howard to see if his office would help.

Dear Attorney General Jeffery Howard:

*I am writing in regard to the Compagna-Psaradelis homi-
cides of 1973. Having been injured during a homicide investigation in 1975, I am retired, as is Chief Robert Baker, on
whose behalf I am writing this letter.*

*Being dedicated police officers, Chief Baker and I have
been extensively involved in these homicides for twenty years.
Over the past eighteen years we have tried unsuccessfully to
interest some law enforcement agency in continuing this inves-*

tigation. As the years go by, the case becomes history and no one is interested.

At the outset in 1973 Assistant Attorney Robert Johmson III was assigned. New Hampshire State Police Detective Lieutenant R. Wilson was assigned as lead investigator.

About five months ago I wrote to Attorney John Davis of your office in reference to this case. In February of this year, Chief Baker and I came to your office and spoke with your head prosecutor, detailing our knowledge and interest in the case. He advised us that he would look into the matter and assign a man to investigate, explaining that we would hear from him shortly. However, to this date we have heard nothing.

I was informed on June 1, 1993, that your office had turned the case back to Sergeant Roland Lamy of the New Hampshire State Police. Chief Baker and I feel we are getting the run around, having spoken with Sergeant Lamy six months ago, to no avail.

I would like to make an appointment with your office soon. I feel strongly that Chief Baker and I would be able to explain our knowledge of these homicides and why we believe it is a solvable situation. Due to attrition, much evidence may already be lost. I am certain you realize that time is important.

Sir, I look forward to hearing from your office soon. Thank you for taking the time to read my letter.

June 6, 1993

Unsolved Mysteries
Burbank, CA
Dear Sir:

First of all, I want to thank you for sending me the address of psychic George Anderson who was on your program on April 23, 1993. I wrote to him on May 14, 1993, and I am sorry to say that I have not received a reply.

I am searching for information about what is needed to put together an "unsolved mystery" for your program. This case is twenty years old. It is very complicated. It has a little bit of everything in it-rape; homicide of two, fifteen-year-old girls; suicide of a young man; and a parent who has been missing for eighteen years. This case is truly a mystery.

The facts of this investigation cannot be told in just a few pages. As I said, it is very complicated. That is why I would appreciate your advising me what is needed.

I am a retired detective lieutenant from a police department in New Hampshire. I am working on the investigation with Robert Baker, a retired chief of police. The investigation involves a double homicide that took place in 1973 and it could lead to a third homicide.

Since about 1977 Chief Baker and I have been trying to find some law enforcement agency or investigator who would continue with this investigation and bring this case to a conclusion. So far, we have had negative results.

This is a solvable case. Our income is very limited and we realize that if we don't solve the case now, it will never be solved. Time is running out. Maybe Unsolved Mysteries is part of the answer to these crimes.

I would appreciate your advising me about what you need to create this story for your program.

I want to thank you for taking the time to read this letter. I hope to have a reply from you in the near future.

27

June 21, 1993

I received a phone call from Assistant Attorney General Michael Ramsdell.

"Lieutenant Horak, the attorney general gave me your letter to read. I want you to know that I'll help you and Chief Baker with investigation of the Compagna-Psaradelis homicides."

"Do you really mean that, Attorney Ramsdell?"

"Yes, I do. I'll be in touch with you soon."

July 6, 1993

Since I hadn't heard from Attorney Ramsdell, I called to see how things were going. Attorney Ramsdell apologized for not being in touch. He had been very busy working on two homicides. He promised to call in a couple of days to set up an appointment to talk about the case.

July 13, 1993

Attorney Ramsdell hadn't called to set up an appointment to talk with me, so I called him.

"Attorney Ramsdell, this is Lieutenant Horak. Do you have any good news for me?"

"Well, Lieutenant, I've been in touch with Detective Sergeant Roland Lamy. We looked over the Compagna-Psaradelis case and we both agree that you, Chief Baker, and the other investigators did a super job with the case. You covered the case thoroughly and didn't leave a stone unturned. Sergeant Lamy and I agree that there are no suspects or leads in the case."

"Hold on right there, Attorney Ramsdell. You aren't going to do that to us. The state police and the attorney general's office haven't done anything on this case in the past eighteen years. How can you know the facts of the case if you haven't worked on it in all that time?"

"Wait a minute, Lieutenant. I told you I wanted to talk with you and Chief Baker about the case. I can see you on July 15 at 1:30 p.m. Is that date good for you?"

"Yes, Attorney Ramsdell. We'll be there."

July 15, 1993

Chief Baker and I rode together to the State House for meeting with Attorney Ramsdell. We made sure to take the confidential report we sent to the state police in August 1992, although we couldn't divulge the name of the person who gave us the information because they were afraid of being harmed or having their property damaged. We promised that their name would not be revealed and we couldn't break that promise.

When we arrived at Attorney Ramsdell's office, he wasted little time and got right down to business.

"As you can see, I have the books on the Compagna-Psaradelis murders right here. I have one set from the Merrimack Police Department and the another set from the state police. I want you to know that I've read the entire case and I agree with the state police. The case has been investigated and there are no suspects or leads in the case that I can see. What do you expect from me?"

"Well, Attorney Ramsdell, I can't speak for Chief Baker, but as far as I'm concerned, I want you people to help us place or eliminate possible suspects we have in the case."

"Lieutenant Horak, let me ask you a question."

"Go ahead, Attorney Ramsdell, ask your question."

"Lieutenant, if you've had suspects in this case for all these years, why did you wait until now to go after them? Why didn't you and others go after these suspects years ago?"

"Attorney Ramsdell, did you read the case books?"

"Lieutenant, I've already told you and Chief Baker that I just finished reading the entire case."

"Well, Attorney Ramsdell, if you've read the case, how can you ask a question like that? I want you to pick up any one of those books and flip through the pages. Pay attention to the investigators' names listed in the upper-right corner of each page."

"What is that supposed to prove, Lieutenant Horak?"

"Well, Attorney Ramsdell, it should tell you a lot. For one thing, after the first few months of investigating the Compagna-Psaradelis murders, most of the people working on the case faded away, leaving just Chief Baker and me. Even when the whole investigative unit was together, there were suspects.

"Take Tom Jefferson as an example. I wanted to charge him with the statutory rape of Diane Compagna that took place on July 4, 1973. I was the only one who kept pushing that. Everyone from the district court, the county attorney, and right up to the attorney general's office said it couldn't be done. It took three years and a new attorney general to charge and convict Tom Jefferson.

"Now, let's talk about suspects. The chief and I think the person who murdered Diane Compagna and Anne Psaradelis knew the girls. If you'll read the case or let Chief Baker and I go over the details with you, you'll understand who the suspects are and why we consider them suspects.

"Attorney Ramsdell, have you looked over the photographs of the crime scene?"

"Yes, I have."

"Well, Attorney Ramsdell, look at the photograph of the victim who was found nude in the pine grove setting. Pay attention to the poor girl's body. She was lying on a pair of jeans so the pine needles wouldn't hurt her. Look at where her other clothes are. They weren't ripped or thrown around the area. They're a short distance from her right hand.

"Now, Attorney Ramsdell, look at the girl's body itself. Doesn't it appear that she's just lying on the ground? There's no sign of a struggle. If she was being raped and in fear, her body would most likely show she was fighting her attacker, but it doesn't.

"Put these things together and it tells you that the girl knew her killers.

"Now, Attorney Ramsdell, look at the photograph of the second girl, that tells another story."

"What does it tell you, Lieutenant Horak?"

"Well, Attorney Ramsdell, the photograph of the second girls shows that she was running for her life. That tells us there had to be more than one killer at the scene."

"Why do you say that, Lieutenant?"

"Come on, Attorney Ramsdell, how could one person control two girls? There was no sign of anyone being tied up or beaten. You have one girl with all her clothes off and the other one with her clothes on. You have two different crime scene settings. Chief Baker and I still believe the killers were known to their victims.

"Now, I'll try to answer your question about why we didn't solve this crime years ago. For one thing, I was injured during another homicide investigation in October 1975. After a few months I came back to work and worked four hours a day for nearly a year when Chief Pelletier forced me to retire in November 1976.

"No one has worked on the Compagna-Psaradelis murder case since 1976, except Chief Baker and me. We've tried all these years to find some law enforcement agency interested enough to bring this case to a conclusion. Oh, there have been lots of people who said they would look into the case, but that never happened.

"Attorney Ramsdell, take the Merrimack Police Department as an example. I'll bet I've talked with just about everyone on the department about the Compagna-Psaradelis case. I asked for their help and even told them the names of people to re-interview who could help with the case. A lot of them said they would help, but they never did. Others said they wouldn't dare get involved because of problems they might have within the department.

"Attorney Ramsdell, if the truth was known, all the books that contain the Compagna-Psaradelis investigation were thrown in the bottom of a closet and they stayed there for years.

"Attorney Ramsdell, Chief Baker and I have stayed with this case for the past twenty years. We've done everything possible to find some person interested enough to finish this case. It can be solved. It just needs someone in law enforcement who isn't afraid of hard work to do it. God knows, we've tried to find that person. We're not giving up until this case is solved.

"Attorney Ramsdell, now, I hope you understand why this case hasn't been solved all these years. Do you think Chief Baker and I didn't have anything else to do all these years?

"While we're talking, Attorney Ramsdell, can we have a copy of the third book of the investigation from the Merrimack Police Department? That book is more complete than the books at the state police."

"Yes, Lieutenant, I'll give you a copy of the book, but I can't give you photographs or financial records."

"That will be fine. Thank you.

"Attorney Ramsdell, I'll send you some of the reports that we've made regarding the investigation. We've tried to be fair and let you and the state police know what we've done regarding the case. We hope that you and the state police will help us bring this case to a conclusion."

"Lieutenant, I'll be in touch with the state police. We'll contact you and Chief Baker if and when we need anything."

Chief Baker and I stopped for coffee and a sandwich on our drive back to Candia. While we were eating, we discussed our meeting with Attorney Ramsdell.

"To tell you the truth, Chief, I thought Attorney Ramsdell was going to slam the book cover shut on the case when we walked in the door. I'm sure he's going to back up the state police. I doubt if any of them will listen to two retired police officers. I hate to say this, Chief, but our struggle with this investigation is far from over."

"I feel the same way, Lieutenant. I'm sure they look at the two of us and say, 'I'm not going to listen to those two guys. They aren't law enforcement officers.' Really, what difference does it make who works on the case as long as the case gets solved? They can take all the credit for solving the case, I don't care about that."

"Chief Baker, what did you think when Attorney Ramsdell said that Jim Psaradelis has stayed in touch with his wife all these years and that the state police and attorney general's office have also stayed in touch with her?"

"I don't believe that any more than you do, Lieutenant Horak."

"To tell you the truth, Chief Baker, I spoke with Mrs. Psaradelis a few months ago. She didn't mention anything about any law enforcement agency keeping in touch with her. I'll make a point of stopping by and talking with Mrs. Psaradelis soon. I'll ask her if the state police or attorney general's office has contacted her."

July 31, 1993

I was in Mrs. Psaradelis' neighborhood, so I stopped by to talk with her.

"Hello, Mrs. Psaradelis, it's been a while since I've talked with you. Would you mind if I asked you a couple of questions?"

"Lieutenant Horak, have you located my husband?"

"No, Mrs. Psaradelis, we haven't located him at this time, but when I do, I'll advise you. Speaking about your husband, Mrs. Psaradelis, I heard a rumor that Jim has been in contact with you all these years. Is that true?"

"No, Lieutenant, that's not true. I have had no contact with my husband since he left. After all this time, I don't want to hear from him. I'm sure my children feel the same way."

"Mrs. Psaradelis, has anyone from the state police or attorney general's office been in contact with you regarding your husband?"

"No, Lieutenant, I haven't spoken to anyone from the state police or attorney general's office in years. I can't say if any of my children have talked to them, but I don't think they have."

"Mrs. Psaradelis, there's nothing new regarding the girls, but we're still working on the investigation. If anything turns up, I'll notify you."

28

I still hadn't received a reply to the letter I wrote George Anderson, but I did receive a letter from *Unsolved Mysteries.* The message was short and to the point.

> *Dear Mr. Horak:*
>
> *Received your letter, but have been unable to reach you by telephone. Please call me at (800) 555-5555, extension 206, so we can discuss your case further. I need information to help us decide if we can move ahead.*

When I called Mr. Johnson that afternoon, he asked for a brief capsulated version of the investigation. I sent the material to him right away.

August 9, 1993

I wrote another letter to the attorney general, hoping he could move things along a little faster.

> *Dear Attorney General Jeffery Howard:*
>
> *The Compagna-Psaradelis homicide case is now twenty years old. It could have been solved long before this. For some unknown reason, the various law enforcement agencies haven't done a thing on this case in the past eighteen years. Robert Baker and I are both retired police officers. We've been trying*

to find someone interested enough to help us with this case, but most people look at the case as being twenty years old and don't seem to care.

Over the years we have contacted various investigators from the Merrimack Police Department and other agencies, asking for their help in solving the two murders. None of them have taken any action.

Chief Joseph Devine of the Merrimack Police Department was contacted as recently as November 1992 regarding the homicides of Diane Compagna and Anne Psaradelis. His response was, "That's not my problem."

We contacted the New Hampshire State Police by mail and in person as recently as November 1992. Sergeant Roland Lamy stated that he would look at the case and get back to us.

They all tell us one thing, but never respond with help toward the investigation.

We've sent three letters to your office regarding this case. When we spoke with your head investigator, he advised that he would pull the case, read it over and get back to us. This never happened.

In July 1993, we spoke with Assistant Attorney General Michael Ramsdell, both by telephone and in person, regarding this case. He gave us some encouragement that your office might help us. In Attorney Ramsdell's letter of July 28, 1993, he advised that he gave the state police copies of the list and materials we gave him. He stated that he would let us know if and when anything further develops.

Sir, this is a complicated case. Someone reading the case thoroughly couldn't even begin to tell the direction in which the investigation should go. Robert Baker and I know this case better than anyone. The person assigned to investigate this case really needs to talk the case over with us. Letting us know if and when anything further develops won't help anyone.

It sounds like we are receiving another stall tactic and that no one really wants to investigate. I can't believe that a double

*homicide that happened twenty years ago isn't just as impor-
tant as one that took place today.*

*Even though we are retired, we are dedicated men. We will
stick with the case until it is solved. We have spent all kinds of
time and money over the years and offered our help to anyone
who would take the time and effort to solve the case.*

*If you would give us an appointment with you, I am sure we
could relate the need to have this case investigated properly.
We realize that you are busy and that your investigative unit is
overloaded with cases. If you cannot afford to assign an investigator, I wonder if you would consider appointing Chief Baker
and me to investigate this case and bring it to a conclusion?*

*The entire case should be reviewed before the prime sus-
pect or anyone else is contacted. We would also appreciate being able to view the film of the crime scene that was taken in
1973 by the New Hampshire State Police.*

*I want to thank you for taking the time to read this letter.
We hope you understand our need to solve this crime and give
us an early reply.*

<u>August 10, 1993</u>

I decided to visit Mrs. Compagna to let her know how the case was
going.

"Hello, Lieutenant Horak. We were just talking about you a couple
of days ago."

"Oh, what did I do now, Mrs. Compagna?"

"My husband and I have been talking about the police reopening
the investigation. We feel the case shouldn't be investigated any further. All it would do is bring up old memories and we don't care for
that."

"I'll tell you something, Mrs. Compagna, Chief Baker and I have
been investigating this case and trying to solve it for the past twenty
years. We can't give up until it's solved. Have you heard anything that
might help in solving the case?"

"No, but I've heard that Mrs. Psaradelis has been in touch with her
husband over the years."

"That isn't true, Mrs. Compagna. I've already checked out that rumor."

"I wish you luck in solving the case, but tell me something, Lieutenant Horak, why, after twenty years, do the police want to solve this case. If the case can be solved now, why didn't they solve it years ago?"

"Mrs. Compagna, I don't understand why you would ask such a question. I think you know better than anyone else how much time and effort Chief Baker and I have put into trying to solve this crime. I think that no matter how anyone feels, solving the murders of Diane and Anne comes before everything else.

"Mrs. Compagna, as far as the crime not being solved years ago, I think you should ask the law enforcement investigators from the Merrimack Police Department and the state police that question. There have always been suspects in the case and they should have placed them or eliminated them as suspects. Chief Baker and I have been trying to do that for the past twenty years. We won't give up until that's accomplished."

<u>August 11, 1993</u>

It was time to write a letter to Assistant Attorney General Michael Ramsdell.

Dear Attorney Ramsdell:

Thank you for returning the list and materials I requested. I am listing below things that Chief Baker and I have done regarding the Compagna-Psaradelis murder case.

1. August 5, 1993 - Sent a second letter to Unsolved Mysteries

2. August 5, 1993 - Sent a second letter to George Anderson (psychic)

3. August 6, 1993 - Received a letter from Unsolved Mysteries.

4. August 3, 1993 - Spoke with Ann Psaradelis at her home

5. August 8, 1993 - Spoke with Dorothy Compagna at her home
6. August 10, 1993 - Sent a letter to chief of police in Alliston, Massachusetts

Chief Baker and I wonder what the state police and attorney general's office are going to do. We thought that someone would contact us so that we could sit down and talk over the case. Just reading the case isn't going to tell the investigator which direction to go. As I have said before, no one knows this case better than we do. Other than Chief Baker and me, no law enforcement agency has done any work on this case in the past eighteen years.

We feel that we are sending you information and trying to keep you abreast of what we are doing. It would be nice if you treated us the same way in return.

Somehow, we are going to do everything possible to bring this case to a conclusion. Of course, that means to solve it by whatever means required.

<u>August 18, 1993</u>

I received a letter from Attorney Ramsdell. He wasn't happy. The attorney general gave him my letter dated August 9 and asked Ramsdell to reply to my concerns. In his response Attorney Ramsdell advised that Chief Baker and I could not be appointed to investigate the Compagna-Psaradelis case. He seemed pretty upset that I used the term "stall tactics" in the letter. He replied that no one was trying to stall anything.

When we first contacted Attorney Ramsdell, we thought we would get some help, but we're not sure anymore. Chief Baker and I felt like thorns in everyone's side, but if someone would just help us place or eliminate the suspects and help us solve the case, we would disappear.

<u>September 1, 1993</u>

It was time to write a few more letters.

Dear Attorney Michael Ramsdell:

JOSEPH A. HORAK

Thank you for your letter of August 18, 1993, and the paperwork we requested.

Enclosed you will find some paperwork and some photographs that should be added to the case.

As you can see, we have been attempting to have this case put on the Unsolved Mysteries program. There have to be people out there who have information on the case. This might help bring them out of the woodwork.

This is the month that the girls were found twenty years ago in a wooded area in Candia, New Hampshire. It would probably be good to hit the news media with some kind of story. It might bring forward some information that would shed light on the case. It really can be solved.

It would be helpful if we knew what was going on regarding the state police investigation. We still feel that our talking to the investigator would be beneficial to his investigation.

Unsolved Mysteries
Burbank, CA
Dear Mr. Johnson:

I am writing in reference to my letter of August 8, 1993, and the Compagna-Psaradelis homicides of 1973.

I have enclosed a brief capsulated version of the investigation. I hope it sparks your interest enough to help us.

This case can be solved with the help of Unsolved Mysteries. Some people out there have knowledge about the case and for some reason have been reluctant to come forward all these years.

If you need any special information, please contact me. We hope we can move this project along.

29

JUSTICE DENIED

September 15, 1993

I drove to Candia to spend some time with Chief Baker.

"Good morning, Chief Baker, I'm here to take you away from your little country store. Is there anyone who can cover for you today?"

"My son can take care of the store. What's up, Lieutenant?"

"Well, Chief, on September 29 it will be twenty years since the girls were found murdered. We have to spark public interest in the story to help us solve the murders. I think we should go to Dover and speak with someone from *Foster's Daily Democrat*. Maybe they'll do a story on the Compagna-Psaradelis murders. Then, I think we should head down to Manchester to see if someone from the Union Leader will write a story. It sure would help."

"That's a good idea. I know someone at the Union Leader. I think he'll help us."

We had good luck at *Foster's Daily Democrat*. Their staff reporter interviewed Chief Baker and me, and we gave her some photographs for the story. They planned to run the article as close to September 29 as possible, to point out that the bodies were discovered twenty years ago on that date.

Chief Baker's friend at the *Union Leader* was in a meeting when we arrived in Manchester. Since the chief had to get back to his store, I volunteered to call the paper later to make an appointment. I called the paper several times before I was able to actually talk with someone. Finally, on September 22 I spoke with the city editor. He invited Chief Baker and me to come to his office to talk about the case.

"Come in, gentlemen, and tell me what I can do for you."

"Sir, here's some paperwork that you can look over. Please feel free to ask any questions."

"Chief Baker, do you know why you're here? It's because of Lieutenant Horak. He was very sincere and dedicated to solving these murders. I could tell that from his voice. I'm going to assign a staff re-porter to the story. We'll contact you with the details."

Later that afternoon the reporter called and asked for more infor-mation on the Compagna-Psaradelis investigation. She also asked the chief and me to meet her and a photographer at 9:00 a.m. the next day at New Boston Road to take pictures of the crime scene.

September 23, 1993

I stopped by Chief Baker's country store early in the morning.

"Chief Baker, I hope you don't mind my coming over so early. I thought we could go to the crime scene and make sure everything is OK, so we can take the reporter and photographer into the woods without any problems. I told the reporter to wear boots and old clothes."

Chief Baker and I drove to New Boston Road and prepared for the reporter and photographer's arrival. They got there on schedule at 9:00 a.m. It didn't take long to take the pictures and gather the information they needed for the story.

"I guess we have everything we need, Lieutenant Horak. We want to thank you for taking the time to come out here to show us the crime scene and answer our questions. We'll do our best to put the story in the paper as close to September 29 as possible."

The Union Leader

"THERE IS NOTHING SO POWERFUL AS TRUTH" — DANIEL WEBSTER

MANCHESTER, N.H. — MONDAY, SEPTEMBER 27, 1993   ©1993, UNION LEADER CORP.   45¢ - NEWSSTAND

1973 Murder Mystery

STILL TRACKING the killer of two 15-year-old girls from Merrimack are retired Merrimack Detective-Lieutenant Joseph Horak, left, and retired Candia Police Chief Robert Baker, in the woods where the bodies were found 20 years ago, on Sept. 28, 1973.
George Naum/Union Leader

Retired Detectives Still Hunting Killer Of Merrimack Girls

By NANCY MEERSMAN
Union Leader Staff

CANDIA — What started as a day at the beach turned into a double murder. Twenty years later, two police officers still work in hopes of finding a killer and solving the crime.

Diane Compagna and Anne Psaradelis, two 15-year-olds from Merrimack, both had told their mothers they planned to sleep over at the other's house. Instead, they gathered towels, bathing suits and beach bags and hitchhiked to Hampton Beach.

It was a misadventure that couldn't have gone more wrong.

The next day at the beach, Diane and Anne said acquaintances they had spent the night on the floor in someone's cottage where a male, his sister and a young child were staying. Around 4:30 that afternoon they were seen near the Hampton Beach Casino. That was the last anyone saw them alive.

About 16 weeks later, on Sept. 28, 1973, a hunter found two bodies in a pine forest off New Boston Road in Candia. The next day, the decomposed corpses were identified as the missing Merrimack girls.

MURDER MYSTERY, Page 6

MURDER MYSTERY
(Continued From Page One)

The crime inexplicably received little media attention at the time. Twenty years later, few people remember much, if anything, about the hideous double murder — except for two long-retired former police officers who are determined their questions will be answered someday.

Robert Baker, who retired as Candia police chief in 1981, and Joseph Horak, a detective lieutenant with the Merrimack Police Department who retired with a disabling injury in 1978, did not stop agonizing over the mystery when they turned in their badges.

They think the case is still solvable and that eventually they will know how the girls died and who killed them.

"I can't let go of it," said Horak, 64, who keeps in touch with the families and visits the girls' graves every year on the anniversary of the day they were found.

"I think about the case every day. I really feel the person who did this is local and the girls knew the person," Horak said. "This is a person who has taken two lives. You don't know if the person could take more, or has taken more."

"It happened during my watch," said Baker, 59. "I'd like to know if it's somebody in town."

Baker and Horak believe the two girls were killed where they were found because it was too far from the road to drag a body or bodies. They think the killer was someone who gave Anne and Diane a ride home from the beach, perhaps someone they knew.

They theorize at least one of the victims went willingly into the woods.

One body was found nude on a bed of pine needles, her blue jeans folded under her back. The rest of her clothing was found neatly folded nearby.

The other body was sprawled several feet away near a stone wall. Baker and Horak said it looked as if she was running away and someone grabbed her from behind, causing the ties on her halter to come undone.

They think one was killed first. The other victim might have come to see why her friend didn't come out of the woods and stumbled upon a violent scene. Possibly the killer went to the car to get the second victim so there would be no witnesses. The investigators say it is also possible two men were involved.

The cause of death isn't known. Baker said he had the remains "X-rayed from stem to stern" at a hospital, but no injuries to bones were detected. The victims might have been strangled, or stabbed and bled to death, he said.

Other events occurred that may have been related to the double homicide. Several months after the bodies were found, a young man who knew the girls committed suicide. Two years later, a close relative of one of the victims disappeared.

The former police officers believe there are people who have information about what happened. Perhaps the witnesses were teenagers at the time and were afraid to come forward, but now as adults they would feel differently. More than 500 people were interviewed 20 years ago, including all of the victims' schoolmates.

When the case was fresh a woman would call up to say she knew who did it but was afraid of being harmed. They wonder where she is now.

The retired officers want people who might know something to contact them by writing, either Horak at 25 Long Pond Road, Dunbarton 03054; or Baker at P.O. Box 161, Candia 03034.

Compagna's mother, Dorothy Compagna, said Thursday the death of her daughter is too painful to talk about. "It's just opening a wound," she said. The Union Leader was unable to contact Psaradelis' parents.

Assistant Attorney General Michael Ramsdell said he has personally reviewed the case and State Police are now reviewing it.

Investigators could retrace all the old leads, but it appears they have been exhausted because the work done by Baker, Horak and others was so thorough, he said.

ANNA PSARADELIS

"Frankly, it's a case that doesn't have many viable leads. That's a tribute to them because of the work they did early on in the case," said Ramsdell.

He said State Police will be following up on a new information that came to authorities from an individual who was in jail.

Anything Baker and Horak could turn up would be welcome, said Ramsdell. "Obviously, anything that can be done to generate any interest in a case can only prove to be positive," he said. "Anything they can do that might turn into a tangible lead, we're thankful for."

DIANE COMPAGNA

Figure 23: 1993 Newspaper article

241

JOSEPH A. HORAK

<u>September 27, 1993</u>

The *Union Leader* ran our story on the front page. The headline read: <u>1973 Murder Mystery - Retired Detectives Still Hunting Killer of Merrimack Girls.</u>

This is what the reporter wrote:

Candia - What started as a day at the beach turned into a double murder. Twenty years later, two police officers still work in hope of finding a killer and solving the crime.

Diane Compagna and Anne Psaradelis, two fifteen-year-olds from Merrimack, both had told their mothers they planned to sleep over at the other's house. Instead, they gathered towels, bathing suits, and beach bags, and hitchhiked to Hampton Beach.

It was a misadventure that couldn't have gone more wrong.

The next day at the beach, Diane and Anne told acquaintances they had spent the night on the floor in someone's cottage where a male, his sister and a young child were staying. Around 4:30 p.m. that afternoon they were seen near the Hampton Beach Casino. That was the last time anyone saw them alive.

About ten weeks later, on September 29, 1973, a hunter found two bodies in a pine forest off New Boston Road in Candia. The next day, the decomposed corpses were identified as the missing Merrimack girls.

The crime inexplicably received little media attention at the time. Twenty years later, few people remember much, if anything, about the hideous double murder - except for two long-retired former police officers. They think the case is still solvable and that eventually they will know how the girls died and who killed them.

"I can't let go of it," said Horak, sixty-four, who keeps in touch with the families and visits the girls' graves every year on the anniversary of the day they were found.

Figure 24: 1993 Newspaper article on murders

JOSEPH A. HORAK

"I think about the case every day. I really feel the person who did this is local and the girls knew the person," Horak said. "This is a person who has taken two lives. You don't know if the person could take more, or has taken more."

"It happened on my watch," said Baker, fifty-nine. "I'd like to know if it's somebody in town."

Baker and Horak believe the two girls were killed where they were found because it was too far from the road to drag a body or bodies. They think the killer was someone who gave Diane and Anne a ride home from the beach, perhaps someone they knew.

They theorize at least one of the victims went into the woods willingly.

One body was found nude on a bed of pine needles, her blue jeans folded under her back. The rest of her clothing was found neatly folded near by.

The other body was sprawled several hundred feet away near a stone wall. Baker and Horak said it looked as if she was running away and someone grabbed her from behind, causing the ties on her halter to come undone.

They think one was killed first. The other victim might have come to see why her friend didn't come out of the woods and stumbled upon a violent scene. Possibly the killer went to the car to get the second victim so there would be no witnesses. The investigators say it is possible that two men were involved.

The cause of death isn't known. Baker said he had the remains "X-rayed from stem to stern" at a hospital, but no injuries to bones were detected. The victims might have been strangled or stabbed and bled to death, he said.

Other events occurred that may have been related to the double homicide. Several months after the bodies were found, a young man who knew the girls committed suicide. Two years later, a close relative of one of the victims disappeared.

The former police officers believe there are people who have information about what happened. Perhaps the witnesses were teenagers at the time and were afraid to come forward, but now as adults they would feel differently.

JUSTICE DENIED

More than five hundred people were interviewed twenty years ago, including all of the victims' school mates.

When the case was fresh a woman would call up to say she knew who did it but was afraid of being harmed. They wonder where she is now.

The retired officers want people who might know something to contact them.

Compagna's mother, Dorothy Compagna, said Thursday the death of her daughter is too painful to talk about. "It's just opening a wound," she said.

The Union Leader was unable to contact Psaradelis' parents.

Assistant Attorney General Michael Ramsdell said he has personally reviewed the case and the state police are now reviewing it.

Investigators could retrace all the old leads, but it appears they have been exhausted because the work done by Baker, Horak and others was so thorough, he said.

"Frankly, it's a case that doesn't have many viable leads. That's a tribute to them because of the work they did early on in the case," said Ramsdell.

He said state police will be following up on new information that came to authorities from an individual who was in jail.

"Anything Baker and Horak could turn up would be welcome," said Ramsdell. "Obviously, anything that can be done to generate any interest in a case can only prove positive," he said. "Anything they can do that might turn into a tangible lead we're thankful for."

Foster's Daily Democrat also ran our story, however, there was a part of the article we didn't think was true. Chief Baker and I found this excerpt from the story objectionable.

State police and the attorney general's office have been investigating the murders, but the trail has run cold, said Mike Ramsdell, a senior assistant attorney general.

He said state police and his office have sifted through thousands of pages of information and interviews, and discovered a small lead in the case which they will pursue.

"There are some things that can be done, but I don't want to sound too optimistic about this, either," said Ramsdell.

He said his office and state police have many unsolved cases they are continuing to investigate. Police work hard to solve these cases, especially one such as the Compagna-Psaradelis murder, but police have their hands full investigating recent crimes, said Ramsdell.

"They've been given an amazing amount of time, if you ask me, for a case that's twenty years old," Ramsdell said.

He said police investigated the alleged rape, but they never gathered sufficient information to charge anyone with rape. A check on a national criminal information network showed the man accused of rape was never arrested or charged with the crime.

In addition, the missing father and the suicide of the girls' friend are dead ends to the investigators, he said.

State Police Sergeant Roland Lamy has been reviewing the case. It is collected in three volumes of interviews from several police agencies, and must be reviewed line by line to get a cohesive picture, he said.

Lamy said the information provided by Horak and Baker has "brought up some good points," which have been considered in his review.

Ramsdell said police will need a big lead in order to crack the case, and despite a lot of fine police work, that big lead has not materialized.

Baker and Horak said they appreciate all the work state police and the attorney general's office have done, they want anyone with information about the case to contact police or themselves as soon as possible.

That was some piece they added to our story on Diane Compagna and Anne Psaradelis. The remarks Assistant Attorney General Ramsdell and Sergeant Roland Lamy made in the story made us look like we didn't know what we were talking about. What were they trying to do, make us look bad? They weren't telling the truth. How could they honestly say they had been working on the Compagna-Psaradelis homicide for the past twenty years?

JUSTICE DENIED

How could the state police and attorney general's office say that there wasn't sufficient information gathered to charge anyone with rape. If no one was ever charged or arrested on a charge of rape, how would his name ever end up on the National Criminal Information Network? Why would the network show that the man was never charged or arrested for rape? It didn't make sense.

We also objected to the section in the article where Attorney Ramsdell stated that the missing father and the suicide of the girls' friend are dead ends to investigators. How in the world could either of them have said such a thing? Both Chief Baker and I knew the missing father and the suicide of the girls' friend were not dead ends to investigators.

The August 1992 confidential report and other reports we sent to the state police were proof that the suicide should be investigated further.

As far as the missing father was concerned, Chief Baker and I were pretty sure we located Jim Psaradelis in May 1993. We advised both the state police and attorney general's office and even gave them the address where he was supposed to be living.

One thing the article did say that was true is that they hoped a witness's conscience had been nagging him or her enough for the past twenty years that they would help. Chief Baker and I wondered if we would receive phone calls or letters regarding the story on our girls. We hoped the articles would turn up some leads.

30

September 28, 1993

I received a letter from Chief John Pelletier. I thought it was strange because I hadn't heard from him since he forced me out of the police department.

Dear Joe:

Good picture and a good story in today's Union Leader. Glad to see you looking so good.

Whereas you are still interested in the murders, I want to tell you that about two years ago I read a story about a murder in Cape Cod that happened around the same time our two girls were found. A dead girl was found on the Cape. Her clothing had been folded very neatly and was lying next to her.

I called the Merrimack Police Department and left word for Miller about this, but he didn't call back.

Also, as you may remember, one father came in every day checking to see if we had found the girls. The same man was checked out because he was parked in Nashua near a foot bridge the school children used. They found a box of porno books in his trunk.

Good luck.

September 28, 1993

I was vacationing at Pawley's Island in South Carolina. A few hours after I arrived, I received a phone call.

"Hello, Lieutenant Horak, this is Nancy from the *Union Leader*. I'm sorry to bother you, but I'm calling in regard to the Compagna-Psaradelis story we just did for you. We've been contacted by the people from *A Current Affair* and they want to do a story on your investigation. They requested that you call them."

"Thanks, Nancy, I'll call right away."

I called *A Current Affair* and spoke with Santanna Luci. She seemed interested in doing a story about our investigation. During the next six days I received four phone calls and a Federal Express letter from *A Current Affair*. I sent all the information they requested. Now, all I could do was wait.

October 9, 1993

I received a phone call from Santanna Luci from *A Current Affair*. She wanted me to talk with the families of Diane Compagna and Anne Psaradelis, and some of the girls' school friends to get approval for *A Current Affair* to interview them on October 14. Chief Baker and I were scheduled for interviews at the crime scene on October 13 at 9:00 a.m.

I cut short my vacation in South Carolina and headed back to New Hampshire to line things up for *A Current Affair*.

October 10, 1993

I arrived in New Hampshire and immediately contacted Chief Baker. I needed his help in arranging the interviews for *A Current Affair*. The first person we spoke with was Mrs. Psaradelis.

"Mrs. Psaradelis, *A Current Affair* is doing a story on Diane and Anne. We hope it will help solve their murders. Would you consent to an interview with them?"

"Yes, Lieutenant, I'll allow them to interview me. The only thing is, I don't like the photograph you used in the newspaper story. I'll give you another one on Monday."

"Remember, Mrs. Psaradelis, people will be here at 9:00 a.m. on October 14 to interview you. If it would make you feel better, Chief Baker and I could be here with you."

"Would you mind being here, Lieutenant? I might be a little nervous."

"No, that will be fine. You can have one or two of your daughters here during the interview, if it would make you feel better."

Chief Baker and I stopped by the Compagna home, but no one was home. We couldn't afford to waste time, so we headed to Raymond to talk with Richard Felton who wrote us a letter about the Compagna-Psaradelis murders. We were doubtful about his being able to help us because he was only five years old when the girls were murdered. When we arrived at the Felton home, Richard's mother answered the door.

"Mrs. Felton, is your son Richard at home?"

"Yes, he is. Why do you want him?"

"Well, Mrs. Felton, this is Chief Robert Baker and I'm Lieutenant Horak. Your son sent each of us a letter stating that he had some information on the murders of Diane Compagna and Anne Psaradelis."

"Lieutenant, my son couldn't possibly know anything about those murders. Richard read the newspaper story and just wanted to be helpful in giving his own ideas about what he thought might have happened. I'll make sure this never happens again. I'm sorry he caused all this trouble."

Instead of going back to the Compagna home, the chief and I stopped at a shopping center and used a pay phone to call them. I waited in the car while Chief Baker placed the call. I couldn't hear the conversation, but I could tell by the look on his face that the chief wasn't happy.

"What happened, Chief? You look a little upset."

"Well, Lieutenant, Marcel Compagna answered the telephone and I told him who I was. I asked if he and his wife would consent to being interviewed by the people from *A Current Affair*. I told him they were doing a story on the murder of the girls and that it might help in solving the case. Mr. Compagna started swearing and yelling at me. He said that he wouldn't allow anyone to interview them and that they were going to sue both of us. I told Marcel Compagna that I didn't call to argue. He said, 'Don't you hang up.' I said, 'Have a nice day,' and hung up."

Although the Compagnas had refused to be interviewed, the other arrangements for *A Current Affair* went smoothly. Mrs. Psaradelis and several others agreed to be interviewed on October 14, and Chief Baker and I were prepared for our interview on October 13.

October 12, 1993

I received a phone call from Santanna Luci of *A Current Affair*.

"Lieutenant Horak, I'm sorry to have to tell you that the Compagna-Psaradelis story has been put on hold."

"You have to be kidding, Ms. Luci. We've worked hard to pull things together for you, I even came back from South Carolina to make sure we had everything you need to do the story. What happened?"

"Well, Lieutenant, the man who was going to do the story had to go out on another assignment, but we'll do your story when he comes back. I'll stay in touch."

That was a shocker. I couldn't believe they had postponed our story out of the blue. Something was wrong somewhere. Now I had to undo all the plans we had made. Mrs. Psaradelis was the first person I contacted.

"Lieutenant, I don't know if I should let you in the house or even talk to you."

"Mrs. Psaradelis, what in the world is wrong?"

"Well, Lieutenant, I received a telephone call from Dorothy and Marcel Compagna last night. My daughter Ellen and the rest of the family came to my house and talked about *A Current Affair*, Chief Baker, and you. They think you're a liar and that I would be making a big mistake to allow anyone to interview me regarding the deaths of the girls. They said it would hurt them, the grandchildren, and my husband."

"Mrs. Psaradelis, do you really think that I'm a liar and that Chief Baker and I have been trying to solve the murders because we haven't had anything better to do with our time and lives?"

"Well, Lieutenant, the Compagnas are probably right and my daughter Ellen agrees with them. Last night we all agreed that we won't help, aid, give or do anything that will help you and Chief Baker with the investigation of this case. We also agreed that the investigators can do what they want, but we won't give you any help."

"You know, Mrs. Psaradelis, we're only trying to solve this case that's now twenty years old. If it was my daughter who was murdered, I would be thankful there were still people out there trying to find the people who murdered her. This case can be solved, Mrs. Psaradelis. I've always believed that and still do. *A Current Affair* could have helped us. It might have brought out someone who has knowledge of the crime. I'm sorry you feel that you can't help us now. I think it was more than wrong for the Compagnas to pressure you and change your mind about helping us.

"Mrs. Psaradelis, I want you to know that I understand how you feel, but I have to tell you that solving the murder of your daughter and Diane has to come above everything else, so Chief Baker and I will do whatever it takes to solve the case. It would have been great to have had your cooperation, but I'll respect the way you feel. I won't bother you anymore."

"Lieutenant Horak, can I have Anne's yearbook that you borrowed the other day?"

"Yes, Mrs. Psaradelis, I'll bring it back tomorrow."

I rode over to talk with Chief Baker. Maybe, together, we could figure out what was going on and why everyone was shutting the door in our faces over the Compagna-Psaradelis murder investigation.

The chief and I talked for several hours, but didn't come up with any answers. It felt like the two of us were against the world, but somehow we had to continue until the case was solved. Although we probably wouldn't have any friends by the time we were done, we decided the best thing to do was to keep plugging away and solve the case ourselves.

October 17, 1993

I cut wood all day. After cleaning up, I was about to sit down to dinner when the phone rang.

"Hello, is this Lieutenant Horak?"

"Yes, it is."

"Well, this is Ellen Psaradelis. I'm a sister to Anne Psaradelis, the victim in your investigation. I would like to talk with you for a few minutes, so please don't hang up."

"What is it you want, Ellen?"

"My mother and sisters are very upset about your investigating Anne's homicide twenty years after her death. I think you and Chief Baker must have something to gain by doing this and I want to know what it is."

"I don't know what you're after, Ellen, but the investigation into the murders of your sister Anne and Diane Compagna has been going on since July 12, 1973, and the investigation will continue until the case is solved. I guess, to use your expression, if we have anything to gain, it would be the satisfaction of knowing that the killers were found and punished for the terrible crime they committed.

"You know, Ellen, you've had me on the phone for over an hour and asked me all kinds of questions. Now, I want to ask you a question. Are you recording our conversation? If you are, it's against the law, unless you tell the person they're being taped. So, you'd better not record anything that we've said."

"Lieutenant, I want you to know that I've heard from my father. I'm not going to say when he called, but I will tell you he left because of family problems and now he wants to come back to his family. I don't want to make any problems for my father and I don't want this mess dragged up again after all these years. I can understand why the investigation is going on, but my family is not going to help you in any way."

"Well, Ellen, we've talked for nearly two hours and I have to go. As I said before, I hope you haven't recorded this telephone call, because if you have, you'll have problems."

"Well, Lieutenant, you might receive a call from my two sisters, they'll probably call Chief Baker, too."

That was some phone call. The last time I spoke with Ellen Psaradelis was when she was a young girl. She probably didn't even remember talking with me about her sister Anne.

JOSEPH A. HORAK

31

October 18, 1993

I spent the day writing letters and getting caught up on my paper-work. One of the letters I wrote was to *A Current Affair*.

Dear Ms. Luci:

As you can well imagine, I was quite shocked and disap-pointed when you advised me that the Compagna-Psaradelis story was not going forward.

Chief Robert Baker, retired, and I were pleased that the Union Leader contacted us and advised that your agency was willing to do a story for television. That would have really helped move our investigation forward.

Robert Baker and I have spent a lot of time and effort find-ing the people you wanted to interview. We feel you have let us down.

We feel this is a good story for television, even though the parents of the girls might not want to be interviewed. This is a solvable case. There are still people who would grant you in-terviews regarding this investigation, including Chief Baker and myself.

The reason we accepted your interest in doing this story was that we felt it would truly aid us in bringing the person or persons responsible for this crime to justice. There are people out there who have information about the crime and they probably live all around the country after all these years.

As you know, we have been investigating this case for the past twenty years. It has been filled with discouragement and negative results from every law enforcement agency we have dealt with over the years. Since the case has received very little media attention, no one has come forward with information that would aid in solving this case.

If Chief Baker and I stop our investigation of the crime, it will never be solved. We hope you won't let this happen. We would appreciate your going forward with the story as you stated you would. We would also appreciate your telling us if anyone contacted you regarding not doing the story for television.

Thank you again for considering this double murder for your program. We hope you will continue with the story and help us solve this crime.

I decided to take Anne's yearbook back to Mrs. Psaradelis because Chief Baker and I didn't need any more problems.

"Hello, Mrs. Psaradelis, may I come in? I've brought back your daughter's yearbook and I want to thank you for letting me borrow it."

"My daughters would probably be mad if they knew I let you in, but come in anyway, Lieutenant. You know my daughters are upset about your investigating the death of their sister. They don't want me to talk with you, Chief Baker, or anyone else from the police about the case. Lieutenant, I don't want you to bring up my husband's name in regard to this case. I just want to forget him and so do my children. I would like you to keep me informed about what is going on with your investigation, but I'm not going to help you in any way."

"You know, Mrs. Psaradelis, it's a two-way street. If you expect Chief Baker and me to keep in touch with you and tell you what is going on, then you have to help us in any way you can. That's only fair.

"By the way, Mrs. Psaradelis, your daughter Ellen called me last night and kept me on the phone for at least two hours. She said that her two other sisters would also be calling to find out what is going on."

"Oh, by the way, Lieutenant, my daughters and a neighbor told me that you and Chief Baker have something about the girls coming on *Unsolved Mysteries* this Wednesday night."

"That isn't true, Mrs. Psaradelis."

"My daughters told me you're a liar and warned me not to believe you. They said that *TV Guide's* listing for *Unsolved Mysteries* this Wednesday is about your case."

"Mrs. Psaradelis, we don't have any such thing coming on television. Why would I lie to you? I've never lied to you. When I tell you that Chief Baker and I do not have anything coming on *Unsolved Mysteries* or any other crime program at this time, that is true. I'll tell you what I'll do. You and your daughters watch *Unsolved Mysteries* Wednesday night. If the story of Diane Compagna and Anne Psaradelis comes on, I'll give you enough money to take out a full-page ad on the front page of the *Union Leader* saying, 'Lieutenant Horak is a first-class liar.' If you find that you and your daughters are wrong, then you know you can trust me. Fair enough?"

"OK, I'll watch the program Wednesday night."

"Well, you'll see that I've always told you the truth, no matter what the others might say. Mrs. Psaradelis, I'm going to ask you to think about four questions. Don't answer them, just think about them to yourself. Perhaps the answers might help you understand why Chief Baker and I have to continue with this investigation.

"1. Why hasn't this case been solved? 2. Why isn't any law enforcement agency willing to help solve this crime? 3. Why hasn't anyone with knowledge of who committed this crime come forward?

4. Why are there still so many unanswered questions?

"I have to get going, Mrs. Psaradelis. If you reconsider and decide to help us, please contact me."

October 12, 1993

Chief Baker and I decided to talk with Captain Tom Winn of major crime unit again. When we arrived at state police headquarters, we

257

were informed that Captain Winn had retired and that Captain John Barthelmes was now in charge of the unit.

"Captain Barthelmes, this is Chief Robert Baker, retired, and I'm Detective Lieutenant Joseph Horak, retired. We would like to talk with you about the 1973 murders of Diane Compagna and Anne Psaradelis. About a year ago we spoke with Captain Winn and Detective Sergeant Roland Lamy about the case. I spent at least four hours detailing the Compagna-Psaradelis case to Sergeant Lamy. He told me that if he could find the case number, he would pull the file, read it, and get back to me in a week. I gave Sergeant Lamy the case number the same day we talked. Even though Chief Baker and I have made phone calls and written to him for over a year, we still haven't received a reply."

"I'll have to agree, Lieutenant Horak, a year is a long time to wait for an answer. I'm aware of this situation and I'll have to take part of the blame."

"Captain Barthelmes, there are a couple of other things that we are disturbed about. I'm sure you know that we had a story run in the *Union Leader* on September 27, 1993, regarding the Compagna-Psaradelis murders. Two things bothered us. How can the state police and attorney general's office say they have been working on this investigation for the past twenty years when it isn't true? The second thing we want to talk about is how anyone can say that there was never anyone arrested or convicted of rape in this investigation."

"Well, Lieutenant, no one has been charged, arrested or convicted of rape in connection with the Compagna-Psaradelis case."

"That is not true, Captain Barthelmes. In fact, here's a copy of the superior court record showing the arrest, trial and conviction of Tom Jefferson for statutory rape."

"Well, Lieutenant, Sergeant Lamy will be going over the case and reporting his findings to me. Once that's done, and Assistant Attorney General Michael Ramsdell finishes the case he's trying, the five of us will sit down and discuss your case. Then we'll tell you what we will or won't do."

Chief Baker and I didn't think we were going to get very far with Captain Barthelmes, especially since he backed up Sergeant Lamy by taking the blame for his not getting back to us for over a year.

October 20, 1993

I watched the episode of *Unsolved Mysteries* that the Compagnas and Psaradelises were convinced was about their daughters. The story was about two girls who were murdered in New Hampshire, but it wasn't Diane and Anne's story. They were two different girls who were found murdered in two different places on different days. As soon as the program was over, my phone rang.

"Is this Lieutenant Horak?"

"Yes, it is. Who's calling?"

"What are you doing?"

"What do you mean, what am I doing?"

"You know. What are you doing? Come on, Joe, you know what you're doing."

Although the caller hadn't identified himself, I recognized his voice. It was Mike Compagna.

"Listen, Mike, I don't know what your problem is, but Chief Baker and I have been trying to solve the murders of your sister Diane and Anne Psaradelis for the past twenty years. We've always tried to keep in touch with your parents, as well as the Psaradelises. We've let them know everything that was going on with the investigation."

"Well, you're hurting everyone. We'll stop you, no matter what it takes."

"Mike, I'm not going to argue with you. I just want you to know that Chief Baker and I will continue to work on this case until it's solved. I'm going to hang up now. Good night."

The phone call was a threat if I ever heard one. I knew I would need to be careful in the future, because no one can predict what people will do. One of my friends even suggested that I start carrying a gun, if I wasn't already carrying one.

32

JOSEPH A. HORAK

October 26, 1993

Captain Barthelmes:
Please be advised that I am sending more paperwork regarding the Compagna-Psaradelis case. If possible, I would appreciate your having a copy made for Assistant Attorney General Michael Ramsdell so that he will have it for his records.

Again, I hope you will see your way clear to have this case investigated. I understand that Prime Time is going to air a story about the January 8, 1989, murder of a young man at the Peterborough Texaco Station in Peterborough, New Hampshire.

I have enclosed a confidential memo regarding a possible suspect in this case and my reasons for giving you this information. This might not mean anything, but it would be worth checking out.

November 10, 1993

Unsolved Mysteries
Dear Mr. Johnson:
I first started writing to you in June 1993 regarding the Compagna-Psaradelis homicides that took place twenty years ago, in 1973. I was requesting help from you and Unsolved Mysteries in the form of your doing a story on the murders of the two girls for your program. You sounded interested.

I have since written to you several times, sent the information you requested, and offered help in any way that Chief Baker and I could. We have been trying to obtain the aid of some law enforcement person who would help us with this in-vestigation. It seems like no one wants to get involved.

If, for some unknown reason, you have decided not to help us with this story, could you please advise us if some person or agency has requested that you not do the story for us?

I would appreciate your giving us some kind of reply.

November 10, 1993

A Current Affair
Dear Ms. Luci:

I wrote you a letter dated October 18, 1993, regarding your agency advising me that the Compagna-Psaradelis story was not going forward.

Chief Baker and I spent a lot of time trying to contact the people you requested so that you could put your story together, and you let us down. As you can well imagine, we are disap-pointed in your handling of this story. With your help, I am sure the case could have been solved.

I know that, for some unknown reason, the families of the murdered girls do not want to help us solve this crime.

I can understand if you truly didn't want to do this story, but I think it would make us feel a lot better if you would be honest with us and tell us why you didn't want to do the story. Did some person or agency request that you not to do the story?

While I was writing letters, I received a telephone call from Nancy of the *Union Leader*.

"Hello, Lieutenant Horak, I'm calling to find out if anything has developed regarding the story we did for you about Diane Compagna and Anne Psaradelis."

"Nancy, we received a few letters. I was told that the state police received a few letters too, but we were never told about their contents. Chief Baker and I are checking out the letters we received and we're still working on the investigation."

"Lieutenant, have you heard from the court?"

"Why do you ask that, Nancy?"

"Well, Lieutenant, I heard that both the Compagnas and Psaradelises were in court this morning to stop you and Chief Baker from investigating the murders any further."

"No, Nancy, I haven't heard anything like that from anyone. I doubt that Chief Baker has either. He would have called me."

"Lieutenant, if this should happen, please contact me and we can tell the rest of the story."

"OK, Nancy, I'll contact you if anything turns up. Thank you for calling."

November 10, 1993

Dear Chief Pelletier

I thought I would let you know what I found out about the girl who was murdered in Cape Cod. I just heard from a police department in that area and they advised me that the only homicide that took place in that time span was in 1965. The female victim was all cut up. They do not know of any crime where the victim's clothes were folded neatly near her body.

I don't know where this case is going, Chief. It's like we have the whole system against us. You would think we're the criminals.

As I told you before, I approached Chief Joseph Devine some time ago and asked for his help in the investigation of the girls' murders. His reply was, "That's not my problem." Since then, it has been brought to my attention that the deputy chief has instructed the officers not to help Chief Baker and me with the Compagna-Psaradelis murders.

Chief Baker and I have contacted A Current Affair and Unsolved Mysteries. We thought they were going to do the story for us, but all of a sudden they backed off and won't reply to any letters we send them.

I have even received a telephone call from the staff reporter of the Union Leader advising me that she heard that the parents of the victims were in court trying to stop us from investigating the case any further. So far, we haven't heard a thing from any court or attorney.

We aren't going to give up. Do you have any suggestions about what we should do now?

November 17, 1993

Days went by and I wasn't making any headway with the case. I decided to write another letter to Captain John Barthelmes.

Dear Captain John Barthelmes:

I am sending you more paperwork regarding the Compagna-Psaradelis murders.

I would like to know if it would be possible for Chief Baker and me to view the state police video tape of the crime scene, made in 1973. It sure would be appreciated.

We hope to hear from you soon about what will be done or won't be done by your office. No matter what, Captain, we have to stay with this case until it is solved.

November 20, 1993

I received another letter from Chief Pelletier, it was good of him to take the time to write. I was sure he wanted the case solved as much as Chief Baker and I did. I had always liked Chief Pelletier and enjoyed working for him. If it hadn't been for Lieutenant Bennett, I probably would have still been with the Merrimack Police Department.

Hi, Joe:

I am about to open the door to your problems. Why don't you and Chief Baker go to Concord and get private investigator licenses and start your own detective agency? With licenses you would be legal investigators, not just retired police officers. It would give you a lot more weight.

Call the agency anything you want and get letterhead printed. You should get better results when you try to get information.

JOSEPH A. HORAK

Have you contacted America's Most Wanted? The program started with missing children. Since your victims were children, the program might jump on the story.

Forget the parents and do your best to keep it between you and Chief Baker. If America's Most Wanted picks it up, don't tell anyone until the day the story airs.

Good luck, Joe. You're not one to give up, so gung ho.

I thought it was pretty nice of the chief to give me his advice. If I had continued with the police department while he was still there, I think we could have solved the case years ago. I think he realizes that too.

That same day I received a letter from my old friend, Sergeant Trask. I was glad to hear from him because I had been trying to contact him for a couple of weeks.

Dear Joe:

My wife said you called and couldn't get in touch with me.

I saw the article in the newspaper and was very impressed with it. It brought back memories of a very impressive investigation by you and not much by anybody else, including the state police.

It has bothered me that this investigation has gathered dust for so many years and that the only people doing anything are you and Chief Baker. Two young lives were snuffed out by someone who is still walking around in our midst. There's even a possibility that he might do it again, if he hasn't already.

Having reviewed the entire case a number of times with you, I believe, as I have always believed, that this case is solvable. It is too bad that those in authority don't feel as you do and reopen the investigation of a case that has never been closed, nor should it be.

However, Joe, I feel that there is nothing I can add to the case that you have put so much of your life into. I don't feel that all the other investigators combined have put as much into this case as you have. I have always felt that someone out there does not want this case solved because of something in your reports and you know what that is.

I will consent to be interviewed by A Current Affair if it will help. I do not think it will, because no one is willing to assist you in the law enforcement community and the families of the girls don't want old wounds to be opened, which I understand to a point.

There is someone out there who knows, like you and I do. They need to come forward and give the one bit of information that will solve the case. If I can help you in this regard, I will do what I can.

I think that you are up against a stone wall of people who don't want this case reopened or dusted off. Remember, if I can help, I will do whatever I can.

Keep in touch, Joe.

That was the most sincere letter anyone could ever receive from a friend. I was sure it wasn't just a lot of words.

November 22, 1993

"Hello, Lieutenant Horak, this is Sergeant Lamy. Captain John Barthelmes asked me to call and advise you that Lieutenant Wiggins will be involved in the case. I've been instructed to tell you that Assistant Attorney General Michael Ramsdell has a court case coming up. As soon as the case is finished, a meeting will be set up with Attorney Ramsdell, Captain Barthelmes, Lieutenant Wiggins, Chief Baker, you and myself. Once we talk the case over, we'll tell you and Chief Baker what the state police will or won't do regarding the investigation."

"You know, Sergeant Lamy, *A Current Affair* is doing a story on this case."

"I know that, Lieutenant. I've read about it in some of the reports you sent to headquarters."

November 24, 1993

I decided to write a short note to Captain John Barthelmes.

JOSEPH A. HORAK

Dear Captain John Barthelmes:

I am sure you have read the paperwork I have sent to you and that you are aware that the people from A Current Affair want to do a story on the girls. If you or anyone from your department would be interested in being involved with this story, please let me know. As soon as I know the date and time of the filming, I will let you know.

November 28, 1993

I decided to write one more letter to *Unsolved Mysteries*, bypassing Mr. Johnson since he refused to answer any of the letters I wrote to him.

Unsolved Mysteries
Burbank, California
Dear Sir:

I am writing this letter in regard to an unsolved double homicide that occurred twenty years ago.

I first started writing to you in June 1993. I was, then, and still am, requesting help from Unsolved Mysteries in the form of your doing a story on the Compagna and Psaradelis girls' homicides. When I first talked with people from your program, they sounded very interested in doing the story, now they don't even reply to my letters.

Sir, I am asking you to help us at this time because time is running out. If we don't solve it now, it will never be solved because any suspect, suspects, or people with knowledge will be dead or hard to find.

The families of the victims, for some unknown reason, do not want us to continue with the investigation, but I, for one, have to bring the person or persons who committed this crime to justice.

We really would appreciate your help and hope you will do the story.

JUSTICE DENIED

I couldn't believe how many letters we had written to different people over the years. Nearly everyone backed off helping us. There had to be some reason for this.

33

<u>December 9, 1993</u>

We still hadn't met with the investigators from the state police and attorney general's office, so I decided to write a note to Assistant Attorney General Michael Ramsdell to move him along.

Dear Attorney Ramsdell:

I received a telephone call from Detective Sergeant Roland Lamy sometime ago, regarding a meeting with you and all persons concerned with the Compagna-Psaradelis investigation.

We really don't seem to be making much headway. I realize that your department and the state police are busy, but the weeks and months seem to slip by and we are no farther ahead with the case than we were in August.

I, for one, want to place or eliminate our prime suspect and, somehow, bring this case to a conclusion.

I hope to receive a reply from you in the near future.

We had started dealing with "*A Current Affair*" on September 28, 1993, and we still didn't know if they were doing the story. They must have received pressure from someone not to do the story. I probably shouldn't have told the state police and others that "*A Current Affair*" was interested in the investigation. I decided to write a letter to the director of "*A Current Affair*."

JUSTICE DENIED

Dear Sir:

On September 28, 1993, I received a telephone call from Santanna Luci who is employed by your company. I was advised that "A Current Affair" was interested in doing a story on the Compagna-Psaradelis homicide that occurred in July 1973. She also stated that they were interested in why two retired police officers were still working on the case after all these years.

Chief Robert Baker, retired, and I gave Ms. Luci the information she required. Ms. Luci advised that she would contact us after she reviewed the information.

Ms. Luci contacted us again, requesting that we arrange interviews with various people involved with the story. We contacted the appropriate people and the interviews were scheduled for the early part of October 1993.

The day before the interviews were to take place, Ms. Luci informed me that the story was not going forward. On October 18, I wrote to Ms. Luci and advised how shocked and disappointed we were that the Compagna-Psaradelis story would not be done.

Ms. Luci called me on October 20. When I asked why the story was not going forward, Ms. Luci advised that they were going to do the story at a later date.

At that time, I advised Ms. Luci that one of the parents of the victims who had previously consented to be interviewed had changed her mind. I also told Ms. Luci that both of the girls' families had decided they would no longer cooperate with the police or anyone else regarding the investigation. Ms. Luci stated that she needed an interview with at least one of the parents and asked for their phone numbers. She intended to contact them and call me back. This never happened, so I assume that "A Current Affair" will not be doing the story.

Sir, this is still a good story for television, even though the parents of the girls might not want to be interviewed. This is a solvable case. There are still people out there who will consent to interviews, including Chief Baker and myself.

JOSEPH A. HORAK

The reason we accepted your interest in doing this story was that we felt it would aid us in bringing the person or persons who committed this crime to justice.

I would appreciate your advising whether or not you have decided to do this story. If you have decided not to do this story, was it because a person or agency contacted you?

I thought a program such as yours was there to help solve crimes and to keep the public informed about current events.

The days passed quickly and still there was no meeting scheduled with the state police and the attorney general's office. It was time to write another letter to the state police and try to get some help.

Dear Colonel Lynn Presby:

I am writing in regard to the Compagna-Psaradelis homicides of 1973. For the past seventeen or so years, I have been unable to obtain the help of any law enforcement officer or agency to help investigate this case and bring it to a conclusion.

As far as I am concerned, this case can be solved. There is, and always has been, a prime suspect. Over the years, I have approached various law enforcement officers, requesting help with this investigation. The results have been negative.

When I approached the chief of police in the town where the victims lived and asked for his help, his response was, "That's not my problem." Something is wrong.

When I approached the chief of police in the town where the victims were murdered and asked for his help, his response was, "I cannot investigate homicides." Something is wrong.

When I approached various people from the major crime unit of the state police and asked for help, their response was, "When we review the case, we'll tell you what we will or won't do." Something is wrong.

When I approached various members of the attorney general's office and asked for help, their response was, "If and

when we or the state police need anything, we'll contact you."
Something is wrong.

When two different television programs, such as A Current Affair and Unsolved Mysteries, are interested in doing the story, then they pull out, something is wrong.

After all these years, when the parents of both victims want Chief Baker and me stopped from investigating the case any longer, something is wrong.

Colonel, I know that I am a retired police officer and that what I know or don't know doesn't carry very much weight with anyone from law enforcement; but, even though I am retired, I am dedicated to bringing this case to a conclusion. I truly need your help.

I don't care who gets credit for solving the case.

If I don't receive help from law enforcement, I will use whatever means it takes to solve this case.

If you want me to make an appointment to talk over the case with you, I am willing to meet with you at your convenience. If you need any information in this regard, I will make sure you receive it.

I hope to receive your reply.

I mailed the letter to Colonel Presby, then headed to Candia to talk with Chief Baker.

"Good morning, Chief, how are things going here at your country store? Good, I hope. I thought I'd give you a copy of the letter I just mailed to State Police Headquarters. If we don't receive help from this, I think we should write to the governor. We've tried everyone else, we might as well go all the way to the top of the ladder."

"Good idea, Lieutenant. I'm with you all the way."

December 21, 1993

I received a letter from the state police.
Detective Lieutenant Joseph Horak:

I write in response to your letter of December 14, 1993, wherein you offer your assistance concerning homicides which occurred some years ago.

I have forwarded your correspondence to Captain John Barthelmes, our Investigative Services Bureau Commander, to be reviewed at that level. Where your letter does not outline facts about any particular case, you might consider documenting any facts or information and forwarding the same to Captain John Barthelmes.

Thank you for your continuing interest in these homicide cases. If we can be of further assistance in the future, please let us know.

That was a nice letter from Colonel Lynn Presby. I only wish that Detective Sergeant Lamy and Captain Barthelmes had told him that Chief Baker and I have sent all kinds of reports to them. All the letter did was throw us back to square one. I didn't care for that.

<u>December 22, 1993</u>

Since one of the crime programs had just covered a homicide that took place in Peterborough in 1989, I made an appointment to talk with the police chief there. His name was Chief Quinten Estey.

"Thanks for seeing me, Chief Estey. Chief Robert Baker, retired from the Candia Police Department, and I are working on a double homicide that is twenty years old. I know you had a homicide case on one of the crime shows recently and I wonder if you could give me information about how you were able to obtain their services."

"Well, Lieutenant, I contacted several different television programs that work on unsolved cases. *Prime Time* was the only one I had any luck with. I'll give you the name and address of the program so you can write to them. Maybe they'll help you."

"Chief Estey, did you have any kind of response from the show?"

"Well, we received about twenty leads."

"I would say that was pretty good, Chief. That's twenty leads you wouldn't have had without *Prime Time* helping you."

"While we're at it, Chief Estey, has anyone from the state police contacted you regarding the information I sent them on your homicide investigation?"

"No, Lieutenant, I haven't heard a thing."

"Chief, I sent that information to the state police on October 23. They've had plenty of time to tell you about it. I have a copy of it in my car. I'll get it for you. It's a letter with the name of a possible suspect. He sure fits the composite drawing to a <u>T</u>. It would be worth checking out.

"Good luck with your case, Chief Estey. Thank you for taking the time to talk with me. If I need to, would you mind my coming back to talk with you again?"

"Lieutenant Horak, you can come back any time you want and thanks for the information."

When I got home, I wrote to *Prime Time* to see if they would do a program on the Compagna-Psaradelis story.

Dear Sir:

I am searching for information about what you need to put together an unsolved mystery for your program.

The case in question is twenty years old. It is a double homicide of two, fifteen-year-old girls. This case is very complicated because it has a little bit of everything in it - rape, suicide, murder, and a parent who has been missing for over eighteen years. It is truly a mystery.

I am a retired detective lieutenant from the Merrimack Police Department. I am working with retired Chief of Police Robert Baker from Candia, New Hampshire. The investigation involves a double homicide that took place in 1973. It is possible that the investigation could lead to a third homicide.

Since 1973 we have been trying to find some law enforcement agency or investigator to help us. So far we have had negative results.

This is a solvable case. Our income is very limited. We realize that if we don't solve the case ourselves, it will never be solved. Time is running out. Maybe Prime Time is part of the key to bringing this case to a conclusion and ending twenty-one long hard years of fighting the system.

JOSEPH A. HORAK

If you are interested in doing the story, these are some of the areas we would like you to cover.

1. *Area where a rape took place in July 1973.*
2. *Girls reported missing on July 12, 1973, where the girls spent the night on July 11, 1973, and with whom.*
3. *Where the victims were last seen alive.*
4. *Crime scene - September 29, 1973.*
5. *Funeral home in Candia, New Hampshire.*
6. *Funeral home in Merrimack, New Hampshire.*
7. *Cemeteries where victims were buried.*
8. *Girls who knew victims in school.*
9. *Former police officers who worked on the case*
10. *Former employer of one of the victims*
11. *Retired police officers still working on the case.*
12. *Would like people with information about the case to come forward.*
13. *The investigators would like to place or eliminate any suspect or suspects.*

I would appreciate your advising if you are interested in doing this story. To be honest with you, we really need your help. I hope to receive an early reply.

34

December 23, 1993

There was no sense in begging law enforcement to help us, it was apparent they weren't going to do anything about the Compagna-Psaradelis murders. That was pretty sad. I was sure they thought Chief Baker and I were just going to fade away, but we weren't going to do that. It was time to write to the governor.

Dear Governor Steve Merrill:

I remember your reaching out to the citizens of New Hampshire when you ran for Governor and I, for one, listened to you.

I am writing to you because I am reaching out for help.

In July 1973 Diane Compagna and Anne Psaradelis were reported missing. In September 1973 the bodies of the two girls were found in a wooded area of Candia, New Hampshire, and a homicide investigation was started.

It is now December 1993 and the murders still remain unsolved. Chief Robert Baker, retired from the Candia Police Department, and I have been working on this case for twenty years. Having been injured in a homicide investigation, I was retired in November 1976. Although Chief Baker and I are retired from service, we are dedicated police officers.

In the past eighteen years we have tried to find some law enforcement officer or person who would be interested enough to continue with our investigation and bring it to a conclusion. Thus far, we have had negative results.

We have tried to obtain assistance from local police departments right up through the state police and attorney general's office. The results have been the same - negative.

Governor, this is pretty discouraging because this case can be solved. There has always been, and still is, a prime suspect or suspects. There isn't any law enforcement person interested enough to help investigate and bring this case to a conclusion.

For some unknown reason, it seems like people in law enforcement do not want the case solved. We sought the aid of television programs, such as A Current Affair and Unsolved Mysteries, but at the last minute they backed off doing the story.

If possible, Chief Baker and I would like to make an appointment with you to talk over the case. If this is possible, we would appreciate your talking with us before you contact any of the various law enforcement people or agencies.

I want to thank you for taking the time to read this letter. I look forward to a reply in the near future.

I took a quick trip to Candia to let Chief Baker read the letter before I mailed it to the governor.

"Well, Chief Baker, I thought it was time to take that last giant step up to the top of the ladder. We've tried everything else and it looks like Governor Steve Merrill is our last hope. Take a look at this letter I wrote to him."

Chief Baker quickly read my letter.

"That's good, Lieutenant, but it will only help if the governor talks with us before he contacts the attorney general or the state police. I guess only time will tell."

December 27, 1993

In a few days it would be 1994. I decided to write one more letter to Colonel Presby, answering his letter of December 21.

Dear Colonel Presby:

I want to thank you for your letter of December 21, which was in reply to my letter dated December 14.

Colonel, I have been dealing directly with various members of your investigative services bureau since November 1992, regarding the Compagna-Psaradelis murders. Chief Baker and I have spoken with Captain Tom Winn, Sergeant Roland Lamy, Captain John Barthelmes, and various attorneys from the attorney general's office.

Weeks and months have gone by and we are no closer to obtaining help from any law enforcement person or agency than we were in November 1992.

As I stated in my letter, something has to be wrong when you can't find anyone in law enforcement to help solve a double murder.

After working twenty years on this case, I find that I cannot walk away from it. If I can't find someone in law enforcement to help Chief Baker and me, then we will have to find another way. We will do whatever it takes to solve this case.

Colonel, thank you for taking the time to read my letters and especially for answering them.

The days passed into another new year. I wondered what kind of a year this would be for the Compagna Psaradelis murder investigation. I hoped it would be better than the last twenty-one years have been.

I was sure that all the law enforcement people that Chief Baker and I had been dealing with, especially these past few years, felt that they had shut down the investigation. I hoped my letter to the governor would light a fire under all of them and give them a real incentive to work hard and place or eliminate our prime and secondary suspects.

The only thing that bothered me was whether they would really put their best foot forward or just do a token investigation to get everyone off their backs.

January 12, 1994

JOSEPH A. HORAK

It was my birthday. I received a birthday card in the mail and a letter from Governor Steve Merrill.

Dear Mr. Horak:

Thank you for your letter regarding the Compagna-Psaradelis homicide investigation. Your dedication to this investigation after all these years as expressed in your letter is impressive.

After discussing the matter with Attorney General Jeffery Howard, I have been assured that his office and the New Hampshire State Police are actively working on the investigation. Furthermore, the prosecutor assigned to the investigation and the head of the state police major crime unit are willing to meet with you, as they have in the past, to discuss any new ideas you may have regarding the investigation.

Again, thank you for taking the time to bring this matter to my attention. I hope this letter satisfies your concerns.

It was good of the governor to write back, but he did what I asked him not to do - <u>please do not contact any law enforcement people or agencies until you speak with us</u>.

I had a bad feeling about this, but I hoped I was wrong. All we could do was wait and see.

The governor's letter changed my whole day. I decided to drive to Candia and talk with Chief Baker.

"Hello, Lieutenant Horak, what are you doing way over here on a day like this?"

"Well, Chief, I received a letter from Governor Steve Merrill, regarding the letter I wrote to him on December 23."

I gave Chief Baker the governor's letter to read.

"Nice letter, Lieutenant, but the governor talked with the attorney general and the state police, even though you asked him to talk with us before contacting any law enforcement people or agencies."

"I know, Chief Baker, that's what concerns me. I feel like we're going to run right into a brick wall. I'm beginning to wonder what we can do if we get the same response we've received in the past from the attorney general's office and the state police. I'll tell you one thing, I've been a fighter all my life and I won't back down. I'll find some way to get this case solved. You have a country store to worry about, Chief, so I have to be careful not to hurt you or your business. I've been told by a few people connected with law enforcement that I should carry a gun. There's probably a lot of truth in that."

"Lieutenant, you know that I'll stick with the investigation, no matter what it takes."

January 13, 1994

I received a telephone call from Sergeant Roland Lamy.

"Lieutenant Horak, this is Sergeant Lamy. I've been instructed to call and tell you that a meeting has been set up in the attorney general's office for tomorrow at 1:00 p.m. This meeting will be with Senior Assistant Attorney General Michael Ramsdell, Lieutenant Arthur Wiggins, Chief Baker, you, and me."

"OK, Sergeant, we'll be there. Thanks for the call."

I was sure the meeting was called as a direct response to my letter to the governor. We were pleased that the governor had responded so quickly.

January 14, 1994

Chief Baker and I met at 10:00 a.m. so that we could talk things over before heading to Concord for the meeting. It was a big day for us. We hoped we would finally get some help, but I didn't feel good about the meeting. The governor's letter had stated that the prosecutor assigned to the investigation and the head of the state police major crime unit were willing to talk with us, but we hadn't seen Captain John Barthelmes since the time we went to State Police Headquarters and spoke with him about the remarks the state police added to the stories we had put in *Foster's Daily Democrat* and the *Union Leader*. Another reason I didn't feel good about the meeting was that I didn't think Captain Barthelmes was too thrilled when I handed him the superior court papers showing that there was, in fact, an arrest and conviction of Tom Jefferson for statutory rape.

JOSEPH A. HORAK

Chief Baker and I arrived early because we were afraid they might cancel the meeting if we weren't right on time. Sergeant Lamy and Lieutenant Wiggins greeted us and showed us into the conference room where the meeting would be held. It had one long table and a dozen chairs. When Attorney Ramsdell entered the room, he sat right next to me, then Sergeant Lamy and Lieutenant Wiggins sat directly across the table from me. I felt boxed in. Chief Baker sat on my side of the table, but closer to the other end.

Attorney Ramsdell started things off.

"I guess we're ready to get started.

"Lieutenant Horak, I don't like you. Look at this big stack of letters you've written to police departments, the state police, the attorney general's office and the governor. You're a liar and you're making me look bad in front of my boss."

"I'm going to tell all of you - Lieutenant Wiggins, Attorney Ramsdell and Sergeant Lamy-if you people had helped us investigate the Compagna-Psaradelis case, I wouldn't have written all those letters. Let me tell you something, and I'm more than sincere in what I'm going to say - if you think you have a lot of letters in your hand now, you'll be holding ten times that number if we don't receive help from some law enforcement officer or agency. That isn't a threat of any kind, it's a promise. Chief Baker and I didn't come here to argue. We thought this was going to be a professional meeting about a double homicide that should be solved."

"We're not after Chief Baker. He didn't write the letters, you did, Lieutenant Horak."

"Hey, like I just told you, I'll write ten times the number of letters you're holding in your hand if I have to."

"Enough, enough. Let's get down to business."

"Sergeant Lamy, I think we've been more than fair to the state police and attorney general's office. In fact, I contacted you in November 1992 and talked the case over with you. You said, "I'll pull the case, read it over, and get back to you in a week." After waiting a year and many telephone calls and letters, that never happened."

"Lieutenant Horak, you are a liar. You write one thing to me and another thing to the attorney general. You make me look bad."

"Well, Attorney Ramsdell, when you first contacted me, you said you wanted to help us with this case. To be honest with you, I can't think of one thing you've done to advance this investigation."

"Lieutenant Horak, you wrote a report, dated August 1992, regarding information that a so-called reliable person gave you about two people who could have some knowledge of who was involved in the Compagna-Psaradelis murders."

"That is correct, Sergeant Lamy."

"Well, we want to know who that reliable person is, because we don't believe there is any such person."

"Sergeant Lamy, I would have no reason to make up false information. If you read the report, you will know that way back in August 1992 you had this report that you're talking about. Why have you waited until January 1994 to question it?

"As I told you in the report, this is a reliable person. He or she does not want to get involved because they know the people in question. I've tried many times to talk with this person to see if they would come forward, but they're afraid for themselves, their family, and their property. This person has also had a heart attack and will not get involved. When this person gave me the information, I promised they would not have to get involved. I do not intend to break that promise.

"I can't understand why the state police investigators haven't interviewed the people listed in my report of August 1992."

"Well, Lieutenant, none of us believes there is any such person. We won't do one thing with this investigation until you tell us the name and address of this reliable person."

"Let me ask you a question, Sergeant Lamy. Say that I'm just John Smith, Jones or whatever. Suppose I'm in a restaurant or a store and I see two men that I either know or don't know. I hear these two men talking about pulling a bank holdup at the First National Bank on Main Street here in Concord tomorrow at 2:00 p.m. I obtain the plate number of their vehicle and have a good description of each of the men. Now, I either see a state trooper on Thorndike Street or I call your headquarters and give the information I have regarding a possible bank holdup. As a detective with the state police or a local police department, what would you do with the information?"

"Well, Lieutenant, I would probably stake out the bank."

"OK, Sergeant Lamy. Now, tell me why the information I wrote in the report of August 1992 isn't just as important and valuable as the information given to you on a possible bank holdup taking place tomorrow? Think about it, Sergeant Lamy, it's the same thing, both pieces of information should be checked out."

"Well, Lieutenant, we're not going to do anything unless you give us the name of this person so we can check him out. You are a liar, Lieutenant Horak."

"I know one thing, Attorney Ramsdell, you are not going to call me a liar again. If you don't like me, that's your problem, but I am not giving you this person's name."

"Lieutenant, let me ask you this question. If you could have us do one thing for you in this case, what would it be?"

"Sergeant Lamy, I would like you to place or eliminate our prime suspect in this investigation."

"Shame on you, Lieutenant Horak. How can you settle for just eliminating the prime suspect? How about any other suspects you have?"

"Hold on, Sergeant, you gave me one choice, and one choice only. Of course, I would like to place or eliminate any and all suspects. Let me ask you a question, Sergeant Lamy. You know who our prime suspect is in this case. Do you think he's a prime suspect?"

"Yes, he could be, Lieutenant."

"I guess there's no sense in our talking any more because I cannot give you the name of the person who gave me the information in my August 1992 report."

"Lieutenant Horak, if you provide us with the name of the reliable person and give us a written idea of what you consider to be the best single lead that can be pursued in this investigation, we will investigate it. If you don't, we will not investigate this case any further."

The meeting ended in a stalemate. On the way home, Chief Baker and I talked about what was said.

"Chief Baker, that wasn't really a meeting to solve the Compagna-Psaradelis murder case, it was more like a chew-out-Lieutenant-Horak session. I don't think Attorney Ramsdell acted very professionally. We didn't accomplish one thing."

"You know, Lieutenant, they didn't ask me anything."

"They weren't fair. They knew we couldn't reveal the name of the person who gave us the information cited in our August 1992 report. They just wanted to box us in so they could end the investigation.

"That was the first time Lieutenant Wiggins was involved in the investigation. He didn't have anything to say, except to tell us to send our reports to Attorney Ramsdell, not the state police. I can tell you, he won't do one thing to help solve this case.

"Chief, we'll have to think about what to do next. We've been to the top of the ladder, now we're back on the ground again."

35

February 14, 1994

Dear Chief Pelletier:
    I am writing in regard to "our girls" and the investigation of their murders. I hope you will be able to give me some advice about the direction I should take at this point in time.
    On December 14 and 27, 1993, I wrote letters to Colonel Lynn Presby of the New Hampshire State Police, and on December 27 I wrote to Governor Steve Merrill. The letters were in regard to obtaining help with the investigation of these two murders.
    On January 14, 1994, Chief Baker and I attended a meeting in Concord with Assistant Attorney Michael Ramsdell, Sergeant Roland Lamy, and Lieutenant Arthur Wiggins, regarding the Compagna-Psaradelis case and what they would do or not do to further the investigation.
    To be honest with you, those attending the meeting were pretty hostile toward me. I thought we were going to talk about the case and what the attorney general's office and state police would do to help with the investigation, but the cards were stacked against us. Assistant Attorney General Ramsdell kept telling me that he didn't like me, that I was a liar, and that I was trying to make him look bad in front of his boss. Attorney Ramsdell, Sergeant Lamy and Lieutenant Wiggins were upset because I had written so many letters to the attorney general,

Colonel Presby and the governor. I told them that if someone from law enforcement had helped with the investigation, I wouldn't have written the letters.

After a tense meeting, they told me that Chief Baker and I could pick one thing for them to do, but they wouldn't get to it for at least four months. They don't want us to send any more letters or reports to the state police, instead they asked us to send them to Attorney Ramsdell.

In August 1992 I sent a report to the state police about two people who are believed to have information about who murdered the girls. This information came from a reliable person who does not want to be identified because they are afraid that they, their family, or their property may be harmed. The state police and attorney general's office want to know the name of this person or they will not investigate the case further. They stated that they have cases needing more attention than this twenty-year-old homicide.

I tried to be up front with them and told the state police and attorney general's office about the various television programs that we have contacted. I think that was a mistake. They admitted that they had dealt with these programs and I believe they are the ones who have stopped the companies from doing the story.

Is there any way you can obtain the address of America's Most Wanted for me? I thought it might be a good idea to try them and not tell anyone about it, as you suggested.

As you can see, I am in Oklahoma at the present time, but I am still working on the case and will be returning to New Hampshire pretty soon.

<u>February 19, 1994</u>
Chief Pelletier replied to my letter.

Dear Joe:

JOSEPH A. HORAK

Sorry to have to say it, but it appears that no one feels you have the right to investigate the case. You are no longer a police officer and do not hold a private investigator's license. If Chief Baker could get the Candia chief of police interested enough to work on the case, he might be able to get things done - you know, get a copy of the whole investigation from the attorney general's files.

You must remember that mistakes could have been made that no one intends to own up to. They would not want mistakes to come out in the open that would make them look foolish.

To be in touch with America's Most Wanted, you should contact John Walsh. His address is enclosed.

I want to wish you all kinds of luck, Joe.

I immediately wrote a letter to Raymond Joseph at *America's Most Wanted.*

February 22, 1994

It had been five weeks since Chief Baker and I met with the attorney general's office. I was sure Attorney Ramsdell and the others felt that they had boxed us in so that the investigation couldn't go any farther. I was not going to let that happen, so I wrote him another letter.

Dear Attorney Ramsdell:

I am writing in regard to our meeting on January 14, 1994. I must say that I was disappointed with this meeting. I thought it was going to conducted in a professional manner and that Chief Baker and I would get some help from you and the state police. The meeting was far from professional. I thought it was one-sided and I didn't appreciate your calling me a liar several times during our talk.

Regarding the person who gave me the information that reflected that two people appear to have knowledge or information about the murders of Diane Compagna and Anne Psaradelis, you, as well as the state police, received a copy of our report dated August 1992. During our meeting, you implied that

286

we didn't have any such person. You also stated that if we didn't identify the person and let the state police investigators interview them, the investigation would end.

As I stated in the meeting and in our report of August 1992, this person is reliable. During the past six weeks, I have approached this person again, but they are still afraid to be interviewed for fear of being harmed.

Chief Baker and I feel that you boxed us into a corner, but we are never going to be satisfied with closing this case until our prime suspect is either placed or eliminated. As you know, there is another possible suspect, but Chief Baker and I have always felt that our prime suspect is the person who took the lives of the two girls. He had motive, opportunity, and was also under threat of being arrested for rape. Whoever took the lives of the two girls knew them, even Sergeant Lamy agrees with that.

I know that your office and the state police investigative office are busy with all kinds of cases. I realize that this case is twenty years old, but it means as much as any homicide that took place as recently as yesterday.

Chief Baker and I would appreciate any help you can provide to bring this case to a conclusion. That means to help us place or eliminate our prime suspect and any other suspects.

We know that, for some unknown reason, the family members of the victims do not want the case investigated any further. Why? We know that we had several television programs willing to do a story about the investigation, but they backed away. Why? Something is wrong.

There is also something wrong when no law enforcement person or agency is willing to help solve this double homicide. I, for one, am not giving up on this investigation. I will do whatever it takes to solve the case.

If you need anything from us, you can contact Chief Baker in case I am out of town.

I wondered what kind of response I would receive from Attorney Ramsdell. One thing was for sure, he didn't like me, but that shouldn't enter into the picture. Solving the murders of Diane Compagna and Anne Psaradelis took priority in my book, regardless of anyone's feelings - and that goes for the attorney general's office, the state police, and even the families of the victims.

We all knew how the system worked sometimes and I had to be careful not to get Chief Baker into trouble. He had a small country store and couldn't afford to have problems with anyone.

February 28, 1994

I received a reply from Assistant Attorney General Michael Ramsdell.

Dear Mr. Horak:

Having read your letter dated February 22, 1994, let me respond by again stating that if you provide the state with the name of the individual who you believe possesses information regarding the two men who have knowledge or information about who murdered Diane Compagna and Anne Psaradelis, we will pursue that lead. However, absent your cooperation in providing us with the individual's name, we are unable to continue to investigate that particular lead.

Additionally, I will reiterate the offer we made to you during our last meeting. That is, if you provide us with a written idea of what you consider to be the single best lead that can be pursued in this investigation, we will pursue that lead. However, simply claiming repeatedly that this investigation could be or should be solved does nothing to advance the prospect of a successful conclusion being reached.

I do not doubt your sincerity in wanting these homicides to be solved. You must understand, however, that your input can only be helpful if you truly cooperate with us. As long as you continue to claim to possess helpful information, but refuse to share it with us, the information will be of no assistance to anyone.

JUSTICE DENIED

I hope you will rethink your position regarding the name of the individual that you claim may have valuable information. If so, do not hesitate to contact me.
cc: Lieutenant Arthur Wiggins

That was some letter. He wanted to make me the scapegoat in this investigation. Attorney Ramsdell had the names of the two people who are supposed to have knowledge or information about who murdered the two girls. Why didn't he or the state police check it out? It was easier for them to close the case, saying I wouldn't give them the individual who furnished the names of these two people.

It bothered me that the state police and attorney general's office stated that they had been investigating this case for twenty years. In November 1992, Detective Sergeant Roland Lamy had no idea what the case number was or even where the case was stored. I was sure Attorney Ramsdell had never heard of the Compagna-Psaradelis murder case until 1993. I also knew that I was a thorn in his side, but that was not a reason why they couldn't continue the investigation and place or eliminate the prime suspect. Even Sergeant Lamy admitted he was a good suspect.

If they had read the entire case, they would have known there had been an arrest and conviction of rape connected to the case. Yet, their remarks to the media in September 1993 reflected that no one was arrested and convicted of rape.

I didn't understand how Attorney Ramsdell could make the statement that, <u>your input can only be helpful if you truly cooperate with us. As long as you continue to possess helpful information, but refuse to share it with us, the information will be of no assistance to anyone</u>.

No one was more cooperative than Chief Baker and I. We sent all kinds of reports to both the state police and the attorney general's office. We spent our own money, time and energy. We offered our time and knowledge to help any law enforcement agency with the investigation. It was law enforcement that was withholding information and not offering assistance to solve the Compagna-Psaradelis murders.

Sergeant Lamy told Chief Baker and me that they had a possible suspect in the case, but he hasn't said who it was or why this person was a suspect. If they have a suspect, why don't they go after him? Having a suspect and not doing anything about it sounded strange to me.

36

April 2, 1994

John Walsh of *America's Most Wanted* had not replied to my letter, so I decided to write again.

Dear Mr. Walsh,

I wrote to you on February 22, 1994, and sent you paperwork regarding the Compagna-Psaradelis homicides of 1973. I was asking for your help.

Mr.Walsh, I can't understand how the people who run shows on television, such as A Current Affair, Case Closed, Unsolved Mysteries, and America's Most Wanted, can air stories on crimes that have been committed and ask the public to come forward with information that would lead to the person or persons who committed such crimes and not be interested in our story. I thought programs such as yours would be happy to help with the case I wrote to you about.

I know that you have probably contacted the New Hampshire State Police or the attorney general's office regarding their viewpoint and feelings about the case. These agencies are not willing to place or eliminate any suspect or suspects. It's as though they don't want the case solved because we have been pushing them to do it.

There has to be something wrong when you can't get help from law enforcement or a program such as yours. I can't be-

lieve that someone won't at least meet with me and talk over the case.

Mr.Walsh, a double homicide case that occurred twenty years ago involving two, fifteen-year-old girls is just as important as a homicide that was committed yesterday. Won't you please help us with this investigation by doing the story? It could help bring people forward with information about the case. There are people out there with that knowledge.

Mr. Walsh, I hope you will reply to this letter.

I wrote a letter to Chief Quinten Estey, hoping to get some advice about how to move the investigation along when no one was willing to help.

Dear Chief Estey:

I was pleased to read in the newspapers that you are moving along with your investigation into the murder that took place in your town in 1989. I am sure, in time, you will solve it. If I can be of any help, please let me know.

You may remember, I talked with you some time ago about the Compagna-Psaradelis murders and the problems Chief Robert Baker, retired, and I were having in trying to find some law enforcement person or agency to help bring this case to a conclusion.

At the present time, we are at a standstill or so-called road block as far as the investigation goes. We have received no help from law enforcement or crime shows, such as A Current Affair, Case Closed, Unsolved Mysteries, and America's Most Wanted. Many of these companies gave us the impression that they would help with the story, but, for some unknown reason, they backed off.

The attorney general's office and the state police have boxed us in, so that the investigation cannot continue. I would appreciate your giving me any thoughts you may have about the direction you would take to move this case forward so it can be solved.

JUSTICE DENIED

Chief Baker and I have tried to cooperate with the attorney general's office and the state police, but they make it look like we won't cooperate with them.

We really don't care who solves the case, we just want it solved. Any suggestions would be appreciated.

May 3, 1994

Chief Quinten Estey did not reply to my letter. I supposed he didn't want to get involved. It seemed like another door had been closed.

No one answered my letters or returned my phone calls. Nothing was happening, until I received a call from Peggy Linderman.

"Lieutenant Horak, this is Peggy Linderman with *America's Most Wanted* in Washington, D.C. I would like more facts about the Compagna-Psaradelis murders and I would like to talk with you about the investigation."

I answered Ms. Linderman's questions and began giving her details about the investigation, then our conversation was cut short. Ms. Linderman had to attend a meeting, but she promised to call back the next day at 9:15 a.m. to complete our conversation.

Two days passed and Ms. Linderman hadn't called. If I wanted them to do the story, I decided I would have to keep after them. I couldn't afford a telephone call to Washington, D.C., but it had to be made.

"Hello, Ms. Linderman, this is Lieutenant Horak. I thought you were going to call me back. I waited all day for your call and even stayed by the phone until 10:00 p.m."

"Lieutenant, your name is on the list. I would have called back."

"Ms. Linderman, may I ask you a few questions that have been on my mind since our last phone conversation?"

"Go ahead, Lieutenant, ask them."

"First of all, isn't solving homicides or crimes more important than the feelings of people? Number two, how about all the time and effort that has been put into the investigation over the past twenty years? Number three, does every investigation have the cooperation of the victim, the victim's family and others? If not, does this stop the investigation? Number four, don't we owe it to the victims, and society it-self, to solve the crime and possibly stop this person from doing it again? And finally, how can *America's Most Wanted* or any other crime program that reaches out to the public for information or help in locating wanted people not reach out themselves and help solve a crime such as the Compagna-Psaradelis murders?"

"Well, Lieutenant, *America's Most Wanted* does not want to hurt or cause pain to the families of victims. We are not like some of the other crime programs. We cannot do this story unless the parents of the victims want it done. If you'll give me the phone numbers and ad-dresses of the families, I'll contact you by letter to advise you if we will do the story or not."

June 2, 1994
I had heard nothing from Peggy Linderman, even though I wrote to her on May 14, so I decided to write to the executive producer of *America's Most Wanted* to see if I could get any kind of help.

> *Dear Sir:*
> *I am writing to you in regard to the Compagna-Psaradelis homicides that took place in July 1973. We need the help of a crime program such as yours to bring this case to a conclu-sion.*
> *In the past we have contacted Peggy Linderman in your Washington, D.C., office, regarding your program doing a story on the two murdered girls. Ms. Linderman was advised that, for some unknown reason, the parents of the victims would not cooperate or consent to be interviewed. Ms. Linder-man advised that the parents had to be willing or they would not do the story. She requested their phone numbers and ad-dresses, stating she would contact each of the parents, then ad-vise me by letter if America's Most Wanted would do the story. That has not happened.*
> *I wrote to Ms. Linderman on May 14, 1994, requesting in-formation in this regard and still have not received a reply.*

JUSTICE DENIED

Sir, we really need your help. Won't you please help us solve this terrible crime?

July 1994

Weeks passed and I didn't hear one word from any of the crime programs I contacted. They must have been pressured by someone or some agency not to help Chief Baker and me with the investigation. I even wrote to the lead investigator with *A Current Affair*, but he didn't have the decency to reply to my letter.

The Compagna-Psaradelis investigation started in July 1973. That was twenty-one years ago. During that time Chief Robert Baker and I put our time, energy and sweat into trying to solve the murders of "our girls." There wasn't a day that went by that we didn't think of them and try to find a way to solve this crime. We never knew the girls when they were alive, but after working on the investigation so long, we felt that we knew them quite well.

We knew that Diane Compagna and Anne Psaradelis wanted their killer found and brought to justice. Once that was done, we were sure the girls could rest in peace.

October 28, 1994

Chief Baker and I considered that the Compagna-Psaradelis murder investigation was shut down.

There wasn't a single person in law enforcement who would help us. We wondered why.

There wasn't one crime program that would help us. We wondered why.

There were people out there who were friends of Diane and Anne. They had information and knowledge of who murdered the girls, but they wouldn't come forward and help end the nightmare. We wondered why.

We just couldn't let all these people walk away from a crime that could be solved. The least they could do was place or eliminate any and all suspects, we did have a couple of them. I contacted Chief Baker to discuss the matter.

"Hello, Chief, this is Lieutenant Horak. I think it's about time we did some serious talking. I don't know about you, but I'm not going to step aside and let the Compagna-Psaradelis murders just fade away. There has to be something we can do."

"Lieutenant Horak, do you know what I've been thinking?"

"No, Chief, what is it?"

"You and I have worked hard over the years to find someone to help solve this crime. We've talked to everyone - from the local police department right up to the governor's office - only to be back where we were twenty-one years ago.

"Lieutenant Horak, I think we should write a book and tell the whole story. Maybe that's the only way this crime will be solved."

"Chief Baker, your thoughts must be on the same track as mine. To be honest with you, I've already started a book. You have a lot to lose with your little country store and I don't want to cause trouble for you. Of course, I don't need problems either, but we made a promise years ago that we would stick with the investigation until the killers were caught.

"I would say that writing a book is like a last hurrah. If we finish the book, and we will, I hope we can find someone to publish it. If it sells, I'd like to see a reward given to the person who comes forward with information that leads to the arrest and conviction of the killers. I would like to have the reward offer become part of the book. Maybe even the publisher will contribute something toward it."

37

It doesn't seem possible that it has taken me nearly a year to write this story with the hope that it brings someone forward that has the information we need to help solve these murders. I often think, how will Chief Baker and I ever be able to place or eliminate our prime suspects, or any other suspects for that matter? We sure haven't had any cooperation from anyone connected with law enforcement in the past twenty years and that is pretty sad.

September 1995

"Hello, Lieutenant, this is Chief Baker. I thought I would give you a call and find out how the manuscript is coming along and when it will be published."

"Well Chief, as you know, I sent the manuscript in to the publisher and the book *TRUTH AND JUSTICE: A Detective's Dilemma* should be out on the market on or before the 29th of September. We set this date of September 29th as this would be the anniversary of the date the bodies of Diane Compagna and Anne Psaradelis were found over in your town. We thought that this might generate more interest and help to bring someone forward that would help us with the investigation."

"Lieutenant, that was a good idea. Will you please keep me informed as to any progress you make? You know I will do anything I can to help solve the murders of our girls. I am like you - I won't give up on the case until the killers are caught and brought to justice."

"OK Chief, I'll keep in touch with you."

JOSEPH A. HORAK

Figure 25: 1995 Newspaper article

September 15, 1995

The days were going by pretty fast and I was doing everything possible to promote our book. If everything stays on schedule, within the next two weeks the book should be on the bookshelves in stores throughout the country. Oh, I know a lot of people will be upset with Chief Baker and me, but we really have tried to obtain the assistance we needed and still need from every police officer or law enforcement agency we could think of. Over the past 20 years or so, the results have been pretty negative.

There's the phone. I wonder who's calling. I rarely ever receive a phone call. "Mr. Horak, this is Ron Jacobs from your publishing company. I am sorry to have to inform you that your book has been delayed and won't come out until December."

Boy, am I discouraged. We sure planned on the book coming out for the 29th of September and now all that time and money we spent on promoting the book is gone, but there's not much we can do about it.

The weeks and months passed by. December 3rd would be here tomorrow and still no books. I guess we'll just have to wait it out and to continue promoting the book.

JUSTICE DENIED

<u>December 28, 1995</u>

The phone is ringing.

"It is for you, Joe."

"Hello, is this Lieutenant Horak?"

"Yes, it is."

"This is your friend Sergeant Rousseau from Merrimack. I thought you might be interested in knowing that Thomas Jefferson, one of your prime suspects in the Compagna-Psaradelis homicides, shot himself a couple of days ago and is on the critical list."

"You have to be kidding me. What happened?"

"Lieutenant, Jefferson shot himself in the head with a .22 caliber rifle he is still alive and is in the Trauma Center down in Nashua. Lieutenant Stavenger from the Merrimack Police Department investigated the shooting/suicide attempt. Jefferson apparently stated that he had been depressed recently and shot himself in the head in an attempt to kill himself.

"Lieutenant Stavenger made the statement, 'It's not uncommon to see suicide attempts this time of the year. The holidays take dysfunctional families and place them in a situation where they have to function as a family.'"

"That really is some kind of a statement by the Lieutenant. Sergeant Rousseau, I wonder if Lieutenant Stavenger tried to obtain any kind of a statement or a dying declaration from Jefferson in regards to the Compagna-Psaradelis murders? This sure was the perfect time to do this since Jefferson most likely would have realized that he was dying and might have wanted to clear his conscience of the murders if, in fact, he was involved in them.

"Sergeant Rousseau, I just can't believe Jefferson tried to take his life because the Christmas holidays were coming up or that he was lonely. There had to be something more to it than that. I am sure he knew that my book was coming out on the market any day now."

"Lieutenant, I just thought that you might be interested because I am sure that this shooting will not be investigated any further."

"Sergeant Rousseau, you know that I am more than interested in this information. I agree with you that Jefferson should be interviewed in regards to the reason he shot himself and of course as to any involvement he might of had in the murders of Diane Compagna and Anne Psaradelis.

"Sergeant, Jefferson could very well die if he is still on the critical list and we might never have another chance like this to place or eliminate him as being involved in the murders. I will, of course, make arrangements to come up to New Hampshire as soon as possible. Chief Baker and I haven't been working on this investigation for the past 22 years just to let an opportunity like this pass us by. We just might come up with the answers we have been searching for all these years. I really don't have the money, but it has to be done. I should be back up there by tomorrow night. I will make contact with you and Chief Baker as soon as I arrive."

I guess I should make a phone call to Chief Baker and advise him that Tom Jefferson apparently attempted to take his own life. There is a chance that we could finally bring this 22 year old case to a conclusion. In a court of law, a <u>dying</u> <u>declaration</u> made by a criminal or by the victim of a crime <u>who</u> <u>believes</u> <u>they</u> <u>are</u> <u>dying</u>, is admissible as sworn testimony by the deceased, the theory being that a man or woman would want to clear his or her conscience before they go to meet their Maker and has no reason to lie when he/she's on his/her deathbed. A dying person can't be punished any further for whatever crimes he/she may have committed. At least, not here on earth. Even if the criminal or victim later recovers, any statement that was made while the person <u>believed</u> he/she was dying is admissible under the same rule, so if Thomas Jefferson confessed to the murder of Diane Compagna and Anne Psaradelis, we had him, even if he survived his suicide attempt.

"Hello, Chief Baker?"

"Yes, it is."

"It's just me."

"What, are you back in New Hampshire?"

"No, Chief, but something has happened. Tom Jefferson shot himself a few days ago and is in critical condition down at the Trauma Center in Nashua. I am making arrangements to come up there and I should arrive around 10:00 p.m., tomorrow night. Chief, I am really excited about this and anxious to interview Jefferson. I hope he is holding his own, as this might be the only chance we will ever have to solve the murders of Diane and Anne. Sergeant Rousseau, who used to be with the Merrimack Police Department called me today and advised me of the attempted suicide. The Sergeant has always shown a great interest in helping to solve these murders and I am sure he will do anything in his power to help us bring this case to a conclusion. I better make this short, Chief. I have a lot to do, but I should be able to make it over to see you on Saturday. In the meantime, you could be checking around to see if you can find out anything about the attempted suicide incident and you could also try to obtain any newspaper articles that might mention anything about Jefferson or anything else that might be connected."

"OK, Lieutenant, I'll see you on Saturday. Have a safe trip."

December 30, 1995

"Hello, Sergeant Rousseau. This is Joe Horak. I tried calling you last night. I arrived back here late and you were either out or fast asleep, I decided I would call you first thing this morning, so here I am. Are you going to be home and more important than that, is our Tom Jefferson still alive and do you know his condition?"

"Lieutenant, Jefferson is alive, but he's still in critical condition. He could go either way at this point."

"OK, Sergeant. I will see you in about 25 minutes. By the way, three boxes were delivered to me yesterday and they contained the advance copies of my book. It sure seems strange to me, or is it just a coincidence, that the attempted suicide and the book coming out, both take place within the same week. It sure is interesting."

I drove directly to Sergeant Rousseau's home.

"It didn't take you long to get here, Lieutenant. Come on in and get out of the cold and snow. Just give me a minute to put the dogs in the other room."

"Take your time, Sergeant."

"You know me and those big dogs - if anyone is going to get bit, it's me. Lieutenant, do you want a cup of coffee or something to drink?"

"No, thanks. I just think we need to talk about Tom Jefferson. You can fill me in on everything you know from start to finish. You know, Sergeant, we really have to give a lot of serious thought as to just how we are going to interview Jefferson. This really has to be done right, because this will be our only chance to obtain some kind of a statement from him and either place or eliminate him as a suspect. If he is still alive and on the critical list, we sure can't afford to have any kind of a flaw in the interview if, in fact, we are allowed to have one. We are really going to have to try and find someone from a law enforcement agency who is still in law enforcement that will help us. The problem being that if you, Chief Baker and I interview Jefferson and he, by chance, gives a dying declaration about being involved and then dies, no one in law enforcement would believe us, so there has to be someone still active in law enforcement present during the interview. Otherwise, they will say we made it up just so the case would be cleared and that sure wouldn't be true. All we want is to solve the murders as we promised the girls we would."

"I will tell you one thing, Lieutenant - I doubt very much that you will find anyone in law enforcement who will help you with this investigation. However, there are those who are concerned about how bad you make them look in your book. They sure don't like you."

"To be honest with you, Sergeant, Chief Baker and I haven't tried to hurt anyone in law enforcement or anyone else. All we ever wanted was to place or eliminate any and all suspects and solve the murders. If someone from law enforcement had helped us, I am sure I never would have written a book. It is pretty sad when you think about it - the same suspects we had 22 years ago are still the prime suspects today. I sure don't call that good police work."

"Lieutenant, I have various people within the State Police that I can talk with and see if they won't help. As you have said, they won't do anything to help you and Chief Baker, but maybe they will help me."

"It is worth a try, Sergeant. See what you can do, as we really need to find someone from law enforcement who will help us interview Tom Jefferson.

"Well, Sergeant, I better head over to Candia and talk with Chief Baker. I guess the main thing at this point is to find someone from some law enforcement agency that will help with the interview of Tom Jefferson. I will call you later on tonight. Do what you can and we will do the same."

I drove to Candia. "What do you say, Chief Baker? How are things going? Isn't this really something about Tom Jefferson trying to take his own life? I wish we could just go to the hospital and interview him, but as you know, we aren't liked very well by law enforcement and we really would be foolish to try and interview Jefferson by ourselves, because if we were lucky enough to obtain any statements and Jefferson died, they would never accept the statements as being true.

"Chief, Sergeant Rousseau is going to make contact with various people within the State Police and see if they will help us in regards to this interview with Tom Jefferson and you and I can attempt to find someone from various other law enforcement agencies that might be willing to help."

Sergeant Rousseau, Chief Baker and I chased around for the next couple of days trying to contact various law enforcement officers and results have been negative.

The days slipped by and how we wanted to interview Tom Jefferson. We knew that he was still alive and apparently gaining in health and strength. We also knew that as each day passed that Jefferson would be harder to deal with, since we were sure he knew he would live.

We still hadn't found anyone from any of the law enforcement agencies that would help and some of the reasons given were - How bad does Horak's book make law enforcement look? It is near election time and we don't want the Sheriff, Governor or anyone else to look bad. If you want to pay for the investigation, we will do it and place the fee in the investigative fund, as we don't have very much in it. You could contact this or that person from another agency and they might help you.

During the course of trying to find someone from a law enforcement agency to help us, I, for one, ran into several retired police officers I had worked with and most of their remarks reflected the verbiage we had already heard, "We doubt that anyone from law enforcement will help because they haven't in the past 20 years."

The way things have been going, I really believe that is true but I still think a double homicide committed 22 years ago is just as important as one committed today, when the criminals are still running loose and might kill again with the right provocation.

Sergeant Rousseau really wasn't having any luck trying to find someone from the State Police that would help. He did say that I am not liked because I have caused problems over this investigation and that I refuse to tell who the informant is in regards to a letter that I had sent to the State Police and Attorney General's Office in August of 1992, which reflected that this person knew two people that had information about who took the lives of Diane Compagna and Anne Psaradelis. I promised the person who gave me this information that I would not reveal their name or anything else that might reflect who they are. This information should have been checked out and still should be checked out. Chief Baker and I feel that this is just a poor excuse that is being used to stop the murder investigation from being proceeding any farther.

Oh, Sergeant Rousseau located a couple of people from the State Police that stated they would help with the investigation, but so far nothing positive has taken place.

I found out that Tom Jefferson had been released from the hospital and was staying with his sister until he could get back on his feet. I knew that we lost that chance to interview Jefferson while he was in the frame of mind where he thought he was going to die.

<u>January 4, 1996</u>

I made contact with the State Police by telephone and spoke with Corporal Dan Kelly from the major crime unit, requesting his help in interviewing Tom Jefferson in regards to the Compagna-Psaradelis homicides of 1973. I advised him that Jefferson had attempted suicide and was recovering and that he should have been interviewed before this, but Chief Baker and I haven't had any luck in finding someone from law enforcement that would help us accomplish that.

Corporal Kelly stated that he would like to help, but that he was working on another homicide case and he would have to check with his boss, Lieutenant Wiggins, and see if he would let him come off his present assignment in order to help. He further advised me that he would call me back and let me know if he could help.

January 5, 1996

It is 9:00 a.m. I guess I will head over to Candia, speak with Chief Baker and then we can make a phone call to Corporal Kelly and see if he is going to help us with the interview of Tom Jefferson.

"Good morning, Chief Baker. I thought I would come over and talk a little about the case and call Corporal Kelly. He seemed sincere in wanting to help us with the interview of Jefferson, but since Lieutenant Wiggins is his boss, I guess it will be up to him. I have a bad feeling and I hope I am wrong, but Lieutenant Wiggins doesn't like me and I bet he won't let the corporal help us. I sure hope I'm wrong."

Later in the day, I said to Chief Baker, "You know, Chief, we have been calling State Police Headquarters and the beeper number that Corporal Kelly gave me all day and there's no response from the corporal. It's almost 3:00 p.m. Why don't I call once again and then we can go over near the crime scene. I know the snow is deep over there, but I just want to see if there has been anyone going in there. It is strange but every time we go over there I can still feel death lingering in the air. I guess it will be that way until we can solve the murders.

"Well, let's make the phone call.

"Hello, could I please speak with Corporal Kelly? This is Lieutenant Horak calling.

"Just a minute. I'll see if he's in."

"Corporal, how did you make out with your boss in regards to helping us with the Compagna-Psaradelis investigation?"

"Well, Lieutenant, I approached Lieutenant Wiggins about you and Chief Baker requesting my help with the Compagna-Psaradelis homicide case and the Lieutenant wanted to know if I cleared it with Assistant Attorney General Michael Ramsdell. I told the Lieutenant that I hadn't. Lieutenant Horak, I am going to have to check this out and I will get back to you."

JOSEPH A. HORAK

"Well, Chief Baker, it doesn't look like we will receive any help from the State Police. Corporal Kelly is going to have to check with Assistant Attorney General Ramsdell and he doesn't like us, so I am sure he won't let Corporal Kelly help us. It's really too bad, but I guess we'll just have to wait for an answer from Corporal Kelly.

"Chief, why don't we take a quick trip over to the crime scene and then I can head back to Merrimack and see Sergeant Rousseau. Maybe he has had some luck in finding someone that will help us."

We drove over to the gravel pit. "Chief, where did that house come from? That sure is a big home and it backs almost into the crime scene."

"I guess it must have been built in the past few months. I haven't been over here in a while."

"Chief, there is no sense in slowing down or stopping. All we will do is get the people upset and there's no need of that. I might as well drop you back at the store and head down to Merrimack. Let me know if you hear anything from Corporal Kelly and if he contacts me, I'll call you."

Back in Merrimack, I greeted Sergeant Rousseau. "You look tired and cold, Sergeant Rousseau. By the looks of it, you have had a rough day."

"Yes, Lieutenant, I have been busy plowing snow and I have also been in contact with various members of the State Police. I think that I might be able to get someone to help us. I'll let you and Chief Baker know the minute I find someone that will help."

"Thanks Sergeant. I'll get going. You go in, take a hot bath and get some rest. I really appreciate everything you are doing to help us with this investigation."

January 7, 1996

"Good morning Sergeant Rousseau, I know it is early and Sunday morning but I wanted to talk with you about our investigation of the Compagna-Psaradelis murders. To be honest with you, I am pretty discouraged that we can't find someone to help us with the investigation. Tom Jefferson really should be interviewed <u>now</u>. Actually, he really should have been interviewed properly the night of December 22,

306

1995 when he shot himself. That was really the time that he was most likely to talk. You know, there is a time and a place for everything and I think they sure missed a good opportunity to either place or eliminate Tom Jefferson as a suspect.

"You know, Sergeant, Corporal Kelly from the State Police was going to try and help us, but when he talked with his boss, Lieutenant Wiggins, he was asked if he had checked with Assistant Attorney General Michael Ramsdell and he replied 'no.' Corporal Kelly was going to check with Attorney Ramsdell and then get back to either Chief Baker or myself but this never happened."

"You know Lieutenant, no one in law enforcement is going to help you because you have made them look bad and they don't like that."

"Sergeant, I had or have no intention to hurt anyone or make them look bad. Help was needed over the past 22 years and is still needed. It shouldn't make any difference if the person seeking help is liked or not, the main thing is to solve the murders, even if they are 22 years old.

"Sergeant, I have been here a little over a week, trying to find someone that would help us to interview Tom Jefferson and as you know, results have been negative just as they have been for the past 20 years. Oh, Chief Baker, you and I could have interviewed Jefferson, but we didn't want to hurt or spoil the investigation, thus Jefferson hasn't been interviewed and it doesn't appear that he will be. It is too bad, because they could place or eliminate him as a suspect, end the case or move onto another suspect, if that would be the case. To say they don't like me sure doesn't cut it.

"Sergeant, I spent well over a thousand dollars to come up here and get this interview done. It sure was a waste of time and money. Just more of the same old thing, no one is interested enough to help solve these murders, not because they can't be solved, but because they think I make them look bad. Sergeant, you know as well as I do that there are people out there that have information about who murdered the two girls. I just wish they would be brave enough to come forward. If they don't want to deal with Chief Baker and me, let us hope they will contact someone from the State or local police. The main thing is to solve the murders. Sergeant, there is a blizzard that is supposed to hit the New England area early tonight, so I am going to leave and head back to Oklahoma. I just hope I miss the storm.

"Chief Baker and I will not give up on the case and I hope you will follow through on this end and try to get someone to interview Tom Jefferson. I will help in anyway I can and if you have any questions or need me to come back, just write or call."

"Lieutenant, I have a meeting with the Major in the next few days and maybe I can get us some help. I'll keep in touch. Have a safe trip."

The snow has already started. I didn't think it would start until early this evening. It is a good thing I am flying out of here in 45 minutes.

We sure were lucky to get out of Boston. The snow is really coming down and I wonder if we will get out of Cincinnati. We should be there in another 20 minutes. We are about to land and you can't see out onto the wings of the plane. There are gale winds and heavy snow.

The whole airport is closing down. It looks like I am going to be stuck here like everyone else. Maybe I should have stayed in New Hampshire until the storm was over. Oh, well, I'll just have to make the best of it.

Since I am stuck here, I might as well make good use of my time and write a letter to Governor Steve Merrill and Colonel Lynn Presby.

January 7, 1996

Dear Colonel Presby,

On December 28, 1995, I received a telephone call from an ex-police officer from the town of Merrimack, New Hampshire advising me that one of the prime suspects in a double homicide case (1973) had shot himself in the head and was in critical condition at a hospital down in Nashua.

Chief Robert Baker, Retired, and I have been working on this investigation for the past 22 years, so I contacted him and advised that I would make arrangements to fly back to New Hampshire, but I didn't arrive until the 29th.

Since the suspect was conscious and yet still in critical condition, this was surely the best time to interview him. Since Chief Baker and I are both retired, we felt it was only proper that we should contact someone from law enforcement and seek their help in making this interview possible and hopefully to solve these murders after all these years.

I spent a thousand dollars for air fare and to rent a car in order to help bring this case to a conclusion. Chief Baker and I sought help from various law enforcement agencies, just as we have all these years, and results were negative, as they have been all these years. It is pretty sad when members of law enforcement won't help to place or eliminate a suspect in a double homicide because they don't like us, don't have money in the budget or for political reasons.

Like with every investigation, you often have to interview the suspect at the right time and under the right conditions. I really feel that law enforcement should have acted right away and interviewed the suspect, and I wonder now if anyone will interview him, or will have any luck since time has a way of changing things.

Thank you for taking the time to read this letter and I hope someone from law enforcement will be interested enough to bring this case to a conclusion.

Boy, that snow is really coming down and all I can see on the Arrival and Departure chart is, "*Cancel, Cancel, Cancel.*" Guess I am stuck here for the night like hundreds of other people.

I might as well use some more of my time to write a letter to Governor Steve Merrill.

Well, now that those letters are done, maybe I will try and get some sleep and that will eat up some of the time until they start moving people out of here.

I finally made it back to Oklahoma. What a trip, between being snowed in and the negative results from my trip to New Hampshire, and now that I am back, I found out that my publishing company went out of business. I wonder what can happen next.

January 24, 1996

Who can be calling me this early in the morning? "Hello, Lieutenant, is that you?"

"Is that you, Sergeant Rousseau?"

"Yes, Lieutenant, I am calling to let you know that I have had several meetings with members of the State Police Major Crime Unit and it appears that they, along with several members of the Attorney General's Office, will work on this case (Compagna-Psaradelis) and bring it to a conclusion. They will place or eliminate any and all suspects.

"Lieutenant you are not liked because you have created problems for a lot of people in the various law enforcement agencies by writing letters about the Compagna-Psaradelis investigation that made them look bad. I believe that the State Police and Attorney General's Office will go forward with the investigation but they don't want you or Chief Baker involved."

"Sergeant, Chief Baker and I don't care who solves the murders as long as they are solved."

February 1, 1996

"Telephone for you, Joe. It's Sergeant Rousseau from Merrimack, New Hampshire."

"Hi there, Sergeant Rousseau. Is everything OK and what is going on as far as Tom Jefferson goes? I sure hope you have some good news for me."

"There's really not too much news, Lieutenant, but I do like to keep in touch with you. I have had contact with the State Police and they, along with the Attorney General's Office, are going to finish the investigation in regards to the Compagna-Psaradelis murders.

"Lieutenant, they are in the process of making copies of the paperwork that is involved with the investigation. Once they have that done, they will move along with the investigation."

"That is really great news, Sergeant, but I hope they really put all their effort into investigating and that they aren't just doing a token investigation. I really hope they have good luck. I will do anything and everything that I can to help any of them and I am sure you and Chief Baker feel the same way. Keep in touch and I will do the same."

JUSTICE DENIED

<u>February 3, 1996</u>

The mail just came. I wonder if I have anything that is good. Usually it is the same old junk mail.

Well, here is a letter from the State Police. It sure isn't junk mail. It's dated January 30, 1996. That sure didn't take long to get here. Sometimes it takes seven or eight days for a letter from the East coast to get here.

Dear Mr. Horak:

I am in receipt of your letter to Governor Steve Merrill dated January 8, 1996. I have reviewed our correspondence and discussed the status of the Compagna-Psaradelis homicides with Colonel Lynn Presby and Lieutenant Wiggins, New Hampshire State Police Major Crime Unit.

As you know, in 1993 the State Police undertook a review of the Compagna-Psaradelis homicides. The investigators determined that the original investigation left many unanswered questions and unresolved issues, including the inability to eliminate individuals that could have committed this crime. However, the initial investigation uncovered no evidence to link anyone to these homicides.

In 1994, you attended a meeting with members of the Attorney General's Office Criminal Bureau and investigators from the State Police Major Crime Unit. At that meeting you indicated that an unnamed source had provided you with information, but you refused to share the informant's identity. Unfortunately, your assistance on this matter has not been forthcoming.

Corporal James Hughes is the investigator assigned to the Compagna-Psaradelis homicides. He is currently pursuing a number of leads, which I am hopeful will move this investigation toward a successful conclusion. If I can be of further assistance, please do not hesitate to contact me.

That was a nice letter but I do not agree with the contents and I will have to write a reply to the State Police within the next few days .

311

JOSEPH A. HORAK

<u>February 6, 1996</u>
I guess it is time for me to write a reply to the State Police.

Dear Captain John Barthelmes:

I am in receipt of your letter written on behalf of Colonel Lynn Presby dated January 30, 1996, this being in regards to the letters I had sent to Governor Steve Merrill and Colonel Presby.

I know that I am probably a pain in the neck, but I can never let go of this case until it has been solved. I, of course, will do anything to help bring this case to a conclusion, For the past 22 years I have attempted to find someone from law enforcement that would have enough courage to step forward and finish this investigation.

There have always been suspects in the case and these suspects have never been eliminated.

You mentioned that in 1993 the State Police undertook a review of the Compagna-Psaradelis homicides and that the investigators determined that the original investigation left many unanswered questions and unresolved issues, including the inability to eliminate individuals that could have committed this crime. However, the initial investigation uncovered no evidence to link anyone to these homicides.

Captain Barthelmes, I have to disagree. Thomas Jefferson has always been a suspect and still is. Has anyone even taken the time to find out why he tried to take his own life on December 22, 1995? I even spent a thousand dollars and came back up to New Hampshire to try and interview Jefferson. Chief Baker and I realized that we had to do things right and that we would have to try and get some help from someone in law enforcement in order not to spoil any evidence that might be obtained in regards to these murders. It is pretty sad that we couldn't find anyone to help because they don't like me, want me to pay for the investigation, or it is election time and no one wants to make anyone look bad.

Yes, in 1994 I attended a meeting with members of the Attorney General's Office Criminal Bureau, investigators from the State Police Crime Unit and Chief Robert Baker. To be honest with you, Captain, that meeting was a waste of time and effort. I, for one, thought this meeting was going to help move the investigation forward and help bring this case to a conclusion but that wasn't the case. All it really turned out to be was a time to "Chew Out Joe Horak," tell him he was a liar and that he was making everyone look bad.

Yes, Captain, there was talk about an unnamed source that had provided me with information about two men that have knowledge about who took the lives of the two girls. This person does not want to get involved because they are in fear of harm to themselves, their family or property. I can't and won't release this person's name any more than you would if you were in the same position I am in. I will say that I sent the State Police a letter in 1992 advising them of this information and if investigators from either the Attorney General's Office and State Police had any problems with the information, why did they wait two years to question it?

All Chief Baker and I ever wanted was to have the killers caught and that is still our goal. I want you to know that I would do anything to help anyone from the Attorney General's Office, State Police or any other law enforcement agency. I do think it is time to place or eliminate any and all suspects in the case once and for all.

May 16, 1996

Who can that be calling me this early in the morning?

"Hello, Lieutenant Horak, is that you?"

"Is that you, Sergeant Rousseau?"

"Yes, Lieutenant. I was wondering if you have heard anything from the Attorney General or the State Police in regards to Tom Jefferson."

"Not a word, Sergeant, how about you? Have you heard from anyone?"

"No, Lieutenant, I haven't heard a single thing. The last time I spoke with the State Police, they stated that once they made copies of the case and reviewed it, that they would then interview Jefferson."

"You know, Sergeant, they have been saying that for years, and I mean 20 or so years. I am pretty sick of all these so-called promises of help, which are just a bunch of words that don't mean a thing to them. Look at how they acted when I came back from Oklahoma in December. We tried everyone from the Attorney General's office, the State Police and various Sheriff Departments in order to find someone that would interview Tom Jefferson and attempt to obtain a "Dying Declaration" from him. As usual, a lot of promises, but nothing is ever done to move this investigation forward.

"You're right, Lieutenant, what can I say? If I hear anything from anyone that someone from the State is really investigating this case, I will let you know."

1996

Is Chief Baker there? This is Lieutenant Horak calling.

Hold on Lieutenant, "I'll get him for you."

Hello Lieutenant, "What's going on, are you still out in Oklahoma or are you back in New Hampshire?" Is there anything new on our case?

Yes Chief, "I am still out in Oklahoma; but I wanted to call you and let you know, "How small the world is."

What do you mean by that Lieutenant?

Well Chief, it's this, "I have a daughter-in-law who has four or five sisters, a few days ago she received a telephone call from her mother back in New Hampshire. Her mother told her that one of her sisters was going with this guy and he got her pregnant.

She said, "You have to be kidding Mom, who is the guy?"

Her mother replied, "Some guy by the name of Tom."

"Where is he from?", her mother replied, "Merrimack, New Hampshire."

"I know lots of guys named Tom in Merrimack, what's his last name?, Virginia, "I am pretty sure it is Jefferson, Tom Jefferson."

You guessed it Chief, "Our prime suspect in the Compagna/ Psaradelis murders."

Chief, at some point in time they were reading a copy of "TRUTH & JUSTICE" and the connection was made to me. Would you believe, he walked away from her sister and went back to his wife. It sure makes you wonder how many women he has used or hurt over the years.

I guess you can now understand why I said, "How small the world is." I bet this doesn't happen in very many cases such as ours."

It doesn't appear that anyone in New Hampshire is going to help us, but I am sure you will stick with me until we bring Jefferson to Justice.

Keep in touch Chief, I'll see you soon.

October 10, 1996

I guess I can finally make that phone call to Chief Baker even though it's after ten o'clock.

"Hello, Chief Baker, is that you?"

"Is that you, Lieutenant Horak?"

"Yes, Chief, I am sorry to be calling you so late, but I have just come back from Oklahoma and I was thinking that we really need to get together and decide what course of action we should take to solve our murder case. I have decided to stay in New Hampshire until we solve the murders and bring our suspects to justice. It sure doesn't look like any-one else will do it. How about my coming over to see you in the morning? On the way, I can stop off at Merrimack. Maybe I will luck out and find Sergeant Rousseau in his office. Will you be in the store on Friday?

"Yes, Lieutenant, I'll see you then."

Good, Sergeant Rousseau's truck is parked in front of the office, he must be there.

"Hi, Sergeant Rousseau."

"Hey, Lieutenant Horak, what are you doing here in New Hampshire? The last time I spoke with you, you were out in Oklahoma."

"I was, Sergeant, but I have come back here with the hope that we can finish the Compagna/Psaradelis case. I guess I really need to be here, since there isn't anyone connected with law enforcement that is going to finish it."

"Well, you know, Lieutenant Horak, no one likes you because they say you make everyone look bad and they sure don't like that."

"Sergeant, I don't mean to make anyone look bad, but on the other hand, if someone would take the time and effort to place or eliminate any and all suspects in the investigation, especially Wayne Powers and Tom Jefferson, then Chief Baker and I wouldn't be writing letters to the Governor, Attorney General, State Police and others. Chief Baker and I will _not_ give up. We promised the girls we would catch their killers. It has already taken twenty-three years and we will stick with the investigation for another twenty-three years if necessary."

"Lieutenant, you know, you are never going to get Tom Jefferson. He has turned his whole life around. He has his own business now, he's adding onto his house and has lots of money. You are never going to get him."

"Sergeant Rousseau, I really don't understand the way you think. You know, just as I know, that Tom Jefferson and Wayne Powers are responsible for the murders of Diane and Anne. How can you think that we should give up on this investigation just because _you_ feel Jefferson has turned his life around. If he did, in fact, murder the two girls, he deserves to be brought to justice and made to pay for the crime."

"Lieutenant, I'll still say that your never going to get Tom Jefferson because he has turned his whole life around and no one is really interested in bringing up the Compagna/Psaradelis murder case after all these years."

"Hi, Chief Baker, it has been quite awhile since I have seen you. How are things going with you and your country store?"

"Things are going good, Lieutenant. What brings you back here, other than our murder case?"

"You said it right there Chief, we just can't let our promise to Diane and Anne fall by the wayside and besides, the killer(s) deserve to be brought to justice. You and I are going to sit down and talk about our investigation as it stands today and then decide what course of action we will take. It is hard to know what to do because we really have tried everything possible and we are getting close to being at the end of the line and that isn't good. Chief, before I head back, I would appreciate it if you would go over to the crime scene with me again. I always have that feeling that some day we will come across a piece of evidence that will help us solve these murders."

"That is OK by me, Lieutenant. My son will be back here in about an hour and we can go then."

"Chief, you know this crime scene really hasn't changed in all these years. I don't know about you, but I can still smell and feel death in the air and that sure isn't a good feeling.

Every time we come here, I can almost feel the girls telling us not to give up on our promise to them and you know we will keep that promise and bring the killer(s) to justice."

"Well, let's look around. Well, Lieutenant, we have gone through the whole area and nothing has really changed and we have even said a little prayer, unless there is something else you want to do."

"No, Chief, I guess you better get back to your store and I will head back to Greenfield. Oh, by the way, I will start writing those letters to the Governor, Attorney General, etc., maybe we will have some luck yet. I do know we just have to keep trying."

The days, weeks and months go by and it is hard for me to believe that we are into January of 1997 and we are no further ahead with this investigation than we were in July of 1973.

March 3, 1997

Dear Chief Baker:

I just wanted to keep you abreast of things, I decided that I would draft a letter that I could send to both the Compagna and Psaradelises. I have part of it done, thought I would let

317

you know what I have drafted so far and maybe you could add to it. I just wanted them to know that a story has been written in regards to the investigation into the murders of their children.

March 2, 1997
Dear Marcel and Dorothy:
    I hope this letter finds you both well and that things are going alright. I sent you the material from Canada and I hope you were able to square it away. My not being able to understand the language sure doesn't help me.
    I am writing this letter for two reasons and the first one being Canada, the one I have already spoken about. I hope you will take the time to read over my second reason.
    You know folks, I have been with you in heart, thoughts and actions since July 12, 1973 when you reported Diane and Anne Psaradelis as missing and the death of the two girls touched my life just as it did yours, but in different ways. Chief Baker and I promised Diane and Anne that we would never give up on the investigation until their killer or killers were brought to justice.
    Here we are, almost into March 1997 and nearly 24 years since I started the missing persons report. We have always had suspects and the same suspects we had nearly 24 years ago are still our prime suspects today.
    This investigation has been and still is a hard road to travel on. It has been full of discouragement, encouragement, time, money, hurt and sadness. Chief Baker and I still travel this road in hope of bringing the people responsible for the murders to justice. We have tried every avenue and knocked on every door to any agency we felt might give us the aid and assistance we need to bring this investigation to a close.
    Our promise to Diane and Anne remains with us and we will continue to do whatever we can to keep our promise to the girls.
    After all these years of trying to find help from the local police departments and all the way up the ladder to the Governor's Office, crime shows etc., the only hope we had to ever bringing this case to a conclusion was to take that last giant step and that was to write a book, with the hope that it might help to bring someone forward that would furnish us with the information we need to bring the killer or killers to justice.

JUSTICE DENIED

Chief, As you can tell, this is just a rough draft, I really would like to have both families help us as they have done in the past, it is really hard for me to understand why they won't help us. If my daughter was murdered, I would be thankful to know that two people were still working on the investigation and wouldn't stop until their killers were brought to justice.

I'll drop over and speak with you in person in regards to any thoughts we should add or take out from the letter.

May 20, 1997

I guess I'll go out and check the mail, we should receive some replies from some of the letters we have sent out.

Hey, there is a letter addressed to James Horak. I wonder if it is for me. It has the correct address, so maybe they just made an error in the first name. I'll just go ahead and open it.

Dear Mr. Horak,

I am writing to you in regards to the Compagna/Psaradelis murder case. I recently contacted the Merrimack Police Department in connection to a long forgotten memory about the case. Lieutenant Milligan called me back and asked for further details. He asked that I write a statement for the police files, which I did. A copy of this statement is attached.

My parents, who still live in Merrimack, found out you had written a book and purchased a copy. I finished it 2 days ago. I had already contacted the police and written a statement before I ever knew of your book.

My long time high school boyfriend, Tim Decato, was the cousin of this Powers boy who committed suicide (you reference him in your book as Wayne Powers). I know factually he was one of two men who killed the girls. My ex-boyfriend knows the identity of the other killer and knows details about this case he shouldn't know. All of this was explained to Lieutenant Milligan. He asked that I not contact anyone I know in Merrimack, as he planned to pay a visit to a few people I know there. He wanted it to be a surprise visit. I had recently spoken with Tim Decato about my memories - 20 years ago and he told me his cousin had confessed to him, that he was involved in the girls' murder.

After submitting my statement to the Merrimack Police Department, I have not received an adequate explanation of what has taken place due to my statement. My involvement has resulted in harassing phone calls, in which my local Police Department and the phone company are involved. Strangely, the kind of calls I receive are exactly of the same nature of calls made to the victim's families (according to your book). No words, just someone on the line who waits, sometimes for over a minute, and then hangs up. The phone company has notified me that the caller "Knows what he is doing" as the person calls from different districts and cities every time he calls, so there is no matching codes. I have received at least twenty calls.

Anyway, please read my statement. I was touched by your integrity and sincerity in trying to solve this case. I believe I can help. I personally know people who have vital information. I believe the murderer should be identified and prosecuted to the full extent of the law.

As I state in the written document, I am in the Human Services field. I'm a psychotherapist and finishing my Ph.D. in Clinical Psychology. I posses great empathy and concern for others. What happened in this case is atrocious!

I would like to speak with you about several things I know about this case. It has been weighing heavily on my mind. Please call me at (phone #). I currently live in California. If you leave your number, I will call you.

That was really quite an interesting letter and one that Chief Baker and I have waited for the past twenty-four years.

<u>May 21, 1997</u>

320

I think I should make a phone call to Chief Baker and tell him about the letter I received from this Lisa J. Rosa, and I probably should read him parts of the statement she had given to the Merrimack Police Department and then to me.

"Hello, Chief Baker, is that you?"

"Yes, Lieutenant, what's up, have you turned up anything new on our investigation?"

"Well, Chief, I received a four page letter from a woman out in California. She talks about the Compagna/Psaradelis murders and of how she contacted the Merrimack Police Department, spoke with a Detective Michael Milligan and sent him a statement in regards to what she knows about the people who apparently murdered Diane Compagna and Anne Psaradelis. She somehow heard about me and the book *"TRUTH & JUSTICE"*. I am going to tell you parts of her statement now, and when I come over, I'll let you read the entire statement. Chief, it really is a very good statement, it contains twelve pages. Lisa J. Rosa sure sounds like she knows what she is talking about. During this whole investigation, I have never known or heard the name Lisa."

"That sounds pretty good, Lieutenant. Please keep me posted. Please bring her letter and the statement over. I'll be anxious to read it."

May 23, 1997

Good morning Chief Baker."

"Lieutenant, what brings you over here this time of the morning?"

"Well, Chief, I wanted to talk with you in person about Lisa Rosa, her letter and the statement she gave to Lieutenant Milligan of the Merrimack PD. I also wanted you to read the statement Lisa wrote in regards to the murder of Diane and Anne. Chief, that statement from Lisa J. Rosa is dated April 19, 1997."

Dear Detective Milligan:

Per your request, I am making a written statement regarding the information I discussed with you on Monday, April 21, 1997. To reiterate, this information concerns the double mur-

JOSEPH A. HORAK

der of a Diane Compagna and Anne Psaradelis. I apologize for the delay in submitting this statement to you, but I have been greatly disturbed over this issue and have found it difficult to perform this task. I will, with a clear mind and to the best of my recollection, outline the information presented to me and all events concerning this issue.

I lived in Merrimack, New Hampshire from the spring of 1973 until the summer of 1978, at which time I moved to California. In the Fall of 1976 (September, I believe) I met and began dating Tim Decato, a resident of Merrimack, NH. We had a committed and monogamous relationship for 2½ years; we continued our relationship long distance when I moved to California. During the years I spent with Tim, I became very close to his nuclear and extended family. Even after our relationship terminated, I remained close to his parents for many years. Between the years of 1978 and 1986, I returned to Merrimack at least once a year to visit my family, and often visited the Decato's as well. I believe the last time I saw Tim Decato was around the summer of 1984.

After I had dated Tim for over a year, probably late in 1977, he confided in me and told me he knew who had killed the two murdered victims, previously mentioned. This is what I recall of that conversation. We were in his car and he said, "I know who killed those girls". I made some comment confirming the girls he was speaking of. He was visibly disturbed. He stated that his cousin confessed to him that he, and another man had committed these murders. He then told me that his cousin committed suicide shortly after. When I asked why his cousin would do this, he replied "he was fucked up and things got out of control". By "fucked up", I confirmed that he meant his cousin was high on drugs, not that his cousin was diagnosed with a mental illness.

I also confirmed this was not a premeditated murder. At the time Tim was emotionally upset about this and I was equally disturbed and shaken. I can't say why I did not say anything at the time, but I believe it had to do with my young age and my concerns for and the closeness to Tim Decato, at that point in my life.

Until last Thursday evening, April 17th, I believe around 11:00 p.m. Western Standard Time, I had forgotten or repressed the conversation I had with Tim Decato in 1977. I cannot say what triggered this memory, but as I was lying down, between wakefulness and sleep, I started to have bad dreams and all of a sudden the murder and the conversation I had with Tim Decato came flooding back. The only thing I could think was whether the parents and the families of these two young girls ever knew what really happened. I have worked with families who have suffered tremendous loss and I know the "not knowing" is a horrific trauma that can haunt for a lifetime. I felt compelled to call the Merrimack Police Department immediately, to give them all the information I had, in hopes that somehow it would be able to stop the haunting and maybe bring closure and eventual peace to the survivors of these murder victims.

At approximately 11:05 p.m., I called the Merrimack Police Department. I spoke with an officer who connected me to someone who was familiar with the case. I relayed my story and provided my name, address and home phone number. In telling my story, I could only remember one victim's last name (Psaradelis) but did not know how to spell it. With the officer on the phone, I searched old Merrimack High School yearbooks in an attempt to find this information. I was quite upset at the time. The officer assured me it would be in the police files. He then informed me that he was going to write a report, on the basis of our phone conversation, and stated that I might be contacted by the police for further questioning.

For some reason I felt it was urgent to try and identify Tim's cousin. I made up my mind to call Tim Decato. I had not spoken to him in over 10 years. I believed, for several reasons, it was best to call him immediately(in the middle of the night) by professing to have a terrible nightmare which was connected to our 1977 conversation. I reasoned that he would be less suspicious if I called late at night, due to a bad dream VS calling mid-day and asking questions. I also felt he would be less guarded and defensive in his response if he had recently awoken from a deep sleep. In this scenario, I was hoping he might relay details that might otherwise be left unsaid.

At approximately 12:00 am (WST), I called Tim Decato. He lives in Merrimack. He was groggy when he answered the phone. When I identified myself, he asked why I was calling him at 4:00 a.m. I will try to recall this conversation as close verbatim as possible.

L: "I'm really flipped out. I just had a bad nightmare about something you told me about a long time ago. Do you remember the conversation we had about the two Merrimack girls who were murdered?"

T. "Yeah, what about it?"

L. "It was Robert who killed those girls, wasn't it, wasn't it?" (I intentionally sounded extremely distressed).

T.   "No, no - it was his older brother."

L. "Didn't you say he died?"

T "Yeah - he killed himself about six months after the murders."

L. "After he confessed to killing those two girls to you?"

T"I never said he confessed anything to me."

L. "Then how do you know how he did it?"

T. Everyone knew, it was common knowledge. Why do you think the police stopped investigating the murders after he was dead?"

L. "You told me he didn't do it alone and someone else was involved in murdering those girls. Who's the other guy?"

T "You don't know him."

L. (Sounding emotionally overwhelmed) "But do I know his brothers or sisters?"

T. "He doesn't have any."

L. "You know who this guy is and you never said anything!"

T. "Look, he's married now and he's got kids."

L. *"So what! Like that absolves him?" He's responsible for murdering two teenage girls."*

T. *"That was a long time ago."*

(When I realized he wasn't going to volunteer any further information, I tried to get him emotionally upset about the death of his cousin).

L. *"You must have been pissed! Your cousin couldn't live with himself after what he'd done, so he took his own life! This other guy got off scot-free and now he's married and has children. Doesn't that make you furious?"*

T. *"No, not at all. My cousin just couldn't handle it and this guy can, that's the only difference."*

It was very bone chilling to hear him make that statement I realized I no longer knew who Tim Decato was. By this time, he was wide awake and wasn't going to say any more about it. He started to make small talk. He asked me where I was living and I foolishly replied. I was trying to sound natural and nonchalant. I did not tell him and definitely didn't insinuate that I had called the police, or would ever call the police. I kept to my original story of being so terrified by my dream and the memory, that I needed to talk with him. We talked about my family and his family. He asked me if I was married and I replied I was not. I took this opportunity to confirm the last name of his cousin Powers.

L. *"Didn't your cousin Robert marry Mary?*

T. *"Yeah, Mary Johnson. They've got two kids; one is in college now and the other is only 6 years old."*

As soon as I hung up, I called the Merrimack Police Department back. I spoke with the officer I had previously spoken to. I informed him that I had a conversation with Tim Decato, he seemed skeptical and asked me for Tim's telephone number, as backup evidence, and I promptly provided him with that information.

The next day, April 18th, I called my parents from work. I asked the names of the two local papers (Nashua Telegraph and the Manchester Union Leader). I very briefly explained to my parents why I was asking, and told them I wanted to access the newspapers' archived records of the murder. My father became very angry with me, stating I had no right to bring up this past case. He stated I might hurt someone because of it. I retorted that I had every right to report what I knew, that it was right and honorable thing to do, and the only person who might get hurt would be a man who brutally murdered two teenage girls.

I hope this rather extensive statement is clear and informative. The whole ordeal has been very upsetting and time consuming. Nevertheless, I believe it is well worth it if I can help identify the killer. I do intend on calling you. Should you have any questions in the mean time, please feel free to call me at the telephone number I have already given you.

"Chief Baker, it is a good statement and I truly feel it is the "*key*" to open the door that will allow us to solve these murders. We just have to find someone from the Attorney General's Office or the State Police that feels the same way we do and that is no easy task.

"Chief, I think that I will write to the Governor, the Attorney General and the State Police in regards to this new information we have just received from Lisa Rosa and I will also send them a copy of her letter and statement. I almost forgot to tell you, Chief, Lisa has already been receiving harassing phone calls since she contacted the Merrimack Police Department and she believes these calls are connected to the murders of Diane Compagna and Anne Psaradelis. She is also in fear of her own safety."

May 29, 1997

The Hon. Jeanne Shaheen, Governor of New Hampshire
State House
Concord, New Hampshire 03301

RE: COMPAGNA/PSARADELIS Homicide of 1973
  "NEW DEVELOPMENTS"

Dear Governor Shaheen:

I am writing this letter to you because there have been new developments in the Compagna/Psaradelis homicide case.

I have been in contact with Ms Lisa J. Rosa, M.A. who lives in California in regards to these new developments and I hope you will take time to read over her statement that she has made in regards to the murders of Diane Compagna and Anne Psaradelis.

Governor Shaheen, it is really time to bring this 24 year old double homicide case to a conclusion. To be honest with you, I am in fear for the safety of Lisa Rosa. Since she gave this information to the Merrimack Police Department she has been receiving harassing phone calls daily on a regular basis and she believes these are tied in with the case.

The one person that she mentions in her statement and the one that has taken his own life, is in fact one of my suspects. The other one being Tom Jefferson DOB 03/17/54 who is often between the Merrimack, New Hampshire and the California areas.

Governor, I am sending this information to your new Attorney General Philip McLaughlin and I pray that he will move this investigation forward before it causes Lisa Rosa or someone else injury or even death. Please know that Chief Robert Baker and I will assist you or anyone else with this investigation.

I would appreciate your letting me know if this investigation will be done and I really do feel that the safety of Lisa Rosa is at stake.

Sincerely,
Joseph A. Horak
Lieutenant/Detective Ret.

<u>May 29, 1997</u>
Attorney General Philip McLaughlin
State House

JOSEPH A. HORAK

Concord, New Hampshire 03301

RE: COMPAGNA/PSARADELIS Homicide case of 1973 (NEW DEVELOPMENTS)

Dear Attorney McLaughlin:
I am writing this letter to you because there are some new developments in the Compagna/Psaradelis investigation.

I am in contact with one Lisa J. Rosa, M.A. who lives in California in regards to these new developments and I hope you will take the time to read over her statement that she made in regards to the murders of Diane Compagna and Anne Psaradelis. I would appreciate it if you would ask the State Police to let you see a copy of the letter I sent to them in 1992 and you will find that it ties in with the statement from Lisa J. Rosa.

Ms Rosa contacted the Merrimack Police Department and spoke with Lieutenant/Detective Michael Milligan about the case and giving him a statement. Since this time, Ms Rosa has been receiving harassing phone calls on a daily basis, she believes this ties in with the Compagna/Psaradelis murders.

The one person she mentions in her statement and the one that took his own life is in fact of my suspects. The other one being Tom Jefferson DOB 03/17/54 who is often between Merrimack, New Hampshire and the California areas.

Ms Rosa is concerned about her own safety and I am just as concerned for her or anyone else that might come forward with information.

I would appreciate it if you would assign someone to the case, it not be Michael Ramsdell, as Chief Baker and I haven't had much luck with trying to have him move this investigation along.

Please know that Chief Baker and I will help you in any way we can and I hope you will advise me if you will investigate this case.

Sincerely,
Joseph A. Horak Det./Lt (Ret.)

June 22, 1997
The days and weeks slip by, a month has gone by and no response from either the Governor or Attorney General, I guess it is time to write to them again, might as well sit down and do it right now while I have the time.

Governor Jeanne Shaheen, Governor of New Hampshire
State House
Concord, New Hampshire 03301

Dear Governor Shaheen:
I know that your days and nights must be filled with business and decisions of every kind, and I really hate to add to your workload. As you know, I have written to you a few times about the Compagna Psaradelis murders of 1973, sending you a copy of my book, Truth & Justice: A Detective's Dilemma, and an additional Chapter written since the book was published. Most recently I wrote to you regarding new developments in the case.
Governor, I am very concerned about Lisa Rosa, who has come forward with information that could help in solving the 1973 murders of these two young girls. I have been in contact with Ms Rosa both by mail and by phone. I understand that she has been receiving harassing phone calls since her contact with Lt./Det. Michael Milligan of the Merrimack Police Department, Merrimack, New Hampshire. Since Tom Jefferson the primary suspect in this case does go between Merrimack, New Hampshire and Oceanside, California, he could very well be the one placing the phone calls to her.
I know that I have advised you several times that Chief Robert Baker and I have had two prime suspects in this investigation, the same ones since 1973. It is hard for me to understand why someone in law enforcement won't have the courage

329

to step forward and bring this case to a conclusion. To be honest with you, Governor Shaheen, I think it is going to take a person such as you, who has the power to demand that this case be investigated and solved. Chief Baker and I know that our suspects, Wayne Powers and Tom Jefferson are the ones responsible for the murders of these two young girls.

I believe that Lisa Rosa has opened the door that would allow the placing or eliminating of these suspects at last. It is time the surviving murderer be brought to justice. Would you please demand that this case be investigated and moved forward. All it would take is for people like Tim Decato, Bruce Clark, Jason Powers, John King and other friends of Jefferson and Powers to be interviewed by the proper authorities. Please don't let the door Lisa Rosa has opened, shut and disappear forever. It would be a credit to you, any law enforcement agency or officer, or anyone else to solve the murders of two 15 year old girls after 24 years.

At some point, Governor, I am sure the news media will pick up on these new developments in the Compagna/Psaradelis murders and will wonder why something isn't really being done to bring the people responsible to justice, especially when they have been suspects for twenty-four years.

I would appreciate a reply from you. Lisa Rosa will cooperate with the investigators in any way possible, as will Chief Baker and I. Thank you for taking the time to read my letter.
Sincerely,
Joseph A. Horak Det./Lt. Retired

<u>August 13, 1997</u>
A letter from the Attorney Generals Office.

RE: Compagna/Psaradelis Murders

Dear Mr. Horak:

JUSTICE DENIED

Governor Jeanne Shaheen's Office has asked me to re-spond to your letter to the Governor dated June 22, 1997. In your letter, you reference information you obtained from Lisa Rosa. Please forward a copy of the information that you have received from Ms Rosa. After I have read and reviewed the in-formation, I will contact the New Hampshire State Police Ma-jor Crime Unit and share the information with them. As you are well aware, all information that you provide to me will be diligently followed up by investigators.

I look forward to receiving the information.
Sincerely,
Michael D. Ramsdell
Associate Attorney General

August 16, 1997

I guess I should write to Governor Jeanne Shaheen again and reply to the letter I just received from Associate Attorney General Michael D. Ramsdell, in regards to the Compagna/Psaradelis case.

Dear Governor Shaheen:

I wrote to you in January (1996) and requested your help in regards to the murders of Diane Compagna and Anne Psaradelis that took place in July of 1973. I did receive a re-ply from you and you advised me that as soon as you appointed a new attorney general that you would have him help with the case.

Governor, I sent you and your new Attorney General (Philip McLaughlin) letters in May and June, I advised you of a woman (Lisa J Rosa, M.A.) that came forward after 24 years and has put her own life on the line in order to help bring the killer or killers of these two girls to justice. I have sent you a copy of her statement given to the Merrimack Police Depart-ment as well as to myself. I have advised you, as well as Attor-ney General Philip McLaughlin, that this woman has been re-ceiving harassing phone calls since she contacted the Merri-mack Police Department and she believes these calls are con-

nected to the Compagna/Psaradelis murders. She is in fear of her own safety or even her life. She has never heard from the Merrimack Police Department, the Attorney General or you. I haven't had any reply from anyone in regards to my letters or statement from Lisa Rosa that I sent to you or the attorney general.

There has to be something wrong, Governor, when justice cannot be given in the case of these two young 15 year old girls that were murdered and no one seems to care about Lisa Rosa, who could be harmed through fear, threats or even death.

How is it possible to have two suspects in this murder case since September 1973 and here it is nearly September 1997 and these people are still our "prime suspects"? The suspects in this case should be placed or eliminated to everyone's satisfaction. Chief Baker and I are 99% sure that these suspects are our killers. In 1973 we tried to have these two suspects placed or eliminated as suspects and no one was really interested.

In August of 1992 a letter was sent to the State Police with information about two men that have knowledge about who murdered the Compagna/Psaradelis girls. One of these two men was the brother to one of our suspects. This information was never checked out. In 1994, there was a meeting at the State House in Concord, New Hampshire and people from both the Attorney General's office and the State Police, as well as Chief Baker and myself. They didn't believe the information in the letter and stated that they would not investigate the murders any further unless we told them who the informant was that gave the information, and of course we couldn't do that, any more than they could tell us such information if they were in the same position we were. If they thought something was wrong with the letter and the information it contained, why did they wait two years to question it?

In April 1997, Lisa J. Rosa comes forward, contacts the Merrimack Police Department and gives a written statement, our "Prime Suspects" are brought into the picture once again. Still no one from law enforcement will come forward to help and they sure aren't interested in the safety of Lisa J. Rosa or even bringing the killers of these two young girls to justice.

It shouldn't make any difference if I am liked or not liked by anyone. This case can be solved and justice should prevail. If Chief Baker and I could talk with you or the Attorney General in person, I am sure you would have a clearer picture of why these people are our suspects and why we know this case can be solved. We have lived this case for the past 24 years, I sure hope you won't allow it to move into 25th or more years.

Governor, won't you please help by demanding that any and all suspects in this case be placed or eliminated and just as important, protect Lisa J. Rosa from harm or even death.

I hope you will reply to my letter and extend the help that is needed to solve these murders and let us finally put this case to rest. I know it would mean a lot to the victims, the families, society and us.

Sincerely,

Joseph A. Horak,

Lt/Det., Ret.

August 27, 1997

I wonder who can be calling me at this time of night. I'm sure it must be some kind of a problem.

"Hello."

"Is that you, Lieutenant Horak?"

"Yes, it is. Who is calling?"

"It's Lisa Rosa. I'm calling you to let you know that I called Merrimack, New Hampshire last night. It was about 3:00 a.m. I woke up Tim Decato and we talked about the murders of the two girls and I wanted you to know some of the answers to some of the questions I asked him.

"He said he didn't know any Tom.

"He said, 'Oh, yeah, I know Tom Jefferson.'

"He said Tom was a little kid.

"He said you have the wrong person.

"He said, 'None of your business.'

"He said Wayne Powers and Tom Jefferson never hung around each other.

"He said he last saw Tom Jefferson in the hospital after he shot himself.

"He said Tom Jefferson shot himself because he was having trouble with his family.

"He said, 'You aren't going to the police.'

"He said, 'It's none of your business.'

"He said, 'I don't know anything. Don't get me involved.'

"Lieutenant Horak, I will call you again and let you know if I hear anything from the Governor, State Police, Lieutenant Milligan or anyone else."

"Thanks for calling, Lisa. I am really proud of you for coming forward and helping with this investigation. I know that you are more than concerned about your own safety, but I also know that you have stated that you will do what ever it takes to help me and others until the people responsible for the murders of Diane and Anne are brought to justice."

I guess I will draft some kind of an article that Chief Baker and I can put into the newspaper as we are fast approaching the anniversary date as to when the girls were found murdered. It doesn't seem possible that all these years have passed and the murders remain unsolved.

"Lieutenant Horak, that is really a great article that you have written up in regards to the Compagna/Psaradelis murders. If we can get it into the Manchester Union Leader, I am sure everyone would read it and there would be a lot of questions asked as to why this case hasn't been solved. I'll contact Nancy from the Union Leader and ask her if she could add this article to a story she might come up with that would draw the interest of the public. Maybe then, this investigation could be moved forward."

Nancy Meersman, Staff Reporter
The Union Leader
100 William Lobe Drive

JUSTICE DENIED

Manchester, NH 03103

Ref: Compagna - Psaradelis Homicides of 1973

Dear Nancy:

I know that Chief Baker, Retired, has been in contact with you in regards to this case. After 24 years, it is time to bring this case to a conclusion with the arrest of the person or persons responsible for these murders.

We need your help and that of your paper in making this possible. The enclosed paperwork is true, no matter what anyone night say. There is no reason for either Chief Baker or me to lie.

We have had two suspects right from the start of the homicide investigation and they are still our prime *suspects after 24 years.*

In August of 1992, information was passed on to the State Police, via letter, in regards to two people that have information as to who murdered the two girls, Diane Compagna and Anne Psaradelis. The information involves the same suspects we have had all these years. Nothing was ever done with it.

In May of 1997, a person came forward with information that opens the door to catching the killer or killers - (same suspects). This person has been receiving harassing phone calls since they made contact with the Merrimack Police Department. (April, 1997).

We have truly tried to find someone in law enforcement that would have the courage to step forward and finish this investigation - so far, no takers.

If you and your paper can help us, it would be appreciated. If you use the article, could you the same photograph you took in the September 27th, 1993 for the article you did on the investigation?

If you find you can't or won't do the article, please send my paperwork back and I'll find another newspaper that will. I just thought that since the Union Leader helped before, they would want to finish the story.

If you should decide to help us, and you think it best that Chief Baker and I should not be put on the list of people that they could contact, just delete our names. We just want the case solved as it should be. Thank you.
Sincerely,
Joe Horak

WHAT HAPPENED TO OUR GIRLS
Compagna-Psaradelis Murders of 1973

New Hampshire has a motto: LIVE FREE OR DIE. How about adding, JUSTICE FOR ALL. Are these just words? Do victims, witnesses, investigators and society all deserve equal justice under our system? Does this same system protect us from Fear, Harm, and Discrimination?

MISSING PERSONS:
DIANE COMPAGNA and ANN PSARADELIS
81 Days Later: Double Homicide Discovered
September 30, 1973:
Diane Compagna/Ann Psaradelis case actually
starts July 4, 1973

24 years later - July 12, 1997- Murders remain unsolved and for the past 24 years, *the same suspects have never been placed or eliminated as suspects.*
The long road to justice - will it stop on a dead end road? It's up to you and the investigators dedicated to following through with their investigation, no matter how long it takes or how rough and difficult the road might be to travel on.

JUSTICE DENIED

Being murdered could happen to *anyone;* your daughter, son, father, mother, spouse or friend, and it could take place *anywhere, at any time.*

Protect And Serve - Justice For Everyone - these are but a few of the terms we hear from our law enforcement agencies, judicial system, and even our elected officials.

The Compagna-Psaradelis murders remain unsolved because these poor girls aren't receiving the justice they *deserve, justice that should be applied equally to everyone,* including them.

On July 12, 1973, two young girls, Diane Compagna and Anne Psaradelis, both fifteen, were reported as missing. After 81 days of searching, hoping, and praying, the poor young teenagers were found to have been murdered in a wooded area in Candia, New Hampshire. This was a sad day for family, friends and even law enforcement officers.

PROMISES, PROMISES, PROMISES

We all make promises at one time or another, but do we keep these promises or let them fall by the wayside? Chief Robert Baker, Retired, and I, Lt/Det. Joe Horak, Retired, stood over the bodies of the two young girls and made a promise that we would stay with the investigation into their murders until their killer or killers were caught, no matter if it took *a week, a month, a year, or a lifetime.* There have been suspects in this investigation from the very beginning. *Twenty-four years have passed* - the same suspects we had in 1973 are still our prime suspects today. [July 12, 1997] Pretty sad when you think about it.

Chief Baker and I [Horak] have heard all kinds of promises made in regards to placing or eliminating any and all suspects in the murders of Diane Compagna and Anne Psaradelis. They were not promises that were kept. They were just empty words.

When you go to the <u>Chief of Police in Merrimack</u>, New Hampshire [where both girls lived and where they were reported as missing] and ask for his help in the matter and all you hear is, "Not my problem," something is wrong.

When you go to the <u>Chief of Police in Candia</u>, New Hampshire, [where the girls' bodies were discovered] and ask for his help in placing or eliminating the suspects, and all you hear is, "I cannot investigate homicides," something is wrong.

When you go to the <u>Sheriff's Department</u> and ask for their help, and all you hear is, "If you want to pay for the investigation, we will do it. It's election time and we don't want to cause any trouble for the Governor or the Sheriff," something is wrong.

When you go to the <u>State Police</u> and ask them for help and all you hear is, "We agree with you. There are things that should be checked out. We will look into it. If and when we need you, you will be contacted," or "We will get back to you," and no further contact is made, something is wrong.

When you go to the <u>Attorney General's office</u> and ask for help in regards to the Compagna-Psaradelis homicides of 1973 and all you hear is. "We have been in touch with the State Police and we agree with them - there are no suspects in this case. Tell us who your informant is or we won't do any investigating in regards to this case. You are making everyone look bad and you are a liar," something is wrong.

When you go to the <u>Governor's Office</u> and ask for help in regards to the Compagna-Psaradelis homicide investigation and you don't receive any real satisfaction, something is wrong.

When you interest some of these so-called <u>crime shows</u> in airing the case and they back off for some unknown reason, something is very wrong.

JUSTICE DENIED

In May 1997, after waiting nearly 24 years for someone to come forward with a phone call or a letter, someone *has* come forward with *new developments* in the case that open the door towards finally getting the case solved. The Merrimack Police Department, the New Hampshire Attorney General and the Governor have all been advised of the new information, and they have also been advised that the person who came forward has been receiving harassing phone calls since the time they spoke with the Merrimack Police.

Will the various law enforcement agencies do anything to help bring this case to a conclusion by placing or eliminating the suspect(s)? Will they make use of these *new developments* that have been brought out after 24 years? Chief Baker and I [Horak] hope they will. The person who has come forward possesses the kind of uncommon courage not often seen in this day and age. This person deserves a lot of praise, and deserves to be free from any form or harassment, harm or injury.

There are others who know what happened to Diane Compagna and Anne Psaradelis. *You know who you are.* Why don't you come forward with the information you've been holding onto for the past 24 years and help bring the killer(s) to justice? I know Diane Compagna and .Anne Psaradelis could at last rest in peace if that happened. And it's certain Chief Baker and I could.

Please don't let this investigation stop at a dead end road. The system should work for everyone, so come forward with any information that might help.

You may contact:

Robert Baker 388 Deerfield Rd. Candia, NH 03034
Joe Horak
New Hampshire Attorney General's Office
Governor Shaheen of New Hampshire

"Telephone for you Lieutenant Horak."

JOSEPH A. HORAK

"Hello."

"Is that you, Lieutenant?"

"Yes, Chief. What's going on? Anything new on our case?"

"No, I just wanted you to know that I took the article you wrote and contacted Nancy from the *Union Leader*, talked with her about wanting her help in regards to putting this article on the Compagna-Psaradelis murders into the paper. Nancy advised me that they would not put the article in the paper."

"I really can't understand that Chief because at one time she did call me and wanted some information on the case, she said that, if the time ever came, she would do the other half of the story, and now she doesn't want anything to do with it. Chief, she might be afraid that if she does the story, that in the future they might not help her or the paper with any other good stories."

"You might be right, Lieutenant. I guess we will have to find someone else that is willing to help us."

"Chief, I have been thinking about writing a letter to United States Attorney General Janet Reno, maybe she would help us. It's sure worth a try."

October 1, 1997

The Honorable Janet Reno
Attorney General of the United States
Justice Department
Washington, D.C. 20530

Dear Attorney General Reno:

My name is Joseph A. Horak and I am a retired police Lieutenant-Detective. During my time as a police officer there was a double murder of two young 15 year old girls out of Merrimack, New Hampshire that was committed in Candia, New Hampshire in July of 1973. The murders have never been solved. I am 99% sure of who the people are that are responsible for these murders. I have never been able to find anyone from law enforcement or any government agency that would help me to place or eliminate these people.

I was injured during another homicide investigation and had to retire in November of 1976. After retirement, I, along with Chief Robert Baker (Retired) spent a lot of time and money investigating this case and we live with this case 365 days a year. We stood over the bodies of the two young victims and made a promise to them that we would catch their killer or killers if it took a week, a month, a year or a lifetime.

The prime suspect in these crimes has a family and friends that live in Oceanside, California, so it is possible that he, friends or someone from his family could be making and is responsible for the harassing phone calls to Ms Lisa J. Rosa. (See enclosed statement of Lisa J. Rosa.)

Oh, we have heard lots of promises of investigators and other law enforcement officers that stated they would help with the investigation and help place or eliminate our "Prime Suspects" but that is all they were, "PROMISES". When everyone refused to help solve this case or were afraid to help, I decided the only thing I could do was to write a book, (TRUTH & JUSTICE), hopeful that it might help to bring someone forward that had information about the murders that would help to bring this investigation to a close with the arrest and conviction of the people responsible. This is a solvable case.

For the past 24 years we have tried everyone from law enforcement that we could contact. We have tried the judicial system, the news media and the crime shows. The results have been negative. It seems that people are afraid and don't want to get involved.

Since we have tried every possible avenue in the state and know that this woman (Lisa J. Rosa) from California came forward with knowledge about the case, this is no longer a State problem, but an interstate problem. We would appreciate it if the Justice Department would intervene and help bring this case to a conclusion.
Sincerely,

JOSEPH A. HORAK

Joseph A. Horak
Lieutenant/Det., Ret.

<u>December 15, 1997</u>

Dear Mr. Horak:
Thank you for your letter regarding the Compagna/Psaradelis Murders. Your dedication in this case is admirable and my hopes are with you that justice does indeed prevail. To best assist you, I recommend that all pertinent information regarding this case that has yet to be sent to the Attorney General be forwarded to that office. It would greater serve yourself and Chief Baker to continue from this point through the Attorney General.

Again, thank you for your letter and more importantly for your dedication to your duty as a police officer. Please do not hesitate to forward updates to my office regarding your progress.
Sincerely,
Jeanne Shaheen
Governor

<u>December 29, 1997</u>

I think I will stop by the Compagna home and find out any thoughts that Mrs. Compagna might have in regards to the letter I sent her telling about this woman from California that just came forward with information about the people responsible for the murder of her daughter and Anne Psaradelis.

Guess I will pull over to the side of the road since Mrs. Compagna is just taking the mail out of the mail box.

"Hello, Mrs. Compagna."

"What are you doing back in New Hampshire, Joe?"

"Mrs. Compagna, I came back to New Hampshire to finish the investigation in regards to the murders of your daughter and Anne Psaradelis."

"Joe, why don't you get on with your own life. We have moved on with ours. We, as well as the Psaradelis family, are not going to help you or the police in any way. We aren't going to let you put us in the position of having to live this thing all over again. If you are so smart, why didn't you solve this case years ago?"

"Mrs. Compagna, how can you make a remark like that? You know we have had two prime suspects from the very start and you know that Chief Baker and I have tried all these years to find someone in law enforcement that would finish the case. You know, Mrs. Compagna, I, of course, feel bad about the Psaradelis family and your loss, but it really doesn't make any difference what you or anyone else thinks or wants. The most important thing is for the killer or killers to be brought to justice. Chief Baker and I have worked on this case for the past twenty-four years and we are not about to walk away from it. You. know who murdered the girls, just as I do. Jefferson is the killer and he will be brought to justice.

"By the way, Mrs. Compagna, I sent you a letter in regards to a woman from California that contacted the Merrimack Police Department with knowledge she has about the murders and the people responsible. I also asked you if the Merrimack Police or anyone else had contacted you and advised you of the new developments in the case and I never received any reply from you. I also advised you that if you were not told about this new development that you could contact the department and they would advise you."

"Yes, Joe, I did receive that letter and I did go to the Merrimack Police Department and spoke with the Chief about this so-called information and he replied, 'There is no such person.'"

"Well, Mrs. Compagna, there is such a person and she is alive and well, in fact she used to live in Merrimack. You believe what you want, Mrs. Compagna but Chief Baker and I are going to finish this case."

"You know, Joe, the Psaradelis family went with us up to the State Police Headquarters in Concord and we spoke with Sergeant Roland Lamy about the investigation and he told us not to worry, that the State Police would no longer investigate this case. We are not going to help you in any way or help anyone else. You do whatever you have to do, but we will not help you in anyway."

"Mrs. Compagna, don't you want the people responsible for taking the lives of Diane and Anne caught?"

"Of course we do, but we will not help you in anyway."

"Well, Mrs. Compagna, thanks for taking the time to talk with me."

It sure doesn't seem possible that it is January 10, 1998. It makes you wonder where all the weeks, months and years have gone since the start of this murder investigation. So far, the investigation has been a tough one and as each year passes, it seems to get worse. Chief Baker and I wonder if justice will prevail in this case. We have tried to find someone that could or would put 100% of their time and energy in trying to solve these two murders, but no takers so far.

February 7, 1998

Dear Attorney Ramsdell:

As you know, Chief Robert Baker and I have been in contact with you since August of 1993 in regards to the Compagna/Psaradelis murders. It is now February, 1998 and we are no closer to placing Wayne Powers and Tom Jefferson or eliminating them as suspects. Chief Baker and I are 99% sure these people are responsible for the murders of the two girls.

We have had lots of promises from you and the State Police that this case would be investigated and it appears that these were just promises. We have furnished you and the State Police with a list of people that are supposed to have knowledge about who murdered the two girls and we have also advised you that Ms. Lisa Rosa came forward with information about the murders. As of this date no one from any law enforcement agency has contacted any of these people or even contacted Tom Jefferson.

It is hard for me to understand why someone won't step forward and finish this investigation. It makes me wonder if justice will prevail.

JUSTICE DENIED

I never knew of or have heard of Lisa J. Rosa until she contacted me in May of 1997. She had contacted Det./Lt. Michael Milligan of the Merrimack Police Department in April of 1997 and she never heard from him again. I spoke with Mrs. Dorothy Compagna the other day and she advised me that she had spoken with the Merrimack Police and they advised her that there is no such person as Lisa Rosa. Something is sure wrong because there is such a person and I wonder why no one will contact her and find out everything she knows about the murders.

If it would help, Chief Baker and I would like to come up to your office and talk over the case.

Thank you again for your letters and time, and we really would like to have justice prevail in this case.
Sincerely,
Joseph Horak,Lt./Det., Ret.

February 15, 1998

Dear Attorney Rudman:
I don't know if you remember me or not but my name is Joseph Horak and I am a retired Lieutenant/Detective out of Merrimack, New Hampshire.

In 1973 you were the Attorney General for the State of New Hampshire and on the 29th of September, 1973 you and your office were advised of a double murder that had taken place in Candia, New Hampshire and the young victims "COMPAGNA and PSARADELIS" came from Merrimack.

I know that you have spent most of your life in connection with law enforcement, as well as representing the people from our state. Chief Baker, Ret., and I really need your help in regards to the investigation of the Compagna-Psaradelis murders. You are really our last hope of ever being able to solve these murders and since this took place while you were Attorney General, we thought you might help us.

JOSEPH A. HORAK

We have had two suspects from the very start and here we are nearly 25 years later and our suspects remain the same. We have tried to obtain help from various law enforcement people and agencies all these years, and have received lots of promises, but no one really helped. We are 99% sure our suspects are the killers and even people in law enforcement will admit they could be, but will do nothing to place or eliminate them as suspects.

I could write pages and pages, Attorney Rudman, but all they would ask, is could you some how help us in getting someone from law enforcement that would really investigate it the way it should be investigated. We know this case can be solved, we even have a woman who came forward in April of 1997, and told the Merrimack Police Department that she knows who the killers are, but they and other law enforcement agencies have yet to contact her. The only thing that happened was that after this woman contacted the Police Department, she started receiving harassing phone calls and she is in fear of her own safety and life.

Over the years Chief Baker and I have tried to obtain help from the local police departments, Sheriff Departments, the Attorney General's Office, Governors, Crime Shows, etc. Not one person has done anything on this investigation. Again, I ask your could you please help us in some way. I would be happy to talk over the case with you if you would take the time to listen to the facts of the investigation.
Sincerely,
Joseph Horak, Lieutenant/Detective, Ret.

February 17, 1998

Dear Lt. Horak
While I continue to appreciate your concern for the above referenced matter, I do not believe that having you and Mr. Baker come to my office for a meeting is the best way for this investigation to progress. Rather, I will discuss your concerns

with Lt. David Eastman, Commander of the New Hampshire State Police Major Crime Unit. If investigators believe that your information may be advantageous, you will be contacted by those investigators.
Sincerely,
Michael D. Ramsdell
Associate Attorney General
Chief, Homicide Unit

February 25, 1998

Re: Compagna/Psaradelis Murders
Senator Judd Gregg
United States Congress 20530

Dear Senator Gregg:
    My name is Joseph A. Horak and I am a retired police Lieutenant/Detective. During my time as a police officer there was a double murder of two young 15 year old girls out of Merrimack, New Hampshire in July of 1973. The murders have never been solved and I am 99% sure of who the people are that are responsible for these murders, I have never been able to find anyone from law enforcement or any government agency that would help me to place or eliminate these people.
    Chief Robert Baker retired and I have been working on the Compagna/Psaradelis murder investigation for nearly 25 years and we have had the same two suspects for the same amount of time. People from law enforcement will admit that our prime suspects could be suspects but will not do anything to place or eliminate these people as suspects and they apparently will not investigate this case any further, lots of promises, but no investigation.
    In April, 1997 a Lisa J. Rosa came forward and contacted the Merrimack Police Department in regards to the murders of the Compagna/Psaradelis girls. Ms. Rosa comes from California and she was advised to send a statement and not say any-

thing to anyone. Since Ms Rosa contacted the police in regards to this matter, she has been receiving harassing phone calls, and is in fear of her own safety and life. She believes these calls are connected with the murders.

Over the years, Chief Baker and I have tried to obtain help from local police departments, Sheriff departments, the State Police, the Attorney General, the Governor, Crime Shows, etc. Not one person has done anything to move this investigation forward.

On October 1, 1997 and again on February 15, 1998 I wrote to U.S. Attorney General Janet Reno and was asking for some help in regards to this murder case that no one is willing to investigate. I really don't know if Attorney General Reno is receiving my letters or not.

Senator Gregg, I realize that these murders are 25 years old, but justice should prevail in this case just as it should in any other murder case, be it a day old or 25 years old.

Ms Rosa did come forward on her own after 24 years. She is from California and is in fear of her own safety and life. I feel that this has now become an interstate investigation and I am hopeful that the Justice Department would at least contact Ms Rosa and talk with her in regards to the murders and her fear of harm or worse.

I know that you are more than busy, but this is really the last chance to ever having these murders solved and we should remember that someone's life could be in jeopardy should anyone fail to take some kind of action. I would really appreciate it if you could talk this matter over with Attorney General Janet Reno and see if she couldn't have someone look into this matter. I am sure it would mean a lot to the victims, their family members, society and of course Chief Baker and myself.

I want to thank you for taking the time to read this letter and I would appreciate some kind of a reply.

Sincerely,

Joseph Horak

Lieutenant/Detective, Retired

JUSTICE DENIED

March 30, 1998

Dear Lt. Horak
    Thank you for your correspondence expressing your concerns regarding the 1973 unsolved murders of two young girls from Merrimack, New Hampshire.
    I certainly can appreciate your desire to see these cases resolved, however, this is a matter which comes under the jurisdiction of the State. In an effort to be of some assistance to you, I have forwarded your correspondence to New Hampshire Attorney General, Philip McLaughlin, as the decision on whether or not to reopen the case would need to be made by his office after reviewing the new information which has come forward. I have asked that his office contact you directly regarding your concerns. I hope this will prove helpful.
    If you feel I can be of assistance in the future with a federal issue, please do not hesitate to let me know.
    Sincerely,
    Judd Gregg, U.S. Senator
March 31, 1998

William Jefferson Clinton
President of the United States
The White House
Washington D.C. 20530

Dear Mr. President:
    I am writing this letter to you for two reasons and the first one is because I feel that you are doing a great job for the people of our country as well as the people of the world. You are not only doing a good job, but you stand up for the rights and needs of everyone, you believe in justice for all, as well as the basic needs of everyone be they rich or poor.

JOSEPH A. HORAK

Sometimes the road gets pretty rough to travel on, but you are one of those men in life that can push forward and accomplish just about any task or problem you encounter.

Mr. President, my second reason for writing to you is a major concern to me and it involves "JUSTICE FOR EVERYONE." I truly believe in this kind of justice, no matter what it might involve.

My name is Joseph A. Horak and I am a retired Lieutenant/ Detective from the Merrimack Police Department in Merrimack, New Hampshire. I am having a major problem with "Justice For Everyone and Justice Will Prevail."

In July of 1973 two young 15 year old girls, Diane Compagna and Anne Psaradelis, were murdered. The victims came from Merrimack and were found murdered in Candia, New Hampshire. I could write pages and pages about this investigation, but I will try to sum it up for you.

Chief Robert Baker and I have had two prime suspects in regards to these murders since 1973 and here it is, nearly April 1998. The same two suspects remain our suspects today. We wonder if justice will prevail in this case and it appears that the only way this will happen is if you would in some way help us to bring these people to justice.

Mr. President, for nearly 25 years we have tried to obtain the help from some law enforcement person or agency. We have tried the local police departments, county attorney, sheriff departments, state police, attorney generals, governors, senators etc. After all these years there still is not a single person who has the courage to step forward and really work on the investigation. They are either afraid to or don't want to get involved.

In April, 1997 one Lisa J. Rosa came forward with information about the murders of the two girls. She made contact with the Merrimack Police Department, spoke with a detective, explained who she was and what she knew about the murders. Ms Rosa was advised to send a statement in regards to what information she had and that it would be put with the case.

She was further advised not to talk with anyone from Merri-mack about the case.

The following morning Lisa Rosa started receiving harassing phone calls and she believes these are tied in with the murders. I have written to the local police departments, the State Police, Attorney General and the Governor advising them that a human life is in jeopardy should anyone fail to take action in this case.

Mr. President, won't you please help us bring this case to a conclusion, help to keep Lisa J. Rosa free from threats, harm or even death? Don't let 25 years of investigation go down the so called drain. Justice should prevail, no matter what.

I want to thank you for taking the time to read my letter and I hope you will reply to my plea for help.
Sincerely,
Joseph A. Horak, Lieutenant/Detective Ret.

April 10, 1998

The Honorable Bob Smith
United States Senate
Washington, D.C. 20510-2903

Dear Senator Smith:
I am writing in response to your letter to United States Attorney Gagnon dated March 31, 1998, regarding a letter you received from Joseph Horak on March 12, 1998.

Please be advised that I have spoken to Lieutenant David Eastman of the New Hampshire State Police in regard to this matter. Lieutenant Eastman has advised me that both the State Police and the New Hampshire Attorney General have active cases in regard to this matter. Lieutenant Eastman was well aware of the case and of the new information which Mr. Horak believes recently came to light. I have forwarded to Lieutenant Eastman a copy of the material which Mr. Horak sent to you.

Please be further advised that in any event there does not appear to be any basis for federal jurisdiction over this matter. If I may be of further assistance please do not hesitate to call.
Yours truly,
Paul M. Gagnon United States Attorney

<u>May 3, 1998</u>

Michael Milligan, Lieutenant/Detective
Merrimack Police Department
Baboosic Lake Road
Merrimack, NH 03054

Dear Lieutenant Milligan:
I am writing to you in regards to the Compagna/Psaradelis murders of 1973 and as you know, I have written to you in the past about this case, but for some unknown reason you didn't reply.

It has been just over a year since Lisa J. Rosa, M.A., contacted you in regards to information she has in reference to the murders of the two girls. I know that you are aware that Lisa has been receiving harassing phone calls since she came forward and believes these are connected to the murders.

Lisa has been in contact with me since the early part of May, 1997 and is going to stay with the investigation until the case is solved no matter how long it takes. She won't be scared off by anyone. Lisa, as well as Chief Robert Baker, Ret., and I, cannot understand why someone active in law enforcement hasn't contacted her in regards to what she knows about the murders and why she is in fear of her own safety. A year is sure a long time for someone to wait to hear from some investigator interested enough to want to solve a double murder.

Lieutenant, I would be more than willing to help you or anyone else bring this case to a conclusion with the arrest of

the people responsible. We are 99% sure that our prime sus-
pects are responsible for the murders. It would be a credit to
you or anyone else interested enough to solve the murders. I
don't want any credit, I just want to see the case solved and
will stick with the case for another 25 years if I have to.
    I hope you will reply to this letter.
Sincerely,
Joseph A. Horak
Lieutenant/Detective Ret.

May 3, 1998

Lieutenant David Eastman
Major Crime Unit
New Hampshire State Police

Re: Compagna/Psaradelis Murders

Dear Lieutenant Eastman:
    As you know, I had contacted you on October 1, 1997 and
again on February 7, 1998 and here it is May 3. 1998, this be-
ing in regards to the Compagna/Psaradelis murder investiga-
tion, as well as Lisa J. Rosa, M.A. who has. information about
who murdered the two girls, as well as the fact that she has
been receiving harassing phone calls ever since she had con-
tacted a detective from the Merrimack Police Department,
Merrimack, New Hampshire. The days, weeks and months pass
by and there doesn't seem to be any movement towards placing
or eliminating the prime suspects or making any attempt to
contact Lisa J. Rosa who has information about the case and
the killers of the two victims. Lisa J. Rosa furnished the Mer-
rimack Police Department with a statement of what she knows
about the murders and all she has received since then was
harassing phone calls and the fear of being harmed or worse.
Something is sure wrong when people disregard this investiga-

tion and the information that Ms. Rosa has furnished to the police as well as myself, it makes me wonder if justice will prevail in this case.

Lieutenant, July 12, 1998 starts the 26th year of this investigation and I sure hope it isn't going to take another 25 years to bring the killers to justice. I, for one, will continue on until this case is solved and I am sure that Chief Robert Baker feels the same way, won't you please help with this investigation, promises sure don't help.

I hope you will let me know if you will help and of any new developments in the case.
Sincerely,
Joseph A. Horak
Lieutenant/Detective Ret.

<u>May 8, 1998</u>
What do you know, a letter from Lieutenant Michael. Milligan, a surprise.

Dear Mr. Horak,
I would like to clarify something in your letter of May 3rd addressed to me.

The agencies with current jurisdiction over the case you are referring to in your letter are the New Hampshire Attorney General's Office and the New Hampshire State Police, Major Crimes Unit, not the Merrimack Police Department.

Any comments or concerns should be addressed to those agencies.
Sincerely,
Michael R. Milligan
Det./Lt. Michael R. Milligan
For: Joseph R. Devine
Chief of Police

Boy, that's not much of a reply. If Lieutenant Milligan felt that way, why did he ask Lisa Rosa to send him a statement in regards to information she had about the Compagna/Psaradelis murders, and why did he give Lisa Rosa the impression he was going to interview some of the people that she had talked with him about? I think if he felt that the Merrimack Police Department didn't have any jurisdiction in regards to the Compagna/Psaradelis investigation that he should have referred Lisa Rosa to the Attorney General or the State Police. I would really like to know what Lt. Milligan did with the statement he received from Lisa Rosa and why did it take well over a year for someone in law enforcement to contact her, especially when she had knowledge about the murders and she was in fear of her own safety?

It is hard for me to understand why there isn't a single person that is connected with the Merrimack Police Department that isn't interested in bringing the people responsible for the murders of Diane Compagna and Anne Psaradelis to justice. The two young girls came from Merrimack and our department was involved in this investigation from the very start of the "Missing Person" stage and you would think that the detectives would want to finish the investigation and bringing the killers to justice.

May 12, 1998

A letter from Warren Rudman. I wonder if he will be able to help us with this investigation. It sure would help, as it doesn't look like anyone in the state is interested enough to have justice prevail in this case.

Dear Joe:

I have your letter of May 5. Since I no longer hold office, I am sure you understand there is nothing I can do directly. I can also tell you that there is absolutely no chance that the federal government through the Justice Department would take any interest in this matter, absent a request from a New Hampshire law enforcement agency.

I remember the case very well and share your frustration that it has never been solved. It was one of the few homicides

JOSEPH A. HORAK

that occurred during my tenure as Attorney General in which the perpetrators have not been brought to justice.

Unless the Attorney General of New Hampshire is willing to take an interest in this case, it will be difficult to reopen. To that end, I have written to Attorney General Phil McLaughlin enclosing your letters. I know Phil quite well and I can assure you that if there is any validity to the so-called new evidence provided by Lisa J. Rosa, he will take appropriate action.
My best to you.
Sincerely,
Warren B. Rudman

May 21, 1998

Re: Compagna/Psaradelis Murders

Dear Lt. Horak,

The Attorney General has requested that I personally re-spond to your inquiry regarding the investigation into the above-referenced homicides. Please rest assured that a homi-cide prosecutor will be assigned to review these matters anew, and to address the concerns expressed in your letter dated May 5, 1998.

The prosecutor assigned to these matters will contact you once he/she becomes familiar with the file. Thank you for your persistence in the pursuit of justice. We look forward to assist-ing you in any way possible.
Sincerely,
John P. Kacavas
Chief Homicide Unit

May 23, 1998

Re: Compagna/Psaradelis Murders

Dear Attorney Kacavas:

JUSTICE DENIED

I received your letter of May 21, 1998 and I more than appreciate your taking more than an interest in the murders of these two young 15 year old girls. Please know that Chief Robert Baker, Ret. and I will help you in anyway we can. We are 99% sure that the two prime suspects we have had for the past 25 years are in fact the people responsible for taking the lives of the two victims.

Thanks again for your offer of help.
Sincerely,
Joseph A. Horak,
Lieutenant/Detective Ret.

June 29. 1998
A note from Lisa Rosa.

Dear Joe:

Sorry it's taken me so long to get back with you. The semester recently finished and then my boss went on vacation and left me in charge.

I began a long letter to the Governor of NH on May 27th and just haven't finished it yet. I'm going to try (very hard) to send it this week. Of course, I'll send you a copy of the final product.

I wanted to let you know that I have not forgot you or the case. As I previously promised, I intend to help you as much as I can in solving this murder. With me, you just have to be patient. Eventually, I find the time to get things done that have been sitting on the back burner.

Take good care of yourself, and I'll be writing soon with a copy of the letter to the Governor.
Warmly,
Lisa Rosa

June 29, 1998

Dear Lt. Horak,

JOSEPH A. HORAK

Just a short note to pass along a copy of the response I received from the U. S. Department of Justice regarding the investigation of two unsolved murder cases. It was a pleasure to look into this matter and I hope you will find the information provided helpful.

Sincerely,
Judd Gregg
U.S. Senator

June 19, 1998

The Honorable Judd Gregg
United States Senator
125 N. Main Street
Concord, New Hampshire 03301

Dear Senator Gregg:
I am writing in reply to your letter of May 12, 1998, to the Office of Legislative Affairs, which passed along correspondence you received from Joseph A. Horak regarding the reopening of an investigation into two unsolved murders which occurred in New Hampshire in 1973.

We have received Mr. Horak's correspondence, as well as additional materials he has sent us, and discussed the matter by telephone with him and with John Kacavas, Chief of Homicide in the New Hampshire Attorney General's Office, who has also received correspondence from Mr. Horak. Mr. Horak's principal concerns, as we understand them, are first, a perceived lack of interest in this case on the part of law enforcement; and second, a desire that the Federal government become involved.

We have been informed by Mr. Kacavas that a prosecutor from his office has been assigned to review the matter along with appropriate personnel from the New Hampshire State Police. After that review, a determination will be made by the

New Hampshire Attorney General's Office whether or not there is sufficient evidence to prosecute the matter. Mr. Kacavas also assures us that the New Hampshire Attorney General's Office will meet with Mr. Horak to discuss their determination.

Mr. Horak believes that the Federal government should become involved in this matter on the ground that a person with information about the case, who lives outside New Hampshire, has recently stepped forward. According to Mr. Horak, this person made a statement to the local New Hampshire police, but has not been further interviewed by that department, and has received harassing phone calls since making that report. We understand from Mr. Horak that these harassing calls do not contain threats, and are under investigation by the local police department where the person lives. We have reviewed these facts, and nothing known to us at this time indicates a basis for Federal law enforcement or prosecutorial jurisdiction. We believe that the matter remains one for state and local investigation and, if appropriate, prosecution, and it seems to us that the New Hampshire Attorney General's Office has outlined an appropriate course of action.

Please do not hesitate to contact me if you have further questions on this matter.

Sincerely,

John C. Keeney

Acting Assistant Attorney General

June 23, 1998

Telephone call for you Lieutenant Horak.

"Hello, who am I speaking with?"

"Lieutenant Horak this is John Kissinger from the Attorney Generals' Office and I work in the Chief Homicide Unit. I am calling in regards to the letter that Attorney John P. Kacavas wrote on May 21, 1998 in regards to the Compagna/Psaradelis Murders. I have had a chance to read over most of the case and I would like to know if you and Chief Robert Baker would agree to coming up to the Attorney

General's Office, along with several other people from his office and the State Police. Since you and Chief Baker have worked so long on the investigation, we thought you might be able to give us some ideas as to your thoughts in regards to moving this investigation forward.

"Lieutenant Horak, would it be agreeable to you and Chief Baker if we set the meeting up for Monday the 6th of July [1998]? The meeting will start at 1020 a.m., if that is all right with you."

"Attorney Kissinger, that will be fine. We will see you on July 6th. Thank you for the call. I sure hope we can move this investigation forward."

I guess I better call Chief Baker and advise him of this meeting with the Attorney General's Office on July 6.

"Hello, is that you, Chief Baker?"

"Yes, Lieutenant, what's going on?"

Chief, I just wanted you to know that I just received a telephone call from Assistant Attorney John C. Kissinger, we have a meeting on July 6, 1998 at 10:00 a.m. up in Concord with people from the Attorney General's office and the State Police."

"That sounds good, Lieutenant."

"Chief, I do think that we need to be up in Concord early on the 6th. We sure don't want to give them any reason to cancel the meeting or to say we didn't show up. I just hope that we have a good meeting and that it doesn't turn out to be like that last meeting we had up there. It sure was a disaster. We will just have to wait and see what happens. I am sure I'll be over to see you before we go to Concord and we can talk about our thoughts in regards to moving the investigation forward."

"See you later, Lieutenant, and thanks for calling."

July 6, 1998

"Well, Chief Baker, are you ready to head up to Concord?"

"Yes, Lieutenant, I just hope we have some good results."

"I guess we better get going. We don't want to be late."

"Lieutenant Horak, this is Sergeant David Parenteau and I am Assistant Attorney General John C. Kissinger. Won't you Chief Baker come into the conference room?"

"Lieutenant, we want you to know that we are new people working on this case. You need to forget about the others you have worked with, and you don't need to be writing letters. You and Chief Baker know more about the case than we do and you probably have more paperwork on the case. We would appreciate it if you would give us a copy of the papers that you believe we might not have. We would like you to tell us about the case, and any thoughts you might have in regards to suspects, and any other thoughts you might have about the case."

Chief Baker and I talked with Attorney Kissinger and Sergeant Parenteau for about four hours. They seemed to listen and appreciate our thoughts. We talked about the suspects, the letter of 1992 that spoke about two people that had knowledge about who the people were who murdered the two girls. We even talked about Lisa J. Rosa and the fact that we believed she was the key to moving this investigation forward. We talked about the various people that are believed to know who the killer(s) are and as to how these various people should be approached.

The results of the meeting would only be told by time and as to if anyone would use the information Lisa J. Rosa came forward with, and if the various people we listed were interviewed and results obtained.

Chief Baker and I advised Attorney Kissinger that we would give them reports of the investigation and photographs of the crime scene, that we would appreciate it if they made copies of everything and returned them to us in 30 days, as we needed to put them back into the case file.

I asked Attorney Kissinger if he would give us a letter reflecting that we had this meeting today. He advised us that they weren't going to write letters, that we would be advised of any progress in the case.

The meeting ended and Chief Baker and I headed back to Candia. "What did you think of the meeting Chief?"

"Well, I think it went good. They seemed to listen to our thoughts and probably learned a lot about the case. I really hope they will move this case forward."

"I guess we will just have to wait and see. Well, Chief, I better head home but I'll be in touch."

<u>July 8 , 1998</u>

"What are you doing over here, Lieutenant Horak?"

"Well, Chief Baker, I just received a note from Lisa Rosa, as well as a copy of a letter she wrote to Governor Jeanne Shaheen. I thought I would come over and read the letter to you and then we could talk about its contents."

<u>June 29, 1998</u>

Dear Governor Shaheen:

I am greatly disturbed by the events surrounding my state-ment to the Merrimack Police Department, dated April 3, 1997, regarding the Compagna/Psaradelis murders which took place in 1973. Attached you will find a letter from Joseph Horak, the initial murder investigator and a copy of my state-ment. Hopefully, this will refresh your memory regarding this issue.

I am a psychotherapist and am in the process of completing my Ph.D. in Clinical Psychology. Perhaps my familiarity with the effects of trauma, coupled with my sensitivity and empathy towards traumatized individuals, will explain my involvement in this case. Last year, I had a horrifying experience. For no particular reason that I can discern, a repressed memory came forth. I had never recalled this incident until that very mo-ment. The memory was of a very disturbing conversation I had in 1976/77 with Tim Decato, a Merrimack man, that I was dating at the time. I was 16 or 17 years old.

We had been dating over 1 year and were very close. Perhaps this, coupled with his anxiety and guilty feel-ings, is why he confided in me. He told me he knew the identity of the murderers who killed Diane Compagna and Anne

Psaradelis. This was a local and heinous crime that terrorized my community. I knew Anne Psaradelis' younger sister, Ellen. Needless to say, I was shocked by what he said. (Please read the attached statement I wrote which was requested by the Merrimack P.D.)

I am writing to you to explain important events that have taken place since that time and to urge you to get involved in the shadowy mishandling of this investigation. After I sent the requested statement to the Merrimack Police Department, I began receiving disturbing telephone calls. The first day, I received eight calls where the caller was on the line but would not speak. The second day the same thing was repeated. I contacted the local police, due to the timeliness of the two events, sending a statement to the police about suspected killers and receiving ongoing numerous, harassing phone calls. I also called the phone company and, given the circumstances, they immediately put a trap on my phone line. What I soon found out from the phone company was the person who was calling "knew what he was doing". I was told he never used the same phone twice. Furthermore, he never called from the same district twice. Therefore, tracking this individual would be extremely difficult. Normally, the phone company will put a trap on a line only for two weeks. Nevertheless, given the calls initially continued for over a month, and the odd circumstances, the phone company extended the trap. I'd call them every few days to determine if they had made a match. At one point, I was told that 5 new traps had been set up, given some calls began to match districts. Then the calls stopped. The trap was taken off my line.

In the meanwhile, I contacted Sergeant Milligan, the individual who took my statement over the phone. I told him about the calls and their intensity, and frankly stated I was frightened for my safety. The situation was very unnerving. Even with this information, nothing was done. When I initially spoke with Sergeant Milligan, he asked me not to talk with anyone in Merrimack about this, as he wanted to pay a few surprise visits to the people mentioned in my statement. Yet no such visits *the people mentioned in my statement. Yet no such visits were ever made.*

At this time I had a friend do some research about this murder. She found a few newspaper articles and sent them to me. I also called the Manchester paper, requesting research on the same. At about this time, my parents, who live in Merrimack, told me a book was written about these murders by the initial investigator. It was being distributed by a Merrimack family, and my father purchased a copy. After reading it, he sent it to me.

I was greatly disturbed while reading this book. It was horrific. The girls' corpses were found deep in the woods. One body was naked and the other partially disrobed. The decay of the one girl's body left a chemical residue, like the shadow of the corpse, in the pine needles where the body was found. This haunted me!

Meanwhile, I waited and waited but the Merrimack Police Department never got back to me, as they promised. I decided it was time to talk to people I knew from Merrimack. I learned much about the families of the murder victims. I ached as I heard the nightmare that had become their life. I knew I had to try to do something. It was at this time, that I contacted Joe Horak, the man who had written the book and had been trying to solve this case for over 20 years. From Joe, I heard even more disturbing facts. One of his prime suspects was indeed Tim Decato's cousin. People who had knowledge of the events leading up to the murders, had been some of my best friends. It hurt. I decided I would help Joe Horak, in any way I could, to bring this case to justice.

My initial contact with Joe began around May of last year. Interestingly, after Joe and I had made phone contact a few times, the calls started again. The same pattern was followed. Joe told me that the families of the murdered victims received exactly the same type of calls shortly after the murders, so I finally decided to call Tim Decato once more. Our conversation was brief. I tried to engage him but he was defensive. He had previously told me that the remaining person, who had mur-dered the girls, was now married and had a family. (As men-tioned in my statement, Tim's cousin confessed to him that he and another person committed the murders. Soon after, his cousin committed suicide by shooting himself in the head.) Nevertheless, I was told by Tim Decato that I had no right to get involved in "stirring things up" and causing grief for this poor family man. I reminded him that the girls who were mur-dered didn't get a second chance; they never married or had children. For God's sake, they never even finished high school. As a test, I told him about the threatening phone calls. I said if they continued I would have to call the police. He was horrified. He angrily told me that in no way should I speak with the police. I simply stated, "I just want the calls to stop." Our phone conversation ended. Interestingly, so did the calls. I think this strongly suggests that Tim Decato knows not only the identity of the killer(s) but has current contact with the one still living. There are other people who I strongly believe know the identity of this murderer. Yet the Merrimack Police Depart-ment continue to do nothing. From what I understand, they have stalled and bungled this case since the beginning. Inter-esting to note, is that one of the prime suspects was, at the time, close friends with individuals who had joined the Merri-mack Police Department. The other suspect was indeed Tim Decato's cousin.

There is more than enough critical information and evi-dence to try the remaining suspected killer. He was found guilty of raping Diane Compagna, one of the victims. The rape took place a month or so before her death. There are witnesses who testified that she believed she was pregnant. The guilty party contacted her friends and openly threatened her safety if she continued to state she was pregnant. These events took place the week before the murders. Why? Was this heinous crime allowed to fall through the cracks, especially when there are two retired police investigators who are still actively trying to solve this case?

I hope you can understand my angst. I've dedicated my life to helping people cope with the emotionally overwhelming circumstances of their lives. Certainly, the events of this case have caused immense psychological damage to the families of the murder victims. Yet they're not even entitled to the truth? When Diane Compagnas' mother asked the Merrimack Police Department why she was not told about the new evidence regarding my statement, they told her I did not exist. I assure you, I do, and I strongly believe that the conclusion to this case would be immensely healing to those involved.

Please give serious thought to what I am saying. Never before have I been involved in anything of this nature, but the time has come for someone to demand that justice, for these poor murdered girls and their families, be served.

Thank you very much for your time and Patience in reading this lengthy account. Without the provided details, I was not sure you would see the gravity of the situation.

Sincerely,

Lisa J. Rosa, M.A.

"Lieutenant, that's really some letter that Lisa wrote to the Governor, I wonder if it will help to put pressure on any law enforcement agency to investigate this case the way it should be investigated and bring the killer(s) to justice?"

"I sure hope so, Chief Baker, we sure need a break. We have really had a rough road to travel and of course, are not liked by many people connected with law enforcement. We really haven't tried to hurt or embarrass anyone, Chief. All we ever wanted was to have the case solved.

"You know, Chief, we really have tried about every way possible to solve these murders. I can only think of one thing that we have never done or tried to do."

"What is that, Lieutenant?"

"Well, Chief, we have never tried an offer of a "REWARD". I know that we don't have any money to try this approach, but maybe if we contacted one of the companies here in Merrimack, one of them might help. A member of one of the victims' families works for An-heuser-Busch, Inc. It sure can't hurt to write a letter. Maybe they would consider helping us by offering a reward leading to the arrest and conviction of the people responsible for the murders. It's worth a try, Chief. I will write a letter to them in the next few days."

Mr. August Busch IV
CEO Anheuser-Eusch, Inc.
Saint Louis, MO

Dear Mr. Busch:
Within the next few weeks a sad anniversary will pass. Twenty-five years ago, two young Merrimack, New Hampshire girls were brutally murdered. These many years later, the memories of the crime have been dulled by the passage of time and the need for family and friends to move ahead with their lives. Forgetting is often a kindness to those in pain, but to me, it is the enemy. For twenty-five years I have sought to bring the murderers to justice.

Please allow me to introduce myself. I am Joseph Horak, Merrimack Police Lieutenant/Detective, Retired. Throughout my entire life I have worked to ensure justice. One night years ago I vowed to the spirit of the two young girls - Diane Compagna and her friend Anne Psaradelis - that I would not rest until the men who took their lives had paid for that deed.

I was a member of the investigating team, I worked closely with then Chief Robert Baker to gather evidence and pursue prosecution. From almost the very beginning we identified two suspects, however, charges have never been filed. We know, from long investigations and documentation, that the individuals who have information necessary to the criminal proceedings have always been hesitant to step forward. We have tried for so long to convince them of the need to do so.

And so I find myself writing this letter. Time is running out, Many in the community have either forgotten or never knew of the incident. Bob Baker and I are seniors now, and have very little time left to see our promise to the girls fulfilled. Nor do we have the financial leverage to offer a reward for the "Information leading to the arrest and conviction of the suspects."

Anheuser-Busch has always had a reputation for its community services. Its concern for the needs of its employees and the community are well known. Knowing this, I come to you with a request. Please consider "carrying the torch" with us. We sincerely believe that the only course of action left is to bring this case before the public once again by offering a reward for the information so long withheld.

We do not wish to receive such monies in hand, but hope that you could establish a fund and administer payment when the established terms of the reward are met.

Chief Baker and I are willing to meet with you at a time convenient to you to present our case and answer any of your concerns. Life is precious and the lives of our children are perhaps the most precious. To have the loss of these two 15 year old girls fade into oblivion without resolution would be a crime in itself. Closure is needed - for families, the community, the investigators and the perpetrators.

Michael Compagna, who is the brother to Diane Compagna, is employed at your Merrimack facility, would be pleased to have these murders solved, as we all would be.

I hope to hear from you soon so that we may discuss this request.
Respectfully submitted,
Joseph Horak,
Lieutenant/Det., Ret.

July 23, 1998

Re: Compagna/Psaradelis Murders

Dear Attorney Kissinger:
I hope that you received the reports and photographs that I left in your office. I requested that you return a copy of every-

thing I sent to you along with the photographs within 30 days so that we can put them back into the case file.

Chief Baker and I were talking about the investigation and of your offer of help. We thought it might help both you and Sergeant David Parenteau if you were able to view the crime scene located in a wooded area off the New Boston Road in Candia. We felt this might help you to better understand what took place and along with all the information that we gave you, it would give you more of a complete picture and thus help you with your investigation of the murders.

Attorney Kissinger, the 29th of September 1998 will start the 26th year of this investigation into the murders of Diane Compagna and Anne Psaradelis. We were thinking about putting an article in the newspaper, unless you and Sergeant Parenteau would put an article in the papers yourselves. It is felt that this could help to bring someone forward that might have information in regards to the murders.

I did send that letter to you I received from Lisa J. Rosa as we stated we would. We will help in any way we can and hope you will reply to this letter.
Sincerely,
Joseph A. Horak,
Lieutenant, Detective Ret.

August 7, 1998
A letter from Lisa Rosa.

Dear Joe:

Just a quick note to let you know that I have not heard from the Governor's office, nor from either Attorney John Kissinger or Sergeant David Parenteau. I will definitely contact you if I hear from anyone, plus I will send you a copy of any correspondence I receive. Could you send me a phone number where I can reach you in case I need to contact you? I don't have a number for you in New Hampshire.

I'm glad they are finally starting to respond. It's certainly about time! I agree with you, I think the souls of Diane Compagna and Anne Psaradelis could finally rest if this case was finally tried and justice for their murders was served.

I don't know if I mentioned it, but I had surgery in July. Luckily, it was outpatient surgery and I'm finally beginning to feel better. Please be rest assured that I will do anything in my power to help in this case. I can't always respond immediately, given my schedule, but I will always respond. I also wanted to say I'm glad you appreciate my effort. Rarely does effort for doing the right thing ever get acknowledged, and I know you know what I mean.

Take care of yourself,
Lisa Rosa

August 20, 1998

"It's for you, Lieutenant. Lisa Rosa calling from California."

"Hello, Lisa. Is that you?"

"Yes, Lieutenant Horak. I just wanted you to know that when I came home tonight, I found a message from Sergeant Parenteau from the New Hampshire State Police on my answering machine. He stated that he would call again Tuesday. I did call back and left a message for Sergeant Parenteau as he wasn't there. I will let you know what happens once I make contact with him."

"Thanks for calling, Lisa. I really more than appreciate your having come forward with information about the case. You are a brave woman. There aren't too many around today who would have the courage to get involved in a murder case like this. I hope you will stay with the case until we bring the killer(s} to justice. Thanks again."

September 2, 1998

Re: Compagna/Psaradelis Murders

Dear Attorney Kissinger:

I have sent you a few letters and for some reason you haven't responded.

It has been just about two months since I gave you the photographs of the Compagna/Psaradelis crime scene that Chief Baker had taken. It seems strange that in this day and age that it should take two months to make copies of the photographs. I would appreciate it if you would send back our photographs so that we can put them back in the case file.

I have asked you about the 29th of September, this day starts the 26th year of this investigation. Chief Baker and I would like to put something into the newspaper and or on the radio. We still would like to do this unless you and Sergeant Parenteau are going to put something out to the news media yourselves. I would appreciate it if you would let us know your feelings on the subject.

I understand that Lisa Rosa has been contacted. Could you advise us if you had good results or if they were negative?

I know that the weeks and months are starting to fly by and something really positive needs to happen. We sure aren't going to let this investigation stop on a dead end street.

I hope you will reply to this letter and if anything turns up on our end, we will contact you.
Sincerely,
Joseph Horak,
Lieutenant/Det., Ret.

September 15, 1998

Re; Compagna/Psaradelis Murders

Dear Attorney Kissinger:
I want to thank you for your letter of September 10, 1998 in which you explained the delay in answering my letters. I also appreciate your contacting the State Lab to make sure the copies of the photographs are made and sent back to me.

JOSEPH A. HORAK

Chief Baker and I really wanted to put something out to the news media in regards to September 29th and the fact that this starts the 26th year of the investigation into the murders of the two girls. At this point in time, we will go along with your point of view that such action would not advance the interests of the investigation and could potentially have a negative consequence for the investigation. The only thing that does bother us is the fact that over the years, law enforcement has brought many, many unsolved murder cases before the public and always talks about every other case but for the double murder investigation of Compagna/Psaradelis. It sure makes a person wonder why.

We know that Lisa Rosa has been contacted via telephone in regards to this investigation. We really don't need the details, but we would appreciate a few words from you or Sergeant Parenteau, as to if what she knows or doesn't know is of any value towards moving this investigation along.

You know, Attorney Kissinger, this investigation into Thomas Jefferson and Wayne Powers as being prime suspects for the past 25 years in regards to the murders of the two girls is pretty sad when you think about it. It is really hard to understand why someone won't place or eliminate them as the people responsible for the murders, the same thing goes for others who have knowledge about the crime.
Sincerely,
Joseph Horak,
Lieutenant/Detective Retired

September 29, 1998

A letter from Lisa Rosa and it looks like it might be interesting and I hope it will contain good news.

Dear Joe:

Just a quick note. I finally did speak with David Parenteau on Sept. 4, 1998. We talked for well over 1 hour and discussed many things about the case. He explained to me that the inves-

tigation has been handed over to him and is considered an active investigation. The problem he explained, was that he has to delay work on this case every time he is given a new case. He also stated the NH State Police Dept. is very small and understaffed.

He asked me specific questions about my statement, stating these would be the questions that I would be asked. I assume he means in court or in a deposition. He did not tape the conversation but took notes. He well understands the delicacy of this case regarding the refusal of people to come forward with information. He also realizes there is a large peer group involved and once he questions just one person he knows the word will spread to others, warning them in advance not to cooperate. He asked me if I could suggest a person to whom he could speak to that was outside this inner group. He also asked me to provide him with a detailed account of all that has happened since my initial statement to the Merrimack Police. He doesn't have a copy of the letter I wrote to the Governor, and requested a copy of that as well. Therefore, I told him I would review all my notes (you'll be glad to know I have saved everything, including quoted conversations I had with Tim Decato), and write him an extensive account of all I feel is relevant, along with a copy of my letter to the Governor, as well as any other document I believe will shed light on the situation. I also told him, per your suggestions, about the timeliness of the phone calls. When I explained that the kind of calls I received were identical to the victims families, he was not very impressed.. I then explicitly stated that Tim Decato threatened me regarding speaking to the police, and I stated I would have no choice if the harassing phone calls continued. He was very interested when I told him the calls stopped immediately after speaking with Tim Decato. He definitely saw the significance of that and now believes that the calls may well be related to the case. What I want to do now, is re-read your book and take notes, then speak with you regarding the identity of certain characters. I have re-read most of your letters to refresh my memory on certain issues. As usual, my schedule is more than hectic. This year I am seeing clients at a mental health facility, taking classes; and working as close to full-time as I can. Both of my classes and the clinic are very time demanding. I already feel behind. Hence the delay in writing you this letter. I don't know exactly when I can get to the book and notes, and write David back, but I hope I can do it before the month ends. Therefore, be expecting a call from me. At that time I can give you more details about my conversation with David.

As an aside, I have purchased a gun and am a very good shot. My good friend purchased the gun from his friend, who is a retired police officer. He is getting paperwork in order so the purchase is completely legal. He has taught me gun safety and took me to an indoor shooting range for gun practice. Being a visual-spatial type person, my aim is quite good. With a .38 special, at about 25 feet, I was able to shoot all but one shot within the black inner circles of the bulls-eye. We also practiced with other guns he owned, my performance was similar with different guns, bigger and smaller. I feel confident that I can handle a gun and be effective with it if it should ever come down to that. Better safe than sorry.

That's all for now. If you want to talk, please feel free to give me a call. Given my hectic schedule, I'm not available Monday, Tuesday or Thursday evenings.
Take care,
Lisa Rosa

November 23, 1998

Re: Compagna/Psaradelis Murders

Dear Governor Shaheen:
I know that "Live Free Or Die" is the motto for the state of New Hampshire, how ever, I wonder what the words "Justice For Everyone" means to you and everyone else within the state.

JUSTICE DENIED

Chief Robert Baker and I have worked on this investigation of the Compagna/Psaradelis murders for the past 25 years and we have sought help from local police departments, state police, sheriff departments, Attorney Generals, Governors, the Justice Department, and right up to President William Jefferson Clinton. I am sorry to say that in all these years that we have been investigating and begging for some help in placing or eliminating the two prime suspects we have had from the very start, all we have had is a lot of talk and promises, which haven't meant very much. As you know, promises are easily made and are not always kept. Sometimes promises are just used as a way of putting off a course of action that really should have been taken care of.

Lisa J. Rosa, from California, came forward with information about the people who are responsible for the murders of these two young girls in 1997, and it wasn't until over a year had gone by that someone from the State Police finally contacted her. He spoke with her for about an hour. She has never heard from any law enforcement person since, and the two suspects still remain our prime suspects. Something is sure wrong.

Governor, I could write pages and pages, but they would add up to the fact that we are begging for your help with this investigation. We aren't going to let this case slip through the cracks, and even if it takes another 25 years, we will stick with the investigation. We do wonder if we shouldn't take our dilemma to the public and maybe this might help us to bring the killers to justice and finally bring this case to a close.

Chief Baker and I believe that if you were to allow us to come to your office and talk with you in person, you would understand why our suspects are "prime suspects." There isn't anyone in the state that knows this case any better than Chief Baker and myself, other than the two suspects. We would appreciate would reply to this letter.
Sincerely,
Joseph Horak

JOSEPH A. HORAK

Lieutenant/Det., Ret.

<u>December 22, 1998</u>
Hey, a letter from the office of the Governor.

Dear Mr. Horak:
   Your letter dated 11/23/98 was received by the Governor's Office of Citizen Affairs. Because your concern is important to us, I would like to take this opportunity to address the issues you raise in your letter.
   To best assist you, I have forwarded your letter to the Office of the Attorney General and asked that your letter be reviewed. Governor Shaheen is deferring to the judgement of the Attorney General in this matter, and it is asked that all future correspondence be directed to that office.

Sincerely,
Nick Clemons
Special Assistant for Citizen Affairs

<u>January 11, 1999</u>

RE: Compagna/Psaradelis Murders

Dear Lieutenant Horak:
   I have been asked to respond to your letter to Governor Shaheen dated November 23, 1998, in regards to the Compagna/Psaradelis murders. As you are aware from our discussions and correspondence during the Summer and Fall of last year, I have been working with Sergeant David Parenteau of the New Hampshire State Police on this case. Both Sergeant Parenteau and I have followed up on information provided by Ms. Rosa, and the investigation into these murders is ongoing.
   I share your hope that the investigation will lead to the discovery of the person or persons responsible for these murders. Very truly yours,

JUSTICE DENIED

John C. Kissinger
Assistant Attorney General

January 23, 1999

RE: Compagna/Psaradelis Murders of 1973

Dear Attorney John C. Kissinger:
I want to thank you for your letter of January 11, 1999, in regards to the Compagna/Psaradelis murders. However, I am somewhat discouraged over your remark, "that you and Sergeant Parenteau have followed up on the information provided by Lisa Rosa." To be honest with you, I know that contact was finally made with Ms. Rosa and that the phone call lasted about an hour, and Lisa has never heard from you again. As far as I can tell, nothing has really been done to place or eliminate Tom Jefferson and Wayne Powers as the people responsible for taking the lives of the two victims in this case. If I am wrong, I would really appreciate it if you would advise me or Chief Baker as to just how these two men were either placed or eliminated. It is also noted that none of the people from the list of names we gave you in regards to having knowledge about the murders and the people responsible have never been approached by anyone in law enforcement.

Attorney Kissinger, I have never received the rest of the pictures that you were given in regards to this investigation. I would appreciate having them back.
It is approaching that time when it looks like I will have to start writing to various people connected with law enforcement, in an attempt to get some help with this investigation. Chief Baker and I have been seeking this kind of help for all these many years and this investigation hasn't moved an inch in all this time, something is sure wrong. Especially since we have had two prime suspects from nearly day one.

JOSEPH A. HORAK

At the present time I am in Oklahoma, I am re-writing my book "TRUTH & JUSTICE" and using true names, but of course not using the names of our two suspects. Maybe this will help to bring some interest from the public and law enforcement. I know that Chief Baker and I are not going to walk away from this investigation until the people responsible are brought to justice.

We really hoped you and Sergeant Parenteau would help us with this investigation, but as the months slip by, it looks like that really isn't going to happen.

Sincerely yours,

Joseph Horak Lt/Det. Ret.

January 29, 1999

RE: Compagna/Psaradelis Murders of 1973

Dear Mr. Clemons:

I want to thank you for your letter of December 22, 1998, but I do wonder how your office is really going to help Chief Robert Baker and I. It is hard for me to know how to deal with your office because I have written in the past and never received any reply.

To be honest with you, Mr. Clemons, for the past 26 years we have sought help from local police departments, sheriff departments, state police, Attorney General's, United States Attorney General, Senators, Justice Department and right up to President William Jefferson Clinton. Justice should be for everyone. The poor victims, family members and society sure aren't receiving the justice in this case they deserve. Not liking me or Chief Baker is not a good enough reason for law enforcement not to do their job and place or eliminate any and all suspects in this or any other investigation. Twenty-six years is sure a long time to fight the system. Whatever happened to "Protect and to Serve," as well as "Justice for all?"

JUSTICE DENIED

Attached to this letter is a three page memo that was written a couple of years ago and the facts then are pretty much the same today. Not much has changed and our "Prime Suspects" still remain our prime suspects. We do owe the victims, family members and society a finished investigation with the arrest and conviction of the people responsible.

At the present time I am out in Oklahoma. If you need more information, you can contact me or Chief Baker. We appreciate help you can give us.
Sincerely,
Joseph Horak
Lieutenant/Detective Retired

March 26, 1999

Dear Joe:

I am so sorry to hear about your heart attack. You've been through quite a lot. I'm going to do something I don't normally do outside my profession, and talk to you about psychological issues. I realize how committed you are to solving this murder but it is NOT more important than your health, or your life. It also should not be your life, but only a part of it. Your dedication to and investment in solving this horrible murder is commendable, and your integrity outstanding. These are very, very fine human qualities. Don't let them become consumed and eventually extinguished because of this case. As you know, in this contemporary society, these qualities are rare. The world needs people like you, not only to pay honor to the dead, but to help the living. There are so many worthy organizations that need help from people like you, in order to fight for those who can not fight for themselves. I think of child organizations, programs for the elderly and the disabled. It goes on and on. Don't misunderstand me. By no means am I suggesting you stop working on this case. I just don't want you to lose sight of how precious life is, only to find, when it is too late, that you never really lived it. Take time to enjoy the simple things in life; take time for yourself Allow yourself to relax from time to time. Find your peace with the world, not for someone else, but for you.

Regarding the case, I haven't heard from anybody. This is probably due to the fact that I still have not written David Paranteau. I have had no time this year to work on this, given my job, my clinical practice and my school. I average four hours of sleep per night. I can do no more than I am doing right now. My school semester ends in May and my clinic commitment ends in June, at which point I intend to take some time for myself, to regenerate. After that, I will be willing to help you in any way I can. I will contact David Paranteau again at that time. Please, really pay attention to what I've said. It's probably hard to hear and I'm sure others have said similar things to you, but I do know what I'm talking about. It's time for you to take care of yourself.
Be well,
Lisa Rosa

RE: Compagna/Psaradelis Murders of 1973

Dear Governor Shaheen:
Time is running out for Chief Robert Baker and me. The Chief's health isn't very good and I have just had a massive heart attack.

I started writing to you about the Compagna/Psaradelis murder investigation in November of 1996 and before that it was Governor Steve Merrill, etc. It is hard for us to understand how twenty-six years have gone by and the same suspects we had from the very start are still our prime suspects today.

Actually there isn't a perfect crime and the Compagna/Psaradelis murders are one of those many cases that are allowed to fall into the cracks. No one bothers to reach down to pick them up, so the killer or killers get off scot-free. Many investigators don't want to investigate a case once it cools down or gets cold even though they aren't supposed to do that They often use the excuse that they can't be bothered with older cases because they have more recent cases to investigate or they don't have the manpower This is really a poor excuse since most departments have increased their staff, but they sure have enough help to investigate a less serious crime or complaint.

There are lots of people connected with law enforcement that would like to see Chief Baker and me walk away from the Compagna/Psaradelis investigation, but we will never let that happen. We are dedicated to working on this case until the people responsible for the murders arc brought to justice.

Governor Shaheen, for the past twenty-six years we have been in contact with various people from local police departments, sheriff departments, state police, Attorney Generals, Governors, Senators, Justice Department and right up to President William Jefferson Clinton. We are sorry to say that there hasn't been a single person that has moved the Compagna/Psaradelis investigation forward in regards to placing or eliminating our two prime suspects or any other suspects and this should have been done years ago. Chief Baker and I realize that we are not liked by many people within law enforcement because they claim we make them look bad and we don't think that is a good enough reason for them not to investigate the Compagna/Psaradelis murders. Liking us or not liking us should play no part in this investigation and the main concern for everyone associated with this Investigation should be to bring the people responsible for the murders to justice.

As you know Governor, a book ("TRUTH & JUSTICE") was written in 1995 in regards to the Compagna/Psaradelis murders with the hope that someone would read it who had information about the murders and would come forward and help law enforcement bring the people responsible to justice. In November of 1992 we received information in regards to two people that had knowledge about the crime and two possible suspects and we were unable to find anyone that would interview them, it was easier for everyone to say that they would not check these people out unless we told them who gave us the information. We couldn't give this information because the person who gave it was in fear of their personal safety; and the safety of their family and property. In April of 1997 a woman came forward, contacted the Merrimack Police Department in regards to knowledge she has about the murders. The information was passed on to the State Police, the Attorney General and you, Governor. A year went by and no one made any attempt to contact this woman even when they were advised that she was receiving harassing phone calls and was in fear of her own safety Finally she was contacted by telephone, spoke with the investigator for an hour and she has never heard from anyone in law enforcement again, and our two prime suspects remain our prime suspects. Two years have now passed and the investigation hasn't moved forward at all. I am updating my book and bringing the story up to July 2001.

We are disturbed over this investigation because after twenty-six years of investigation and trying to place or eliminate our two prime suspects, we realize that there is no one within the State of New Hampshire who will really do anything to solve these murders. We have tried the Justice Department and others and all we hear is, 'we cannot help you, there is no Federal crime or violation." "Contact your Attorney General and State Police". The end results is negative. The system has let the victims, families, society and us down and the people responsible get away scot-free. Is it too much to expect law enforcement to place or eliminate any and all suspects in this or any other case?

As Governor, it would mean a lot to you, the victims, families and the state if this twenty-six year old double murder was solved and the people responsible brought to justice. What makes this case special is that people can get away with murder and there are so many people that say it is someone else's job and not theirs. Please don't let twenty-six years of investigation become wasted years and allow the people responsible to get away scot-free.

JUSTICE DENIED

I hope you will reply to my letter.
Sincerely,
Joseph A. Horak,
Detective Lieutenant Ret

April 10, 1999

"Telephone call for you, Lieutenant Horak. It's Chief Baker from Candia."

"Hello Chief Baker, is that you?"

"Yes, Lieutenant. I'm calling to find out how you are coming along after your heart attack. It is hard for me to believe that you ever had a heart attack, you have always been so healthy. Before I forget to tell you, I recently had a heart attack myself, as well as a quadruple by-pass. I am feeling better, it just takes time and. as you know, trust in God and having a good attitude."

"Chief, I am doing OK, but I am sure shocked to hear that you have had heart problems yourself. It sounds like we better think of something we can do about Wayne Powers and Tom Jefferson because if we don't find away to place or eliminate them as suspects, no one within the State of New Hampshire will ever do it. Chief, time is running out for us, our health has sure slipped this year and I am sure that the various people we have been dealing with in regards to the murders of Diane Compagna and Anne Psaradelis feel that they have shut the door Lisa J. Rosa has opened and will not answer our letters or investigate this case any further.

"Chief, I have sent out several letters to various people in the past few months including the Governor and the only one that has replied was Lisa Rosa and she stated that she hasn't heard from anyone from the state since she was interviewed by Sergeant Parenteau by telephone months and months ago. Lisa said that she would help us in anyway she could and would not back off because of any pressure or threats from anyone.

"Well, Chief, I think I better let you hang the phone up and get some rest. If you can think of anything we can do to move this investigation forward, please let me know. If you need anything just pick up the phone and let me know. You know I would help you in anyway, just as I know you would help me. I do know that we can't let 26 years of investigation become wasted years and have Powers and Jefferson get away with the crime of murder. There is also the promise we made to the victims and we need to keep that promise. It would sure make everyone feel that the justice system does work for everyone, even through it took 26 years."

May 9, 1999
No reply from anyone in the state.

May 20, 1999

RE: Compagna/Psaradelis Murders of 1973

Dear Attorney Kissinger:
As you know, I last wrote to you on January 23, 1999 and I never received a reply or even received the rest of the pictures taken of the crime scene, that I gave you in July of 1998. I would appreciate it if you would return the pictures as you agreed to do. I really would like to put them back into the case.
The way things have been going, it appears that you and Sergeant David Parenteau are not going to do anything in re-gards to placing or eliminating the two prime suspects we have had for the past 27 years and that is pretty sad, because they are the responsible people.
I am still in touch with Lisa Rosa and she has never heard from anyone connected with law enforcement since Sergeant Parenteau spoke with her last September. Lisa is really the key to open the door that will lead to having justice prevail in this investigation.
I have just finished re-writing my book "TRUTH & JUSTICE" and have brought the story up to July, 2001, since I have used mostly the true names of persons, places and things, the story should be more of an interest to the general public and I hope it will bring someone forward that has information and knowledge about the crime and the people responsible.

384

Maybe the only way this murder investigation will ever be solved, will be from pressure coming from the general public or concerned people like Lisa Rosa.

In your last letter you stated that you and Sergeant Parenteau followed up on the information that we obtained from Lisa Rosa, I sure would appreciate it if you would advise Chief Baker and me, just how these suspects were placed or eliminated. We would appreciate knowing what kind of action you took and any results you had. We would like to know if you interviewed anyone from the list of people we gave you that know and have information about the people that are responsible for the murders of these two young girls. As far as we can tell, no one has been interviewed from the list we gave you.

I am hopeful that when my book is published that it will help us to solve the murders, since there really isn't anyone in law enforcement that will do it.

Sincerely yours,
Joseph A. Horak
Lieutenant/Detective Ret.

May 20, 1999

Dear Bledsoe:

Even though I have never been to a football game, the "Patriots" are what I call "My Team." Speaking about the Patriots, I am well aware that you and the other members of the team not only play football, but that you help people and organizations in their various causes.

I hope you will read this letter and the material I am sending along with it. I find that I am a "Patriot", but in a different way. Since the New England Patriots are a team that sticks together in all the good and bad times, I thought you might un-

derstand my plight and the reason I am seeking the help of you and your team mates. After 26 years, I find that this is my last chance to keep a promise I made in October of 1973, this being in regards to the Compagna/Psaradelis murders of 1973.

Within the next few weeks a sad anniversary will pass. Twenty-six years ago, two young Merrimack, New Hampshire girls were brutally murdered. These many years later the memories of the crime have dulled by the passage of time and the need for family and friends to move ahead with their lives. forgetting is often a kindness to those in pain. But to me, it is the enemy. In twenty-six years I have sought to bring the murderers to justice.

Please allow me to introduce myself. I am Joseph Horak, Merrimack, New Hampshire, a retired Lieutenant/Detective.

Throughout my entire life I have worked to ensure justice. One night years ago, I vowed to the spirit of two young 15 year old girls, Diane Compagna and her friend Anne Psaradelis that I would not rest until the men who took their lives were brought to justice. I was a member of the investigation team. I worked closely with Chief Robert Baker to gather evidence and pursue prosecution. From the very beginning we had identified two suspects, however criminal proceedings have never been filed. We know from long investigations and documentations, that these individuals who have information necessary to the criminal proceedings have been hesitant to step forward. We have tried for so long to convince them of the need to do so.

And so, I find myself writing this letter. Time is running out. Many in the community have forgotten or never knew of the incident. Chief Baker and I are seniors now and have very little time left to see our promise to the girls fulfilled, nor do we have the financial leverage to offer a reward for "information leading to the arrest and conviction" of the suspects. The so-called "team of patriots" that I belonged to, walked away from this investigation years and years ago. We have spent the past twenty-six years trying to find someone that would help us to bring the suspects to justice. We have tried Local Police Departments, Sheriff Departments, State Police,

Attorney Generals, Governors, Senators, Justice Department, Janet Reno and right up to President William Jefferson Clinton. The results for the most part have been negative.

Knowing this, I come to you with a request, from you and your team members. Please consider "Carrying the Torch of Justice" with us. We sincerely believe that the only course of action left is to bring this case before the public once again by offering a reward for critical information so long withheld.

We do not wish to receive such money in hand, but hope that you and your teammates could establish a fund and administer payment when the established terms of the reward are met. We know that many of the team have children and families and if it were one of their own, they would want the people responsible brought to justice.

Chief Baker and I would be willing to meet with you at a time convenient to you, to present our case and answer any of your concerns. Life is to precious and the lives of our children are the most precious of all. To have the loss of these two 15 year old girls fade into oblivion without resolution would be a crime in itself. Closure is needed for the families, the community, the investigators and everyone else that has been touched by this case.

I hope to hear from you soon, so that we may discuss this request of help. I may be reached at 603 478-0441.

Sincerely yours,
Joseph A. Horak
Lieutenant/Detective Retired

June 2, 1999

RE: Compagna/Psaradelis Murders

Dear Mr. Horak:

As I stated to you in my letter of January 11, 1999, New Hampshire State Police Sergeant David Parenteau and I have followed up on the information provided by Lisa Rosa. I would be glad to discuss this investigation with you and I urge you to give me a call. I apologize for not returning the remainder of the crime pictures to you. I will contact the forensic laboratory and have them returned.

I continue to share your hope that the investigation will lead to the discovery of the person or persons responsible for these murders.

Very truly yours,
John C. Kissinger
Assistant Attorney General

January 5, 2000

Dear Mr. Horak

The Governor's Office is in receipt of your letters regarding the investigation into the Compagna/Psaradelis homicides. Governor Shaheen has asked that I review and reply to your letter dated December 28, 1999.

I have forwarded a copy of your letter to the office of the Attorney General and asked that your letter and concerns be addressed in a timely manner. We realize that the investigation has not proceeded at the pace you would prefer but the Governor is confident that the Department of Justice is being diligent in its pursuit of justice in this homicide.

JUSTICE DENIED

Governor Shaheen is deferring to the judgement of the Attorney General in regards to this matter and we request that all further correspondence be directed to this office. You may reach the Attorney General at 271-3671 or by addressing the Criminal Justice Bureau in writing at: New Hampshire Department of Justice 33 Capital Street Concord, New Hampshire 03301-6397.

Thank you for your inquiry.
Sincerely,
Jill Burke
Special Assistant for Citizens Affairs

January 8, 2000

Dear Ms. Burke:

I received your letter of January 5, 2000 in regards to a letter I wrote to Governor Jeanne Shaheen dated December 28, 1999, this being in reference to the Compagna/Psaradelis homicides of 1973.

I really can't understand why you ended up with my letter to the Governor because I am sure you couldn't even begin to understand any concerns that I have in regards to this murder investigation or any request for help that I have requested. In the past I have been contacted via mail by a few different people from your office and the results were the same as what I just received from you. No results, just pass the letter onto another department and the weeks, months and years pass by and the case remains unsolved. I did request a meeting with the Governor and as usual, no mention of any reply to this request.

In regards to a remark you made in your letter, "We realize that the investigation has not proceeded at the pace that you would prefer but the Governor is confident that the Department of Justice is being diligent in its pursuit of justice in this homicide." I think that the pace of this investigation does not proceed at the pace I would prefer, don't you yourself think that over twenty-six years is more than enough time or is it going to take another twenty-six or more years. Chief Baker and I spent nearly five years with Attorney Michael Ramsdell from the Attorney General's Office.

The investigation didn't move an inch and the same suspects we had from the very beginning are still our prime suspects today. Thank you for your reply, but it sure doesn't answer my letter or offer any real help towards moving this investigation forward.

Sincerely,
Joseph Horak
Lieutenant/Detective Ret.

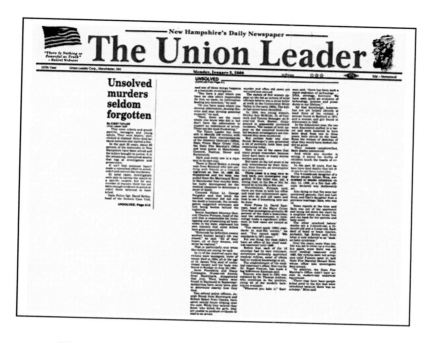

Figure 26: Union Leader article - 28 years later

JOSEPH A. HORAK

January 10, 2000

I cannot believe it, 10:00 a.m. already, I better make that phone call to Chief Baker.

Hello Chief, just me calling. I wanted you to know that I received a telephone call from a reporter in Hartford, Connecticut.

What is the world did he want and how did he get your telephone number?

Chief, do you remember the article that we were trying to get the Union Leader to do on the Compagna/Psaradelis murders, and it ended up being part of the story the State Police came out with on January 3, 2000, this was in regards to old unsolved murder cases.

How could I forget Lieutenant, they really didn't put our article in the paper, actually they made a mess out of it, they couldn't even put the correct name of the town where the poor girls were found murdered.

Well anyway, this reporter is a man by the name of Kevin Canfield and he works for the Hartford Courant, he gave me his telephone number 1 800 524-4242 Ext. 6289 and also his E-Mail CANFIELD @ COURANT.COM and he told me the paper does four or five "Unsolved older murder cases every month."

Mr. Canfield told me he read about our case in the newspaper and they wanted to do the story, he called me back several times and wanted more information, which of course I gave to him.

You know Chief, if this reporter does a good job at writing an article on our investigation, it could help to bring attention to someone else that would want to do another story or come forward with knowledge about the murders and those responsible.

I don't know if we should ask the State Police and the Attorney General's Office if they would like to be a part of the interview in regards to this case. I think back at how many times we have set things up so that we could bring attention to the Compagna/Psaradelis murder investigation before the public. As you know, we have tried some of the so-called crime shows, television stations, newspapers and just about everyone of them backed away from doing any story, which wasn't fair. When I would ask these various places why they backed off from doing the story or article, they would never give us a decent answer, it was always things like, the reporter or the camera crew were assigned to do another story, your story is to hot to handle, there was always the, "We will get back to you" and of course that never happens.

Well Chief, I'll let you get back to work on your truck, this reporter sounds more than interested in doing the story, so I'll keep you advised as to any progress in that direction, I know that he wants to interview us in person.

Thanks for calling Lieutenant.

January 17, 2000

RE: Compagna/Psaradelis Homicide of 1973

Dear Governor Shaheen:

I sent you a letter on December 28, 1999 in regards to the Compagna/Psaradelis homicide investigation. I also requested that you allow Chief Baker and me the chance to talk with you in person. This investigation has been going on for the past twenty-seven years as you know. In the various letters I have sent you in regards to this case I have mentioned the names of Tom Jefferson and Wayne Powers and I of course have to protect the true name of the suspect or suspects, and I would hope that anyone else who would obtain this information would do the same.

Governor, I have never received any reply from you in regards to my request that you allow Chief Baker and I to meet with you. I often see that you allow all kinds of people both young and old to meet with you in regards to various things. It is hard for me to understand why you won't grant us the same privilege of speaking with you in person, after all, a double murder of two young girls should rate being near the top of the list.

Governor, I did receive a letter from Ms. Jill Burke who is one of the Special Assistances for Citizen Affairs.

JOSEPH A. HORAK

This letter she sent does not help to move this investigation forward in anyway, it just pushes the case back into the hands of the people that won't really do anything to solve the murders. (We dealt with the then Assistant Attorney General Michael Ramsdell for nearly five years in regards to this case and results were negative, as they have been all these years.)

In Ms. Burke's letter she made a remark that wasn't appreciated, "We realize that the investigation has not proceeded at the pace you would prefer etc." I really think that twenty-seven years isn't a slow pace for any investigation, especially this one. I don't think Ms. Burke should have been given the letter I sent to you since she isn't connected with law enforcement and the letter had the prime suspects name in it.

It is hard for Chief Baker and I to understand how we can have two prime suspects in this case and there isn't a single person connected with law enforcement within the State of New Hampshire that will put in the time and effort that is needed to bring the people responsible to justice, especially since we are 99% sure these people are the killers. How would you feel if one of these victims had been one of your daughters, I am sure you would want her killer caught even if it took a lifetime.

Governor, we really would appreciate your letting us talk with you in person, this case can be solved and we won't quit until it is.

Sincerely,
Joseph Horak
Lieutenant/Detective Ret.

March 1, 2000

Dear Detective Mark Fuhrman:
 "I Need Your Help"

Re: Compagna/Psaradelis Murders of 1973

JUSTICE DENIED

Please allow me to introduce myself, I am Joseph A. Horak, a Lieutenant/Detective Retired. Chief Robert Baker and I have been working on the Compagna/Psaradelis murder investigation for the past twenty-seven years. We have always had two prime suspects in this case. Throughout the years we have tried to find someone in law enforcement who would help us bring the killer or killers to justice. It took from 1973 to 1977 to have the suspect in the rape of Diane Compagna that took place on July 4, 1973, tried and convicted. There were various people who were not very pleased to see me accomplish this.

The man who was tried and found guilty of the crime was Tom Jefferson. He is also one of the prime suspects in the Compagna/Psaradelis murders and has been from 1973 up to the present time. My second prime suspect in this investigation is Wayne Powers (deceased) from Merrimack, New Hampshire.

The girls bodies were found in a wooded area off the New Boston Road in Candia, New Hampshire on September 29, 1973, and were identified on September 30th. Wayne Powers was at work on September 30th, when he received a telephone call. What ever was said to Wayne during this phone call, caused Wayne to flip out so badly that he had to receive medical attention.

Two days later, (October 2, 1973) he was admitted to the hospital with a mental breakdown. Twenty-six days later, Wayne came home from the hospital and on the morning of November 9th, he shot and killed himself. The investigation into Wayne's death revealed that something happened to him in the early part of July that changed his life forever. Powers and Jefferson were friends, not good friends, but friends. Both Powers and Jefferson were off from work on July 12, 1973. The girls were alive and well on the 12th over at Hampton Beach between 4:30 p.m. and 5:30 p.m., it is believed that the two girls were murdered that night.

The motive that Tom Jefferson would have had for killing Diane Compagna is three fold.

JOSEPH A. HORAK

a. *He would have lost his job.*
b. *He would have been arrested, tried and probably sent to prison for raping her.*
c. *The most important fact was that Tom Jefferson was going with a woman who was in the middle of a divorce and he wanted to marry her. Note: Tom Jefferson married Cathy Michaels nine days before the bodies of the girls were found in Candia. Jefferson was married on September 21, 1973.*

> *Detective Fuhrman, various people from law enforcement agencies such as local police departments, State Police, Attorney General's Office , Governor's Office were contacted.*
>
> *The various so called "Crime Shows" were contacted over the years in an effort to find someone that would help Chief Baker and me to either place or eliminate our suspects, as well as any other suspects that came to our attention. Plenty of people stated that they would help, but these only turned out to be empty promises. No one really ever helped us and thus Wayne Powers and Thomas Jefferson remain our prime suspects.*
>
> *Even people within the State Police and Attorney General's Office will admit that these people could be suspects, but they never would do anything to place or eliminate them as suspects.*
>
> *In August of 1992, Chief Baker and I sent a letter to the New Hampshire State Police advising them that we had an informant, who demanded anonymity, that he knew of two people that had information about the murders of the two girls (Diane Compagna and Anne Psaradelis) and that Wayne Powers was one of the men involved in the murders, also that these two men were related to the deceased Wayne Powers. One of the men being Jason Powers, brother of Wayne and the other man , Bruce Smith who is the brother-in law. The letter was sent in August of 1992 and the State Police and Attorney General's Office never questioned the letter until 1994. (Why? This letter was brought up at a meeting at the State House in 1994 and*

they advised Chief Baker and me (Horak) that they didn't believe there was any such informant, that we had made up this person, which of course was not true. All I really heard was that I was a liar and was making everyone look bad. Both members of the State Police and Attorney General's Office stated they would not do anything about working on this investigation until we revealed the name of the informant.

They were advised that we couldn't do this anymore then they could if they were in the same position.

In December of 1995, Tom Jefferson tried to take his own life by shooting himself. Even though I couldn't afford it, I came back to New Hampshire hopeful that we might be able to obtain a "Dying Declaration" from Jefferson since he was dying.

Upon my arrival back in New Hampshire, I met with Chief Baker and former Merrimack Police Sergeant George Rousseau. We talked about trying to obtain a Dying Declaration from Jefferson, if he was involved in the two murders. We knew he was, but we needed the assistance of an active police officer, as we knew no one would believe us if we obtained one and the suspect died. We each contacted various people from different law enforcement agencies in an attempt to find someone that would help us. All we heard were things like, "We don't like Joe, how bad does his book make us look, if he wants to pay for the investigation, we will investigate it. It is election time and we don't want to make the Sheriff or Governor look bad." We were astonished by this attitude because if they eliminated any and all suspects and got nothing, they were doing their job; if they were able to place the suspect, they were still doing their job and the murders would have been solved and those responsible arrested. I spent 10 days in New Hampshire trying to find someone that would help. It was a waste of time, money and effort, just as it has been all these years. It shouldn't make any difference if they don't like me, Chief Baker or anyone else, catching the killer or killers should be above everything else.

JOSEPH A. HORAK

I returned to Oklahoma without a "Dying Declaration" from Tom Jefferson, I wrote letters to the Governor and State Police. I was advised that the case would be investigated and brought to a conclusion. This was never done, because our two prime suspects have never been placed or eliminated by either the State Police or the Attorney General's Office.

Here we are, it is 2000 and Wayne Powers and Tom Jefferson are still our prime suspects, pretty sad when you think about it.

In May of 1997, I received a letter and a statement from Lisa J. Rosa who lives in California. Lisa had just finished giving some of the information to Lieutenant/Detective Michael Milligan from the Merrimack Police Department, in regards to the murders of Diane Compagna and Anne Psaradelis. After making that call, she has never heard from Lieutenant Milligan again, however Lisa started receiving harassing phone calls the very next day.

Lisa found out that I was one of the Detective's on the case, she sent me a letter, a copy of her statement and she advised me about the harassing phone calls and believes they are connected to the murders of the two girls, she further stated that she was in fear of her safety and life, stated that she was so concerned that she contacted the San Francisco Police Department and made a report.

I wrote letters to the Governor, Attorney General and the State Police, sent each of them a copy of Lisa's statement and advised them that she fears for her own safety and life.

One year later, Ms. Rosa received a telephone call from the New Hampshire State Police and she has never heard from anyone connected with law enforcement again. No one seems interested in her safety or the knowledge she has about the murders.

Lisa went with a Tim Decato who is the cousin to Wayne Powers around 1975, and he told Lisa that his cousin (Wayne) had confessed to him that he was involved in the murders of the girls, Compagna and Psaradelis. Decato knows who the killers are, just as others like Jason Powers, Bruce Smith, Greg Iverson, Earl Iverson Mark Decato and others. It would take a little pressure to be put on these people, and give them the chance to tell the truth, or maybe later on they could be charged with aiding the killer or killers.

Chief Baker and I are now seniors, we have both had major heart attacks, we have very little money and time is running out for us. We promised the victims that we would bring their killers to justice. We have been through the entire system, from local Police Departments, Sheriff Departments, County Attorneys, State Police, Attorney Generals, Senators, Governors, Justice Department, Janet Reno and right up to President William Jefferson Clinton, results have been negative for the most part.

I am writing to you because we have watched you in regards to the O.J. Simpson murder investigation and have knowledge of your now being a Private Investigator working on various older homicide cases. We have no way of paying you for your services, but this case can be solved. If you were to investigate our case and solve it, this could be an aid to you in your new area of employment.

To be honest with you Mr. Fuhrman, you are our last hope of ever having this case solved. Will you please consider our request and we will help you in anyway we can, no one knows this case any better than we do. We have lived with this case for 27 years.

There isn't anyone connected with law enforcement that will really work on this investigation, Oh, lots of promises, but they are just words that don't mean a thing. We worked with one Assistant Attorney General from 1993 through 1998, all kinds of promises and yet, not a single thing done.

I hope you will reply to this letter and if you need any information, or we can help in anyway, please feel free to call day or night. I want to thank you for taking the time to read this letter. Please know that we are sincere and we really need to keep our promise to the victims, their families and society.

JOSEPH A. HORAK

Sincerely yours,
Joseph A. Horak
Lieutenant/Detective Retired

May 18, 2000

Dear Mr. Horak:

Your letter dated December 28, 1999, and Ms. Jill Burke's reply to you dated January 5, 2000 have been referred to me for review and reply.

I appreciate your expression of interest and concerns in an effective and just resolution to the homicides of Ms. Compagna and Ms. Psaradelis in 1973. The Homicide Unit of the New Hampshire Attorney General's Office is currently reviewing a number of so-called "unsolved" homicides including this one.

This matter is currently assigned to Assistant Attorney General Malinda Lawrence. Ms. Lawrence has a busy trial schedule, as do all members of the Homicide Unit. We hope that the coming months will permit us to turn our attention to these and a number of other unsolved homicides.

I appreciate your anxiety and concern that the continuing investigation of these homicides not be allowed to languish. Unfortunately, our work prosecuting recent homicides has to take precedence over our work on unsolved cases. The members of the Homicide Unit recognize that the priority given to recent cases is frustrating to victims' families and concerned members of the community. We strive, however, to bring our best professional efforts to bear on each of the many matters we are call upon to investigate or litigate.

I accept responsibility for case management and resource decisions made by my predecessors and me. I regret that you do not support those decisions. I believe however that your letter unfairly and inaccurately portrays us as indifferent to the sufferings of homicide victims and their families. Our record in

*prosecuting both recent and unsolved homicides and our posi-
tive, professional relations with law enforcement officers over
the years attest to our caring and professional commitment to
these difficult cases.*

*Please do not hesitate to contact Ms. Lawrence or me if
you have further questions or concerns regarding this matter.*

Very truly yours,
Charles T. Putnam
Senior Assistant Attorney General

June 22, 2000

Dear Lieutenant Horak:

*Senator Judd Gregg forwarded your May 21st communica-
tion to the Department of Justice, who subsequently forwarded
it to the FBI for response directly to you. You are requesting
help in obtaining information from Ms. Lisa J. Rosa, who, you
indicate, may have knowledge about the 1973 double murders
of Diane Compagna and Anne Psaradelis.*

*As you were previously advised in our letter to you dated
December 22, 1997, most murder cases are investigated by law
enforcement authorities at the local or state level. In order for
the FBI to become involved, specific facts must be present to
indicate that a violation of federal law within our investigative
jurisdiction has occurred. Based on a review of the information
you provided in your current communication and in past correspondence, we are unable to identify any violation of federal
law within the investigative jurisdiction of the FBI.*

*We are, therefore, unable to take any investigative action
in this case. However, upon receipt of a request from the state
or local agency investigating this case, we would be willing to
assist by covering out of state leads or making available the
services of our Laboratory and Criminal Justice Information
Services (fingerprint) Divisions.*

Since you indicated that Ms. Rosa fears for her safety, she should report her concerns to the local or state police in California since the FBI does not have the legal authority to provide her personal protection.

Additionally, if she has pertinent information concerning this case, she should contact our San Francisco Office at the address listed below. That Office is responsible for overseeing operations in her
area.

Sincerely yours,
A. Robert Walsh
Legislative Counsel
Office of Public and Congressional Affairs

July 17, 2000

RE: Compagna/Psaradelis Murders of 1973

Dear Chairman Welch:
I want to thank you for taking the time to talk with me in regards to the homicide of Diane Compagna and Anne Psaradelis, that took place in Candia, New Hampshire in 1973.

As you suggested, I have assembled a folder that contains material from the investigation of these murders from 1973-2000. I, of course have a large amount of material in regards to the investigation, but I tried to condense it best I could.

There comes a time after 27 years of investigation when we need to think about moving ahead, and not worry about one organization or another in regards to what they did or didn't do in order to solve this case. We need to find justice on a united front and bring a murderer to justice. These two young 15 year old girls never finished school, married or had a chance to live their lives or anything else.

JUSTICE DENIED

We need to pool our resources together and show the system works, a killer is convicted, wounds healed, and a good look at law enforcement working together for New Hampshire.

Chairman Welch, you asked me what I would like to see accomplished in this investigation.

A. *I would like to have the New Hampshire State Police or FBI conduct DNA Testing on the clothing from the two victims. The State Police hold these items in the evidence room in regards to this case.*

B. *I would like to have Ms. Lisa J. Rosa from California interviewed in person. She really is the key to opening up the door that will lead to the arrest and conviction of the killer. Ms. Rosa could be an asset in regards to Tim Decato from Merrimack, New Hampshire, he knows who the killers are and knows facts that he shouldn't know.*

C. *I would like to see the various people we have listed as having information and knowledge as to who is responsible for the murders interviewed. If possible the polygraph used in some cases. These people are either friends or related to the suspects in this investigation.*

I want to thank you once again for your help and if you need any information or material on this case, please don't hesitate to contact me. I would appreciate it if you could advise me if there is any kind of movement in regards to moving this investigation forward.

Sincerely yours,
Joseph Horak
Lieutenant/Detective Retired

Figure 27: New Boston Road in July 2000

Figure 28: Entrance to gravel pit as it is in July 2000

JUSTICE DENIED

August 7, 2000

Geoffrey C. Bible Chairman & CEO
The Philip Morris Companies, Inc.

Dear Mr. Bible:

I am aware of how The Philip Morris Companies, Inc. touch the lives of people in this country, as well as those of others in every part of the world. I also realize that your companies go well beyond just selling your products and services. You have ventured into various areas such as, Domestic Violence, Humanitarian, being involved in the National Aids Foundation and many other areas, which of course help people in our country, as well as other countries around the world.

Within the next six weeks a sad anniversary will pass. Twenty-seven years ago, two young 15 year old girls from Merrimack, New Hampshire were brutally murdered. These many years later the memories of the crime have been dulled by the passage of time and the need for family and friends to move ahead with their lives. Forgetting is often a kindness to those in pain. But to me, it is the enemy. For the past twenty-seven years I have sought to bring the murderers to justice.

Please allow me to introduce myself. I am Joseph A. Horak, Merrimack Police Lieutenant/Detective, Retired.

Throughout my entire life I have worked to ensure justice. One night many years ago, I vowed to the spirit of the two young girls, Diane Compagna and her friend Anne Psaradelis that I would not rest until the men that took their lives had paid for that deed.

In 1973, I was a member of the investigation team. I worked closely with Chief Robert Baker to gather evidence and pursue prosecution. From the very beginning we identified two suspects, however, charges have never been filed in regards to the murders. We know from long investigations and documentation, that the individuals who have information necessary to the criminal proceedings have always been hesitant to step forward. We have tried for so long to convince them of the need to do so. From 1973 and up to the present time. Chief Robert Baker and I have attempted to find someone connected with law enforcement that would help us to place or eliminate these two men as being responsible for the murders. We have tried to obtain help from the local police departments, sheriff departments, county attorneys, Janet Reno and right up to President William Jefferson Clinton, results have been negative.

And so, I find myself writing this letter to you. Time is running out. Many in the community have either forgotten or have never known of the incident. Chief Baker and I are now "seniors" and have very little time left to see our promise to the girls fulfilled. Nor do we have financial leverage to offer a reward for the "Information leading to the arrest and conviction of the suspects."

I come to you with a request. Please consider "carrying the torch" with us. We sincerely believe that the only course of action left to us, is to bring this case before the public once again by offering a reward for critical information so long withheld.

We do not wish to receive such monies in hand, but hope you would establish a fund and administer payment when the established terms of the reward are met.

Chief Baker and I are willing to meet with you at a time and place convenient to you, in order to present our case and answer any questions or concerns you might have. Life is precious and the lives of our children perhaps the most precious.

To have the loss of these two 15 year old girls fade into oblivion without resolution would be a crime in itself. Closure is needed for families, the community, the investigators and the perpetrators.

Mr. Bible, I hope to hear from you soon so that we may discuss this request. I may be reached at 1 603 478-0441, or you could contact Chief Baker at 1 603 483-8659.

Respectfully submitted,

JUSTICE DENIED

Joseph A. Horak
Lieutenant/Detective Ret.

<u>August 10, 2000</u>

Diane P. Scarponi
Foster Daily Democrat

RE: COMPAGNA/PSARADELIS Murders of 1973

Dear Ms Scarponi:

In 1973, Chief Robert Baker Retired and I spoke with you about doing an article for us in regards to the murders of Diane Compagna and her friend Anne Psaradelis that took place in Candia, New Hampshire in 1973. You did write a story on the murders and it was great. You advised us that if we needed help in the future, that we could contact you.

Diane, we would like to do another story, it will not be on the murders itself, but on the investigation. And so, I find myself writing this letter to you. Time is running out' Many in the community have either forgotten or never heard of the incident. Chief Baker and I are now "seniors" and have very little time left to see our promise to the girls fulfilled. To have the loss of these girls fade into oblivion without resolution would be a crime within itself.

From 1973 and up to the present time, Chief Baker and I have attempted to find someone connected with law enforcement that would help us to place or eliminate the two men we have as prime suspects since November of 1973.

We start the 28th year of this investigation this year. We have tried to obtain help from the local police departments and right up to President William Jefferson Clinton, for the most part, results have been negative.

a. One of the prime suspects was convicted of statutory rape in regards to one of the victims in this case that took place on July 4, 1973.

b. *In November of 1992, the state police were advised of two men that are believed to have information about the murders and the people responsible. This has never been checked out by law enforcement.*

c. *On December 22, 1995, one of the prime suspects attempted to take his own life by shooting himself in the head. Chief Baker, former Sergeant George Rousseau and I tried to find someone or agency connected with law enforcement that would interview the suspect in an attempt to obtain a "Dying Declaration." We received a lot of promises, but not a single person or agency would interview the suspect. The suspect did recover and has never been questioned about the shooting and or the two murders.*

d. *In April of 1997, a woman from California contacted the Merrimack Police Department and spoke with a detective. She advised him of who she was and that she had information about the murders of Compagna and Psaradelis. This woman contacted me in May of 1997 about the murders and sent me a copy of her statement, she had sent to the Merrimack detective in April. I made a copy of this woman's letter, copies of her statement.*

I sent copies to Governor Jeanne Shaheen, Attorney General Philip McLoughlin and the State Police. I also advised them that this woman was in fear of her own safety and even her life. It took over a year before someone from the State Police contacted her by telephone, this woman has never heard from anyone connected with law enforcement again and the information she provided has never been checked out.

Diane, I think I have given you enough information so that you could make a decision as to if you will or will not be able to do a story on this subject. We thought that since you helped us in 1993, that we should give you the story now, that is if you wanted to do it.

I hope you will reply to this letter, if you need more information. Chief Baker and I would be willing to talk with you at anytime and will help in anyway we can.

JUSTICE DENIED

Thank you for taking the time to read this letter.

Sincerely yours,
Joseph A. Horak
Lieutenant/Detective Ret.

August 20, 2000

RE: Compagna/Psaradelis Murders of 1973

Dear Chairman David Welch:
   As you know, I sent you a folder that contained material from the investigation of these murders from 1973-2000. I tried to condense the material as best I could. I am sure you realize that I have the complete case in regards to this investigation.
   I know that you and other members of the Criminal Justice Committee are more than busy, but a month has passed and I haven't received a single word from anyone. There comes a time when after twenty-seven years of investigation we need to find away to gain the attention of someone in this so-called, "inner circle." Receiving promises from Governors, Attorney Generals, the State Police and others that the prime suspects would be placed or eliminated as the people responsible for the murders of these two young 15 year old girls has been that, just a lot of promises. Chief Baker and I have tried for years to find a governor or attorney general that would allow us to interview them in person and so far we have had negative results.
   These two 15 year old girls aren't receiving the justice they truly deserve.
   Two things I would have liked done by you and your committee would have been to have the clothing of the victims checked by the State Police of FBI in regards to DNA testing.
   The other one would be to have Ms Lisa J. Rosa interviewed in person, she really is the key that will open the door

that will lead to the arrest and conviction of the one killer that is still alive.

If you and your committee cannot help us in regards to this investigation, I would appreciate your sending me back the material on the case that I sent you.

I hope you will reply to this letter and I want to thank you again for taking the time to talk with me and the interest you took in regards to this investigation.

Sincerely yours,
Joseph A. Horak
Lieutenant/Detective Ret.

September 7, 2000

Dear Rep. Charles Bass:
Within the next few weeks a sad anniversary will pass. Twenty-seven years ago, two young girls from Merrimack, New Hampshire were brutally murdered. These many years later the memories of the crime have been dulled by the passage of time and the need for family and friends to move ahead with their lives. Forgetting is often a kindness to those in pain. But to me, it is the enemy. For the past twenty-seven years I have sought to bring the murderers to justice.

Please allow me to introduce myself. I am Joseph A. Horak, Merrimack Police Department Lieutenant/Detective Retired. Throughout my entire life I have worked to ensure justice. One night many years ago, I vowed to the spirit of Diane Compagna and her friend Anne Psaradelis that I would not rest until their killers had paid for that deed.

In 1973, I was a member of the investigative team. I worked closely with Chief Robert Baker to gather evidence and pursue prosecution. From the very beginning we identified two suspects, however, charges have never been filed in regards to the murders. We know from long investigations and documentation, that individuals who have information necessary to the

410

criminal proceedings have always been hesitant to step forward. We have tried for so long to convince them of the need to do so. From 1973 and up to the present time, Chief Baker and I have attempted to find someone connected with law enforcement that would help us to place or eliminate these two men as being responsible for the murders.

We have tried to obtain help from the local police departments right up to President William Jefferson Clinton, results have been negative for the most part. And so I find myself writing this letter to you. Time is running out, many in the community have either forgotten or never knew of the incident. Chief Baker and I don't have the financial leverage to offer a reward for the information leading to the arrest and conviction of the suspects.

I come to you with a request. Please consider "carrying the torch" with us. We sincerely believe that the only course of action left to us is to find someone such as yourself that believes in family, God and justice for everyone. You are the only one that can help us at this point in time. I know that you were instrumental in regards to the $257,000.00 that was recently awarded to the New Hampshire Justice Department.

Since the New Hampshire Justice Department has just received this large award and it is meant to further justice, it would be appreciated if a small portion of it could be used to bring this case to a conclusion, this case can be solved and the three things that need to be done in order to accomplish this are as follows:

a. DNA testing on the clothes of the two victims.
b. Alive interview with Ms Lisa J. Rosa from California.
c. Interview people that have knowledge about the murders and those responsible.

Chief Baker and I would more than appreciate any help you can give this request. Life is precious and the lives of our children perhaps the most precious of all.

Rep. Bass, if you need any further information please feel free to contact me any time. I hope to hear from you soon, so that we could discuss this request of help.

Yours truly,
Joseph A. Horak
Lieutenant/Detective Ret.

September 7, 2000

Louis C. Carmillen SVP & CFO
The Philip Morris Companies, Inc.
120 Park Avenue New York, NY 10017

Dear Mr. Carmillen:
On August 7th of this year I wrote to Chairman CEO Mr. Geoffrey C. Bible of The Philip Morris Companies, Inc. This being in regards to a request for help and at this point in time, I do not know if he received my letter or not, so I am writing this letter to you with the hope that you would forward a copy of this letter to Mr. Bible.
Within the next three weeks a sad anniversary will pass. Twenty-seven years ago, two young 15 year old girls from Merrimack, New Hampshire were brutally murdered. These many years later the memories of the crime have been dulled by the passage of time and the need for family and friends to move ahead with their lives. Forgetting is often a kindness to those in pain. But to me, it is the enemy. For the past twenty-seven years I have sought to bring the murderers to justice.
Please allow me to introduce myself. I am Joseph A. Horak, Merrimack Police Lieutenant/Detective, Retired. Throughout my entire life I have worked to ensure justice. One night many years ago, I vowed to the spirit of the two young girls - Diane Compagna and her friend Anne Psaradelis that I would not rest until the men who took their lives had paid for that deed.

JUSTICE DENIED

In 1973, I was a member of the investigation team. I worked closely with Chief Robert Baker to gather evidence and pursue prosecution. From the very beginning we identified two suspects, however, charges have never been filed in regards to the murders. We know from long investigations and documentation, that the individuals who have information necessary to the criminal proceedings have always been hesitant to step forward. We have tried for so long to convince them of the need to do so. From 1973 and up to the present time, Chief Robert Baker and I have attempted to fine someone connected with law enforcement that would help us to place or eliminate these two men as being responsible for the murders. We have tried to obtain help from the local police departments, sheriff departments, county attorneys, attorney generals, governors, FBI, Janet Reno and up to President William Jefferson Clinton, results have been negative.

And so, I find myself writing this letter to you & The Philip Morris Companies, Inc.. Time is running out. Many in the community have either forgotten or never known of the incident. Chief Baker and I are now "seniors" and have very little time left to see our promise to the girls fulfilled. Nor do we have financial leverage to offer a reward for the "information leading to the arrest and conviction of the suspects."

I come to you and your company with a request. Please consider "carrying the torch" with us. We sincerely believe that the only course of action left to us, is to bring this case before the public once again by offering a reward for critical information so long withheld. We do not wish to receive such monies in hand, but hope that you would establish a reward fund and administer payment when the terms of the reward are met.

Chief Baker and I are willing to meet with you at a time and place convenient to you, in order to present our case and answer any questions or concerns you might have. Life is precious and the lives of our children perhaps the most precious. To have the loss of these two young girls fade into oblivion without resolution would be a crime in itself. Closure is needed

for families, the community, the investigators and the perpetra-
tors.

Mr. Carmillen, I hope to hear from you so that we may dis-
cuss this request. I may be reached at 1 603 478-0441, or you
could contact Chief Robert Baker at 1 603 483-8659.

Sincerely yours,
Joseph A. Horak
Lieutenant/Detective Ret.

September 8, 2000

RE: Compagna/Psaradelis Murders of 1973

Dear Colonel Gary Sloper:
Within the next three weeks a sad anniversary will pass.
Twenty-seven years ago, two young 15 year old girls from
Merrimack, New Hampshire were brutally murdered in Can-
dia. These many years later the memories of the crime have
been dulled by the passage of time and the need for family and
friends to move ahead with their lives.
Forgetting is often a kindness to those in pain. But to me, it
is the enemy. For the past 27 years we have sought to bring the
murderers to justice.
Colonel, throughout my entire life I have worked to ensure
justice. One night many years ago, I vowed to the spirit of the
two young girls - Diane Compagna and her friend Anne
Psaradelis that I would not rest until the men who took their
lives had paid for that deed.
In 1973 I started this investigation as "two missing girls"
and in September of 1973 it turned into a double homicide of
Diane Compagna and Anne Psaradelis. I was a member of the
investigation team. I worked closely with Chief Robert Baker
together evidence and pursue prosecution. From the very be-
ginning we identified two suspects, however, charges have
never been filed with regards to the murders. We know from

long investigations and documentation that individuals who have information necessary to the criminal proceedings have always been hesitant to step forward.

We have tried for so long to convince them of the need to do so. From 1973 and up to the present time, Chief Baker and I have attempted to find someone connected with law enforcement that would help to place or eliminate these two men as being responsible for the murders. We have tried to obtain help from the local police departments, sheriff departments, county attorneys, state police, attorney generals, governors, senators, Janet Reno and right up to President William Jefferson Clinton, results have been negative.

And so, I find myself writing this letter to you, time is running out. Many in the community have either forgotten or never known of the incident. Chief Baker and I are now "seniors" and have very little time left to see our promise to the girls fulfilled.

Colonel, we know we aren't liked by many people in law enforcement because they say we make them look bad and that isn't true. All we ever wanted and still want is to bring the killers to justice. We are 99% plus sure that our suspects are the people responsible for the murders. Chief Baker and I would like to have an appointment with you so that we can explain just why we know these people are the killers. We know this case can be solved and it would just take the following three things to accomplish it.

a. DNA testing done on the clothing of the two victims.
b. Face to face interview with Ms Lisa J. Rosa.
c. Have the list of people interviewed that we believe have information and knowledge about the murders and those responsible.

Chief Baker and I are willing to meet with you at anytime and place convenient to you, and will answer any concerns or questions you might have. Life is precious and the lives of our children perhaps the most precious. To have the loss of these two 15 year old girls fade into oblivion without resolution would be a crime in itself. Closure is needed for families, the community, the investigators and the perpetrators.

We hope to hear from you and that you will allow us the time to talk with you about the case. I can be reached at 1 603 478-0441. Thank you for taking the time to read this letter.

Respectfully submitted,
Joseph A. Horak
Lieutenant/Detective Ret.

September 13, 2000

RE: Compagna/Psaradelis Murders of 1973

Dear Colonel Sloper:
I want to thank you for taking the time to call me yesterday, September 12th, it was more than appreciated.

I know that I probably talked about so many things in regards to the murders of Diane Compagna and Anne Psaradelis, but I guess I wanted you to be sure that you realized how much time Chief Baker and I have put into this investigation, and that we are sincere in wanting to solve these murders. Our intent has never been to insult or hurt an investigator or agency. We need to keep our promise to the two girls that we would bring their killers to justice.

As you can see, I have put together a folder so that you might look it over and it might help you understand the case from our view, should you talk with your detective's from the Major Crime Unit.

I would appreciate it if you would send me back the material once you are done with it, I have no objection if you wanted to make a copy of it.

I want to thank you once again for taking an interest in this case and I sure hope we can bring the killers to justice.

416

JUSTICE DENIED

Chief Baker and I will help in anyway we can. I am sure that when and if you allow us to talk with you in person, that you will understand why we know this case can be solved.

Respectfully submitted,
Joseph Horak
Lieutenant/Detective Ret.

October 17, 2000

RE: Compagna/Psaradelis Murders of 1973

Dear Colonel Sloper:

It has been over a month since I spoke with you, and you advised me that if I didn't hear from you within that time, that I should contact you. I did however receive a note from Chief Baker advising me that he had received a note from you, and you advised him that he should contact Lieutenant Eastman from the Major Crime Unit.

Colonel, I know that you are more than busy, but I would appreciate it if you would allow me, as well as Chief Baker to meet with you in person, so that we could discuss the murders of the two victims in this case, and to help you understand why our two prime suspects are still our prime suspects after 28 years. We would also like to talk with you about our suggestion as to how these two murders can be solved.

I want to thank you for taking the time to read this letter and I hope you will grant this request.

Sincerely yours,
Joseph Horak
Lieutenant/Detective Ret.

October 21, 2000

Dear Chairman David Welch:

JOSEPH A. HORAK

As you know, I first made contact with you on or about July 17, 2000 and was seeking your help in regards to the Compagna/ Psaradelis murder investigation that has been ongoing since September 29, 1973.

I received your letter of September 14, 2000 along with the material I sent you to look over, in reference to this case. You advised me that you had made a full copy of the material and sent it to Attorney General Philip McLoughlin.

It makes me wonder why you did this, because I am sure the Attorney General, the State Police and the Governor have all known about this information for years and not a single thing has really been done by any person or agency connected with law enforcement to place or eliminate our two prime suspects, that we have had for the past twenty-eight years.

As you know Chairman Welch, I came to you because I really don't know who I can turn to in order to bring the killers of these two girls to justice. Chief Baker and I have tried to obtain help from the local police departments right up to President William Jefferson Clinton and results have been negative and our two prime suspects are allowed to get away with murder.

Chairman Welch, I really don't know what the function of the New Hampshire Justice & Public Safety is.

Since Chief Baker and I have been unable to find a single person or law enforcement agency to really work on this investigation, we wonder why it doesn't fall into the same area as to what the state just went through with the New Hampshire State Supreme Court. There has to be a way to penetrate this so-called, "inner circle".

Chief Baker and I would be willing to meet with you and your committee to talk over this problem and to determine what course of action could be taken in order to have these murders solved.

Thank you for taking the time to read my letter and I hope you will reply to it.

JUSTICE DENIED

Sincerely yours,
Joseph A. Horak
Lieutenant/Detective Ret.

October 22, 2000

RE: Compagna/Psaradelis Murders of 1973

Dear Governor Jeanne Shaheen:
  As you know, I started writing to you in November of 1996 about the Compagna/Psaradelis murder investigation and here we are nearly into November of 2000 and the Compagna/Psaradelis murders still remain unsolved. I always thought that "Justice" was for everyone, but for some reason it doesn't appear that it will happen in this case.
  Governor, I really thought that you would help Chief Baker and I with this case since you yourself have daughters. I really thought you would understand our need to bring the killers to justice. Then there is Lisa J. Rosa from California that came forward in April of 1997 with information about the people responsible for the murders of the two girls, she even wrote you a letter and never received any reply. I am sure she wonders why there isn't anyone connected to law enforcement within the state that will help to bring the killers to justice.
  Chief Baker and I have tried to find some way to talk with you and Attorney General Philip McLoughlin in person several times and for some unknown reason, we have never been able to accomplish that.
  We know that you see and talk with people from every walk of life and just can't understand why you won't allow us to talk with you in person in regards to this investigation.
  We have tried to penetrate the so-called "Inner Circle" for the past 28 years, with no success and we hope that you won't let all these years become wasted years and allow the killers to walk away scot-free. If you should decide to grant our request and let us talk with you in person about this investigation, and

our suggestion of just how this case can be solved, it would be greatly appreciated.

Sincerely yours,
Joseph Horak

October 25, 2000

Dear Lt. Horak:
    I took a great deal of time and effort in reviewing the entire criminal report and files associated with the COMPAGNA/ PSARADELIS murders. It is also quite evident that a host of others have closely scrutinized this case, including Merrimack Police Detectives, State Police Major Crime Investigators and Attorney Generals Office Prosecutors. I agree with you in respect with those I believe have pertinent knowledge/involvement in this case, however I disagree with you in many other areas to certain weight you apply to witness statements and importance of other evidentiary issues.
    Until enough evidence can be obtained to accomplish those ends, arrests and effective prosecutions can't be made. This case will remain open and we will continue to review all the evidence therein in addition to any future substantive leads.
    I would encourage you to direct future correspondence, inquiries, suggestions or information in this matter to Major Barry Hunter, Investigative Services Bureau Commander, or Lieutenant David Eastman, Major Crime Unit Commander.

Very truly yours,
Colonel Gary M. Sloper
Director

November 2000

Dear Mr. Horak:

JUSTICE DENIED

In reply to your letter dated October 21, 2000, several items have been addressed. Let me address your letter specifically:

You wondered why I sent copies of the file you supplied to me, to the Attorney General when I should have known he already had the files. The short answer to what question is: It was important to me, that the Attorney General know what I knew and document the source.

The function of the Criminal Justice & Public Safety Committees described in House Rules:

30c: It shall be the duty of the Committee on Criminal Justice and Public Safety to consider all matters relating to criminal justice, the Department of Corrections, sentencing, drug enforcement, bail, probation, parole, corrections facilities, DWI, domestic violence, firearms, fireworks, police and fire training, victims' assistance and such other matters as may be referred to it.

I have since had a conversation with the Attorney General and he is aware of your interest in this case. While I had addressed particular concerns that you had relayed to me, the Attorney General committed only to the fact of this being an open case and more may come from it.

Given the period of time that this case has endured a while longer cannot hurt since I am sure that the matter is not being ignored.

I would be happy to meet with you and Chief Baker, but for the present I am only a representative-elect and have not given an assignment to any committee. That will take place during the coming month. You have my E-mail address and we can and should keep in touch.

Sincerely,
David A. Welch

JOSEPH A. HORAK

<u>November 19, 2000</u>

RE: Campagna/Psaradelis Murders of 1973

Dear Colonel Gary Sloper:
    I received your letter of October 25, 2000 and I more than appreciated your taking the time and effort to review the files and criminal report associated with the Compagna/Psaradelis murders.
    I am somewhat discouraged, because I really thought that you would have allowed Chief Baker and I the chance to talk over this case with you in person. No one within the state knows more about this than we do. I do disagree with you in regards to the weight you have placed on the State Police Investigators, Attorney Generals Office and the Merrimack Police Detectives in regards to having scrutinized this case closely.

a. The Merrimack Police Detectives haven't worked on this investigation for the past 26 years and they sure haven't placed or eliminated the two prime suspects we have had all this time.
b. The Attorney Generals Office hasn't done a single thing to move this investigation forward, a lot of promises, but no results. We worked with Assistant Attorney General Michael Ramsdell for nearly five years and yet, the two prime suspects remain our prime suspects.
c. The State Police Major Crime Investigators have given us all kinds of promises and yet the two prime suspects remain prime suspects. Like members of the Attorney Generals Office, they admit that our suspects could be suspects. In 1995, Tom Jefferson one of our suspects shot himself in an attempt to take his own life. I came back from Oklahoma in order to try and obtain a "Dying Declaration" from him, we knew that we had to obtain the help of some active law enforcement person and we received no help. All we heard were things like, "We don't like Horak, how bad does he make us look in his book, if you want

to pay for the investigation, we will do it. Our job is to protect the governor and sheriff". The suspect lived and there hasn't been a single person connected with law enforcement that has interviewed him in regards to the murders and as to why he shot himself the night of December 22, 1995. The two prime suspects remain our Prime suspects.

d. In all these years we have never been able to talk with a governor, attorney general, or head of the state police in person. That "INNER CIRCLE" is sure hard to penetrate. Colonel, I really think that 28 years is a long time to have two prime suspects and it is pretty sad to think that there isn't a single law enforcement person interested enough to place or eliminate Tom Jefferson and Wayne Powers as the people responsible for the murders.

Chief Baker and I are not going to walk away from this investigation, as I have said. I wrote a book in 1994 "TRUTH & JUSTICE: A Detective's Dilemma" with the hope it would bring someone forward that had information about the crime and the people responsible, I used fictitious names of people, places and things. I have now re-written the book, using true names of people, places and things and have brought the story July 2001 and am relating how difficult it has been to obtain any help from the so-called "Inner Circle" and as to why Chief Baker and I have stayed with this case for the past 28 years.

Chief Baker and I have been approached by one of the large newspapers from one of the New England States to do a story on this investigation and also another newspaper from one of the southern states. Maybe this will help in some way. We will do what ever it takes to bring the killers to justice.

Again Colonel, I want to thank you for taking the time to talk with me and to answer my letter. If you would reconsider letting us talk with you in person, it would be greatly appreciated.

Sincerely,
Joseph A. Horak

JOSEPH A. HORAK

December 5, 2000

RE: Compagna/Psaradelis Murders of 1973

Dear Major Barry Hunter:
The last letter I received from Colonel Gary M. Sloper was dated October 25, 2000. This being in regards to the Compagna/ Psaradelis murders. The Colonel asked me to direct future correspondence, inquiries, suggestions or information in this matter to you or Lieutenant David Eastman from the Major Crime Unit.

Major, this double homicide is now 28 years old and still remains unsolved. Chief Robert Baker Ret. and I have worked on this investigation all these years and have had and still have two prime suspects that have never been placed or eliminated.

Over the years we have tried to obtain help from various law enforcement agencies and results have been negative for the most part. We have received all kinds of promises from the local police, sheriff departments, state police, attorney generals, various governors. We have requested to speak with several Governors, Attorney Generals, heads of the State Police and others in person and have never been granted that request. No one within the State of New Hampshire knows this case better than we do. Even people from the state police and attorney generals office will admit that our suspects could be the killers, but nothing is ever done to place or eliminate these people as the ones responsible for the murders.

My request from you would be for you to allow Chief Robert Baker and myself the chance to meet with you in person and to be able to discuss this ease with you. I am sure it would take at least a couple of hours, but it would be worth it if this case could be brought to a conclusion.

I would appreciate any consideration you could give us in regards to this request.

Sincerely,
Joseph A. Horak
Lieutenant/Detective Ret.

December 12, 2000

Dear Mr. Horak:
    I am in receipt of your December 5, 2000 letter requesting that I meet with Robert Baker and yourself regarding the Compagna/Psaradelis murder investigation.

    At this time, I am unfamiliar with the case and would therefore, prefer an opportunity to review the investigative file. The process of review will take approximately two to three weeks.

    Once I have completed the review, I will contact you to arrange for a meeting.

    In the meantime, thank you for maintaining interest in the case and I look forward to our future discussions.

Sincerely,
Major Barry J. Hunter
Commander,
Investigative Services Bureau

February 3, 2001

Dear Major Hunter:
    I am sure that you haven't been able to complete your review of the Compagna/Psaradelis murder investigation file. I know that you are more than busy.
    Major, Chief Baker and I have been working on this investigation for nearly 28 years and there isn't anyone that knows the case any better than we do. We just need the time to speak with you in person.

JOSEPH A. HORAK

I want to thank you again for taking an interest in this case; it means a lot to us, the families and society itself.

When you reply to our request, could you please send a copy of the letter to Chief Robert Baker. 388 Deerfield Road, Candia, New Hampshire 03034
Sincerely,
Joseph A. Horak
Lieutenant/Detective Retired

April 9, 2001

Kevin Canfield
Hartford Courant
285 Broad Street
Hartford, Connecticut 86115

RE: Compagna/Psaradelis Murders of 1973

Dear Kevin:

As you know, you contacted me last year in regards to doing a story on the Compagna/Psaradelis murders and also in regards to why Chief Robert Baker and I have stayed with this investigation for all these years. For some unknown reason you advised me that you were not going to do the story. I really couldn't understand that because you called me at least ten or more times because you wanted more information, and of course I gave what ever information you requested.

All these months have gone by and you never did explain the reason you couldn't do the story, especially since you were the one that contacted me in the first place.

I am writing to you at this time to see if you and your paper wouldn't reconsider doing the story as planned, or at least be honest and give us the true reason you decided not to do it.

I hope you will reply to this letter.
Sincerely yours,
Joseph A. Horak
Lieutenant/Detective Retired

June 26, 2001

Dear Lisa:

I hope this letter finds you well and that things are going great for you between school and work. I know that it doesn't give you much time to write letters and I do understand that.

I hope you received the copy of the manuscript, I am sure you can tell I am using most true names of people, places and things. I really think it helps to make it a better story, and as you know it was written with the idea of bringing someone forward like yourself that has knowledge about the murders and those responsible.

Lisa, I know that you came forward in April of 1997 and here it is, June 26, 2001. Someone from the State Police contacted you in 1998, talked with you for about an hour and you have never heard from or talked with anyone connected with law enforcement again.

I know that you must be pretty discouraged to know that you came forward to help in regards to the murders of Diane Compagna and Anne Psaradelis, you put your own safety and life on the line and no one seems to care about what you know or don't know, or even your safety.

Lisa, I know you are a woman of courage and values and I am sure you will stay with this investigation. I am more than proud of you, your beliefs and your desire to follow through with what ever task you are confronted with. I am sure you won't cave in and I know you will help in anyway you can until the people that are responsible for the murders of the two girls are brought to justice.

JOSEPH A. HORAK

I hope you haven't been receiving any more of those har-
assing phone calls, I think we both know who was making
them. If by chance you start receiving those calls again once
the book comes out, please call the FBI Office in San Fran-
cisco. I would also appreciate your letting me know so that I
could do something on this end. I really don't expect that you
will receive any, but we don't know what the reaction will be
with the so-called bad guys.

I'll close for now, but will be in touch with you, remember,
don't give up, justice will prevail.
Thank you for being you and for your help.
Sincerely yours,
Joseph A. Horak
Lieutenant/Detective Retired

<u>July 2, 2001</u>

RE: Compagna/Psaradelis Murders of 1973

Dear Detective Mark Fuhrman:

I wrote a letter to you on March 1, 2000 in regards to the
murders of two young 15 year old girls from Merrimack, New
Hampshire that were found in a wooded area in Candia.
Please find a copy of that letter enclosed. I never received any
reply.

"I Need Your Help!!

This month starts another year of this homicide investiga-
tion and there isn't a single person or law enforcement agency
that will really put in the time and effort that is needed to place
or eliminate the two prime suspects we have had these many
years.

Knowing that you spent a large portion of your life in law
enforcement and homicide investigations, I know you must

have been a dedicated police officer. I realize that you are now a Private Investigator.

Detective Fuhrman, this case can be solved and I know that you could be the person that could place or eliminate the two suspects that are responsible for taking the lives of these two young girls.

If you would take an interest in this investigation, I know it would be a giant step forward, bringing the two suspects to justice and would truly help to give peace of mind to the victims, families, society, us and it could help you in your new career.

I would appreciate some kind of a reply, and if you would help, it great. Chief Baker and I would assist you in anyway we could. No one knows this case any better than we do.
Sincerely yours,
Joseph A. Horak
Lieutenant/Detective Ret.

July 4, 2001

Weather wise, it was going to be one of those nice warm sunny days and I had already made up my mind that I was going over to Candia talk with Chief Baker about our investigation into the murders of Diane Compagna and Anne Psaradelis, our investigation was pretty much at a stand still and that sure wasn't good.

I started up the truck, pointed it in the direction of Manchester and I was on my way. As I drove along, many thoughts were in my mind, after all, today was the 4th of July and 28 years ago Diane Compagna was raped by Tom Jefferson. I often wondered if things would have been different if Diane had told her mother or the police about being raped by Tom Jefferson, I really think it would have, but as we know, that didn't happen.

As I got closer to Candia, I started to run into heavy traffic, I now realized that it was the weekend of the Deerfield Fair. As I pulled onto Deerfield Road, I passed the Maiden Funeral home and headed on towards Chief Baker's store. I slowed down at the next intersection, it was New Boston Road and I just took a left turn, I knew I was now headed towards the crime scene. The town dump was on the right side of the road and the swampy area to my left, all sorts of memories came flooding back and they weren't very good ones. A strange feeling and really not much had changed on the road, a few new homes, but pretty much the same as it was 28 years ago.

Lieutenant, "what do you mean by that?"

Well Chief, "Think about it, most people at this stage of the investigation think we are, "The Bad Guys" and that isn't true. The news media won't help, the so-called crime shows won't help. The local Police Departments, State Police, Attorney Generals, Governors and other agencies really won't help, often a lot of promises, but nothing ever done.

WHO DO YOU TURN TO IN A SITUATION LIKE TH1S?

During this investigation, we really have had only one person that has come forward with information about the murders and the people responsible. That person is Lisa J. Rosa from California and not a single law enforcement officer has talked with her in person, one phone call to her in 4 years does nothing for this investigation.

I have to agree with you Lieutenant.

Chief, since we are both here in your parking lot, why don't we take a few minutes and take our yearly trip over to the crime scene, I know we have been there a hundred times, but there is always a chance the people that committed the murders could return and leave a piece of evidence, those things do happen.

We drove over to the crime scene off the New Boston Road, we had to park on the side of the road, the entrance to the gravel pit was blocked by large boulders. We checked the entire area, nothing unusual, but you could still feel death in the air. We said a small prayer and walked back out onto the road

We got back into the truck and headed back to Deerfield Road and Chief Bakers home.

Lieutenant, how is the manuscript coming along?

Well Chief, I just have to put everything in its proper place, photographs, newspaper clippings, sketches, diagrams and a few other things. Once that is done, it will be ready for the publisher and I sure will be glad when that day comes. I just hope and pray that someone will read the book and will come forward with information about the murders and those responsible.

You know Chief, just because the book will come out, we will of course continue on with our investigation, we will never stop until the people responsible are brought to justice. This story covers a span from July, 1973 to July, 2001. This isn't the whole story and with any luck, we will tell you the rest of the story.

JOSEPH A. HORAK

In Memoriam

Diane Compagna

WHEN I MUST LEAVE YOU

When I must leave you
For a little while-
Please do not grieve
And shed wild tears
And hug your sorrow to you
Through the years,
But start out bravely
With a gallant smile;
And for my sake
And in my name
Live on and do
All things the same,
Feed not your loneliness
On empty days,
But fill each waking hour
In useful ways,
Reach out your hand
In comfort and in cheer
And I in turn will comfort you
And hold you near,
And never, never
Be afraid to die,
For I am waiting for you in the sky!

Anne Rosalie Psaradelis

"We'll shelter her with tenderness, we'll love
    her while we may,
And for the happiness we've known, forever
    grateful stay."
"But should the angels call for her much sooner
    than we've planned,
"We'll brave the bitter grief that comes and try
    to understand."

432

HYPOTHESIS OF A DOUBLE MURDER

This is what Chief Baker and I think happened between July 4th through November 20, 1973. Relying on the evidence and witness statements from investigations into this case. We hope this will help everyone understand who murdered Diane Compagna and her friend Anne Psaradelis.

During the morning and afternoon of Wednesday July 4th, Diane Compagna and Linda Caron spent most of their time watching the parade, then went to an area near the Merrimack High School where the games, rides, concessions and other things had been set up in regards to the 4th of July celebration. It was during this time that Diane noticed two older boys walking around. She looked over to Linda and said, "I think that boy is nice looking." Linda replied, "That's Tom Jefferson, you better watch out for him, he will try to get you into the bushes." Diane looked towards Linda and said, "What do you mean by that?" She advised her that he would try to have sex with her. They continued to walk along and spoke with various people they knew, they were just having a good time.

It was about 4:30 p.m. when Linda turned to Diane and said, "It's getting late, we better head home for supper, then we can come back and stay until the fireworks are set off."

It was about 6:30 p.m. when Linda and Diane arrived back in front of the high school, there was a large crowd, much larger than when they left to go home for supper. They just walked around, talked with some of their friend sand looked for a good spot to watch the fireworks. It was around 9:00 p.m. when the two girls decided to get something to drink and as they headed towards the concession stands, the two girls spotted Tom Jefferson and one of his friends. The two boys must have spotted them at the same time because they headed towards them. Jefferson asked Diane if she wanted to dance and she refused and the two boys walked away.

A short time later Jefferson and his friend came back over to talk with Linda and Diane again. He walked up to Diane and asked her if she wanted to dance and she refused again, he then asked her if she wanted to take a walk and she said she would. They walked towards the rear of the high school leaving Linda and his friend still talking. Diane ended up down in the woods with Jefferson. Once they came out of the woods, he went his way and she went her way. Once back in the area where she had left Linda, she looked around and found her talking with a couple of friends, she headed over where they all were. Diane appeared to be shaken and nervous, she told Linda that Tom Jefferson had just raped her, thought she was pregnant and didn't know what to do or expect.

Diane was going around telling various people that Tom Jefferson had taken her down into the woods near the rear of the high school and raped her. Many of these people Diane spoke with knew Jefferson and they looked around until they found him. They told him that Diane Compagna was going around telling everyone that he raped her. He was more than angry and said, "When I catch up with her, I'll shut her mouth and kick her in the ass."

During the week of July 8th, Jefferson was still looking for Diane. He was in anguish, showing a lot of anger and distress, some of his friends were still coming up to him and saying that Diane Compagna was still going around telling his friends and others that he raped her. He was more than upset because he was going with a woman that was in the middle of a divorce and he wanted to marry her. He had to find Diane as soon as possible and tell her to shut her mouth before she spoiled things for him.

On Wednesday July 11, Marcel Compagna, father of Diane came into the Merrimack Police Station and reported his daughter and her friend Anne Psaradelis as "Missing." There were lots of people that knew the girls had hitch hiked a ride to Hampton Beach, but they never told their parents or the police.

About mid afternoon on Thursday July 12th, Linda Caron was looking for Diane and Anne, she was about to enter Pizza By Golly, a place where most of the kids from town would hang around. They would often have pizza, play some of the games, have a cold drink, or just talk. The kids that went there knew just about everyone and everything that was going on around town. Linda was about to open up the front door when Tom Jefferson came out onto the front porch, he looked at Linda and asked what she was doing there. She looked at him and said she was looking for Diane and Anne Psaradelis because they had been reported as "Missing". She then asked him if he knew where Diane was and he replied that he didn't know any Diane. Linda said, "Yes you do know Diane and she described her." Jefferson said, "Oh, I think I remember her. "He asked why she wanted to know, she again said, "Diane is missing." Jefferson said he had to get going and left without saying anything else.

Thursday, July 12th was sort of a dreary day at Hampton Beach, it was a cool day with dark clouds, the threat of rain and very few people at the beach or in the water. The girls were both alive and well at 4:30 p.m. in the area of the Red Cross Station, they had talked with several girls they knew from town. They were even offered a ride home by some of them. They turned down the offer of a ride, said they wanted to stay awhile. They did not appear to nervous, worried in anyway. They just acted like they always did.

We have to remember three things in regards to the 4th of July incidents she told many of her friends about.

a. Thought Tom Jefferson was good looking even though he raped her.

b. Thought she would never see him again.

c. Thought she was pregnant.

Tom Jefferson and his friend Wayne Powers drove over to Hampton Beach with the idea of locating Diane Compagna. He told Powers that he was really angry, that he had been looking for her all week, as she was running around telling his friends and others that he raped her and that wasn't true. She could spoil things for him and he needed to get things squared away. They arrived at the beach, parked the car and started looking for Diane. It was pretty easy for them to locate Diane and her friend. Hardly anyone in the water and not very many people at the beach itself. Jefferson spotted Diane standing with another girl near the Red Cross Station, they walked across the street and approached the girls, they talked for a few minutes and then Jefferson offered them a ride back home.

Diane was flattered and they accepted the offer of a ride back to Merrimack. Anne got into the back seat of the car with Powers and Diane got into the front seat with Jefferson. The radio was on, they all talked and listened to the music. They had driven for about twenty-five minutes when Jefferson drove off the main highway and entered into Candia. They came up to the next intersection and took a right turn onto Deerfield Road and continued on until they came to another intersection. They took a left turn onto New Boston Road, passed over a small bridge, passed the town dump and continued on until they came to a small opening in a stone wall.

Jefferson pulled into the opening and parked the car in front of a small gravel pit. He shut the motor off, turned around towards Anne and Powers and said that he and Diane were going to take a walk in the woods, that they had some things they needed to talk about. He asked them if they minded staying in the car until they came back.

Anne and Powers said that they didn't mind waiting in the car, so Diane and Jefferson got out of the car and started to walk towards the woods. He put his arm around her and was apparently telling her things that made her feel special, he pulled her close and kissed her a few times. They went through a large opening in a stone wall and took a right turn and followed the wall until they came to a pine grove type setting. He kissed her a few more times, told her various things and more flattery. A couple of hugs, a couple of kisses again and he convinced her to take her clothes off. As Diane took her clothing off, she would fold the clothing neatly and then place it in a small pile on the ground. She then took the pair of jeans she had been wearing and laid them on the ground so that she could lay on them without getting on the pine needles. She laid down on the jeans, he had already taken off his clothes, he got on top of Diane, kissed her a few times and told her things she wanted to hear. They had intercourse, Jefferson was still on top of her and one of two things happened, she might have told him that she thought she was pregnant, or he might have said, "You aren't going to tell the police about the 4th of July are you?" Who ever said what, it outraged him even more. He was already laying on top of her and had complete control over her and her body. He lost control of himself, she was going to cause problems for him. He was more than angry; he put his hands around her neck and strangled her.

He picked himself up off the ground after killing Diane, he looks at what he has done. He is shaking uncontrollably and is sick to his stomach.

He grabs his clothes and starts to put them on and as he does, it is beginning to sink in as to what he has just done. He now realizes that he has to make a quick decision, do I kill both Anne and Powers, I sure don't want to get caught and how am I going to get them both in here and how can I kill them both. One of them might get away.

Jefferson has to do something fast, so he makes his decision, he runs back to the car, out of breath and yells to Anne and Powers, "Come on quick, I need your help, something has happened to Diane." They jump out of the car and Anne says, "What's Wrong?" Jefferson just hollers to them, quick, quick, we have to get back in there and help Diane. He is still more than nervous and excited and thinks to himself, how am I going to be able to kill both of them, or should I just kill Anne and put the fear of God into Powers. Once they pass through the large opening in the stonewall Jefferson allows himself to trip over a rock and falls onto the ground. He tells the others to keep going, he picks himself up and now has both of them in front of him heading into the pine grove where Diane is. As Anne and Powers enter the pine grove area, Anne looks around and notices Diane's body, she is naked and appears to be dead, she panics, doesn't turn around and look at Jefferson or Powers, but runs into the woods. Jefferson rushes past Powers and goes after Anne, she is just about to go over a stone wall when Jefferson grabs her from behind and drags her down onto the ground, Powers is yelling at Jefferson, "What are you doing?" Jefferson strangles Anne, turns towards Powers and says, "You better not say a word to anyone about this, now or ever, or you're next. Now, come on, let's get out of here.

Powers is shaking, crying and yells to Jefferson, "Why did you have to kill the two girls?" He replies, you better shut your mouth, you are part of this now and if I go down, you will go with me, now lets get back to the car and get out of here. They both run back to the car, Powers is still crying and says again, "Why did you have to kill the two girls?" He just looks at Powers and tells him to get into the car. Jefferson backs the car out onto New Boston Road gets out of the area as fast as he can. He is quite nervous and tells Powers several more times that he better not say anything to anyone or he is dead. He'd better not tell anyone that they picked the girls up at the beach or any other place, just keep your mouth shut if you know what is good for you.

It was late by the time Jefferson and Powers made it back to Merrimack, they had driven the back roads with the hope that no one would see them together. Powers got dropped off on Wire Road and Jefferson's parting words to him were, "You better not contact me in anyway, if I need to talk with you, I'll find away to contact you, remember, if I go down, you will go down too and if you say anything to anyone, you will be dead."

The days and weeks slipped by, the police were all over the place looking for the two girls. Powers was having major problems, he didn't know how he could handle the pressure and stress that now hung heavy on his every thought. His school work started to slip, his job wasn't going very well because his mind and thoughts were consumed with Jefferson and the murders. July has passed and it was already mid August. Powers didn't hear a single word from Jefferson, the girls were still missing and everything was weighing heavy on him. He would fight with his friends, school and work going down hill, would read the bible and he was just falling apart. August had come and gone and it was now the middle of September, the two girls still hadn't been found, not a single word from Jefferson and Powers life was now a living hell. He sure didn't know how to handle all the pressure.

On September 29th, Robert Lupien had been scouting the woods near the town dump off the New Boston Road in Candia. He was looking for birds to hunt and came across what he thought was a partially decomposed human body with no clothes on it. The bright clothing on the ground had drawn his attention to the area. He advised the local police of the finding and a search and investigation was conducted of the area. A second body was also found in the area.

JUSTICE DENIED

The crime scene was examined, roped off and because of darkness and the crime scene being so complicated, it was decided to leave the bodies intact and a guard schedule set up to protect the bodies and entire crime scene until the morning when better light would prevail.

On Sunday the 30th, the entire crime scene investigation was conducted and the two bodies were identified as those of Diane Compagna and Anne Psaradelis.

The news media picked up on the murder investigation and the identification of the two victims. They put out a news release on the radio and in the newspapers. Wayne Powers was at work when the news of Diane Compagna and Anne Psaradelis came over the radio. Within five minutes, he received a telephone call and whoever it was and what was said caused Powers to fall apart. He was so bad that they had to take him to the doctors, two days later Powers was brought to the hospital for a mental break down. He was treated in the hospital for 26 days, came home and on November 9th, he shot and killed himself. Jefferson has never been brought to justice for the murders of the two girls. After an intensive investigation, it showed that July 12th changed Wayne Powers life for ever.

Tom Jefferson married that woman he was in fear of losing nine days before the bodies of Diane Compagna and Anne Psaradelis were found.

JOSEPH A. HORAK

EPILOGUE

This book is special because it is written from my heart. Chief Robert Baker and I stood over the bodies of these two young girls and made a promise to them that their murderers would be caught, even if it took 20 years or more. We live with these murders everyday of our lives and we can't believe that 28 years have passed and the murderers haven't been brought to justice.

I have written this story because it is really the last chance to ever have this case solved. When Chief Baker and I die, there isn't any one else interested enough to work on a 28 year or older homicide investigation. This book could help to bring someone forward that has the information we need to help solve these murders, and these people are out there somewhere across the country. To have these murders solved would be a relief to the parents, society, us, and most of all, to the victims themselves.

Life is precious and if taken away by the hands of another, this is morally, spiritually and lawfully wrong and a double homicide of two young girls that was committed 28 years ago is just as important as one that took place as recent as yesterday. To just forget these victims is an unjust to society. To allow murderers to walk free will never give us the freedom to live in peace without fear of our lives. Chief Baker and I will never rest until the killers are brought to justice.

We hope this story will inspire other police officers to follow through with all their investigations no matter how hard the road gets, or how long it takes to solve the crime, never give up.

Chief Baker and I have always known who the killers are that took the lives of Diane Compagna and her friend Anne Psaradelis, after 28 years, we are still searching for new leads. Oh, we know that there are friends, relatives and others out there that know Tom Jefferson and Wayne Powers are responsible for taking the lives of these two young 15 year old girls. You know who you are, just as we do and we need your help.

JUSTICE DENIED

Our plea to you, the killers themselves and/or their families and/or friends and others who might know anything about it at the time of happening, or who were confided to over the years after the murders occurred.

Please come forward, we can't offer you money, but we can offer you such things as Immunity, Safety and Anonymity (for themselves for knowing of the crime and not reporting it.)

It is now July, 2001 and these two girls are not receiving the justice they deserve. The so called "inner circle" is very difficult to penetrate. After 29 years of investigation, the two prime suspects remain suspects, and the system has just about shut down the investigation. The newspapers, crime shows, law enforcement agencies and others have reached that point where they just ignore our letters, and any plea for help. Who do you turn to for justice in a case such as this?

Just maybe, there will be one, two or more people that will come forward with information about the murders and those responsible, just as Lisa Rosa had the courage to come forward and help in the fight for justice.

This is the end of the book, but not the whole story, the investigation will continue.

"There Is Nothing So Powerful As The Truth"
        "DANIEL WEBSTER"

Glossary

ACCOMPLICE: one who aids and abets a lawbreaker in a criminal act, either as a principal or an accessory

APPEAL: A legal proceeding by which a case is brought from a lower court to a higher court for rehearing; 2, to call upon another for corroboration, vindication or decision.

APPREHEND: To seize; to take hold of; arrest

ARREST: to take, seize or arrest a person.

ATTORNEY: one who is legally appointed by another to transact business for him; a legal agent qualified to act for suitors and defendants in legal proceedings

BAIL: Security given for the due appearance of a prisoner in order to obtain his release from imprisonment; the temporary release of a prisoner upon security.

BAILABLE: Entitled to bail; admitting of bail

BAILMAN: One who gives bail for another

BREAKING AND ENTERING: gaining unauthorized, illegal access to another's premises, as by forcing a lock.

BURGLARY: the act of breaking into a building, especially with the intent to steal; the act of breaking into and entering the dwelling house of another at night with felonious intent

CHARGE: Accusation, indictment; a complaint of error, failure or wrong; instructions in points of law given by a court to a jury

COMPLAINT: a formal allegation against a party

COMPLAINANT: the party who makes the complaint in a legal action or proceeding

COURT: A chamber or other place for the administration of justice; a faculty or agency of judgment or evaluation, an assembly or board with legislative or administrative powers.

CRIME: An act or the commission of an act that is forbidden or the omission of a duty that is commanded by public law and that makes the offender liable to punishment by that law; a gross violation of law; criminal activity

CRIMINAL: relating to a crime or its punishment; guilty of a crime; one that has committed a crime

D.O.B.: date of birth

EXIGENT CIRCUMSTANCES: requiring immediate aid or action

FELONY: a grave crime expressly declared to be a felony by statute because of the punishment imposed; a grave crime formerly differing from a misdemeanor under English common law by involving forfeiture in addition to any other punishment

FRISK SEARCH: to search especially for concealed weapons by running the hands rapidly over the clothing and through pockets

JUDGE: a public official authorized to decide questions brought before a court; to sit in judgment; to determine or pronounce after inquiry or interrogation

JURISDICTION: The area in which a certain agency has authority

JUROR: A member of a jury; a person summoned to appear on a jury

JURY: A body of men and women sworn to give a verdict on some matter being submitted to them; a body of men legally selected and sworn to inquire into any matter of fact and to give their verdict accordingly

MISDEMEANOR: A crime less serious than a felony

PAT SEARCH: exactly suited to the purpose or occasion

POLICE FORCE: a body of trained officer and men entrusted by a government with maintenance of public peace and order, enforcement of laws and prevention and detection of crime

PROBABLE CAUSE: a reasonable ground for supposing that a criminal charge is well founded; to test, approve, prove

RELEASE FORM: to set free from restraint, confinement, or servitude; 2. Discharge from obligation or responsibility; relinquishment of a right or claim; an act by which a legal right is discharged

SEARCH WARRANT: a warrant authorizing a search (as of a house) for stolen goods or unlawful possessions (such as gambling implements)

SENTENCE: one formally announced by a court or judged in a criminal proceeding and specifying punishment to be inflicted on the convict; the punishment so imposed

STAKE OUT: watching a fixed object or location

SURVEILLANCE: To watch; to watch over; close watch kept on a person or a group (as by a detective)

SUSPECT: One who is suspected; regarded with suspicion; to have doubts of; distrust; to imagine one to be guilty or culpable on slight evidence or without proof

SUSPECT'S RIGHTS: The Supreme Court ruled that the guarantee of due process required that before any questioning of suspects in police custody, the suspects must be informed of their right to remain silent, that anything they say may be used against them and that they have the right to counsel.

TT ITEM: A message sent by teletype machine

WARRANT: a precept or writ issued by a competent magistrate authorizing an officer to make an arrest, a seizure, or a search to do other acts incident to the administration of justice.

HOMICIDE
RSA 630

630:1 Capital Murder.

1. A person is guilty of capital murder if he knowingly causes the death of

(a) A law enforcement officer or a judicial officer acting in the line of duty or when the death is caused as a consequence of or in retaliation for such person's actions in the line of duty;

(b) Another before, after, while engaged in the commission of, or while attempting to commit kidnapping as that offense is defined in RSA 633:1;

(c) Another by criminally solicited by another for his personal pecuniary gain;

(d) Another after being sentenced to life imprisonment without parole pursuant to RSA 630:1-a, III;

(e) Another before, after, while engaged in the commission of, or while attempting to commit aggravated felonious sexual assault as defined in RSA 632-A:2;

(f) Another before, after, while engaged in the commission of, or while attempting to commit an offense punishable under RSA 318-B:26, I(a) or (b).

II. As used in this section, a "law enforcement officer" is a sheriff or deputy sheriff of any county, a state police officer, a constable or police officer of any city or town, an official or employee of any prison, jail or corrections institution, a probation - parole officer, or a conservation officer.

II-a As used in this section, a "judicial officer" is a judge of a district probate, superior or supreme court; an attorney employed by the department of justice or a municipal prosecutor's office; or a county attorney; or attorney employed by the county attorney.

III. A person convicted of a capital murder may be punished by death.

IV. As used in this section and RSA 630:1-a, 1-b,2,3 and 4, the meaning of "another" does not include a fetus.

V. In no event shall any person under the age of 17 years be culpable of a capital murder.

630:1-a First Degree Murder.

I. A person is guilty of murder in the first degree if he:
    (a) Purposely causes the death of another; or
    (b) Knowingly causes the death of:

(1) Another before, after, while engaged in the commission of, or while attempting to commit felonious sexual assault as defined in RSA 632-A:3;

(2) Another before, after, while engaged in the commission of, or while attempting to commit robbery or burglary while armed with a deadly weapon, the death being caused by the use of such weapon.

(3) Another in perpetrating or attempting to perpetrate arson as defined in RSA 634:1, I, II, or III;

(4) The president or president-elect or vice-president or vice-president-elect of the United States, the governor or governor-elect of New Hampshire or any other state or any member-elect of the congress of the United States, or any candidate for such office after such candidate has been nominated at his party's primary, when such killing is motivated by knowledge of the foregoing capacity of the victim.

II. For the purpose of RSA 630:1-a, I(a), "purposely" shall mean that the actor's conscious object is the death of another, and that his act or acts in furtherance of that object were deliberate and premeditated.

III. A person convicted of a murder in the first degree shall be sentenced to life imprisonment and shall not be eligible for parole at any time.

630:1-b Second Degree Murder.

I. A person is guilty of murder in the second degree if:
    (a) He knowingly causes the death of another; or
    (b) He causes such death recklessly under circumstances manifesting an extreme indifference to the value of human life. Such recklessness and indifference are presumed if the actor causes the death by the use of a deadly weapon in the commission of, or in an attempt to commit, or in immediate flight after committing or attempting to commit any class A felony.

II. Murder in the second degree shall be punishable by imprisonment for life or for such term as the court may order.

630:2 **Manslaughter.**

I. A person is guilty of manslaughter when he causes the death of another:

(a) Under the influence of extreme mental or emotional disturbance caused by extreme provocation but which would otherwise constitute murder; or

(b) Recklessly.

II. Manslaughter shall be punishable by imprisonment for a term of not more than 30 years.

630:3 **Negligent Homicide.**

I. A person is guilty of a class B felony when he causes the death of another negligently.

II. A person is guilty of a class A felony when in consequence of being under the influence of intoxicating liquor or a controlled drug or any combination of intoxicating liquor and controlled drug while operating a propelled vehicle, as defined in RSA 637:9, III or a boat as defined in RSA 270:48, II, he causes the death of another.

III. In addition to any other penalty imposed, if the death of another person resulted from the negligent driving of a motor vehicle, the court may revoke the license or driving privilege of the convicted person for up to 7 years.

CAPITAL PUNISHMENT

New Hampshire has not abused the death penalty in any way. It is the only state east of the Mississippi to use "hanging" as a way of Capital Punishment.

JUSTICE DENIED

The last execution in New Hampshire was in 1939. (Howard Long for murder of a young child.) We have not had one in New Hampshire for the past 61 years.

ACKNOWLEDGEMENTS

The author would like to thank
the following people for their help and
continued support, in regards to the
making of this book and the ongoing
investigation of this case.

Susan Wightman Abaid
Robert Baker
Priscilla Casey
Richard and Katherine Corbin
Karen Day
Michael Fario
Gary and Tracy Francoeur
Dorothy Hildebrand
Tom Hurst
Thomas Hyde
Betty Lloyd
Lisa J. Rosa
Evelyn M. Taylor
Steven Vanderhoff
My son's, Raymond and Richard
And other friends.

JOSEPH A. HORAK

ABOUT THE AUTHOR

Joseph A. Horak was born in Lynn, Massachusetts, in 1929. His entire adult life has been dedicated to public service in the field of law enforcement. Although Mr. Horak is sixty-six years of age and now retired from active service, his dedication still pushes him to solve the horrendous and senseless crime of which you are about to read in "Justice Denied—A Detective's Dilemma" and to finally seek the arrest and conviction of the perpetrator(s). His dedication to the two victims and their families will not cease until this crime is solved.

Mr. Horak's career in law enforcement is quite extensive and broad in accomplishment. His career includes serving as Inspector (Detective), Security Supervisor-Investigator, Detective Lieutenant, Captain, Chief of Police and Deputy U.S. Marshal. Most of his career has been spent in the State of New Hampshire.